I0029602

TOWARDS HUMAN RIGHTS COMPLIANCE IN AUSTRALIAN PRISONS

TOWARDS HUMAN RIGHTS COMPLIANCE IN AUSTRALIAN PRISONS

ANITA MACKAY

Australian
National
University

PRESS

ANU PRESS

Published by ANU Press
The Australian National University
Acton ACT 2601, Australia
Email: anupress@anu.edu.au

Available to download for free at press.anu.edu.au

ISBN (print): 9781760464004
ISBN (online): 9781760464011

WorldCat (print): 1202767710
WorldCat (online): 1202767709

DOI: 10.22459/THRCAP.2020

This title is published under a Creative Commons Attribution-NonCommercial-NoDerivatives 4.0 International (CC BY-NC-ND 4.0).

The full licence terms are available at
creativecommons.org/licenses/by-nc-nd/4.0/legalcode

Cover design and layout by ANU Press

Cover image adapted from photo by Kris Cros on Unsplash

This edition © 2020 ANU Press

Contents

Foreword

In December 2017, Australia ratified the Optional Protocol to the United Nations *Convention against Torture and Other Cruel, Inhuman or Degrading Treatment or Punishment*, and in doing so committed itself to opening up places in which persons are deprived of their liberty to enhanced levels of external independent scrutiny. This very timely book offers a compelling analysis of current issues concerning prison detention in Australia and explores the prerequisites for addressing the problems it identifies.

As this book goes to press, the world is facing the challenge of a global health pandemic on a scale not experienced in recent times. The response has been to try to reduce the spread of infection by ensuring that people 'keep their distance' from each other via imposing restrictions on personal mobility, widely referred to as 'lock downs'. For those in prisons, such restrictions are not a temporary necessity, they are a way of life. But in what are frequently overcrowded prison systems this results in the very opposite of 'distancing', and the physical, health and mental problems resulting from such closed and close confinement, now being glimpsed by the population at large, form the day-to-day reality for many in prison detention. This book probes that reality and explores options for change.

The picture and pattern of prison detention is surveyed in the opening chapter, which are then juxtaposed against Australia's international human rights obligations, including the obligations to establish effective independent visiting mechanisms. It carefully explores existing provisions at the state/territory and Commonwealth level before concluding that there is much to be done to ensure compliance with those international commitments, both procedural and substantive.

There follow a series of chapters that consider prerequisites for addressing these deficiencies, fundamental to which is to reduce reliance on imprisonment. It should be noted that the author is not calling for this merely to address the problems of overcrowding within in the prison system (though naturally it will have this effect). The opening chapter considers what are described as the more generic 'pains of imprisonment' which overcrowding naturally exacerbates. But its amelioration does not remove those pains, and so there remains a human rights imperative to ensure that the prison population is as limited as possible, irrespective of overcrowding. Various strategies are canvassed and practices evaluated, and the case for a reductionist approach made.

Drawing on the earlier analysis, a second prerequisite identified is to bring Australian law into conformity with its international obligations, and various examples of where it falls short are highlighted. Particular focus is placed on there being variable, but invariably relatively weak, systems of human rights protection. Serious issues concerning the extent to which fundamental rights are acknowledged and reflected in the respective Corrections Acts of the states and territories are also highlighted, it being concluded that 'the majority of jurisdictions have neither human rights legislation, nor enforceable rights in corrections legislation. In short, there is no effective legislative protection of human rights for imprisoned people' (Chapter 5). Helpfully, practical suggestions for reform are then given, in both the legislative and regulatory spheres.

A further prerequisite of change, drawing inspiration from the *International Covenant on Civil and Political Rights*, is then considered—this being to ensure that the focus of the prison system is on 'rehabilitation and restoration'. As in so many systems that have grown over many years, there are overlayers of differing conceptions of penal theory and policy which result in confusions and contradictions as to aims and purposes. The author offers a clear path through these complexities and a strategy for implementing a model based on her understanding of the international human rights–based approach.

A fourth prerequisite has a very practical orientation, and that is to assist prison staff to treat detainees in a human rights–compliant manner. This is a very important point, though often misunderstood as suggesting that those working in detention facilities are mistreating detainees. While, unfortunately, this is indeed sometimes the case, the problem is more usually that the systems and structures, resources and facilities stand in the way of realising this objective. That said, there are some powerful structural hurdles based on disparities of power and agency that need to be overcome too, and which are magnified by the use of coercive power within the day-to-day regime of detention.

A final prerequisite is, perhaps, self-evident, but is important nonetheless to emphasise: the need for there to be decent physical conditions of detention. International standards have much to say about this, and have done so for many years. There can, then, hardly be an excuse for such standards not to be known or adhered to and, as the author points out, 'lack of resources is not an acceptable reason for failing to comply with this prerequisite' (Chapter 8). Yet so often it is not. The author then carefully looks at issues arising from both the nature of the 'built environment' and provision of basic necessities before once again concluding that, in Australia, there is huge scope for improvement, as there is in so many other countries too. Once again, practical suggestions are made, particularly regarding detention conditions for Indigenous populations.

The work concludes that there 'is a large gap between the international human rights law applicable to prisons, which Australia has chosen to be bound by, and daily prison operations in individual prisons across Australia' and that 'The picture of Australian prisons painted throughout this book is not positive' (Conclusion). Yet the author has not given in to despair. Rather, throughout this careful and thoughtful presentation and analysis, practical suggestions are made and strategies advocated, imbued with a sense of hopeful optimism that the ratification and implementation of the Optional Protocol to the Convention against Torture—and the promise of enhanced openness and transparency it brings—will help forge a new climate in which positive advances can be made. This is a compelling book with a convincing message.

Sir Malcolm D Evans
4 May 2020

Acknowledgements

I am indebted to my doctoral supervisors, Professor Bronwyn Naylor and Associate Professor Julie Debeljak, who supervised me from 2011–14 and continue to mentor me. The research undertaken for my doctorate formed a solid foundation for this book. I am grateful to Professor Matthew Groves for encouraging me to adapt my research into this book and providing insightful comments on the first draft.

I would particularly like to thank my father, Dr George Mackay, who proofread this book (and my thesis). I am grateful to my partner, Dr Zachary Watts, my family and friends for their unwavering support.

I would also like to thank my colleagues at La Trobe Law School for their enthusiastic encouragement for all aspects of my work, and I acknowledge the financial assistance provided by La Trobe University in the form of a Social Research Platform Grant.

List of Abbreviations

ACT	Australian Capital Territory
AHRC	Australian Human Rights Commission
ALRC	Australian Law Reform Commission
AMC	Alexander Maconochie Centre
The Bangkok Rules	United Nations *Rules for the Treatment of Women Prisoners and Non-Custodial Measures for Women Offenders*
Body of Principles	United Nations *Body of Principles for the Protection of All Persons under Any Form of Detention or Imprisonment*
CAT	*Convention against Torture and Other Cruel, Inhuman or Degrading Treatment or Punishment*
CAT/C	Committee against Torture
Charter	*Charter of Human Rights and Responsibilities Act 2006* (Vic)
CMA	*Corrections Management Act 2007* (ACT)
Constitution	*Commonwealth of Australia Constitution Act 1900*
CRPD	*Convention on the Rights of Persons with Disabilities*
Disabilities Committee	Committee on the Rights of Persons with Disabilities
ECHR	*European Convention for the Protection of Human Rights and Fundamental Freedoms*
ECtHR	European Court of Human Rights
GLM	Good Lives Model of Offender Rehabilitation

Guidelines	*Standard Guidelines for Corrections in Australia*
Guiding Principles	*Guiding Principles for Corrections in Australia*
HMIP	Her Majesty's Inspectorate of Prisons (United Kingdom)
HRA	*Human Rights Act 2004* (ACT)
HR Committee	United Nations Human Rights Committee
ICCPR	*International Covenant on Civil and Political Rights*
IVF	in-vitro fertilisation
JARO	Justice Assurance and Review Office (Victoria)
Kimberley prison	West Kimberley Regional Prison (Western Australia)
The Mandela Rules	United Nations *Standard Minimum Rules for the Treatment of Prisoners* (the Nelson Mandela Rules)
MAP	Melbourne Assessment Prison (Victoria)
NPM	National Preventive Mechanism
NSW	New South Wales
NT	Northern Territory
OCSR	Office of Correctional Services Review (Victoria)
OICS	Office of the Inspector of Custodial Services (Western Australia)
OPCAT	*Optional Protocol to the Convention against Torture and Other Cruel, Inhuman or Degrading Treatment or Punishment*
QHRA	*Human Rights Act 2019* (Qld)
QPC	Queensland Productivity Commission
RCIADIC	Commonwealth Royal Commission into Aboriginal Deaths in Custody
RNR model	Risk-Need-Responsivity model
SARC	Scrutiny of Acts and Regulations Committee (Victoria)

SPT	Subcommittee for the Prevention of Torture and Other Cruel, Inhuman or Degrading Treatment or Punishment
TCID	torture and other cruel, inhuman or degrading treatment or punishment
TMB	treaty monitoring body
TOCI	Tasmanian Office of the Custodial Inspector
UK	United Kingdom
UN	United Nations
USA	United States of America
WA	Western Australia

Table of Cases

Australian Cases

Ali v State of Queensland [2013] QCAT 319 (6 August 2013)

An Inquest into the Death of Steven Claude Freeman [2018] ACTCD 7

Anderson v Pavic [2005] VSCA 244

Assistant Commissioner Condon v Pompano Pty Ltd (2013) 252 CLR 38

Binse v Willians [1998] 1 VR 381

Brazel v Westin & Anor [2013] VSC 527 (3 October 2013)

Callanan v Attendee X [2013] QSC 340

Callanan v Attendee Y [2013] QSC 341

Callanan v Attendee Z [2013] QSC 342

Castles v Secretary to the Department of Justice [2010] VSC 310 (9 July 2010)

Castles v Secretary to the Department of Justice and Others (2010) 28 VR 141

Certain Children v Minister for Families and Children & Ors (No 2) [2017] VSC 251

Clark v Commissioner for Corrective Services [2016] NSWCA 186

Clarkson v Governor of the Metropolitan Reception Prison & Anor (1986) EOC ¶92–153

Collins v State of South Australia [1999] SASC 257

Collins v The Queen [2012] VSCA 163

Craig William John Minogue v Human Rights and Equal Opportunity Commission [1998] FCA 1283 (12 October 1998)

Dale v DPP [2009] VSCA 212

David Harold Eastman v Chief Executive Officer of the Department of Justice and Community Safety [2010] ACTSC 4 (12 January 2010)

Australian Coronial Inquest Findings

Magistrates' Court of Tasmania, *Findings. Deaths in Custody Inquest*, 2001

White, Peter, *Inquest into the Death of Adam Sasha Omerovic*, Coroner's Court of Victoria, 24 January 2014

Canadian Cases

Sauvé v Canada (Attorney-General) [1993] 2 SCR 438

Sauvé v Canada (Chief Electoral Officer) [2002] SCR 519

European Court of Human Rights Cases

Aliev v Ukraine [2003] ECHR 41220/98

Bădilă v Romania [2012] ECHR 31725/04

Bazjaks v Latvia [2010] ECHR 71572/01

Ciorap v Moldova [2007] ECHR 12066/02

Dankevich v Ukraine [2003] 40679/98

Dickson v UK [2007] ECHR 1050

Dybeku v Albania [2007] ECHR 41153/06

Gusev v Russia [2008] ECHR 67542/01

Hirst v United Kingdom (No. 2) (2005) ECHR 74025/01

Husayn (Abu Zubaydah) v Poland [2014] ECHR 7511/13

Iwańczuk v Poland [2001] ECHR 25196/94

Korneykova and Korneykov v Ukraine [2016] ECHR 56660/12

Mayzit v Russia [2005] ECHR 63378/00

Murray v The Netherlands [2016] ECHR 10511/10

Valašinas v Lithuania [2001] ECHR

Van der Ven v the Netherlands [2003] ECHR

Wainwright v United Kingdom [2006] ECHR 12350/04

New Zealand Cases

Attorney-General v Taylor [2018] NZSC 104

Taylor v The Attorney-General and Ors [2013] NZHC 1659 (3 July 2013)

United Kingdom Cases

Raymond v Honey [1983] 1 AC 1

United Nations Committee Against Torture Cases

Jaïdane v Tunisia, Committee against Torture, *Views: Communication No 654/ 2015*, UN Doc CAT/C/61/D/654/2015 (11 August 2017)

United Nations Disabilities Committee Cases

Doolan v Australia, Committee on the Rights of Persons with Disabilities, *Views: Communication No 18/2013*, UN Doc CRPD/C/22/D/18/2013 (30 August 2019)

Leo v Australia, Committee on the Rights of Persons with Disabilities, *Views: Communication No 17/2013*, UN Doc CRPD/C/22/D/17/2013 (30 August 2019)

Noble v Australia, Committee on the Rights of Persons with Disabilities, *Views: Communication No 7/2012*, UN Doc CRPD/C/16/D/7/2012 (15 August - 2 September 2016)

United Nations Human Rights Committee Cases

Brough v Australia, Human Rights Committee, *Views: Communication No 1184/ 2003*, UN Doc CCPR/C/86/D/1184/2003 (17 March 2006)

C v Australia, Human Rights Committee, *Views: Communication No 900/1999*, UN Doc CCPR/C/76/D/900/1999 (13 November 2002)

C v Australia, Human Rights Committee, *Views: Communication No 2216/2012*, 119th sess, UN Doc CCPR/C/119/D/2216/2012 (28 March 2017)

Danyal Shafiq v Australia, Human Rights Committee, *Views: Communication No 1324/2004*, UN Doc CCCPR/C/88/D/1324/2004 (31 October 2006)

G v Australia, Human Rights Committee, *Views: Communication No 2172/2012*, 119th sess, UN Doc CCPR/C/119/D/2172/2012 (17 March 2017)

Hicks v Australia, Human Rights Committee, *Views: Communication No 2005/2010*, UN Doc CCPR/C/115/D/2005/2010 (5 November 2015)

Hill and Hill v Spain, Human Rights Committee, *Views: Communication No 526/93*, UN Doc CCPR/C/59/D/526/1993 (2 April 1997)

Jensen v Australia, Human Rights Committee, *Views: Communication No 762/1997*, UN Doc CCPR/C/71/D/762/1997 (22 March 2001)

Kang v Republic of Korea, Human Rights Committee, *Views: Communication No 878/99*, UN Doc CCPR/C/78/D/878/1999 (15 July 2003)

Lluberas v Uruguay, Human Rights Committee, *Views: Communication No 123/1982*, UN Doc CCPR/C/21/D/123/1982 (25 March 1983)

M.T. v Uzbekistan, Human Rights Committee, *Views: Communication No 2234/2013*, UN Doc CCPR/C/114/D/2234/2013 (23 July 2015)

McTaggart v Jamaica, Human Rights Committee, *Views: Communication No 748/1997*, UN Doc CCPR/C/67/D/748/1997 (3 June 1998)

Mukong v Cameroon, Human Rights Committee, *Views: Communication No 458/91*, UN Doc CCPR/C/51/D/458/1991 (21 July 1994)

Portorreal v Dominican Republic, Human Rights Committee, *Views: Communication No 188/84*, UN Doc CCPR/C/31/D/188/1984 (5 November 1987)

Samathanam v Sri Lanka, Human Rights Committee, *Views: Communication No 2412/2014*, UN Doc CCPR/C/118/D/2412/2014 (28 October 2016)

Suleimenov v Kazakhstan, Human Rights Committee, *Views: Communication No 2146/2012*, UN Doc CCPR/C/119/D/2146/2012 (21 March 2017)

Toonen v Australia, Human Rights Committee, *Views: Communication No 488/1992*, UN Doc CCPR/C/50/D/488/1992 (4 April 1994)

Wanza v Trinidad and Tobago, Human Rights Committee, *Views: Communication No 683/1996*, UN Doc CCPR/C/74/D/683/1995 (26 March 2002)

Wilson v The Philippines, Human Rights Committee, *Views: Communication No 868/99*, UN Doc CCPR/C/79/D/868/1999 (30 October 2003)

Yasseen and Thomas v Guyana, Human Rights Committee, *Views: Communication No 676/1996*, UN Doc CCPR/C/62/D/676/1996 (30 March 1998)

United States of America Cases

Brown v Plata, unreported, Supreme Court of the United States, 23 May 2011

Introduction

In the 1840s, there was a short-lived experiment in prison reform in the penal settlement of Norfolk Island under the leadership of Captain Alexander Maconochie. Maconochie's starting premise was that penal settlement regimes, such as Van Diemen's Land, that focused on cruel treatment damaged not only those who were subject to such regimes, but the society that applied such treatment.[1] This is because people would return to society at least as dangerous as they were beforehand, if not more so. Maconochie opined that 'he had never known a bad man made better by punishment, though he had known many good men made worse'.[2]

Maconochie instead adopted a system intended to, in his own words, 'train them [convicts] to return to society, honest, useful and trustworthy members of it'.[3] His initiatives were extensive and included removing the gallows, allowing the convicts to eat with forks instead of their hands, teaching people to read and providing them with plots for farming produce they could then trade.[4] The men were also organised into groups with accountability for each other's conduct, which was intended to create a sense of social responsibility.[5] He introduced a reward system for good behaviour, with the men given 'marks', the collection of which

---

1   John Barry, 'Alexander Maconochie. 1787–1860' in Hermann Mannheim (ed.), *Pioneers in Criminology* (Patterson Smith Publishing Corporation, 1972) 85–6. This was a conclusion Maconochie reached following a detailed study of the penal system in Van Diemen's Land (Alexander Maconochie, *Report on the State of Prison Discipline in Van Diemen's Land* (London, 1838)): at 88–9.
2   Kenneth Maconochie, 'Captain Alexander Maconochie: Sociologist and Penal Reformer' (2009) 9(3) *The Howard Journal of Criminal Justice* 235, 236.
3   Cited by Barry, above n 1, 91.
4   Ibid 95–6.
5   John Moore, 'Alexander Maconochie's "Mark System"' (2011) 198 *Prison Service Journal* 38, 42; Barry, above n 1, 94.

would then reduce their time in the settlement. The aim was to provide an incentive for responsible behaviour.[6] Loss of marks was the only form of punishment imposed by Maconochie.[7]

People released from Norfolk Island during Maconochie's leadership became known as 'Maconochie's gentlemen',[8] with a reconviction rate of 3 per cent, compared to 9 per cent for those released from Van Diemen's Land.[9] To some extent then, Maconochie was achieving his stated reformist aim, namely, '[i]t is the duty, and even still more the interest of society, in dealing with its criminals, to try earnestly while they are in custody, to reform them'.[10]

Maconochie's experiment was short lived, lasting only from 1840–44, after which he was recalled to London.[11] His reforms were too much of a departure from the prevailing view that punishment should be the focus of imprisonment.[12]

There have been analyses suggesting that there are continuing lessons to be learned from Maconochie as a reformer.[13] Maconochie has been described by Taylor and Rynne as one of five—in their terms—'idealistic prison managers' that 'braved the punitive tide to apply reformative principles'.[14]

---

6   A J W Taylor and John Rynne, 'Exemplary Prisoner Management' (2016) 49(4) *Australian & New Zealand Journal of Criminology* 512, 515.

7   Barry, above n 1, 93.

8   As reflected by the title of Norval Morris's book, *Maconochie's Gentlemen. The Story of Norfolk Island and the Roots of Modern Prison Reform* (Oxford University Press, 2002). K Maconochie makes the point that 'after a year or so a new phrase was born which without further reference could get a man a job anywhere in the Australian colonies—if he could simply say: "I'm one of Captain Maconochie's men"': above n 2, 240.

9   K Maconochie, above n 2, 240.

10   Cited in John Barry, *Alexander Maconochie of Norfolk Island. A Study of a Pioneer in Penal Reform* (Oxford University Press, 1958) 214. This brief overview should not be taken to suggest Maconochie's leadership was entirely humane. He did, for example, use corporal punishment: Moore, above n 5, 44.

11   Barry, above n 1, 97.

12   K Maconochie, above n 2, 236. The start of Maconochie's experiment coincided with the grant of representative legislative institutions in the Australian colonies in 1840. Whether the two are related is unclear, though it has been noted that before 1840 many social and political issues were contested in the courts: David Neal, *The Rule of Law in a Penal Colony: Law and Power in Early New South Wales* (Cambridge University Press, 1992). The advent of some form of representative legislative institutions may have fostered a climate where novel changes could be attempted through other means.

13   See Morris's chapter entitled 'Contemporary Lessons from Maconochie's Experiment' in Morris, above n 8. K Maconochie also notes specific examples where Maconochie's philosophy has been followed since: above n 2, 235.

14   Taylor and Rynne, above n 6, 512.

The Australian Capital Territory named their only prison—opened in 2009—the 'Alexander Maconochie Centre' after Captain Maconochie due to its purported commitment to rehabilitation.[15]

At this distance in time, we are unlikely to be able to fully understand what Maconochie thought himself to be doing or exactly which aspects of his context he was reacting against. It may also seem far-fetched to compare a penal settlement in the 1840s to Australian prisons in 2020.[16] Yet there is at least one clear parallel between the society of which Maconochie was a part and contemporary Australia: both harbour(ed) conflicting opinions about the purposes of imprisonment. Is imprisonment about punishment (which sits at one end of the spectrum) or rehabilitation (which sits at the other)?

Those currently responsible for criminal justice policy in Australia, like Maconochie's contemporaries, valorise punishment (more commonly referred to as 'retribution'). Imprisonment is a central feature of the 'tough on crime' agenda that governments pursue Australia wide. Examples include the abolition of alternative sanctions to prison (such as home detention, which was abolished in Victoria in 2012), mandatory minimum sentences for a range of offences (including murder and sex offences in the Northern Territory), tightening the eligibility for parole (including 'no body, no parole laws' in South Australia, Victoria and the Northern Territory)[17] and 'supermax' prisons being established for certain categories within the prison population (such as the Woodford Correctional Centre in Queensland for members of 'Criminal Motorcycle Gangs').[18]

Predictably, the 'tough on crime' agenda has resulted in prison capacity failing to keep up with increases of the prison population. This is despite extensive investment to expand prison capacity (including 'rapid build' prisons in New South Wales).[19] Detailed statistics are provided in Chapter 1, and may be described as alarming. By way of overview, in the

---

15 Anita Mackay, 'The Road to the ACT's First Prison (the Alexander Maconochie Centre) was Paved with Rehabilitative Intentions' (2012) 11(1) *Canberra Law Review* 33, 52–3.

16 In 2002, Morris drew a parallel between 'supermax' prisons in the United States of America and the Norfolk Island colony prior to Maconochie taking over, noting that '[t]his deep end of the prison system raises similar problems to those that Maconochie confronted in 1840, with the distinction that the passage of years has led us to impose a degree of sensory deprivation on prisoners that Norfolk Island never attained': above n 8, 197–8.

17 These reforms are detailed in Chapter 4.

18 'Supermax' prisons, including Woodford, are discussed in Chapter 8.

19 Detailed in Chapter 4.

period from 2002–16, there have been increases in the imprisonment rate of 81 per cent in South Australia, 78 per cent in the Northern Territory and 74 per cent in Western Australia.[20] Nationally, prisons were operating at 121.2 per cent of capacity in 2016–17 on average (the most recent year for which a reliable national rate is available).[21]

Consequently, the Australian prison system is characterised by overcrowding, increasing levels of violence, lack of adequate treatment for people with mental illness and disability, lack of resources for educational and work programs, and other problems, all of which will be documented throughout this book. All of the above factors make it less likely that Australian prisons can 'reform' (as Maconochie would have put it) or 'rehabilitate' the people moving through them.[22] There is also the question of the damage this is doing to Australian society more broadly, as perceptively identified by Maconochie.

There are two pressing reasons why Australia's current valorisation of punishment and retributive goals of imprisonment, and the prison conditions that stem from this, require attention. The first is that imprisoned people should not be subjected to 'harsh conditions, humiliation or violence'.[23] It is simply unacceptable to degrade and brutalise people, regardless of the crime they may have committed. It is now widely accepted, including by courts, that people are sent to prison *as* punishment, not *for* punishment.[24]

---

20   Don Weatherburn, 'Australian Imprisonment 2002-2016: Crime, Policing and Penal Policy' (2018) 51(4) *Australian & New Zealand Journal of Criminology* 537, 538.
21   Steering Committee for the Review of Government Service Provision, *Report on Government Services 2018, Volume C: Justice* (Commonwealth of Australia, 2018) 8.14, Table 8A.13. The figure is 115.6 per cent for 2017–18, but Victoria, New South Wales (NSW) and South Australia did not provide data and, given that Victoria and NSW operate two of the larger prison systems in Australia, this skews the data: Steering Committee for the Review of Government Service Provision, *Report on Government Services 2019, Part C: Justice* (Commonwealth of Australia, 2019) 8.17.
22   The debates about the ability of prisons to achieve 'rehabilitation' are discussed in Chapter 6.
23   Bronwyn Naylor, 'Human Rights and Respect in Prisons: The Prisoners' Perspective' in Bronwyn Naylor, Julie Debeljak and Anita Mackay (eds), *Human Rights in Closed Environments* (The Federation Press, 2014) 84.
24   *Rich v Secretary of the Department of Justice* [2010] VSC 390, [45]; Bronwyn Naylor and Stan Winford, 'Implementing OPCAT Through Prison Monitoring: The Relevance of Rehabilitation' (2019) 25(1) *Australian Journal of Human Rights* 113, 113.

The second reason is that Australia has international legal obligations relating to the treatment of imprisoned people—obligations that it has voluntarily (and in one case quite recently) committed itself to—that must be complied with. Strategies for compliance with these obligations is the principal concern of this book.

Of particular relevance are Australia's obligations under the *International Covenant on Civil and Political Rights* (ICCPR) to ensure that the 'essential aim' of the prison system should be 'reformation and social rehabilitation' (art 10(3)), and that those deprived of their liberty should be treated with 'humanity and respect for the inherent dignity of the human person' (art 10(1)).[25] Australia has also ratified the *Convention against Torture and Other Cruel, Inhuman or Degrading Treatment or Punishment* (CAT) and is therefore required to prevent torture and 'other acts of cruel, inhuman or degrading treatment or punishment which do not amount to torture' in prisons.[26]

As recently as December 2017, Australia ratified the *Optional Protocol to the Convention against Torture and Other Cruel, Inhuman or Degrading Treatment or Punishment* (OPCAT).[27] The OPCAT establishes a system of monitoring of places where people are deprived of their liberty (defined in art 2, and definitely including prisons) that operates at the international and national level. At the international level, visits are conducted by the Subcommittee for the Prevention of Torture and Other Cruel, Inhuman or Degrading Treatment or Punishment (SPT) (established by art 2). Australia is also expected to establish a national-level National Preventive Mechanism (NPM) that meets the criteria set out in the OPCAT (required under art 3). Both the SPT and NPM are required to ensure the *prevention* of torture, cruel, inhuman or degrading treatment or punishment. This is significantly different from the monitoring currently carried out in Australia by organisations such as Ombudsmen and Coroners, that tends to be predominantly reactive.[28]

---

25   *International Covenant on Civil and Political Rights*, opened for signature 19 December 1966, 999 UNTS 171 (entered into force 23 March 1976) ('ICCPR'). Australia ratified the ICCPR on 23 November 1980.
26   Article 2 defines torture and Article 16 contains the requirement to prevent 'other acts': *Convention against Torture and Other Cruel, Inhuman or Degrading Treatment or Punishment*, opened for signature 10 December 1984, 1465 UNTS 85 (entered into force 26 June 1987) ('CAT'). Australia ratified the CAT on 10 December 1985.
27   *Optional Protocol to the Convention against Torture*, adopted 18 December 1992, UN Doc A/RES/57/199 (entered into force 22 June 2006) ('OPCAT').
28   This is discussed further in Chapter 3.

Often the relevant international human rights contained in these treaties and the OPCAT apply very generally across many sites where people are deprived of their liberty. Therefore, to understand the precise implications of these treaties for the operation of prisons, it is necessary to refer to a large body of additional rules,[29] principles[30] and, particularly, to the views, observations and General Comments of relevant treaty monitoring bodies and United Nations Special Rapporteurs.[31] This book clearly outlines the application of the treaties to Australian prisons and the practical steps required to comply.

Despite these layers of international law, it is possible to condense the requirements down to the position that once a person is imprisoned, while they may be denied their liberty, they maintain all their other rights.[32] There are numerous policies and practices in Australian prisons that do not meet this requirement. For example, people are routinely denied the right to personal safety by exposure to violence, and denied the right to privacy by being forced to use a toilet in front of a cellmate.[33] There are examples of torture and other cruel, inhuman or degrading treatment or punishment in Australian prisons, including:

- imprisoned people being shackled to their hospital beds when seeking medical treatment, including while giving birth or receiving end-of-life care (which is policy in South Australia)[34]

- a woman who was left to give birth in her prison cell in Western Australia alone without medical assistance in 2018, posing significant risks to both her and her baby[35]

---

29   Such as, for example, the United Nations *Standard Minimum Rules for the Treatment of Prisoners* (the Nelson Mandela Rules), UN Doc A/RES/70/175 (17 December 2015).

30   Such as, for example, the United Nations *Basic Principles for the Treatment of Prisoners* and *Body of Principles for the Protection of All Persons under Any Form of Detention or Imprisonment*.

31   Such as, for example, the Human Rights Committee established under the First Optional Protocol to the ICCPR and Committee against Torture established under the CAT. These mechanisms are detailed in Chapter 2. The need to refer to a 'large body' of material to understand the meaning of 'treating prisoners with humanity' in accordance with the ICCPR art 10(1) is identified by Andrew Coyle, *Humanity in Prison. Questions of Definition and Audit* (International Centre for Prison Studies, 2003) 22.

32   *Basic Principles for the Treatment of Prisoners*, Principle 5.

33   More detailed discussion of these matters is found in Chapters 4, 7 and 8. See, eg, Victorian Ombudsman, *Investigation into Deaths and Harms in Custody* (2014); Office of the Inspector of Custodial Services (OICS), *Western Australia's Prison Capacity* (2016) 15.

34   Ombudsman South Australia, *Ombudsman Investigation into the Department of Correctional Services in Relation to the Restraining and Shackling of Prisoners in Hospitals* (2012) 1. This policy is discussed in detail in Chapter 7.

35   OICS, *The Birth at Bandyup Women's Prison in March 2018. Inspector's Summary* (2018). This incident is discussed in detail in Chapter 7.

- a man with a psychosocial disability being kept in solitary confinement for 19 years in a Queensland prison.[36]

To date, much of the academic literature concerning human rights of imprisoned people focuses on the case law concerning situations where state parties have violated their obligations to imprisoned people—that is, the literature examines reactive responses, not proactive ones.[37] This book takes a different approach—one that aligns closely with the preventive objective of the OPCAT. It clarifies the treaty obligations, then asks what Australia *ought* to do to comply with them. In other words, it identifies proactive steps that should be taken to avoid human rights violations.

The proactive steps put forward in this book are categorised into five prerequisites for human rights compliance in Australian prisons:

1. reduce reliance on imprisonment
2. align domestic legislation with Australia's international human rights law obligations
3. shift the focus of imprisonment to the goal of rehabilitation and restoration
4. support prison staff to treat imprisoned people in a human rights–consistent manner
5. ensure decent physical conditions in all prisons.

These prerequisites address the gap between current prison operations and Australia's international human rights law requirements. They will assist policymakers and prison managers in three ways. First, by clearly outlining the international law requirements that apply in prisons. Second, by clarifying the practices that are likely to breach these requirements through detailed consideration of international and domestic case law. Third, by setting out practical steps for reform. The aim is to help Australia, as a party to the OPCAT, prepare for visits by the SPT, and to help individual prisons be better placed when preventive monitoring by the NPM commences.

---

36   Human Rights Watch, *'I Needed Help, Instead I Was Punished': Abuse and Neglect of Prisoners with Disabilities in Australia* (2018) 43. Solitary confinement is discussed in detail in Chapter 7.
37   See, eg, Nigel Rodley and Matt Pollard, *The Treatment of Prisoners Under International Law* (Oxford University Press, 3rd ed, 2009); Tim Owen and Alison Macdonald (eds), *Livingstone, Owen, and Macdonald on Prison Law* (Oxford University Press, 5th ed, 2015).

The book has three parts. The first part explores the gaps between current practice in Australian prisons and Australia's international human rights law obligations and explains the way that the current system of monitoring will need to shift from reactive to preventive. The second part details the national-level, system-wide changes necessary to close those gaps—the first three prerequisites. The remaining two prerequisites can be pursued within individual prisons, and these more micro-level actions are detailed in the third part.

The case for a departure from the prevailing approach to imprisonment in Australia is compelling. It is all the more compelling because there are alternatives available that, if implemented, would benefit both the individuals who are incarcerated and society as a whole. In this respect, the situation is reminiscent—at least in the starting premise and spirit—of the very practical reforms Captain Alexander Maconochie attempted 175 years ago.

Note Concerning Terminology

This book does not use the term 'prisoner' except when quoting other sources. Instead, this book uses the phrases 'imprisoned person' or 'person in prison' to place the shared humanity of people in prison at the forefront of the analysis. It is of the upmost importance that our shared humanity is reinforced if Australia is to act consistently with the dual international human rights law requirements that (1) people do not lose their human rights when imprisoned (other than the right to liberty) and (2) people be treated with 'humanity and respect for the inherent dignity of the human person'. To apply labels—including 'prisoner', 'offender', 'criminal', 'detainee', 'terrorist' and/or 'sex offender'—is to risk subtly justifying substandard, inhumane or less-than-optimal treatment—the very opposite of this book's purpose.

Part 1: Legal, Statistical and Sociological Context for the Operation of Prisons in Australia

1

The Australian Prison Population and Daily Life in Australian Prisons

Introduction

Prisons do not exist in a vacuum. Nor does prison law. The legal and other obligations that apply to prisons are greatly influenced by the society in which those prisons operate and the people that are held in them. This chapter provides the statistical and sociological context for the remainder of the book by providing an overview of key aspects of Australian prisons and imprisoned people.

The first part of the chapter provides a picture of the prison population in Australia. This includes the statistical profile of the Australian prison population, and an outline of the characteristics of this population and some of the ways it differs from the general population.[1] The unifying feature of this distinctiveness is vulnerability: the prison population contains an over-representation of vulnerable segments of the general population, including Indigenous Australians and people with mental health problems and cognitive disability.

---

1   The statistics in this chapter are based on Australian Bureau of Statistics data released in December 2019 drawn from a prison census conducted on 30 June 2019.

The second part of the chapter examines the sociological literature about daily life in Australian prisons. This is important background as to why this particular population requires the human rights protections that form the subject of the remainder of this book.

Men comprise the majority of the Australian prison population and for this reason much of the sociological literature focuses on men's experience of imprisonment. However, because women are one of the fastest growing sub-groups of the Australian prison population and because they have particular vulnerabilities, the first part of this chapter will also outline the statistical profile and vulnerabilities of the female prison population.[2] Selected references will be made to the treatment of women in Australian prisons throughout the remainder of the book. However, it should be noted that women's imprisonment is not the sole focus of this book and imprisoned women's vulnerabilities are sufficiently complex that they alone could be the subject of an entire book.

The Australian Prison Population

The prison population of Australia cannot be completely captured by statistics and simplified categories, but there are three key features. The first is how *many* people are incarcerated, including the trend of these numbers increasing over time (with overcrowding as the corollary). The second is the *disproportionate* imprisonment of members of certain groups of the general population, particularly Indigenous Australians.[3] The third is the characteristics that make people in prison a *vulnerable* group within Australian society.

Vulnerability is the norm rather than the exception in the Australian prison population. This bears out Garland's observations about the function of the prison within what he terms the 'culture of control'.[4] He argues

---

2   The female prison population rose consistently from 2011–18 before dropping by 4 per cent in 2019. The male prison population has been increasing since 2012, but not at as high a rate as the female prison population: Australian Bureau of Statistics, *Prisoners in Australia 2019* (5 December 2019) ('ABS 2019').

3   The first two themes are taken from Garland, who writes, 'imprisonment ceases to be a fate of a few criminal individuals and becomes a shaping institution for whole sectors of the population': David Garland, 'Introduction: The Meaning of Mass Imprisonment' in David Garland (ed), *Mass Imprisonment: Social Causes and Consequences* (SAGE, 2001) 2.

4   This is a framework for understanding developments in crime control in the United States of America (USA) and United Kingdom between 1975 and 2000 that can be generally characterised as involving increasing punitiveness.

that prisons are used as a means of 'segregating the problem populations created by today's economic and social arrangements'.[5] Garland's approach echoes Australian authors, such as Cunneen et al, who argue that prison 'has been reconstituted as a "therapeutic institution" providing a solution not only to serious criminal behaviour but also to behaviour seen as too difficult to manage in the community'.[6]

Imprisonment Statistics and Rates

As at 30 June 2019, there were 43,028 people in Australian prisons (a combination of those who have been sentenced, and those on remand), resulting in an overall imprisonment rate of 219 per 100,000 (409 per 100,000 males and 35 per 100,000 females).[7] Because criminal law, sentencing and prisons are a state/territory responsibility, there are variations in both the imprisonment rate and the growth of imprisonment rates across jurisdictions. The imprisonment rates for each state and territory are provided in Table 1.1 in ascending order (by the overall imprisonment rate), with the male and female imprisonment rates provided in separate columns. These rates are from the annual prison census conducted on 30 June 2019.

Table 1.1: Imprisonment Rates in Australian Jurisdictions as at 30 June 2019

Jurisdiction	Total imprisonment rate per 100,000 of population[8]	Male imprisonment rate per 100,000 of population[9]	Female imprisonment rate per 100,000 of population[10]
Australian Capital Territory	143.2	274.9	19.5
Victoria	157.1	297.8	22.0
Tasmania	164.7	308.4	25.6
South Australia	207.3	394.6	37.9
New South Wales	213.6	404.0	29.7

---

5   Garland, above n 3, 199.
6   Chris Cunneen et al, *Penal Culture and Hyperincarceration. The Revival of the Prison* (Ashgate, 2013) 285–6. A similar argument is made in relation to prisons in the USA by Loïc Waquant, 'Deadly Symbiosis: When Ghetto and Prison Meet and Mesh' in David Garland (ed), *Mass Imprisonment: Social Causes and Consequences* (SAGE, 2001) and, more broadly, David Scott, 'Unequalled in Pain' in David Scott (ed), *Why Prison?* (Cambridge University Press, 2013) 315 and the authors cited therein.
7   ABS 2019, above n 2.
8   Ibid, Table 17.
9   Ibid.
10   Ibid.

Jurisdiction	Total imprisonment rate per 100,000 of population[8]	Male imprisonment rate per 100,000 of population[9]	Female imprisonment rate per 100,000 of population[10]
Queensland	224.8	415.0	42.8
Western Australia	344.7	623.0	70.2
Northern Territory	942.0	1,708.3	128.5
Australia	218.6	409.0	34.9

The Northern Territory's rate of imprisonment is particularly startling.[11] As Scott observed, '[i]n March 2012 the Northern Territory had a prisoner rate of 821 per 100,000, which, if it was a nation in its own right, would be the number one penal incarcerator in the world'.[12] This rate has risen since 2012 and is much higher for males. As Table 1.1 shows, the rate of male imprisonment in the Northern Territory is 1,708.3 per 100,000. To put this into perspective, the *World Prison Brief* lists the highest imprisonment rate in the world as the United States of America's (USA's) rate of 655 per 100,000.[13]

The rate of imprisonment in Australia grew by 10 per cent between 2002 (when it was 152 per 100,000) and 2012 (when it reached 167 per 100,000) before rising higher still to the 2019 rate shown above of 218.6.[14] This has occurred despite overall crime rates declining.[15]

Although the rate of growth varies between states and territories, growth is a common feature across all jurisdictions and is a trend that applies regardless of which political party is in power (explanations for this growth and how it might be addressed are considered in Chapter 4). In the period between 2012 and 2013, the Australian Bureau of Statistics reported an upward trend in all jurisdictions except Western Australia and Tasmania.[16]

---

11   The Northern Territory's imprisonment rate has been higher than the national average for many years. For example, in 2008, the Northern Territory's male imprisonment rate was 1,111.9 per 100,000 while the national average was 320.3 per 100,000: ibid, Table 15.

12   Scott, above n 6, 5.

13   International Centre for Prison Studies, *World Prison Brief* <http://www.prisonstudies.org/world-prison-brief>. Similar to Australia, the USA's rate varies when broken down on a state-by-state basis.

14   Australian Institute of Criminology, *Australian Crime: Facts and Figures: 2013* (2014) Chapter 6 ('AIC 2013').

15   Ibid, Foreword. There are some exceptions to the general trend of declining crime rates. For a detailed discussion see Rick Sarre, 'The Importance of Political Will in the Imprisonment Debate' (2009) 21(1) *Current Issues in Criminal Justice* 154, 157–8 and the statistics in ibid.

16   Australian Bureau of Statistics, *Prisoners in Australia 2013* (2014).

Taking a longer-term perspective, Weatherburn compared the increases in imprisonment rates across jurisdictions between 2002–16 and found an increase of 81 per cent in South Australia, 78 per cent in the Northern Territory and 74 per cent in Western Australia.[17] The Victorian Sentencing Advisory Council documents that the Victorian imprisonment rate increased by 40 per cent between 2002 and 2012.[18]

The consequence of this rapid growth in the prison population is overcrowding, which is an increasing problem in Australian prisons.[19] The Victorian Auditor-General has highlighted that the 'nationally-accepted limit for the safe and efficient operation of the prison system' is a 95 per cent utilisation rate.[20] Yet the Report on Government Services highlights that secure facilities nationally were operating at 121.2 per cent of capacity in 2016–17 (the most recent year for which a reliable national rate is available),[21] with West Australian secure prisons operating at 132.8 per cent capacity in 2018–19.[22] The Victorian Ombudsman referred to overcrowding in Victorian prisons as a 'crisis' in 2014, writing that '[a]s a result of overcrowding, people detained in custody in Victoria face a greater risk of harm than any time in the past decade'.[23]

Overcrowding is a theme that recurs throughout this book because it is a major factor precluding human rights compliance in Australian prisons. It will be seen that overcrowding is itself often a breach of human rights (such as when it leads to two or three people being held in a cell designed for one), but it also indirectly causes or worsens distinct breaches of human rights (such as when the stresses of crowded prisons leads to greater violence).

---

17   Don Weatherburn, 'Australian Imprisonment 2002-2016: Crime, Policing and Penal Policy' (2018) 51(4) *Australian & New Zealand Journal of Criminology* 537, 538.
18   Sentencing Advisory Council, *Victoria's Prison Population 2002–2012* (2013).
19   Termed 'hyperincarceration' by Cunneen et al, above n 6.
20   It was noted in the report that this rate 'allows prison management the flexibility to adequately manage the rehabilitation, human rights and welfare of prisoners. Operating above 95 per cent utilisation compromises the ability of prison management to safely and humanely manage prisoners': Victorian Auditor-General, *Prison Capacity Planning* (2012) 9.
21   Steering Committee for the Review of Government Service Provision, *Report on Government Services 2018, Volume C: Justice* (Commonwealth of Australia, 2018) 8.14, Table 8A.13. The figure is 115.6 per cent for 2017–18, but Victoria, New South Wales and South Australia did not provide data and, given that Victoria and New South Wales operate two of the larger prison systems in Australia, this skews the data: Steering Committee for the Review of Government Service Provision, *Report on Government Services 2019, Part C: Justice* (Commonwealth of Australia, 2019) 8.17.
22   Steering Committee for the Review of Government Service Provision, *Report on Government Services 2020, Volume C: Justice* (Commonwealth of Australia, 2020) Table 8A.13.
23   Victorian Ombudsman, *Investigation into Deaths and Harms in Custody* (2014) 10.

Over-Representation of Certain Population Groups

This section will cover four of the population groups that are over-represented in the Australian prison population: (1) Indigenous Australians, (2) people with mental illness or cognitive disability, (3) people from disadvantaged locations and (4) older people.

The general national picture is captured well by Cunneen et al when noting, 'the rapid increases in imprisonment rates across Australian jurisdictions (and arguably elsewhere) from the mid-1980s onward, while clearly variable and far from uniform across the Australian states and territories, can be seen as predominantly composed of Indigenous men, women and juveniles'.[24] This book does not deal with juveniles, but will deal with the other main sub-groups, as well as some additional aforementioned sub-groups. This is because juvenile detention is a specialised area and under international human rights law, the starting position (that juvenile detention should only be used 'as a measure of last resort and for the shortest appropriate period of time'[25]) is different to the starting position that applies in relation to adult imprisonment (this will be detailed in Chapter 2).

Indigenous Australians

The over-representation of Indigenous Australians in prison is striking. Indigenous people (men and women) make up 28 per cent (11,866) of the national adult prison population despite only comprising 2 per cent of the general adult population.[26] This means that the overall national imprisonment rate of 219 per 100,000 cited above, when broken down by Indigenous status, is 162 for non-Indigenous Australians and 2,349 for Indigenous Australians.[27] It also means that if the imprisonment rates in Table 1.1 were separated by Indigenous and non-Indigenous by jurisdiction, the imprisonment rate for non-Indigenous people would be lower and the difference even more striking. A useful way of characterising the figures is that Indigenous Australians are approximately 13 times more likely to be imprisoned than non-Indigenous Australians.[28]

---

24   Cunneen et al, above n 6, 182. Cunneen defined women and the first three categories as 'Suitable Enemies: Penal Subjects': at Chapter 5.
25   *Convention on the Rights of the Child*, opened for signature 20 November 1989, 1577 UNTS 3 (entered into force 2 September 1990), art 37(b). Australia ratified this Convention on 17 December 1990.
26   ABS 2019, above n 2, Table 2.
27   ABS 2019, above n 2, Table 17.
28   Human Rights Watch, *'I Needed Help, Instead I Was Punished': Abuse and Neglect of Prisoners with Disabilities in Australia* (2018) 20.

The Indigenous imprisonment rate varies around the country. For instance, the imprisonment rate for Indigenous people in Western Australia is 70 per cent higher than the national imprisonment rate.[29] The imprisonment rate for Indigenous people in each of the states and territories is shown (in ascending order) in Table 1.2 alongside the Indigenous proportion of the prison population in each jurisdiction.

Table 1.2: Indigenous Imprisonment Rates in Australian Jurisdictions as at 30 June 2019

Jurisdiction	Indigenous imprisonment rate per 100,000 of population[30]	Indigenous proportion of prison population (%)[31]
Tasmania	777.3	20.2
New South Wales	1,879.9	23.1
Australian Capital Territory	1,944.2	21.9
Queensland	2,098.7	32.8
Victoria	2,267.7	10.4
South Australia	2,551.1	23.8
Northern Territory	2,837.4	83.4
Western Australia	4,105.7	38.6
Australia	2,349.2	27.6

The over-imprisonment of Indigenous people is even more acute when particular communities are examined. For example, in the town of Papunya, Northern Territory, 72 out of the total population of 308 adults (23 per cent) were imprisoned during 2007–08.[32] Such a high imprisonment rate has implications for the entire community.

The Indigenous imprisonment rate is growing rapidly. Between 2004 and 2018, the Indigenous prison population rose by 88 per cent, whereas the remainder of the prison population rose by 28 per cent.[33]

---

29   The Honourable Wayne Martin (Chief Justice of Western Australia), 'Indigenous Incarceration Rates. Strategies for Much Needed Reform' (Speech, 2015) 4. The figures quoted in this speech were from the Australian Bureau of Statistics in 2014 when the rate was 3,663 per 100,000 in Western Australia and 2,174 per 100,000 nationally. For a discussion of possible causes see Hilde Tubex et al, 'Western Australian Penal Culture and Indigenous Over-Representation: Evaluating 25 Years of Law, Policy and Practice' (2018) 43(1) *The University of Western Australia Law Review* 264.
30   ABS 2019, above n 2, Table 17.
31   Ibid, Table 14.
32   Melanie Schwartz, 'Building Communities, Not Prisons: Justice Reinvestment and Indigenous Overimprisonment' (2010) 14(1) *Australian Indigenous Law Review* 2, 4–5.
33   Human Rights Watch, above n 28, 21.

Indigenous women represent the fastest growing sub-group in the Australian prison population overall. Human Rights Watch report that they are '21 times more likely to be incarcerated than their non-indigenous peers'.[34] This rate also varies across jurisdictions. For example, in Western Australia, Indigenous women comprise more than 50 per cent of the female prison population.[35]

Indigenous incarceration was the subject of a recent in-depth inquiry by the Australian Law Reform Commission, which produced a detailed report in December 2017. The report found that over-representation of Indigenous people in prisons is the culmination of over-representation at every stage of the criminal justice system (being arrested, charged, prosecuted and sentenced).[36] The report also found that Indigenous people were disproportionately more likely than non-Indigenous people to receive a custodial sentence, rather than a community-based sentence.[37] The report contained a number of recommendations to address this situation and the main recommendations concerning justice reinvestment will be considered in detail in Chapter 4.[38]

People with Mental Illness or Cognitive Disability

There are high rates of mental illness and cognitive disability across the prison population. The precise proportion of imprisoned people with mental illness varies according to the definition of mental illness used. The Australian Institute of Health and Welfare reports that 35 per cent of male prison entrants and 37 per cent of male prison dischargees fall into the category of 'reported being told by a health professional that they had a mental health condition (including alcohol and other drug use disorders)'. The figures are 65 per cent and 38 per cent respectively for females.[39]

---

34   Ibid 23.

35   Martin, above n 29, 4. The figures quoted in this speech were from the Australian Bureau of Statistics in 2014.

36   The executive summary reports, 'Over-representation increases with the stages of the criminal justice system. In 2016, Aboriginal and Torres Strait Islander people were seven times more likely than non-Indigenous people to be charged with a criminal offence and appear before the courts; 11 times more likely to be held in prison on remand awaiting trial or sentence, and 12.5 times more likely to receive a sentence of imprisonment': Australian Law Reform Commission, *Pathways to Justice—An Inquiry into the Incarceration Rate of Aboriginal and Torres Strait Islander Peoples*, Report No 133 (2017) 26.

37   The executive summary reports, 'Up to 45% of Aboriginal and Torres Strait Islander offenders sentenced in 2015–2016 received a sentence of imprisonment of less than six months. Few received a community-based sentence': ibid.

38   These were recommendations 4-1 and 4-2 contained in Chapter 4 of the report: ibid 137–8.

39   Australian Institute of Health and Welfare, *The Health of Australian Prisoners 2018* (2019) 28. This is based on individuals' responses when 'asked whether they had ever been told that they have a mental health disorder by a doctor, psychiatrist, psychologist or nurse': ibid 137–8.

Other studies range from indicating that 30 per cent of the prison population have been diagnosed with a mental illness[40] to 80 per cent of the prison population having a psychiatric illness over a period of 12 months.[41] One study of females in South Australian prisons, which had an 81 per cent participation rate, found that all respondents had a psychiatric disorder.[42]

Moreover, it has been reported that 20 per cent of the prison population have an intellectual disability,[43] and as many as 80 per cent of imprisoned people have a history of brain trauma (depending on the definition used).[44] A Victorian study reported that 40 per cent of the prison population had an acquired brain injury, compared to 2 per cent of the general population.[45]

These categories overlap. Many people present with comorbidity, such as 'mental or cognitive impairment with a substance abuse disorder', with Cunneen et al arguing that this group, often referred to as those having 'complex needs', is 'a large and neglected group' within the prison population.[46]

Despite a lack of comprehensive data on this subject, it is generally agreed that Indigenous people in prisons also display complex mental health needs.[47] Human Rights Watch reported in 2018 that '[a]bout 73 percent of Aboriginal and Torres Strait Islander men and 86 percent of Aboriginal

---

40   Victoria Herrington and Katrina Clifford, 'Policing Mental Illness: Examining the Police Role in Addressing Mental Ill Health' in Isabelle Bartkowiak-Théron and Nicole Asquith (eds), *Policing Vulnerabilities* (Federation Press, 2012) 117.

41   Tony Butler et al, 'Mental Disorders in Australian Prisoners: A Comparison with a Community Sample' (2006) 40 *Australian and New Zealand Journal of Psychiatry* 272. A NSW study from 2003 found that '[t]he 12-month occurrence of any psychiatric disorder (psychosis, anxiety disorder, affective disorder, substance use disorder, personality disorder or neurasthenia) was 74 per cent amongst prisoners': cited by Cunneen et al, above n 6, 97.

42   Claire O'Connor 'Victims or Offenders? Mental Health Issues in Women's Prisons' (2007) 81 *Precedent* 26, 27.

43   Terese Henning, 'Vulnerable Suspects and Arrest and Investigative Processes' in Isabelle Bartkowiak-Théron and Nicole Asquith (eds), *Policing Vulnerabilities* (Federation Press, 2012) 218.

44   James Huntley, 'Acquired Brain Injury and Vulnerability to the Criminal Justice System' in Isabelle Bartkowiak-Théron, and Nicole Asquith (eds), *Policing Vulnerabilities* (Federation Press, 2012) 173.

45   A 2011 study cited by Gaye Lansdell et al, '"I am Not Drunk, I Have an ABI": Findings From a Qualitative Study into Systematic Challenges in Responding to People with Acquired Brain Injuries in the Justice System' (2018) 25(5) *Psychiatry, Psychology and Law* 737, 737–8.

46   Cunneen et al, above n 6, 99.

47   Robin Jones and Andrew Day, 'Mental Health, Criminal Justice and Culture: Some Ways Forward?' (2011) 19 *Australasian Psychiatry* 325. For an in-depth examination relating to 2,731 persons in the state of NSW see Eileen Baldry et al, *A Predictable and Preventable Path: Aboriginal People with Mental and Cognitive Disabilities in the Criminal Justice System* (UNSW, 2015).

and Torres Strait Islander women in prison have a diagnosed mental health condition'.[48] An older study that broke this down into different types of mental conditions found that 6.6 per cent of Indigenous imprisoned males screened positive for psychosis. A further 13.1 per cent of males and 43.1 per cent of females had mood disorders and 34.4 per cent of males and 58.6 per cent of females had anxiety disorders (the most common of which was posttraumatic stress disorder). Finally, the study found that '[n]early 50% of males and over 85% of Indigenous females reported medium or higher levels of psychological distress'.[49]

Another indicator of mental illness or distress among the prison population is the number reporting a history of self-harm or who are at risk of suicide. Upon prison entry, it has been found that 31 per cent of female entrants and 20 per cent of male entrants report a history of self-harm. When asked if they have had thoughts about harming themselves recently (in the past 12 months), the figures were 16 per cent for females and 14 per cent for males.[50] People are assessed for risk of suicide or self-harm upon prison entry, with five per cent of males and three per cent of females identified as at risk.[51]

The World Health Organization has recognised that the nature of imprisonment is likely to worsen people's mental health if they have problems upon entry, or to cause mental health problems in some people that are healthy upon entry. This is due to factors such as the disciplinary regime, lack of choice about activities and people they spend time with, and limited communication with family and friends.[52] These are aspects of daily life in Australian prisons that are outlined in more detail later in this chapter.

---

48   Human Rights Watch, above n 28, 22.
49   The study was conducted by Butler et al in 2001 and confirmed by Heffernan, Andersen and Kinner to be the largest study in 2009 (although they argue that there were some methodological problems with the study): Edward Heffernan, Kimina Andersen and Stuart Kinner, 'The Insidious Problem Inside: Mental Health Problems of Aboriginal and Torres Strait Islander People in Custody' (2009) 17(17) *Australasian Psychiatry* S41, S42–3. A study of Queensland prisoners referred to by a Senate Committee 'found that 72.8 per cent of men and 86.1 per cent of women has at least one mental health disorder': Senate Legal and Constitutional Affairs References Committee, *Value of a Justice Reinvestment Approach to Criminal Justice in Australia* (2013) 35.
50   Australian Institute of Health and Welfare, n 39, 43–4.
51   Ibid 47.
52   World Health Organization, *Health in Prisons. A WHO Guide to the Essentials in Prison Health* (2007) 134.

Disadvantaged Locations

Prison populations in countries such as the USA, the United Kingdom (UK) and Australia are overwhelmingly drawn from a small number of locations, with Cunneen et al terming this 'imprisonment by postcode'.[53] These are locations with high levels of economic and social disadvantage. The stigma associated with imprisonment, and consequent difficulty in obtaining employment and housing, has a tendency to exacerbate such disadvantage.[54] It has also been observed that prison becomes normalised in such communities, to the extent where it is considered 'a near inevitability'.[55]

The discussions about, and trials of, justice reinvestment have significantly advanced our understanding of the over-representation of people from disadvantaged locations in the prison population. Justice reinvestment is discussed in detail in Chapter 4, but in essence it entails reallocating some of the money spent on imprisonment and investing it, in the form of social assistance, in the localities from which the majority of imprisoned people come. This includes investment in, for example, education and employment assistance programs. The way the relevant communities are identified is by 'justice mapping', which also involves assessing what services are already available in these localities.[56] Justice mapping in Texas, for example, reveals that 'five counties [out of 254] … accounted for more than half of the people imprisoned'. Further, '50 per cent of former prisoners returned to neighbourhoods that accounted for only 15 per cent of the Houston population'.[57]

The same level of detail is not available in Australian data, as noted by the Senate Legal and Constitutional Affairs References Committee during an inquiry into justice reinvestment.[58] However, a study of the 'distribution of disadvantage in Australia' by Vinson compared indicators of disadvantage falling into the categories of (1) social distress, (2) health, (3) community safety, including prison admissions, (4) economic hardship

---

53   Cunneen et al, above n 6, 139.
54   Alison Shinkfield and Joseph Graffam, 'Community Reintegration of Ex-Prisoners' (2009) 53(1) *International Journal of Offender Therapy and Comparative Criminology* 29.
55   Cunneen et al, above n 6, 143, 193.
56   David Brown, Melanie Schwartz and Laura Boseley, 'The Promise of Justice Reinvestment' (2012) 37(2) *Alternative Law Journal* 96, 97.
57   Senate Legal and Constitutional Affairs References Committee, above n 49, 50.
58   Ibid 95–7.

and (5) education, in geographic units around Australia.[59] The study revealed that '1.7% of the geographic counting units in each jurisdiction account for seven times their share of the top ranking positions across all of the indicators'.[60] A separate New South Wales (NSW) survey of people following their release from prison found that '50 per cent of these persons originally from the Sydney area came from and went back to just eight locations in western Sydney'.[61] Finally, the Victorian Ombudsman has observed that a 'quarter of Victoria's prisoners come from just 2 per cent of the State's postcodes and half from just 6 per cent'.[62]

In summary, socio-economic disadvantage is not evenly spread across Australia. The localities from which the prison population comes are disproportionately those that are socio-economically disadvantaged. This contributes to the concentration of socio-economic disadvantage in the prison population, which is one of the vulnerabilities discussed in the next section.

Older People

The Australian population is ageing, and the prison population is ageing at an even greater rate. The Australian Institute of Criminology defines elderly people in prison to be those over 50 years of age, which takes into account that the health of people in prison is generally worse than that of people in the general community. The health of a 50-year-old person in prison is likely to be equivalent to the health of a 60-year-old person in the community.[63]

This particular group within the prison population increased by 84 per cent between 2000 and 2010, such that they comprised 11.2 per cent of the national prison population by 2011.[64] The NSW statistics are illustrative and have been detailed recently by the NSW Inspector of Custodial Services who reported:

---

59   Tony Vinson, *Dropping Off the Edge. The Distribution of Disadvantage in Australia* (Jesuit Social Services/Catholic Social Services Australia, 2007) x. In some jurisdictions the 'geographic units' were Statistical Local Areas, and in others Local Government Areas.
60   Ibid xi.
61   Cunneen et al, above n 6, 141.
62   Victorian Ombudsman, *Investigation into the Rehabilitation and Reintegration of Prisoners in Victoria* (2015) 5.
63   Susan Baidawi et al, *Older Prisoners—A Challenge for Australian Corrections* (Trends and Issues in Crime and Criminal Justice No 426, 2011) 1.
64   Ibid 2.

NSW has seen an overall increase in the prison population of 25 percent for the 10 years 2005-2015. Offenders aged over 55 increased on average 91 percent for this same period. This growth was most marked in the over 65 year olds, with elderly men increasing by approximately 225 percent and the number of elderly women increasing from three to eight percent over the last decade.[65]

It has also been noted that in the past 10 years, there has been a 250 per cent increase in the number of older people incarcerated in the ACT.[66]

The ageing of the prison population is occurring at a faster rate than the ageing of the general population.[67] Explanations for the ageing prison population include sentencing laws (eg, mandatory minimum sentences and reduced options for early release) that mean people are spending longer in prison. It is also because higher proportions of older people are being convicted of offences that have longer sentences attached and due to convictions for historical sexual abuse (which has been given greater national attention recently due to the Royal Commission into Institutional Responses to Child Abuse that reported in 2017).[68]

Vulnerabilities

There are other characteristics of the Australian prison population that provide an important backdrop for the consideration of compliance with international human rights law in prisons. They fall into three categories: (1) general health, (2) socio-economic status and (3) the specific vulnerabilities of women.

---

65   NSW Inspector of Custodial Services, *Old and Inside: Managing Aged Offenders in Custody* (2015) 16. For another report relating to NSW see Chris Angus *Older Prisoners: Trends and Challenges* (NSW Parliamentary Research Service, 2015).
66   ACT Inspector of Correctional Services, *Report of a Review of a Correctional Centre by the ACT Inspector of Correctional Services Healthy Prison Review of the Alexander Maconochie Centre* (2019) 98.
67   Statistics about the general population 'show that the numbers of Australians aged 50 years and over increased by 31 percent over the period 2000–10, comparatively smaller than the 84 percent increase observed in the older prisoner population over the same period': Baidawi, above n 63.
68   Ibid 2–3; NSW Inspector of Custodial Services, above n 65, 16; ACT Inspector of Correctional Services, above n 66, 98.

General Health

In addition to the mental health and disability rates outlined above, imprisoned people as a group tend to have poor overall health when compared to the general population. This contributes to them being classified as 'elderly' at a younger age than people in the wider community. The Australian Institute of Health and Welfare provides the following snapshot:

> Prisoners have higher levels of mental health problems, risky alcohol consumption, tobacco smoking, illicit drug use, chronic disease and communicable diseases than the general population. This means that prisoners have significant and complex health needs, which are often long-term or chronic in nature. The health of prisoners is sufficiently poorer than in the general community such that prisoners are often considered to be geriatric at the age of 50–55.[69]

Drug and alcohol addiction feature prominently among the prison population and at much higher rates than among the general community (three times higher for men and six times higher for women[70]):

- 65 per cent of imprisoned people have used illicit drugs in the 12 months prior to their incarceration[71]
- 46 per cent have injected drugs[72]
- 34 per cent of prison entrants were found to be at risk of a high level of alcohol-related harm in the past 12 months.[73]

Smoking is another relevant addiction, with 75 per cent of people entering prison identifying as smokers.[74] This compares to the national average of 12.2 per cent.[75] This is not surprising given the over-representation in

---

69   References contained in the original quotation are excluded. Australian Institute of Health and Welfare, *The Health of Australian Prisoners 2015* (2015) 2.
70   Australian Institute of Health and Welfare, above n 39, 97.
71   Ibid 92.
72   Ibid 95.
73   Ibid 101. The same report notes the following about how this assessment is made: 'The proportion of prison entrants who are at risk of alcohol-related harm was determined using questions on alcohol consumption from the WHO's Alcohol Use Disorder Identification Test (AUDIT) screening instrument. The consumption component of this instrument (AUDIT-C) contains the three consumption questions from the AUDIT, with each question scoring 0–4. Scores for the three questions are summed, with a maximum possible score of 12. A score of 6 or more indicates a risk of alcohol-related harm.': at 101.
74   Ibid 85.
75   Australian Institute of Health and Welfare, *National Drug Strategy Household Survey 2016 Detailed Findings* (2017) 7.

prison of sub-groups (eg, those with a mental illness, illicit drug users and Indigenous people) that have a high incidence of smoking generally. The Australian Institute of Health and Welfare has found:

- 'people who reported smoking daily were ... twice as likely to have been diagnosed with, or treated for, a mental health condition as those who had never smoked (29% compared with 12.4%)'[76]
- 27 per cent of Indigenous Australians are smokers[77]
- 28 per cent of illicit drug users smoke.[78]

An example of communicable disease is the prevalence of Hepatitis C among the prison population, which stands at 31 per cent nationally.[79] A study of Hepatitis C transmission in Australian prisons found that the highest rate, 42 per cent, was in NSW and the lowest, 21 per cent, was in Western Australia. The Indigenous rate was higher, at 43 per cent, than the non-Indigenous rate of 33 per cent.[80] There is evidence that being incarcerated increases the chances of contracting Hepatitis C. A NSW study, for example, found that one in three injecting drug users in prison contracted the disease.[81]

Socio-Economic Status

Relevant socio-economic indicators for the prison population, as identified by the Australian Institute of Health and Welfare, include poor levels of education, low levels of employment, high levels of homelessness and a significant proportion of people who have a parent who had also been imprisoned.

---

76   Ibid 113. As an illustration, 68 per cent of patients at the Thomas Embling Hospital in Victoria (a secure mental health facility) identified as smokers in a 2013 survey: *Robert Peter De Bruyn v Victorian Institute of Forensic Mental Health* [2016] VSC 111, [32].

77   Ibid 105. These rates are higher in some jurisdictions. For example, in the Northern Territory, 66 per cent of Indigenous males and 47 per cent of Indigenous females are smokers: Marita Hefler, Robyn Hopkins and David Thomas, 'Successes and Unintended Consequences of the Northern Territory's Smoke-Free Prisons Policy: Results From a Process Evaluation' (2016) 26(2) *Public Health Research and Practice* 1, 2.

78   Ibid 9.

79   Australian Institute of Health and Welfare, above n 69, 55.

80   Jack Wallace et al, *Regulating Hepatitis C: Rights and Duties. Preventing Hepatitis C Transmission in Australian Adult Correctional Settings* (La Trobe University, 2009) 9.

81   Kate Dolan et al, 'Incidence and Risk for Acute Hepatitis C Infection During Imprisonment in Australia' (2010) 25 *European Journal of Epidemiology* 2.

Education

It has been found that 33 per cent of Australian prison entrants have not completed Year 10, with 17 per cent of those having completed 'year 8 or below'.[82] Indigenous people entering prison are more likely to have completed 'year 8 or below' with the proportion being 24 per cent.[83] The comparisons the Australian Institute of Health and Welfare make with the general community are broken down by age group. For instance, of people aged between 25 and 34, 24 per cent of non-Indigenous prison entrants and 21 per cent of Indigenous prison entrants have completed only Year 10 or below, compared to 17 per cent of the non-Indigenous and 2 per cent of Indigenous people in the general population.[84]

The Australian Institute of Health and Welfare go on to report that '[b]oth Indigenous (2–4%) and non-Indigenous (6–11%) prison entrants aged 20–44 were less likely than their general community counterparts to have completed Year 12 or equivalent (10–26% and 13–36% respectively)'.[85]

Employment

In the 30 days prior to incarceration, 67 per cent of Indigenous and 50 per cent of non-Indigenous entrants report being unemployed.[86] Approximately 29 per cent of prison entrants report having 'a chronic condition or disability that affected their participation in day-to-day activities', with 22 per cent of females and 15 per cent of males reporting that this impacted on their employment.[87]

Homelessness

The Australian Institute of Health and Welfare has found that '[p]rison entrants were around 66 times more likely to be homeless than people in the general community'.[88] In the four weeks prior to incarceration,

---

82   Australian Institute of Health and Welfare, above n 39, 16. Note that the Australian Institute of Health and Welfare does not provide a breakdown of the education levels for male and female prison entrants.
83   Ibid 17.
84   Australian Institute of Health and Welfare, above n 69, 23. The comparative data is from the earlier Australian Institute of Health and Welfare report because the 2019 report only provides the comparison for tertiary studies.
85   Ibid.
86   Ibid 18.
87   Ibid 78. See also Figure 9.1: ibid 79.
88   Ibid 22.

5 per cent of prison entrants were 'in unconventional housing or sleeping rough', and 37 per cent of Indigenous entrants and 23 per cent of non-Indigenous entrants were in 'short-term/emergency accommodation'.[89]

Parental Imprisonment

The high proportion of people in prison with a parent who had been incarcerated when they were children reveals an inter-generational trend in imprisonment. The stigma and disruption of having a parent incarcerated has social and emotional consequences for children, causing social disadvantage.[90] Eighteen per cent of prison entrants 'reported that 1 or more of their parents or carers had been in prison during their childhood'.[91] The figures for Indigenous prison entrants were higher, with 31 per cent of Indigenous entrants and 11 per cent of non-Indigenous entrants reporting this as their situation.[92]

Women's Vulnerability

It has been established in the preceding discussion that women represent a rapidly growing segment of the Australian prison population, particularly Indigenous women. They also have higher levels of mental illness than male prison entrants and the male levels are disproportionately higher than the general population.

There are some further vulnerabilities specific to women imprisoned in Australia that it is important to emphasise. These are the high rates of victimisation and the high proportion of women who are primary caregivers for dependent children. When these are combined with the higher rates of mental illness, it leads to the conclusion that '[t]he prevalence of histories of abuse and violence and the experience of multiple and complex support needs among women in prison can no longer be overlooked as somehow exceptional or marginal'.[93]

---

89   Ibid. See also Figures 2.8 and 2.9: ibid 23.
90   See, eg, Alannah Burgess and Catherine Flynn, 'Supporting Imprisoned Mothers and Their Children. A Call for Evidence' (2013) 60(1) *Probation Journal* 73.
91   Australian Institute of Health and Welfare, above n 39, 14.
92   Ibid.
93   Ruth McCausland and Eileen Baldry 'Understanding Women Offenders in Prison' in Jane Ireland et al (eds), *The Routledge International Handbook of Forensic Psychology in Secure Settings* (Routledge, 2017) 32.

A national study estimated that between 57 and 90 per cent of women in prison have been victims of childhood sexual abuse.[94] More recent data from Queensland suggests that 37 per cent have been victims of abuse before they turn 16 and 35 per cent before they turn 10.[95]

These rates are even higher among Indigenous women. The Australian Law Reform Commission provides the following up-to-date summary of the research:

> Prison population surveys have revealed high rates of family violence and sexual abuse among incarcerated Aboriginal and Torres Strait Islander women. One Western Australian study suggested that up to 90% of Aboriginal and Torres Strait Islander female prisoners were survivors of family and other violence. A New South Wales study in 2014 revealed that 70% of the Aboriginal and Torres Strait Islander female prisoners disclosed they were survivors of child sexual abuse, with 44% subject to ongoing sexual abuse as adults and 78% experiencing violence as adults.[96]

A number of monitoring bodies have recognised the traumatic impact that standard prison practices—particularly strip searching—can have on women with this history. For example, the Queensland Ombudsman wrote in an investigation of strip searching at the Townsville Women's Correctional Centre that 'research also suggests that, due to the high levels of past sexual abuse among female prisoners, strip searches have the capacity to negatively impact (including re-traumatise) female prisoners more significantly than other parts of the population and may jeopardise attempts at rehabilitation'.[97] The Victorian Ombudsman has also criticised the practice at the Dame Phyllis Frost Centre, reporting:

> this humiliating, degrading and undignified practice persists, described by some women prisoners as a form of sexual assault. It should not be forgotten that many women prisoners are victims of sexual abuse, for whom strip searching has the potential to inflict further trauma.[98]

---

94   Mary Stathopoulos, 'Addressing Women's Victimisation in Custodial Settings' (ACSSA Issues No 13, Australian Institute of Family Studies Australian Centre for the Study of Sexual Assault, 2012) 4.
95   Anti-Discrimination Commission Queensland, *Women in Prison* (2017) 72.
96   Australian Law Reform Commission, above n 36, 351.
97   Queensland Ombudsman, *The Strip Searching of Female Prisoners Report. An Investigation into the Strip Search Practices at Townsville Women's Correctional Centre* (2014) 5.
98   Victorian Ombudsman, *Implementing OPCAT in Victoria: Report and Inspection of the Dame Phyllis Frost Centre* (2017) 5. See also Anti-Discrimination Commission Queensland, above n 95, 72–3; ACT Human Rights and Discrimination Commissioner, *Human Rights Audit on the Conditions of Detention of Women at the Alexander Maconochie Centre* (2014) 68–9.

Two-thirds of women sentenced to imprisonment are primary caregivers for dependent children.[99] These children have to be cared for by relatives during their mother's incarceration, or are taken into the care of the state. Being in prison has a well-recognised differential impact on mothers, with Burgess and Flynn explaining that '[t]hese pre-existing vulnerabilities are further compounded by experiences during the prison sentence, which can negate women's role and confidence as mothers, leading to mental health concerns and fear that they will lose their children's love'.[100]

Concluding Remarks on the Australian Prison Population Profile

The prison population in Australia is increasing, but it is not representative of the broader community. Particular sub-groups, including Indigenous people, women and mentally ill people, are over-represented. This combines with other socio-economic disadvantage and health problems to mean that the prison population is comprised of the most vulnerable and marginalised members of the community.[101] Put another way, those sent to prison are more likely to be disadvantaged in one or more ways and those already disadvantaged groups are becoming increasingly likely to be imprisoned.

The causal factors generating Australia's prison population profile are complex and extend beyond penal policies. They include:

- harsh sentencing policies that lead to increased use of imprisonment and longer sentences[102]
- over-policing of Indigenous communities[103]

---

99 Burgess and Flynn, above n 90, 74.
100 Ibid. The impact of parental incarceration on children is explored in depth in a special issue of *Law in Context* edited by Anna Eriksson and Catherine Flynn (2015) 32.
101 Jill Guthrie, Michael Levy and Cressida Forde, 'Investment in Prisons: An Investment in Social Exclusion. Linking the Theories of Justice Reinvestment and Social Inclusion to Examine Australia's Propensity to Incarcerate' (2013) 1(2) *Griffith Journal of Law & Human Dignity* 254, 263.
102 Such as the 'tough on crime' sentencing reforms introduced in Victoria: Michelle McDonnell and James Farrell, 'Tough, Tougher, Toughest? A New Government's Approach to Sentencing Laws in Victoria' (2012) 37(3) *Alternative Law Journal* 238, 242.
103 Indigenous people are '22 times more likely to be arrested or detained by police than non-Indigenous people': Lorana Bartels, 'Twenty Years On: Indigenous Deaths in Police Custody and Lessons from the Frontline' in Isabelle Bartkowiak-Théron and Nicole Asquith (eds), *Policing Vulnerabilities* (Federation Press, 2012) 181.

- lack of support and community treatment programs for people with mental illness and disabilities[104]
- the changing prevalence of certain types of crimes (although, as noted above, the overall crime rate is not increasing).[105]

The complex vulnerabilities of the Australian prison population, combined with their experiences of daily life in prison that are discussed in the remainder of this chapter, provide compelling justification for the human rights protections examined by the remainder of this book.

Sociological Literature: Daily Life in Australian Prisons

Two studies are considered here. The first is Goffman's characterisation of prisons as a 'total institution', and the second is Sykes's formulation of the 'pains of imprisonment'.[106] Both of these classic sociological analyses date from the 1950s and 1960s, yet continue to provide a pertinent framework for understanding the lives of people in prison.[107] Neither was written in an Australian context, but Australian statistical data is employed to demonstrate their relevance to contemporary Australian prisons.

Total Institution

The prison environment is heavily controlled. Every aspect of people's lives is regulated, including when they can leave their cell, when they can access showers and toilets (in cases where neither are in their cell), and when they eat. Their access to medical services is also regulated, as is what

---

104 In relation to mental illness see chapters 8 and 9 of Senate Select Committee on Mental Health, *A National Approach to Mental Health - From Crisis to Community, First Report* (2006) Chapters 8–9; Guthrie, Levy and Forde, above n 101, 265. In relation to disabilities see Productivity Commission, *Disability Care and Support, Productivity Commission Inquiry Report* (2011) Chapter 2.

105 See, eg, the Victorian Sentencing Advisory Council discussion of increases in 'offences against the person, drug offences and offences against good order': Sentencing Advisory Council, above n 18, 36.

106 Erving Goffman, *Asylums. Essays on the Social Situation of Mental Patients and Other Inmates* (Aldine Publishing Company, 1962); Gresham Sykes, *Society of Captives; A Study of a Maximum Security Prison* (Princeton University Press, 1958).

107 In 2001, Sykes's *Society of Captives* was held to be the top ranked of the three most influential books in penology in the twentieth century: Michael Reisig, 'The Champion, Contender, and Challenger: Top-Ranked Books in Prison Studies' (2001) 81(3) *The Prison Journal* 389. Goffman's 1961 book *Asylums* is still being printed: Seamus Mac Suibhne, 'Erving Goffman's Asylums 50 Years On' (2011) 198 *The British Journal of Psychiatry* 1, 1.

they may possess, when they can communicate with other people (both within and outside the prison), and their participation in activities such as work and education.

Definition

It is the regulated nature of the environment that led Goffman to characterise prisons as 'total institutions', which he defines as having the following characteristics:

> First, all aspects of life are conducted in the same place and under the same single authority. Second, each phase of the member's daily activity is carried on in the immediate company of a large batch of others, all of whom are treated alike and required to do the same thing together. Third, all phases of the day's activities are tightly scheduled, with one activity leading at a prearranged time into the next, the whole sequence of activities being imposed from above by a system of explicit formal rulings and a body of officials. Finally, the various enforced activities are brought together into a single rational plan purportedly designed to fulfil the official aims of the institution.[108]

According to Goffman, when someone enters a prison, they undergo the processes of 'role stripping' and 'mortification', which in essence involves the loss of the role the individual had in society, and a loss of personal autonomy and privacy. As Van Zyl Smit and Snacken explain in relation to contemporary European prisons, these processes begin during the induction procedures when personal effects and clothing are confiscated, people are strip searched and they are given a uniform. The same processes are then reinforced by daily occurrences, such as correspondence being inspected, cells being searched and other security procedures.[109] In addition to these physical elements, there is the requirement for people to mix with others whether they want to or not, something Goffman argues 'can lead an inmate to feel he [sic] is being contaminated by contact with undesirable fellow inmates'.[110]

---

108 Goffman, above n 106, 6. He also classifies other institutions, such as mental institutions, army barracks, aged care homes and boarding schools, as 'total institutions': at 4–5.
109 Dirk Van Zyl Smit and Sonja Snacken, *Principles of European Prison Law and Policy. Penology and Human Rights* (Oxford University Press, 2009) 39. See also ibid 14–35.
110 Goffman, above n 106, 29.

Implications of the 'Total Institution'

There are a number of implications of the 'total institution' aspect of prisons that are relevant to compliance with international human rights law in prisons. The three discussed here are the loss of personal autonomy, abuse of power, and powerlessness caused by rules and disciplinary proceedings. Specific examples of the implications of the 'total institution' on the requirement that imprisoned people be treated with humanity and respect are provided in Chapter 7.

Loss of Personal Autonomy

People lose their ability to make everyday decisions, particularly those that allow them to behave in the way they would when not in prison. Examples of this have occurred in Australian prisons and three of these are as follows. First, an imprisoned person who was of Muslim faith was provided with a vegetarian diet for four months despite the fact that other imprisoned people were provided with halal meat. The person in question was told that halal meat was unavailable.[111] Second, remandees were being woken at 6.00 am daily to be transported to court for their hearing. Transport involved their confinement for between 65 and 80 minutes in small compartments in a prison transport van.[112] Medical evidence was provided to the court that this routine was causing 'psychological and emotional difficulties' and fatigue, and that it was affecting their ability to concentrate and remember things.[113] The Court was satisfied on the basis of this evidence that the accused were unable to participate effectively in their trial, making it an unfair trial.[114] Third, people in Tasmanian prisons were being issued with inadequate amounts of underwear and socks (two pairs of each) upon their arrival in prison that had also previously been used by other people. The Tasmanian Custodial Inspector wrote of this situation, '[i]t is not considered acceptable for prisoners to wear previously used underwear, even if it has been freshly washed'.[115]

---

111 *Ali v State of Queensland* [2013] QCAT 319 (6 August 2013). The Tribunal awarded Mr Ali $3,000 compensation.
112 *R v Benbrika & Ors (Ruling No 20)* (2008) 18 VR 410 [34]–[35].
113 Ibid [82]–[84].
114 Ibid [91]. See also the discussion in Bronwyn Naylor, 'Protecting the Human Rights of Prisoners in Australia' in Paula Gerber and Melissa Castan (eds), *Contemporary Perspectives on Human Rights Law in Australia* (Lawbook Co, 2013) 407; Rebecca Ananian-Walsh, 'A Fair Trial for Accused Terrorists' in Matthew Groves, Janina Boughey and Dan Meagher (eds), *The Legal Protection of Rights in Australia* (Bloomsbury Publishing, 2019).
115 Tasmanian Custodial Inspector, *Inspection of Adult Custodial Services in Tasmania, 2017 Care and Wellbeing Inspection Report* (October 2018) 29.

Some international examples include laundry processes being organised in such a manner that people did not have their own underwear and socks returned to them, and people being forced to use a bucket overnight when they did not have access to a toilet (in many cases in the presence of their cell mate).[116]

A corollary of loss of autonomy is lack of control over, or choice about, who to associate with. This has serious implications for the right to security of the person and the right to freedom of association. Prisons are designed to house members of the community who pose a danger to others. Therefore, it is logical to assume that many of these people also pose a danger to one another (although this is not to suggest that every person in prison represents a danger to others). The risk of violence and harassment is more acute for people who have been convicted of particular offences, such as child sexual abuse.[117] In the case of sexual violence in male prisons, those who are young, those who are perceived to have 'feminine characteristics' and those who are transgender are particular targets.[118] The lack of control over who to share a cell with, and who to associate with on a daily basis, means that people cannot protect themselves from the risk of violence. This poses a threat to the right to security of the person. This theme is developed further in the next section because two of the 'pains of imprisonment' identified by Sykes are deprivation of autonomy and security.

Abuse of Power

Due to the hierarchical nature of 'total institutions', imprisoned people are at risk of abuse of power by staff. This may be either physical or psychological, although it is important to emphasise that not all staff abuse their power. Some staff may hold preconceived views about how punitive the prison environment should be, which tends to lead to staff behaviour that is lacking in respect.[119] Some Australian examples of this include:

116 Her Majesty's Inspectorate of Prisons, *Report on HMP Aberdeen Full Inspection 6 – 10 October 2008* (2009) 8 [2.29]; Independent Monitoring Boards, *'Slopping Out?' A Report on the Lack of In-Cell Sanitation in Her Majesty's Prisons in England and Wales* (National Council for Independent Monitoring Boards, 2010).

117 Dot Goulding, 'Violence and Brutality in Prisons: A West Australian Context' (2007) 18(3) *Current Issues in Criminal Justice* 399, 407.

118 Richard Edney, 'To Keep Me Safe From Harm? Transgender Prisoners and the Experience of Imprisonment' (2004) 9(2) *Deakin Law Review* 327, 332. See also Sam Lynch and Lorana Bartels, 'Transgender Prisoners in Australia: An Examination of the Issues, Law and Policy' (2017) 19 *Flinders Law Journal* 185, 193–4 (mainly referring back to Edney's article).

119 One study found that 61 per cent of prison officers in California consider that the goal of prison should be 'totally punishment': Amy Lerman and Joshua Page, 'The State of the Job: An Embedded Work Role Perspective on Prison Officer Attitudes' (2012) 14(5) *Punishment & Society* 503, 516. Australian prison staff attitudes are discussed in detail in Chapter 7.

- the South Australian policy of shackling people to their hospital beds during treatment, including during end-of-life care and childbirth[120]
- the case of Mr Brough who, as a 16-year-old intellectually disabled Indigenous person, was held in an adult correctional centre in a padded isolation cell with the lights on continuously and, for periods, without any clothes[121]
- Mr Eastman's allegation that he was subjected to verbal abuse by staff in the Alexander Maconochie Centre in the ACT, by, for example, being called 'murderer' and 'idiot'.[122]

People in prison themselves hold varying degrees of informal power. Research about the culture in prisons suggests that hierarchies often form among the population of those who are imprisoned. This leads to increased vulnerability for those at the bottom of the hierarchy (and, as noted above, these people tend to be at most risk of violence). People known as 'prison heavies' have the most power within this hierarchy and tend to be the most violent and feared by others. People in protection units tend to be the least powerful and the most targeted. As one Western Australian imprisoned person commented in an interview, 'when you're in protection you're targeted by mainstream prisoners because they think we're all tramps (paedophiles). So we have to go places like the library or canteen all together on a Friday to cut down the risk of assault'.[123]

Powerlessness

People in a 'total institution' are subject to a multitude of rules that must be followed, and the disciplinary proceedings that result from failure to comply with these rules. In many instances, these rules may serve as a protection from human rights violations—for example, they prohibit people from assaulting prison staff and other imprisoned people.

However, rule violations can lead to restrictions being imposed that circumscribe rights. Two examples are: (1) denial of visits from family members, which may contradict the protections put in place for the family, including the prohibition against 'arbitrary or unlawful interference'

---

120 Ombudsman South Australia, *Ombudsman Investigation into the Department of Correctional Services in Relation to the Restraining and Shackling of Prisoners in Hospitals* (2012).

121 Human Rights Committee, *Views: Communication No 1184/2003*, UN Doc CCPR/C/86/D/1184/2003 (17 March 2006) ('*Brough v Australia*').

122 *Eastman v Chief Executive of the Department of Justice and Community Safety* [2011] ACTSC 33 (4 March 2011) [26]–[40].

123 Goulding, above n 117, 407.

with family and correspondence;[124] and (2) placing people in solitary confinement for prolonged periods, which can lead to violations of arts 10(1) and 10(3) of the ICCPR, as occurred in the case of Mr Brough (mentioned briefly above and discussed in more depth in Chapter 2).

It is also problematic when an imprisoned person neither understands the rules they are subject to, nor the behaviour that is contrary to those rules. This is quite likely in light of the statistics about the prevalence of cognitive disability in the prison population discussed in the first half of this chapter. A relevant example is provided by Owers, who notes, 'when I met a young man with severe learning difficulties and asked how he got to know what the rules of the prison were - "If I get sent down the block, I know I've broken a rule" was the response'.[125]

Such penalties will often be justified for security reasons, but there is also a balance that needs to be achieved between maintenance of security and protection of human rights. The balance is often tipped in favour of security. Critical assessments need to be made about whether this is in fact justified. As Owers warns, 'security can come to have the quality of the parental "because I say so"; the trump card, the excuse rather than the reason'.[126] While ever security remains the 'trump card' in Australian prisons, it will not be possible to achieve human rights compliance.[127]

Pains of Imprisonment

The other main sociological study of significance to this book is by Sykes, who sought to understand prison social structures. His work highlights that the prison's 'brutalising effects bound prisoners to a common identity, displaced their prior identities, and socialised them almost irresistibly into roles and values that would remain consistent whoever entered the milieu'.[128] He was writing in a time when (officially) the

---

124 Articles 17 and 23 of the *International Covenant on Civil and Political Rights*, opened for signature 19 December 1966, 999 UNTS 171 (entered into force 23 March 1976), which are reflected in ss 13 and 17 of the *Charter of Human Rights and Responsibilities Act 2006* (Vic), ss 11 and 12 of the *Human Rights Act 2004* (ACT) and s 25 of the *Human Rights Act 2019* (Qld).

125 Anne Owers, 'Comparative Experiences of Implementing Human Rights in Closed Environments: Monitoring for Rights Protection' in Bronwyn Naylor, Julie Debeljak and Anita Mackay (eds), *Human Rights in Closed Environments* (Federation Press, 2014) 221.

126 Anne Owers, 'Prison Inspection and the Protection of Human Rights' (2004) 2 *European Human Rights Law Review* 107, 109.

127 The emphasis on security in legislation governing Australian prison management is detailed in Chapter 5.

128 Ben Crewe, 'Gresham Sykes' in Keith Hayward, Shadd Maruna and Jayne Mooney (eds), *Fifty Key Thinkers in Criminology* (Routledge, 2010) 136–7.

focus of imprisonment had moved away from the imposition of physical discipline, noting that 'severe bodily suffering has long since disappeared as a significant aspect of the custodians' regime';[129] rather, the suffering people experience is psychological. He argued that such suffering may be categorised into the *deprivation* of all of the following: (1) liberty, (2) goods and services, (3) heterosexual relationships, (4) autonomy and (5) security. These 'pains of imprisonment' are all evident in Australian prisons.

It should be noted that Sykes's 'pains of imprisonment' are still being used in empirical studies of the sociology of imprisonment. A 2017 edited collection entitles the second part 'coping with the pains of imprisonment', which is introduced with an overview of Sykes's five pains of imprisonment as listed above.[130] Crewe has suggested that there are additional pains evident in prisons in the UK, and Shammas, building on Sykes's work, has argued that an open prison in Norway subjects residents to what he terms the 'pains of freedom'.[131] This demonstrates the ongoing relevance of Sykes's formulation.

Deprivation of Liberty

Sykes observed that the 'loss of liberty is a double one—first, by confinement to the institution and second, by confinement within the institution'.[132] This means that people in prison are both unable to leave the prison, and are also unable to freely move about the prison. They are often confined to their cell and do not have any choice about when they access other parts of the prison, such as the common room, outside areas or medical services. This is a feature of the prison as a 'total institution'. This is definitely evident in Australian prisons where the national average of time spent *out* of cells is nine hours per day, and where, in some jurisdictions, it is less (eg, 7.2 hours per day in NSW and 7.7 hours in Tasmania and South Australia).[133]

---

129 Sykes, above n 106, 64.

130 Carla Reeves (ed), *Experiencing Imprisonment. Research on the Experience of Living and Working in Carceral Institutions* (Routledge, 2017) 115–18. A report by the NSW Inspector of Custodial Services also makes a reference to Sykes: NSW Inspector of Custodial Services, *Report No. 1 - The Invisibility of Correctional Officer Work* (2014) 25.

131 Crewe, above n 128. Victor Shammas, 'The Pains of Freedom: Assessing the Ambiguity of Scandinavian Penal Exceptionalism on Norway's Prison Island' (2014) 16(1) *Punishment & Society* 104.

132 Sykes, above n 106, 65.

133 These figures are for secure prisons. Steering Committee for the Review of Government Service Provision (2019), above n 21, Table 8A.13.

Sykes's view of deprivation of liberty also encompasses the deprivation of contact with family members and friends. In addition to limited face-to-face contact, this includes restrictions on phone calls and written contact.[134] It is a common complaint of people in Australian prisons that their contact with people outside the prison is circumscribed, with even the face-to-face contact that does occur bound by rules about no physical contact.[135] This has been a particular issue in relation to funeral attendance in Western Australia.[136]

Further, as Sykes argues, this pain includes the fact that incarceration 'represents a deliberate, moral rejection of the criminal by the free community'.[137] Even though Australian law has abandoned the concept of 'civil death', imprisoned people still lose fundamental elements of citizenship, including the right to vote, if they are sentenced to longer than three years of imprisonment.[138]

Deprivation of Goods and Services

In the prison environment, people are generally not allowed to wear their own clothes, they are provided with furnishings for their cell not of their own choosing, they do not have much control over what they eat or when they exercise, and particular goods (eg, cigarettes and alcohol) are restricted or banned.[139]

Sykes notes that due to the disadvantaged background of many people in prisons (as is evident in the Australian prison population from the discussion in the first part of this chapter), some may argue that they are better off in prison than they would be in the community. However, Sykes emphasises that the pains of imprisonment are to be considered from the perspective of imprisoned people rather than by objective measures, and he notes that 'legitimately or illegitimately, rationally or irrationally, the inmate population defines its present material impoverishment as a painful loss'.[140]

---

134 Sykes, above n 106, 65.
135 Bronwyn Naylor, 'Human Rights and Respect in Prisons: The Prisoners' in Bronwyn Naylor, Julie Debeljak and Anita Mackay (eds), *Human Rights in Closed Environments* (Federation Press, 2014) 101. See generally Office of the Inspector of Custodial Services (OICS), *Contact with Family and Friends While in Custody* (2018).
136 OICS, *Funeral Attendances by Incarcerated People in Western Australia* (2013).
137 Sykes, above n 106, 65.
138 Naylor, above n 114, 395–6. A position upheld by the High Court in *Roach v Electoral Commissioner* (2007) 233 CLR 162. This decision is discussed in Chapter 5.
139 Sykes, above n 106, 68.
140 Ibid.

A good example of this 'pain of imprisonment' in the Australian context is access to cigarettes, something that is of great significance to most people in prisons given that, as noted earlier in this chapter, 75 per cent of people entering prison identify as smokers.[141] Smoking has been described as 'one of the few social pleasures not denied to prisoners', yet this is rapidly changing.[142] Smoking has been banned in prisons in the majority of Australian states and territories, with the Northern Territory becoming the first to ban smoking from 1 July 2013.[143] Queensland, NSW, Victoria, Tasmania and South Australia have followed suit.[144] This leaves the ACT and Western Australia as the only jurisdictions without smoking bans in prisons.[145]

The general effectiveness of such bans is debatable,[146] and an investigation into a riot in Victoria in 2015 found that the introduction of the smoking ban had been the 'catalyst' (although there were other contributing factors).[147] However, the mere fact that bans are being imposed exemplifies the loss of access to goods in the prison environment that is likely to cause people pain. In this instance, it is more than psychological pain, as the physical symptoms of nicotine withdrawal may ensue. As a New Zealand judge commented in the context of the smoking bans imposed in New Zealand prisons, '[f]orcing prisoners into nicotine withdrawal is not humane'.[148]

---

141 Australian Institute of Health and Welfare, above n 39, 85.

142 OICS, *Issues Paper. Smoking in Prison* (2008) 3.

143 Hefler, Hopkins and Thomas, above n 77, 1.

144 Anita Mackay, 'The Human Rights Implications of Smoking Bans in Closed Environments: What Australia May Learn From the International Experience' (2016) 46 *International Journal of Law, Crime and Justice* 13, 14; Premier of South Australia, 'All SA Prisons Successfully Transition to Smoke Free' (Media Release, 26 February 2020).

145 The ACT Drug Strategy Action Plan 2018-2021 released in December 2018 contained the following 'action' about smoking in the prison in the ACT: 'Deliver a comprehensive strategy that will describe actions to be undertaken to address alcohol, tobacco and drug and blood borne viruses issues in ACT correctional centres until 2022'. This was assigned to the ACT Health Directorate: ACT Government, *ACT Drug Strategy Action Plan 2018-2021: A Plan to Minimise Harms from Alcohol, Tobacco and Other Drug Use* (2018) 28. A 2019 review by the ACT Inspector of Correctional Services raised concerns about smokers and non-smokers being required to share cells: above n 66, 107.

146 See Anita Mackay, 'Stubbing Out Smoking in Prisons. Bans are an Ineffective Mechanism' (2014) 39(2) *Alternative Law Journal* 99; Hefler, Hopkins and Thomas, above n 77.

147 Independent Investigation into the Metropolitan Remand Centre Riot, *Final Report* (December 2015) 6. There have also been other riots associated with the introduction of smoking bans: see Mackay, above n 146, 20.

148 *Taylor v The Attorney-General and Ors* [2013] NZHC 1659 (3 July 2013) [31]. Mr Taylor also brought a landmark case about the voting rights of imprisoned people in New Zealand: *Attorney-General v Taylor* [2018] NZSC 104 (9 November 2018).

Deprivation of Heterosexual Relationships

There are two aspects to this particular 'pain of imprisonment', which is based on Sykes's observations in an all-male prison. The first is the denial of the ability to have heterosexual intercourse, which Sykes writes 'is a frustration which weighs heavily and painfully' on people's minds while incarcerated.[149] The second is the lack of contact with women, which impacts on people's identity. Sykes argues that 'since a significant half of his audience is denied him, the inmate's self-image is in danger of becoming half complete, fractured, a monochrome without the hues of reality'.[150]

There has not been much research conducted about sex in Australian prisons. However, a large telephone survey of imprisoned males was conducted in 2007 in Queensland and NSW prisons as part of the 'Sexual Health and Attitudes of Australian Prisoners Study'.[151] This study found that a similar proportion of imprisoned people report being heterosexual (95.7 per cent) as in the general community (97.4 per cent), but that imprisoned people were more likely to disapprove of sex between men (62 per cent) than those in the community (37 per cent).[152] The study also found that '[o]f those who identified as heterosexual, 79.5% of men and 73.9% of women had a regular opposite-sex partner just before prison'.[153] Further, there is strong support among the imprisoned population for overnight visits from spouses and partners (89.5 per cent of men and 77.2 per cent of women), which is generally not allowed in Australian prisons.[154] This supports Sykes's contention that deprivation of heterosexual sex is likely to be a 'pain of imprisonment' among the Australian prison population.

---

149 Sykes, above n 106, 71.
150 Ibid 72.
151 The survey covered 14 per cent of the male prison population in 2007: Juliet Ritchers et al, 'Consensual Sex Between Men and Sexual Violence in Australian Prisons' (2012) 41 *Archives of Sexual Behavior* 517, 518–19.
152 Tony Butler et al, 'Sexual Behaviour and Sexual Health of Australian Prisoners' (2013) 10 *Sexual Health* 64, 66; ibid 523.
153 Butler et al, above n 152, 66.
154 Eva Malacova, 'Attitudes Towards Sex: A Comparison of Prisoners and the General Community' (2011) 8 *Sexual Health* 355, 359. Overnight visits are, however, allowed in four Victorian prisons: Corrections Victoria, Deputy Commissioner's Instruction No: 3.04 'Visits: - Personal - Professional-Adult Parole Board'; Naylor, above n 135, 103.

No research could be located about the problems for identity associated with men having little contact with women in Australian prisons. This particular aspect of this pain of imprisonment may have reduced somewhat since the time Sykes was writing, given that male prisons employ female staff members.[155]

The threat, and incidence, of sexual assault will be discussed below during consideration of deprivation of security in Australian prisons.

Deprivation of Autonomy

The rules in the prison environment are all-encompassing and designed to control every aspect of imprisoned people's behaviour, as shown by the 'total institution' concept. Further, Sykes argues that imprisoned people for the most part are not entitled to know the justification for the rules, which means that they cannot make arguments about the need to change the rules.[156] Sykes describes the combined effect of this situation as follows:

> The frustration of the prisoner's ability to make choices and the frequent refusals to provide an explanation for the regulations and commands descending from the bureaucratic staff involve a profound threat to the prisoner's self-image because they reduce the prisoner to the weak, helpless, dependent status of childhood.[157]

Some Australian examples of the deprivation of autonomy were provided in the preceding section during the discussion of the human rights implications of the 'total institution'. Another example is the use of solitary confinement (which involves deprivation of liberty within the institution). Solitary confinement is common in Australian 'supermax' prisons, as detailed in Chapter 8, but it is also used in mainstream prisons and remand centres. For example, Gucciardo J expressed concern about solitary confinement being imposed on a remandee for 22 or 23 hours per day for a period of 18 months in the Melbourne Remand Centre.[158] The Victorian Ombudsman has also 'identified a number of cases where prisoners held in solitary confinement for up to 23 hours per day had attempted suicide or self-harm'.[159]

---

155 There is no national data on the breakdown of male and female prison officers, but in Victoria, 30 per cent of prison officers are female: Minister for Corrections (Vic), 'All-Female Prison Squad Completes Tactical Training Minister for Corrections' (Media Release, 9 June 2019).
156 Sykes, above n 106, 73–5.
157 Ibid 75.
158 *DPP v Foster & Ors* [2014] VCC 312 [50]–[53].
159 Victorian Ombudsman, above n 23, 40.

Deprivation of Security

The probability of being subjected to aggression or violence in prison is much higher than in the general community.[160] Sykes's observed, following his study, that:

> regardless of the patterns of mutual aid and support which may flourish in the inmate population, there are a sufficient number of outlaws within this group of outlaws to deprive the average prisoner of that sense of security that comes from living among men who can reasonably be expected to abide by the rules of society.[161]

Even if a person has not actually been subjected to violence or aggression, the fear of being so invokes a high degree of anxiety, making this one of the most significant pains of imprisonment. Sykes argues that people in prison are in a constant state of anxiety due to both the prospect of being subjected to violence and aggression, and because of their concern about their own ability to cope with such an occurrence.[162]

The focus of Sykes's analysis was violence by imprisoned people against other imprisoned people, which excludes the violence that may be inflicted by staff towards imprisoned people or vice versa. Given that it is quite difficult to access data about violence involving prison staff in Australian prisons, the focus of the following discussion will be on violence by imprisoned people towards other imprisoned people.[163] This is the most common form of violence in prisons.[164]

---

160 Sykes, above n 106, 77.

161 Ibid.

162 Ibid 78.

163 For example, in the interviews conducted among NSW and Queensland imprisoned people about their experience of sex and sexual violence in prison, the participants were not asked if they were exposed to such violence by staff. The authors wrote, '[m]indful of the need to obtain permission from correctional authorities and cooperation of officers to implement the survey, we did not specifically ask in the interview whether participants had been sexually coerced by, or had consensual contact with, an officer or other member of staff': Ritchers et al, above n 151, 523. Further, the Australian Institute of Health and Welfare data about assault and sexual assault is confined to that perpetrated by other imprisoned people: above n 39, 108–9. The Productivity Commission provides some limited data about the assault of officers by imprisoned people, but not the converse: Steering Committee for the Review of Government Service Provision, above n 22, Table 8A.17. There is brief mention of violence directed at staff in Victorian prisons having 'nearly doubled' in the past five years by the Victorian Ombudsman, above n 23, 37.

164 This analysis also excludes self-harm and suicide as it is concerned with the deprivation of security caused by the threat posed by others. The fact that violence by others is more common is supported by NSW data indicating that 78 per cent of injuries resulting from violence were 'inflicted by others', with 22 per cent being 'self-inflicted': Tony Butler et al, 'Injury Surveillance in the New South Wales Prison System' (2004) 15(2) *Health Promotion Journal of Australia* 151, 152.

The risk of becoming a victim of violence or aggression is high in Australian prisons. A national picture is gained from Australian Institute of Health and Welfare questionnaires that ask people about their experience of violence upon discharge from prison. These questionnaires have found that 11 per cent of people admit to having been physically assaulted and 2 per cent admit to having been sexually assaulted during their incarceration (8 per cent did not respond to the question about sexual assault).[165]

Types of Physical Violence

A more nuanced picture is provided by studies in particular jurisdictions and in relation to particular types of violence. Qualitative research about violence in Western Australian prisons reveals that violence by imprisoned people directed at other imprisoned people falls into three main categories: 'payback', 'predatory' and 'impulsive'/'random' violence.[166]

Predatory violence was acknowledged by participants to be the most severe, thus resulting in the most severe forms of injuries, including death in some instances. 'Predatory' violence is usually associated with attempts to recruit those who are seen to be weaker into a group or gang.[167] It may also be used as a means of accessing goods, such as drugs. This form of violence often encompasses sexual violence.[168] It has also been termed 'standovers' and its use in Western Australian prisons is corroborated by the Office of the Inspector of Custodial Services.[169] Standovers have also been detailed by the Victorian Ombudsman, and one specific example provided is the murder of Carl Williams in the Barwon Prison.[170]

'Payback' violence surrounds punishing a person who is viewed as having 'wronged' the perpetrator in some way. An example included in the Western Australian study describes such a situation. If two people were arrested at the same time and one gave the police incriminating information about the other, then the informer would likely be subjected to payback violence once in prison.[171]

---

165 Australian Institute of Health and Welfare, above n 39, 108–9.
166 Goulding, above n 117, 409.
167 Ibid.
168 Ibid 410.
169 OICS, *Vulnerable and Predatory Prisoners in Western Australia: A Review of Policy and Practice* (2003).
170 Victorian Ombudsman, above n 23, 36–7. See also Victorian Ombudsman, *The Death of Mr Carl Williams at HM Barwon Prison – Investigation into Corrections Victoria* (2012).
171 Goulding, above n 117, 409.

The third category of violence—'impulsive'/'random' violence—may erupt at any time over seemingly trivial matters. It also tends to be the least serious form of violence and may stop as quickly as it started.[172] As one participant in Goulding's study commented, this type of violence is:

> part and parcel of being in prison … someone looks at the wrong crim in the wrong way and can cop a belting, even if you bump into someone accidentally it can be seen as an insult and end up in a fight … that sort of violence is usually no big deal, no one usually dies from that.[173]

Sexual Violence

Research about sexual violence in NSW and Queensland prisons is consistent with the Australian Institute of Health and Welfare data.[174] However, the NSW and Queensland study provides a more nuanced understanding of the extent of the problem. It shows that for some people this had occurred multiple times—three men said this had happened to them 10–30 times, nine said it had occurred six times, and 15 said it had happened two or three times.[175] The study also found that 6.9 per cent of respondents had been threatened with sexual assault, and for 18 people this had occurred between 10 and 300 times.[176]

A study in Western Australian prisons found that the rates were higher, with 14 per cent admitting to having been victims of sexual assault and 23.3 per cent saying they had been pressured to 'perform sexual acts'.[177] This study identified the places within the prison where the risk of sexual assault is highest to be within cells (by the person sharing the cell), in shower blocks and in protection units.[178]

---

172 Ibid 410.
173 Ibid.
174 The study found that 2.6 per cent of people were sexually assaulted during their incarceration: Ritchers et al, above n 151, 521.
175 Ibid.
176 Ibid.
177 Brian Steels and Dot Goulding, *Predator or Prey? An Exploration of the Impact and Incidence of Sexual Assault in West Australian Prisons* (2009) 54.
178 Protection units contain a high concentration of people convicted of sex offences because they need protection from those in the mainstream and they may victimise others in the protection unit: ibid 50–1.

These statistics are likely to represent the 'tip of the iceberg' for a number of reasons.[179] Sexual assault in the community at large is widely acknowledged to be under-reported, with an estimated 30 per cent of cases reported to police.[180] Under-reporting in prison is likely to be exacerbated by certain aspects of the prison population and climate. These include that the majority of imprisoned people disapprove of sex between men and the inmate code of not 'informing' on others. Any breach of this code may cause people to be subject to 'payback' violence, as noted by the Victorian Ombudsman: '[i]n some cases, prisoners have been seriously injured in retaliation for reporting a matter to prison authorities'.[181] The argument that sexual assault is under-reported is supported by the Western Australian study of sexual assault in prisons, which found that 90 per cent of the 150 participants (who had all been formerly imprisoned) indicated that they thought sexual assault was 'grossly under-reported'.[182]

Another factor, critiqued by Minogue, is the public discourse suggesting that sexual violence in prison is in some sense an inevitability and 'tough luck'. This is demonstrated by jokes about prison rape, such as those relating to dropping soap in a prison shower.[183] Views about the inevitability of sexual violence have been expressed by authority figures, including a former NSW Corrective Services Minister.[184] Such discourse is likely to add to the difficulty that victims face in reporting sexual assault to prison authorities.

Overcrowding: Exacerbating the Pains of Imprisonment

As demonstrated by the statistics provided in this chapter and the continuous growth of the Australian prison population, overcrowding is an increasing problem in Australian prisons. This exacerbates the pains of imprisonment in a number of ways.

---

179 It is described in these terms by the Western Australian Office of the Inspector of Custodial Services: OICS, *Western Australia's Prison Capacity* (2016) 16.

180 Australian Institute of Criminology, *Guilty Outcomes in Reported Sexual Assault and Related Offence Incidents* (Crime Facts Info No 162, 2007).

181 Victorian Ombudsman, above n 23, 35.

182 Steels and Goulding, above n 177, 26.

183 Craig Minogue, 'Why Don't I get the Joke? Prison Rape in the Public Discourse' (2011) 36(2) *Alternative Law Journal* 116, 116.

184 Ibid. See also Richard Evans, 'Prison Rape: Is it Okay to Make Jokes About Rape in Prison? (2014) *Arena* 26.

First, as numbers increase, imprisoned people are more likely to have to share a cell with another person/s (many others in the case of dormitory-style prison accommodation that is being introduced in some jurisdictions, as discussed in Chapter 8). This further deprives imprisoned people of autonomy and goods and services because they no longer have any space that they have complete control over.

Second, the increase in numbers increases tension in the prison and, consequently, the chances of being subjected to violence and intimidation. This is a phenomenon recently documented by the Victorian Ombudsman in relation to prisons in Victoria, the report highlighting that 'with overcrowding, Victorian prisons are becoming more violent'.[185] As violence increases, prison management is likely to use 'lock downs' (where all imprisoned people are locked in their cells) more frequently, such that people's deprivation of liberty within the prison is increased. This exposes people to an even greater chance of experiencing violence within cells when they are shared, something found in the Western Australian study of sexual violence to be a particular risk. This was also a concern raised by the Victorian Ombudsman.[186] The violence may lead to greater use of disciplinary measures, such as solitary confinement, which increases the pain associated with deprivation of liberty, goods and services, and autonomy.

Third, in a situation of overcrowding, such goods and services as there are must be shared by a greater number of people. Accordingly, access to educational and work programs, telephone access to contact people outside the prison, exercise areas and common areas (including showers) are all likely to be rationed as the prison population increases.[187]

Fourth, overcrowding has been found to lead to increased deprivation of liberty within the institution and deprivation of autonomy, with some imprisoned people in Victoria being confined for 24 hours per day.[188] This is in breach of the requirement in s 47(1)(a) of the *Corrections Act 1986* (Vic) that people be allowed out of their cells for at least one hour per day.

185 Victorian Ombudsman, above n 23, 34.
186 Ibid 35–6.
187 Naylor, above n 135, 96.
188 Victorian Ombudsman, above n 23, 40.

Fifth, the Australian Institute of Health and Welfare has observed that one of the strategies prisons are using to manage overcrowding is frequent transfer of imprisoned people between facilities. They note that this makes 'continuing health care more difficult'.[189] This is particularly problematic in light of the complex health needs of the prison population outlined in this chapter. It also makes it more difficult for people to maintain regular contact with their family members and friends.

There are very good reasons why overcrowding in Australian prisons must be addressed in order for human rights compliance to be achieved. These are discussed in Chapter 4 (reduce reliance on imprisonment) and Chapter 8 (decent physical conditions). Here it is sufficient to highlight that the consequences of overcrowding contribute to the 'pains of imprisonment' experienced by people in Australian prisons.

Conclusion

The nature of prisons as a 'total institution' and the pains of imprisonment mean that human rights, such to the right to life, personal security, privacy and humane treatment, are abrogated on a regular basis in Australian prisons (as detailed in later chapters of this book). Further, daily life in prison serves to exacerbate the vulnerability and marginalisation of the population that has been documented in this chapter. This is due to the negative impact of imprisonment on mental health and the pains of imprisonment in general, and particularly the high levels of aggression and violence that imprisoned people experience.

Van Zyl Smit and Snacken have argued that practices built on recognition of the human rights of imprisoned people can reduce the 'pains of imprisonment' and inhibit the 'role stripping' and 'mortification' that occur in prisons as 'total institutions'.[190] Therefore, human rights law offers the potential to improve conditions in Australian prisons for the benefit of people imprisoned in them.

---

189 Australian Institute of Health and Welfare, above n 39, 7.
190 Van Zyl Smit and Snacken, above n 109, 41.

2

Australia's International Human Rights Law Obligations

Introduction

Australia has chosen to become a party to a number of international treaties that impose international legal obligations on Australia relating to how prisons are managed. In a federation where prisons are the responsibility of the states and territories (resulting in eight different correction laws and prison systems), the international obligations hold particular significance for ensuring consistent and equal protections across the country.

It is important to note at the outset that there is no international prohibition against imprisonment. International human rights law accepts that states may use imprisonment as a sanction. However, when people are deprived of their liberty in prisons, it does require that they only be 'deprived ... in accordance with such procedure as are established by law'.[1] Therefore, the treaties concern the regulation of imprisonment, rather than preventing states from imprisoning people.

---

1   *International Covenant on Civil and Political Rights*, opened for signature 19 December 1966, 999 UNTS 171 (entered into force 23 March 1976) art 9 ('ICCPR').

The United Nations *Basic Principles for the Treatment of Prisoners* (1990), while containing 'soft' law obligations, is also relevant to understanding the international law position in relation to imprisonment.[2] Principle 5 states:

> Except for those limitations that are demonstrably necessitated by the fact of incarceration, all prisoners shall retain the human rights and fundamental freedoms set out in the Universal Declaration of Human Rights, and, where the State concerned is a party, the International Covenant on Economic, Social and Cultural Rights, and the International Covenant on Civil and Political Rights and the Optional Protocol thereto, as well as such other rights as are set out in other United Nations covenants.

This means that—according to international law—prisons must operate in such a way that all rights, other than the right to liberty (which is necessarily restricted by incarceration), are retained and respected. This is sometimes described as the 'residuum principle'. This principle is that a person sentenced to imprisonment retains all their rights other than those unavoidably lost by virtue of their imprisonment, such as liberty.[3]

Once Australian people are imprisoned, the most relevant international treaties that regulate their rights for the duration of their sentence are the *International Covenant on Civil and Political Rights* (ICCPR), *Convention against Torture and Other Cruel, Inhuman or Degrading Treatment or Punishment* (CAT) and *Convention on the Rights of Persons with Disabilities* (CRPD).[4] The last of these three has particular relevance to Australia given the high proportion of the Australian prison population with mental illness and disabilities (as outlined in Chapter 1).

---

2   'Soft' law is a term used to describe international agreements that have not been negotiated as treaties and are, therefore, not covered by the *Vienna Convention on the Law of Treaties*, opened for signature 23 May 1969, 1155 UNTS 331 (entered into force 27 January 1980). See further Harmut Hillgenberg, 'A Fresh Look at Soft Law' (1999) 10(3) *European Journal of International Law* 499.

3   Bronwyn Naylor 'Protecting the Human Rights of Prisoners in Australia' in Paula Gerber and Melissa Castan (eds), *Contemporary Perspectives on Human Rights Law in Australia* (Lawbook Co, 2013) 396. This principle is also recognised at common law: *Raymond v Honey* [1983] 1 AC 1, 10 (Lord Wilberforce).

4   ICCPR. Australia ratified the ICCPR on 23 November 1980. *Convention against Torture and Other Cruel, Inhuman or Degrading Treatment or Punishment*, opened for signature 10 December 1984, 1465 UNTS 85 (entered into force 26 June 1987) ('CAT'). Australia ratified the CAT on 10 December 1985. *Convention on the Rights of Persons with Disabilities*, opened for signature 30 March 2007, 2515 UNTS 3 (entered into force 3 May 2008) ('CRPD'). Australia ratified the CRPD on 17 July 2008.

This chapter focuses firstly on Australia's international obligations under these three treaties and the other relevant international instruments that provide additional details about their operation, and secondly on the international enforcement mechanisms that are in place to support their implementation.

The domestic incorporation of some of the human rights protections contained in the international treaties is considered separately in Chapter 5. The impact of the international monitoring regime introduced by the *Optional Protocol to the Convention against Torture and Other Cruel, Inhuman or Degrading Treatment or Punishment* (OPCAT) on Australia is discussed in detail in Chapter 3.[5]

Treaty and Other International Law Requirements

There are three main categories of international law. The first—treaties—contain binding legal obligations that state parties agree to when they sign up to a treaty. The second are the so-called 'soft' law obligations referred to in the introduction above that help elaborate the treaty requirements. The third is the General Comments issued by the treaty monitoring bodies (TMBs), which also elaborate the treaty requirements, given that these bodies are responsible for interpreting the treaties.

Treaty Requirements

The treaty requirements that apply to Australian prisons are overlapping and interwoven. That is, while each treaty has a distinct emphasis, they also simultaneously reinforce the requirements in the other treaties.

The three most relevant provisions of the ICCPR addressing the treatment of people once they are imprisoned[6] are:

---

5   *Optional Protocol to the Convention against Torture*, adopted 18 December 1992, UN Doc A/ RES/57/199 (entered into force 22 June 2006) ('OPCAT'). Australia signed the OPCAT on 19 May 2009 and ratified it on 15 December 2017.

6   Article 9(1) of the ICCPR (referred to in the introduction to this chapter) is relevant to the circumstances under which a person is sentenced to imprisonment, rather than what occurs once they are in prison. It provides that '[n]o one shall be deprived of his [sic] liberty except on such grounds and in accordance with such procedure as are established by law'.

1. art 7, which provides that '[n]o one shall be subjected to torture or to cruel, inhuman or degrading treatment or punishment'[7]

2. art 10(1), which provides that '[a]ll persons deprived of their liberty shall be treated with humanity and with respect for the inherent dignity of the human person'

3. art 10(3), which provides that '[t]he penitentiary system shall comprise treatment of prisoners the essential aim of which shall be their reformation and social rehabilitation'.

Other relevant rights provided for in the ICCPR include the right to life (art 6(1)), the right to personal security (art 9(1)), the right to privacy (art 17(1)), the right to culture and religion (arts 18 and 27),[8] and the right to equality before the law and not to be discriminated against (art 26). There is also a prohibition against 'arbitrary or unlawful interference' with family and correspondence that is relevant to imprisoned people's contact with their family members (arts 17 and 23), and a requirement that those on remand be separated from those who have been convicted and be treated 'appropriate to their status as unconvicted' (art 10(2)(a)).

The CAT elaborates on art 7 of the ICCPR by providing a more detailed definition of torture.[9] It also requires state parties to:

- ensure torture is an offence under domestic criminal law[10]

- take 'effective legislative, administrative, judicial or other measures to prevent acts of torture in any territory under its jurisdiction'[11]

---

7   The *Bill of Rights 1689* still applies in the states and territories, and Article 10 of that Bill is roughly equivalent to Article 7 of the ICCPR, providing, '[t]hat excessive baile ought not to be required nor excessive fines imposed nor cruel and unusual punishments inflicted'. Although the Bill of Rights has continued application, and has formed the basis of litigation as recently as the 1990s (see, eg, *Holden v South Australia* (1992) 62 A Crim R 308), it has not provided any relief to imprisoned people in Australia. See further the discussion in Matthew Groves, 'Administrative Segregation of Prisoners: Powers, Principles of Review and Remedies' (1996) 20 *Melbourne University Law Review* 639, 654–8.

8   The United Nations Declaration on the Rights of Indigenous Peoples (a resolution adopted by the United Nations General Assembly on 13 September 2007) elaborates on the rights of Indigenous people to culture, religion and language contained in art 27 of the ICCPR (eg, arts 11 and 18). For a discussion of the relevance of art 27 to Indigenous people in Australian prisons see Emma Henderson and Nicole Shackleton 'Minority Rights Advocacy for Incarcerated Indigenous Australians: The Impact of Article 27 of the ICCPR' (2016) 41(4) *Alternative Law Journal* 244.

9   CAT art 1.

10   Ibid art 4. This requirement was implemented in Australia with the passage of the *Crimes Legislation Amendment (Torture Prohibition and Death Penalty Abolition) Act 2010* (Cth).

11   CAT art 2.

- 'undertake to prevent in any territory under its jurisdiction other acts of cruel, inhuman or degrading treatment or punishment which do not amount to torture'[12]
- ensure that personnel involved in imprisonment be trained about the prohibition of torture.[13]

The CRPD echoes the prohibition of torture and cruel, inhuman, and degrading treatment and punishment found in other treaties (art 15), as well as protecting the rights to privacy (art 22), and home and family (arts 22 and 23). Its definition of people with 'disabilities' includes 'those who have long-term physical, mental, intellectual or sensory impairments'.[14] As outlined in Chapter 1, there is a high prevalence of mental illness and cognitive disability among the people in Australian prisons, meaning many would meet this definition. It may be seen from the discussion about individual communications (below) that the CRPD is becoming increasingly relevant because there have been more successful individual communications concerning Australian prison conditions brought under the CRPD than the ICCPR.

Optional Protocol to the Convention Against Torture

It can be seen from the above that there is a particular emphasis in all three Treaties on prohibiting torture, cruel, inhuman or degrading treatment or punishment. There is a particularly important international mechanism for ensuring the *prevention* of torture, cruel, inhuman or degrading treatment or punishment, set out in the OPCAT. The OPCAT establishes a comprehensive system for international and national inspection of places where people are deprived of their liberty and may be at risk of being subjected to 'torture and other cruel, inhuman or degrading treatment or punishment'.[15] Places of deprivation of liberty include, but are not limited to, prisons.[16]

---

12   Ibid art 16.
13   Ibid art 10(1).
14   CRPD art 1.
15   OPCAT art 1.
16   The definition of 'deprivation of liberty' in the OPCAT is broad and as follows: 'any form of detention or imprisonment or the placement of a person in a public or private custodial setting which that person is not permitted to leave at will by order of any judicial, administrative or other authority': art 4(2).

The dual levels of international and national monitoring are carried out by:

1. the international Subcommittee for the Prevention of Torture and Other Cruel, Inhuman or Degrading Treatment or Punishment (SPT), which is a United Nations (UN) committee of experts and a subcommittee of the Committee against Torture
2. the domestic National Preventive Mechanisms (NPMs) that state parties are required to establish.[17]

In addition to carrying out inspections of places of detention and making recommendations to states, the SPT is required to 'advise and assist' states with the establishment of NPMs.[18] Once established, NPMs are required to regularly inspect places of detention and make recommendations to relevant authorities to 'improve treatment and conditions' therein.[19]

Australia signed the OPCAT on 19 May 2009 and ratified it on 15 December 2017.[20] Between these dates it took two major steps to prepare for ratification. These were (1) the preparation of a National Interest Analysis and (2) consideration of that document by the Joint Standing Committee on Treaties, which recommended Australia ratify the OPCAT.[21] Australia has three years from the date of ratification to set up an NPM.[22] The Australian Human Rights Commission has been carrying out consultations to inform its advice to the government about how OPCAT should be implemented.[23]

---

17   National Preventive Mechanisms (NPMs) are required to be designated within one year of ratification: OPCAT art 17. This period may be extended if a state party makes a declaration pursuant to art 24, which Australia has done.

18   OPCAT art 11.

19   Ibid art 19.

20   Minister for Foreign Affairs and Attorney-General (Cth), 'Ratification of OPCAT Caps Year of Significant Human Rights Achievements for Turnbull Government' (Media Release, 15 December 2017). For a detailed discussion of Australia's 'path' to ratification see Richard Harding, 'Australia's Circuitous Path Towards the Ratification of the OPCAT, 2002-2017: The Challenges of Implementation' (2019) 25(1) *Australian Journal of Human Rights* 4.

21   See Bronwyn Naylor, 'Protecting Human Rights in Detention. Rights, Monitoring and OPCAT' (2016) 41(3) *Alternative Law Journal* 151, 153–4.

22   Australia has made a declaration pursuant to art 24 of the OPCAT which allows state parties to postpone establishment of an NPM for up to three years.

23   Australian Human Rights Commission, *OPCAT: Optional Protocol to the Convention Against Torture* <https://www.humanrights.gov.au/our-work/rights-and-freedoms/projects/opcat-optional-protocol-convention-against-torture>.

With Australia's federal structure, and split responsibility for places of deprivation of liberty between Commonwealth, state and territory governments,[24] it has been apparent since Australia first signed up to OPCAT that more than one organisation may be needed to form an NPM with the necessary coverage.[25] Some countries have multiple organisations comprising their NPM.[26]

The Attorney-General has announced that multiple bodies at the federal, state and territory level will form Australia's NPM, and that the Commonwealth Ombudsman will perform the coordinating role as well as being the NPM for places of deprivation of liberty under the Commonwealth's jurisdiction (eg, immigration detention centres).[27] The Ombudsman's formal role commenced on 1 July 2018.[28] Western Australia has announced that the Office of the Inspector of Custodial Services (OICS) will be the NPM responsible for prisons in that state (as well as other justice system places of deprivation of liberty, such as police cells).[29] Other states and territories have not yet nominated the organisations that they wish to form part of the NPM.

The OPCAT represents a significant change to the monitoring landscape in Australia, which has until now been primarily characterised as reactive, rather than preventive. The changes to the current system of prison monitoring will be explored in detail in Chapter 3. It is nevertheless important to note here that the OPCAT would add the following to the current system:

---

24   The Commonwealth Ombudsman identified 55 existing organisations in a 'baseline assessment' of the current monitoring of places of deprivation of liberty around Australia: Commonwealth Ombudsman, *Commonwealth Ombudsman Implementation of the Optional Protocol to the Convention Against Torture and Other Cruel, Inhuman or Degrading Treatment or Punishment (OPCAT) Baseline Assessment of Australia's OPCAT Readiness Report No. 3/2019* (September 2019) 2.

25   For example, in 2010, Harding and Morgan proposed that there be a central coordinating organisation at the national level (such as the Australian Human Rights Commission), with one organisation in each state and territory: Richard Harding and Neil Morgan, 'OPCAT in the Asia-Pacific and Australasia' (2010) 6(2) *Essex Human Rights Review* 99, 120.

26   New Zealand has five and the United Kingdom has 18. However, McGregor has argued that New Zealand may achieve better implementation of OPCAT with a single NPM: Judy McGregor, 'The Challenges and Limitations of OPCAT National Preventive Mechanisms: Lessons From New Zealand' (2017) 23(3) *Australian Journal of Human Rights* 351. See further in relation to New Zealand Natalie Pierce, 'Implementing Human Rights in Closed Environments: The OPCAT Framework and the New Zealand Experience' in Bronwyn Naylor, Julie Debeljak and Anita Mackay (eds), *Human Rights in Closed Environments* (Federation Press, 2014) 154. For a discussion of NPM models in federations see Ben Buckland and Audrey Olivier-Muralt, 'OPCAT in Federal States: Towards a Better Understanding of NPM Models and Challenges' (2019) 25(1) *Australian Journal of Human Rights* 23.

27   Commonwealth Ombudsman, above n 24, 1.

28   Ibid.

29   The Western Australian Ombudsman will also have NPM responsibilities: ibid 30.

1. international-level scrutiny by an expert committee (the SPT) that may compare the situation in Australian places of detention to that in comparable jurisdictions

2. improved standards of monitoring because NPMs would need to comply with the criteria established under the OPCAT[30]

3. additional coverage of prison-related environments that are not currently monitored by existing monitoring mechanisms, such as vehicles transporting people between prisons[31]

4. comprehensive coordination and oversight at the national level (by the Commonwealth Ombudsman) that would identify gaps and overlaps in monitoring coverage that occur currently within individual places of detention, across different places of detention and across jurisdictions

5. a clear division of responsibility between organisations comprising the NPM in relation to places of deprivation of liberty, rather than the overlapping responsibility that exists currently across places of detention

6. the capacity to compare what is happening in the same environments across the different jurisdictions (eg, to compare prisons in Queensland with prisons in South Australia), which does not occur currently due to each monitoring organisation being limited to one jurisdiction

7. the capacity to compare how various types of closed environments address identical or similar human rights issues. For example, comparison of police custody and prisons, both within and across jurisdictions, and comparison of the way particular groups (such as mentally ill people) are treated across different types of environments.

The NPM offers the most potential for improving the human rights of people in Australian prisons. This is for two reasons. First, the SPT's impact will be limited because it will not visit regularly given the current resourcing levels and number of countries that have signed the OPCAT.[32] Conversely, the NPM will be required to carry out *regular* inspections

---

30 It will be shown in Chapter 3 that existing organisations are not compliant with these criteria.
31 Naylor, above n 21, 154. Naylor notes that this was one of the gaps identified by the National Interest Analysis conducted in 2012. There have been deaths in prison transport vehicles in Australia, for example, the death of Mr Ward in Western Australia, which will be discussed in Chapter 3.
32 Subcommittee on Prevention of Torture and Other Cruel, Inhuman or Degrading Treatment or Punishment, *Fifth Annual Report of the Subcommittee on Prevention of Torture and Other Cruel, Inhuman or Degrading Treatment or Punishment (January – December 2011)* (2012).

because this is one of the OPCAT criteria for NPM operations.[33] Second, in light of the Australian Government's disregard for decisions by the TMBs (discussed later in this chapter), it remains open to question as to what the government's response would be to recommendations made by the SPT.

Other Relevant Instruments

Given the treaty obligations are abstract, there are other relevant international instruments that help to elaborate the meaning of the treaty requirements. These include the UN *Standard Minimum Rules for the Treatment of Prisoners* (the Nelson Mandela Rules) that were updated in 2015 and became known as the Mandela Rules, UN *Rules for the Treatment of Women Prisoners and Non-Custodial Measures for Women Offenders* ('the Bangkok Rules') and UN *Body of Principles for the Protection of All Persons under Any Form of Detention or Imprisonment* ('Body of Principles').[34] None of these constitute binding legal requirements, unlike the Treaties discussed above.

There are also General Comments issued by the relevant TMB responsible for each of the Treaties. Eastman has explained that General Comments 'offer guidance as to how the relevant human rights in the treaty should be interpreted and implemented'.[35] One of the General Comments issued by the UN Human Rights Committee (HR Committee) stipulates that state parties are required to 'indicate in their reports to what extent they are applying the relevant United Nations standards applicable to the treatment of prisoners'. This includes the Mandela Rules and Body of Principles.[36] This emphasises the importance of these instruments.

---

33   OPCAT art 19. This and the other criteria for NPM operations are discussed in detail in Chapter 3.
34   United Nations *Standard Minimum Rules for the Treatment of Prisoners* (the Nelson Mandela Rules), UN Doc A/RES/70/175 (17 December 2015) ('the Mandela Rules'); United Nations *Rules for the Treatment of Women Prisoners and Non-Custodial Measures for Women Offenders*, UN Doc A/RES/ 65/229 (adopted by the General Assembly on 21 December 2010) ('the Bangkok Rules').
35   Kate Eastman, 'Australia's Engagement with the United Nations' in Paula Gerber and Melissa Castan (eds), *Contemporary Perspectives on Human Rights Law in Australia* (Lawbook Co, 2013) 106.
36   United Nations Human Rights Committee, *CCPR General Comment No. 21: Article 10 (Humane Treatment of Persons Deprived of Their Liberty)* (10 April 1992) [5].

The Mandela Rules

The UN Minimum Rules have been in place since 1955 and have been described as 'the best-known and most widely distributed document for improving conditions of detention'.[37] The updates to the Rules in 2015 took into account the wide-ranging developments in international human rights law that had occurred since the Rules were originally introduced in 1955. For example, the Mandela Rules provide specific guidance in relation to the prohibition against torture, cruel, inhuman and degrading treatment or punishment,[38] whereas the 1955 Rules contained no references to torture, cruel, inhuman and degrading treatment or punishment. They also include new Rules about inspections that reflect the OPCAT requirements.[39]

There are a total of 122 Mandela Rules, with many of them several paragraphs long. The rules provide a lot of specific detail that aid compliance with treaty provisions and are to be read in conjunction with the General Comments issued by TMBs. For example, it has been noted that all three aforementioned Treaties prohibit 'torture, cruel, inhuman or degrading treatment or punishment'. The HR Committee has clarified that 'prolonged solitary confinement' may amount to acts within this category (as prohibited by art 7 of the ICCPR).[40] Mandela Rule 44 provides definitions of 'solitary confinement' and 'prolonged solitary confinement' as follows: 'solitary confinement shall refer to the confinement of prisoners for 22 hours or more a day without meaningful human contact. Prolonged solitary confinement shall refer to solitary confinement for a time period in excess of 15 consecutive days'.

Due to the level of detail contained in the rules, it is not possible to catalogue all the topics covered by the rules here. Some selected examples that align with the themes that recur throughout this book are provided in Table 2.1.

---

37 Katrin Tiroch, 'Modernizing the Standard Minimum Rules for the Treatment of Prisoners – A Human Rights Perspective' in *Max Planck Yearbook of United Nations Law, Volume 19, 2015* (Brill, 2016) 281. In the Australian context, they have been cited by Royal Commissions, including the Royal Commission into Aboriginal Deaths in Custody and the Nagle Royal Commission concerning New South Wales prisons conducted in the 1970s: Matthew Groves, 'International Law and Australian Prisoners' (2001) 24(1) *University of New South Wales Law Journal* 17, 27.
38 See, eg, Rules 1, 32 and 43.
39 See Rules 83–5 and discussion by Tiroch, above n 37, 295–6. See Tiroch for a detailed discussion about the process by which the Rules were updated (285–90) and the differences between the 1955 and 2015 Rules (292–304).
40 United Nations Human Rights Committee, *CCPR General Comment No. 20: Article 7 (Prohibition of Torture, or Other Cruel, Inhuman or Degrading Treatment or Punishment)* (10 March 1992) para 6.

Table 2.1: Examples of the Mandela Rules

Mandela Rule number and topic	Text of rule
12, Accommodation	1. Where sleeping accommodation is in individual cells or rooms, each prisoner shall occupy by night a cell or room by himself or herself. If for special reasons, such as temporary overcrowding, it becomes necessary for the central prison administration to make an exception to this rule, it is not desirable to have two prisoners in a cell or room.
24, Health care	1. The provision of health care for prisoners is a State responsibility. Prisoners should enjoy the same standards of health care that are available in the community and should have access to necessary health-care services free of charge without discrimination on the grounds of their legal status. 2. Health-care services should be organized in close relationship to the general public health administration and in a way that ensures continuity of treatment and care, including for HIV, tuberculosis and other infectious diseases, as well as for drug dependence.
47, Use of restraint	1. The use of chains, irons or other instruments of restraint which are inherently degrading or painful shall be prohibited. 2. Other instruments of restraint shall only be used when authorized by law and in the following circumstances: (a) As a precaution against escape during a transfer, provided that they are removed when the prisoner appears before a judicial or administrative authority; (b) By order of the prison director, if other methods of control fail, in order to prevent a prisoner from injuring himself or herself or others or from damaging property; in such instances, the director shall immediately alert the physician or other qualified health-care professionals and report to the higher administrative authority.
52, Bodily searches	Intrusive searches, including strip and body cavity searches, should be undertaken only if absolutely necessary. Prison administrations shall be encouraged to develop and use appropriate alternatives to intrusive searches. Intrusive searches shall be conducted in private and by trained staff of the same sex as the prisoner.
76, Training of prison staff	1. Training referred to in paragraph 2 of rule 75 shall include, at a minimum, training on: (a) Relevant national legislation, regulations and policies, as well as applicable international and regional instruments, the provisions of which must guide the work and interactions of prison staff with inmates; (b) Rights and duties of prison staff in the exercise of their functions, including respecting the human dignity of all prisoners and the prohibition of certain conduct, in particular torture and other cruel, inhuman or degrading treatment or punishment; …

The Mandela Rules (like the 1955 Rules that preceded them) are designed to be adapted to local circumstances by nations and incorporated into their national statutory schemes.[41] The 1955 Rules formed the basis of the *Standard Guidelines for Corrections in Australia* ('Guidelines') that were adopted by the Corrections Ministers conference in 1994 and revised in 2012.[42] The Guidelines were replaced in 2018 by the *Guiding Principles for Corrections in Australia* ('Guiding Principles') which refer to the Mandela Rules as a 'framework' that was 'considered' in their development;[43] however the Guiding Principles are seriously out of alignment with the Mandela Rules on paper, and the policies and practices in Australian prisons that are not human rights compliant increase the chasm even further. The Guiding Principles are also open to the same criticism that was made of the predecessor Guidelines, which is that they have little 'practical value' to imprisoned people and those that scrutinise prisons (such as courts and Ombudsmen) due to their non-binding nature.[44]

In some areas, the Guiding Principles are more out of alignment with the Mandela Rules than the predecessor Guidelines were. Three examples are given here to demonstrate this. The first is the prohibition of use of restraints during labour. The Mandela Rules are clear about this, providing that '[i]nstruments of restraint shall never be used on women during labour, during childbirth and immediately after childbirth' (Rule 48(2)).[45] The Guidelines did not prohibit the use of restraints during childbirth.[46] The Guiding Principles are also silent on the use of restraints during childbirth. They discourage the use of restraints during treatment for 'medical conditions', giving pregnancy as an example, but there is still discretion for restraints to be used where 'there is a serious

---

41   The Mandela Rules, Preliminary Observation 2 paragraph 1, noting: 'In view of the great variety of legal, social, economic and geographical conditions in the world, it is evident that not all of the rules are capable of application in all places and at all times'.

42   The Corrective Services Ministers' Conference (Cth), *Standard Guidelines for Corrections in Australia* (2012) 2 ('Guidelines').

43   Corrective Services Administrators' Conference (Cth), *Guiding Principles for Corrections in Australia* (2018) 6 ('Guiding Principles').

44   Matthew Groves, 'The Second Charters of Prisoners' Rights' in Matthew Groves and Colin Campbell (eds), *Australian Charters of Rights a Decade On* (Federation Press, 2017) 192. This conclusion is supported by Bronwyn Naylor, 'Protecting the Human Rights of Prisoners in Australia' in Paula Gerber and Melissa Castan (eds), *Contemporary Perspectives on Human Rights Law in Australia* (Lawbook Co, 2013) 407. The Preface to the Guidelines indicated their non-binding nature. While the Guiding Principles do not have a similar statement about their status, there is nothing to indicate that they are binding. The purpose is described to be to 'support continuous improvement and reflect the diverse challenges and priorities of correctional services in Australia': ibid.

45   This is repeated in identical terms in Rule 24 of the Bangkok Rules; thus, there can be no doubt as to the international law position on this matter.

46   Restraint is dealt with by Guidelines 1.67–1.69: Guidelines, above n 42.

risk to themselves or others, a substantial risk of restraint or they cannot be restrained by any other means'.[47] The Department of Correctional Services in South Australia has a policy that specifically requires restraints to be used during labour, which has been repeatedly criticised by the South Australian Ombudsman since 2012 for being used irrespective of whether there was a risk of escape, but to no avail.[48]

Second, in relation to solitary confinement, where the Mandela Rule was referred to above, the Guidelines stipulated that 'Prolonged solitary confinement … should not be used'; however, there was no definition of 'prolonged'.[49] The Guiding Principles contain several references to 'segregation' and Principle 3.3.6 requires that a person's mental health be 'recognised and considered' where segregation is 'continued';[50] however, there is no prohibition of prolonged solitary confinement. There is also a principle indicating that one hour per day out of cell time is sufficient and even this has a caveat of 'weather permitting'.[51] According to the Mandela Rule definition of 22 hours a day in a cell constituting 'solitary confinement', under the new Guiding Principles all people in Australian prisons could be subject to this.

A number of Australian jurisdictions have policies that could not be described as anything other than 'prolonged' solitary confinement. For example, in the Woodford prison in Queensland, the policy states, '[o]ut of cell time restricted to at least two daylight hours a day', leading to solitary confinement without access to daylight for 22 hours per day and falling within the Mandela Rules definition of prolonged solitary confinement.[52]

The third is the use of bodily searches, including strip searches. The relevant Mandela Rule (Rule 52, see Table 2.1) is clear that intrusive searches are to be 'undertaken only if absolutely necessary'. The Guidelines limited strip searching to attempts to find contraband and also required that they be

---

47   Guiding Principles, above n 43, Principle 3.1.16.
48   Anita Mackay, 'The Relevance of the United Nations Mandela Rules for Australian Prisons' (2017) 42(4) *Alternative Law Journal* 279, 284.
49   Guidelines, above n 42, Guideline 1.80.
50   Guiding Principles, above n 43, 18.
51   Ibid 12, Principle 2.3.2.
52   The policy is cited by Applegarth J in *Callanan v Attendee Z* [2013] QSC 342, [27]. In relation to the use of solitary confinement in Tasmania see *Pickett v The State of Tasmania* [2011] TASSC 907 (20 April 2011) and in relation to Victoria see *Dale v DPP* [2009] VSCA 212 (21 September 2009). Both cases are discussed in Anita Mackay, 'Human Rights Protections for People with Mental Health and Cognitive Disability in Prisons' (2015) 22(6) *Psychiatry, Psychology and Law* 842, 848 and 860.

conducted by a staff member 'of the same gender, wherever practicable'.[53] The Guiding Principles provide no such restrictions on invasive searches, simply specifying that searches be carried out 'lawfully, in the least invasive manner possible'.[54]

The OICS has recently conducted a review of strip searching in West Australian prisons where it was found that 900,000 strip searches had been conducted in a five-year period, strip searching is routine in 97 per cent of cases (rather than dependent on risk and certainly not only carried out when 'absolutely necessary'), is sometimes used as a means of punishment or control, and causes significant distress and humiliation, particularly to people with a history of abuse.[55] The OICS recommended that routine strip searching be phased out and that instead new technology be explored,[56] but neither of these recommendations are supported by the government.[57]

The Bangkok Rules

The Bangkok Rules are explicitly intended to *supplement* the 1955 Rules (they predate the Mandela Rules) and there are cross-references throughout to the relevant rules that are supplemented.[58] They have been made in recognition of the particular needs of women in prison that were not taken into account when the 1955 Rules were made, as well as the growth in female imprisonment rates since then.[59] The relevance of both of these matters in the Australian context were detailed in Chapter 1.

There are 70 Bangkok Rules and, similar to the Mandela Rules, it is not possible to detail all of them here. However, some illustrations of the Bangkok Rules include the:

- prohibition of strip searching in Rule 20 ('alternative screening methods, such as scans, shall be developed to replace strip searches and invasive body searches, in order to avoid the harmful psychological and possible physical impact of invasive body searches')

---

53   Guidelines, above n 42, Guideline 1.55 and 1.56.
54   Guiding Principles, above n 43, Principle 2.3.12.
55   Office of the Inspector of Custodial Services (OICS), *Strip Searching Practices in Western Australian Prisons* (2019) iii–v.
56   Ibid xi, Recommendations 8 and 10.
57   Ibid 32–33.
58   Preliminary observation 3 states, '3 - The present rules do not in any way replace the Standard Minimum Rules for the Treatment of Prisoners or the Tokyo Rules and, therefore, all relevant provisions contained in those two sets of rules continue to apply to all prisoners and offenders without discrimination': the Bangkok Rules, above n 34. See also Preliminary Observation 13.
59   Ibid, Preliminary Observation 1.

- reference to the specific health needs that women may have that are not relevant to males in Rule 5, for example, sanitary towels
- emphasis that mothers should be able to maintain contact with their children and 'their children's guardians and legal representatives' through visits in Rule 26.

Body of Principles

Unlike the Mandela Rules, the Body of Principles applies to all forms of detention, including imprisonment. Principles 17 and 18 concern access to legal representation, Principles 19 and 20 concern contact with family members, and Principle 30 concerns disciplinary proceedings, including a requirement that review of such decisions be available. The Body of Principles also reiterate a number of treaty requirements. For example, Principle 1 requires humane treatment (echoing art 10(1) of the ICCPR) and Principle 6 prohibits torture, cruel, inhuman or degrading treatment or punishment (echoing art 7 of the ICCPR, art 1 of the CAT and art 15 of the CRPD), with Principle 33 adding to this that an imprisoned person (or their counsel) who is subject to such treatment should 'have the right to make a request or complaint … to the authorities responsible for the administration of the place of detention and to higher authorities and, when necessary, to appropriate authorities vested with reviewing or remedial powers'.

In the same way as the provisions requiring that the rights contained in treaties be reflected in domestic legislation, Principle 7 requires that 'States should prohibit by law any act contrary to the rights and duties contained in these principles, make any such act subject to appropriate sanctions and conduct impartial investigations upon complaints'. This is not something any Australian jurisdiction has complied with, as is demonstrated in Chapter 5.

General Comments

The HR Committee (responsible for monitoring the implementation of the ICCPR) has issued a General Comment on 'Article 10 (Humane Treatment of Persons Deprived of Their Liberty)'.[60] The General Comment provides the following types of elaboration on the ICCPR requirements:

---

60   United Nations Human Rights Committee, above n 36.

> Paragraph 3 considers the interrelationship between Article 10 and the prohibition against torture, or other cruel, inhuman or degrading treatment or punishment contained in Article 7 of the ICCPR. Paragraph 4 declares that Article 10(1) is to be complied with irrespective of the material resources of the State party and 'must be applied without distinction of any kind, such as race, colour, sex, language, religion, political or other opinion, national or social origin, property, birth or other status'.[61]

The HR Committee has also issued a General Comment on 'Article 7 (Prohibition of Torture, or Other Cruel, Inhuman or Degrading Treatment or Punishment)'.[62] Paragraph 4 states, 'nor does the Committee consider it necessary to draw up a list of prohibited acts or to establish sharp distinctions between the different kinds of punishment or treatment; the distinctions depend on the nature, purpose and severity of the treatment applied' and paragraph 6 adds, '[t]he Committee notes that prolonged solitary confinement of the detained or imprisoned person may amount to acts prohibited by article 7'.

The UN Committee against Torture (CAT/C) (responsible for monitoring the implementation of the CAT) has issued a General Comment on 'Implementation of article 2 by States parties'.[63] This Comment reinforces that torture cannot be justified in any circumstances, noting in paragraph 5 that 'the prohibition against torture is absolute and non-derogable'. It goes on to emphasise that '*no exceptional circumstances whatsoever* may be invoked by a State Party to justify acts of torture in any territory under its jurisdiction' (emphasis in original).

The UN Committee on the Rights of Persons with Disabilities (Disabilities Committee) has also issued a General Comment on 'equality and non-discrimination' that mentions that prison staff should be provided with training on the rights of persons with disabilities.[64]

---

61 Anita Mackay, 'Article 10(1) of the International Covenant on Civil and Political Rights (ICCPR) and Australian Prisons' (2017) 23(3) *Australian Journal of Human Rights* 368, 370.

62 United Nations Human Rights Committee, above n 40.

63 United Nations Committee against Torture, *CAT General Comment No. 2 Implementation of Article 2 by States Parties* (24 January 2008).

64 United Nations Committee on the Rights of Persons with Disabilities, *CRPD General Comment No. 6: Equality and Non-Discrimination* (26 April 2018) para 55(e).

International Enforcement Mechanisms

There are three enforcement mechanisms in relation to the treaties that apply to imprisoned people: (1) incorporation of treaty rights into domestic law, (2) periodic reporting by the relevant TMB and (3) individual communications to the relevant TMB.[65]

Special Rapporteurs, which do not form part of the treaty enforcement mechanisms but are established by, and report to, the UN Human Rights Council, also visit countries that are parties to the treaties. The role of Special Rapporteurs is to 'examine, monitor, advise and publicly report on human rights situations' and '[t]hey are not bound by the terms of any particular treaty'.[66]

The Australian Government's response to the views of TMBs in relation to the periodic reporting process and individual communications is relevant here and is discussed near the end of this chapter.

Domestic Implementation

The Treaties impose obligations on state parties to implement the rights domestically. For example, both the ICCPR and CRPD require states 'to adopt such laws or other measures as may be necessary to give effect to the rights recognized in the present Covenant/Convention', and the ICCPR requires that there be 'effective' remedies provided.[67] As noted above, the CAT requires measures to prevent torture, and the CRPD requires that 'public authorities and institutions act in conformity with the present Convention'.[68]

---

65   Of the three treaties considered here, one—the CAT—establishes a process for inter-state complaints: art 21. This is not relevant to protection of imprisoned people; therefore, this enforcement mechanism will not be discussed here. For a discussion of this mechanism see Claudio Grossman, 'Implementing Human Rights in Closed Environments Through the United Nations Convention Against Torture' in Bronwyn Naylor, Julie Debeljak and Anita Mackay (eds), *Human Rights in Closed Environments* (Federation Press, 2014) 141. Another enforcement mechanism not discussed here is the Universal Periodic Review, which has occurred twice for Australia (in 2011 and 2015). See Australian Government Attorney-General's Department, *Australia's Universal Periodic Review* <https://www.ag.gov.au/RightsAndProtections/HumanRights/United-Nations-Human-Rights-Reporting/Pages/Australias-Universal-Periodic-Review.aspx>; Madelaine Chiam, 'International Human Rights Treaties and Institutions in the Protection of Human Rights in Australia' in Matthew Groves, Janina Boughey and Dan Meagher (eds), *The Legal Protection of Rights in Australia* (Bloomsbury Publishing, 2019) 233–6.
66   Eastman, above n 35, 123. See further Surya Subedi, 'Protection of Human Rights Through the Mechanism of UN Special Rapporteurs' (2011) 33(1) *Human Rights Quarterly* 201.
67   ICCPR art 2; CRPD art 4.
68   CAT art 13; CRPD art 4.

To date, Australia has not comprehensively incorporated the rights contained in these Treaties into domestic legislation. The HR Committee regularly highlights the absence of national human rights legislation in Australia. The HR Committee most recently made the following recommendation in December 2017: 'The Committee reiterates its recommendation (see CCPR/C/AUS/CO/5, para. 8) that the State party should adopt comprehensive federal legislation giving full legal effect to all Covenant provisions across all state and territory jurisdictions'.[69]

Three Australian jurisdictions have human rights legislation (the Australian Capital Territory, Victoria and Queensland).[70] However, this legislation does not incorporate all of the international human rights relevant to prisons. Specifically, art 10(3) of the ICCPR has not been incorporated by any of these jurisdictions.[71] Further, in all three jurisdictions, the enforcement mechanisms provide weak protection of the rights contained therein, which arguably cannot be described as 'effective' remedies as required under the ICCPR.

Given the states and territories are responsible for prisons, there is a question about rights protection in corrections legislation around Australia. While some legislation does confer rights, these are often vague and unenforceable.[72]

These matters will be explored in more detail in Chapter 5 because the second prerequisite—align domestic legislation with the international human rights obligations—stems from this requirement for domestic implementation.

Periodic Reporting

The second enforcement mechanism for these Treaties is the requirement to submit periodic reports to the relevant TMB about the implementation of the treaty. These have previously been mentioned as the bodies that

---

69   Human Rights Committee, *Concluding Observations on the Sixth Periodic Report of Australia*, UN Doc CCPR/C/AUS/CO/6 (1 December 2017) 2.
70   *Human Rights Act 2004* (ACT); *Charter of Human Rights and Responsibilities Act 2006* (Vic); *Human Rights Act 2019* (Qld).
71   It should be noted that rehabilitation does feature in the *Corrections Management Act 2007* (ACT), discussed further in Chapter 6.
72   See, eg, *Corrections Act 1986* (Vic) s 47; *Corrections Act 1997* (Tas) s 29.

issue General Comments, but they are the HR Committee in relation to the ICCPR, CAT/C in relation to the CAT, and Disabilities Committee in relation to the CRPD.[73]

Australia has provided six reports under the ICCPR (most recently in 2016, with the next one due in November 2023), six reports under the CAT (most recently on 16 January 2019) and two reports under the CRPD (a combined second and third report was submitted on 7 September 2018).[74]

Following the reporting process, the relevant TMB issues Concluding Observations or Concluding Comments to which the government responds.[75] The HR Committee's most recent Concluding Observations in December 2017 gave considerable attention to imprisonment, with grave concern expressed about Indigenous over-representation, followed by the concerns expressed about the treatment of people in Australian prisons: '[t]he Committee is concerned about reports of prison overcrowding, inadequate mental health-care facilities, solitary confinement and routine strip searches in places of detention (arts. 7 and 10)'.[76] The HR Committee made six recommendations to address these concerns, including that Australia ratify the OPCAT which, as noted above, has now been done.[77] The other recommendations remain unaddressed and many are covered by the prerequisites in this book. For example, the recommendation to 'eliminate overcrowding' may be addressed by the prerequisite to reduce reliance on imprisonment.[78]

Other TMBs have also raised concerns about imprisonment. For example, the CAT/C has raised concerns about overcrowding in prisons, the over-representation of Indigenous people in prisons and inadequate health care

---

73 Pursuant to the ICCPR art 40, reports are required one year after the Covenant entered into force, then on request. Pursuant to the CAT art 19, reports are required every four years. Pursuant to the CRPD art 35, reports are required every four years.

74 Australian Government Attorney-General's Department, *Treaty Body Reporting* <https://www. ag.gov.au/RightsAndProtections/HumanRights/United-Nations-Human-Rights-Reporting/pages/ Treaty-Body-Reporting.aspx>.

75 Secretary-General of the United Nations, *Compilation of Guidelines on the Form and Content of Reports to be Submitted by States Parties to the International Human Rights Treaties*, UN Doc HRI/ GEN/2/Rev.5 (29 May 2008). Recent reports and responses are available at Australian Government, above n 74.

76 Human Rights Committee, above n 69, 8.

77 Ibid.

78 Ibid [42](a).

in prisons.[79] The Disabilities Committee has raised concerns about the use of prison for accommodating people with disabilities who have not been convicted, particularly Indigenous people with disabilities.[80]

It should be noted, however, that Concluding Observations or Comments are not enforceable. The Australian Government's response to TMB Observations and Comments is detailed below.

Individual Communications

The third enforcement mechanism is individual communications to the relevant TMB concerning alleged violations of the rights contained in the Treaties. These communications may be made by anyone who believes their rights have been violated, including people in prison. In relation to the ICCPR and CRPD, this mechanism is provided through the ratification of the Optional Protocols.[81] Under CAT, jurisdiction over individual communications is provided for in the main treaty, but state parties must 'opt in' to this jurisdiction.[82] Australia opted in on 28 January 1993.

There are numerous admissibility criteria that must be established before TMBs gain jurisdiction over individual communications.[83] The most difficult admissibility criterion is establishing that all domestic remedies

---

79   United Nations Committee against Torture, *Concluding Observations of the Committee against Torture: Australia*, UN Doc CAT/C/AUS/CO/3 (22 May 2008) 7.

80   United Nations Committee on the Rights of Persons with Disabilities, *Concluding Observations on the Initial Report of Australia*, UN Doc CRPD/C/AUS/CO/1 (21 October 2013) 4. This has also been the subject of individual communications to the Committee: see Fiona McGaughey, Tamara Tulich and Harry Blagg, 'UN Decision on Marlon Noble Case: Imprisonment of an Aboriginal Man with Intellectual Disability Found Unfit to Stand Trial in Western Australia' (2017) 42(1) *Alternative Law Journal* 67.

81   *First Optional Protocol to the International Covenant on Civil and Political Rights*, 999 UNTS 302, opened for signature 16 December 1966 (entered into force 23 March 1976). In relation to Australia's accession to this Optional Protocol see Hilary Charlesworth, 'Australia's Accession to the First Optional Protocol to the International Covenant on Civil and Political Rights' (1991) 18 *Melbourne University Law Review* 428; *Optional Protocol to the Convention on the Rights of Persons with Disabilities*, opened for signature 30 March 2007, A/RES/61/106 (entered into force 3 May 2008).

82   CAT art 21.

83   Joseph and Castan summarise the criteria under arts 1, 2, 3 and 5 of the Optional Protocol to the ICCPR to include the following: the complaint must be made by an 'individual victim', the matter must be 'within the relevant State's jurisdiction', the event that is the subject of the complaint must have occurred after the Optional Protocol was ratified, and the complaint must not be 'simultaneously before another international tribunal': Sarah Joseph and Melissa Castan, *The International Covenant on Civil and Political Rights. Cases, Materials and Commentary* (Oxford University Press, 3rd ed, 2013) 19.

have been exhausted.[84] Once a communication has been considered, the TMB issues 'views on the merits', which include its conclusion as to which articles have been violated and the appropriate remedy. The state party has 180 days to report to the TMB on the steps taken to remedy any violation.

There have only been four successful communications concerning Australian prison conditions. The first was the complaint by Mr Brough to the HR Committee, which to date is the only successful communication brought under the ICCPR.[85] At the time of the complaint, Mr Brough was a 16-year-old Aboriginal male with a mild intellectual disability who was transferred to an adult correctional facility. For some of the time he was there, he was kept in a padded isolation cell in circumstances that the HR Committee found to be in violation of arts 10(1) and 10(3) of the ICCPR.[86] In making this finding, the HR Committee commented:

> [i]n the circumstances, the author's extended confinement to an isolated cell without any possibility of communication, combined with his exposure to artificial light for prolonged periods and the removal of his clothes and blanket, was not commensurate with his status as a juvenile person in a particularly vulnerable position because of his disability and his status as an Aboriginal. As a consequence, the hardship of the imprisonment was manifestly incompatible with his condition, as demonstrated by his inclination to inflict self-harm and his suicide attempt.[87]

The other three were complaints to the Disabilities Committee under the CRPD by three Indigenous men. Mr Noble was being indefinitely imprisoned in Western Australia because he had been found unfit to

---

84   First Optional Protocol to ICCPR art 5(2)(b); CAT art 22(5)(b); Optional Protocol to CRPD art 2(d). This is 'unless [inter alia] there is no available remedy, or the remedy is futile': Eastman, above n 35, 110.

85   Human Rights Committee, *Views: Communication No 1184/2003*, UN Doc CCPR/C/86/D/1184/2003 (17 March 2006) ('*Brough v Australia*'). There was a communication concerning the imprisonment of Mr Hicks for seven months following his transfer to Australia from Guantanamo Bay, which the Human Rights Committee held to be arbitrary under the ICCPR art 9(1). However, this communication did not concern the conditions of his imprisonment: see Human Rights Committee, *Views: Communication No 2005/2010*, UN Doc CCPR/C/115/D/2005/2010 (5 November 2015) ('*Hicks v Australia*'). Other communications have been found to be inadmissible, such as Human Rights Committee, *Views: Communication No 762/1997*, UN Doc CCPR/C/71/D/762/1997 (22 March 2001) ('*Jensen v Australia*').

86   The requirement for treatment with humanity and respect for human dignity, and the requirement for rehabilitation.

87   Human Rights Committee, *Views: Communication No 1184/2003*, UN Doc CCPR/C/86/D/1184/2003 (17 March 2006) ('*Brough v Australia*') [9.4].

stand trial due to his disabilities. The Disabilities Committee found that Australia's treatment of Mr Noble violated arts 5(1), 12, 13, 14(1) (b), 14(2) and 15 of the CRPD.[88] This communication is discussed in detail in Chapter 7. McGaughey et al provide a succinct summary of the Committee's findings:

> The Committee found that Mr Noble's right to a fair trial was fully suspended by the application of the CLMIA Act [*Criminal Law (Mentally Impaired Accused) Act 1996* (WA)], depriving him of the protection and equal benefit of the law – a violation of Article 5 (1) and (2) of the Convention. They also found that the lack of support to exercise his rights to access to justice and a fair trial resulted in a violation of Articles 12 (2) and (3), and 13 (1). His detention was considered to amount to a violation of Article 14 (1) (b) which provides that 'the existence of a disability shall in no case justify a deprivation of liberty'. Finally, the Committee declared that Mr Noble's indefinite detention amounted to inhuman and degrading treatment under Article 15 of the Convention.[89]

The communications by Mr Leo and Mr Doolan both concerned treatment in the Northern Territory. Both men were found unfit to stand trial and were detained in the Alice Springs Correctional Centre in maximum security, with long periods in solitary confinement, for the total time of five years and 10 months and four years and nine months respectively.[90] When not in solitary confinement, the men were not separated from those who had been convicted; they were subject to involuntary treatment and the supervision orders that they were subject to were indefinite.[91]

Similar to the views expressed in response to Mr Noble's communication, the Disabilities Committee found that arts 5, 12, 13, 14 and 15 of the CRPD had been violated by Australia in both instances.[92] Also similar to the views expressed in response to Mr Noble's communication, it was the

---

88   Committee on the Rights of Persons with Disabilities, *Views: Communication No 7/2012*, UN Doc CRPD/C/16/D/7/2012 (15 August - 2 September 2016) ('*Noble v Australia*') [8.10].

89   McGaughey, Tulich and Blagg, above n 80, 68.

90   Committee on the Rights of Persons with Disabilities, *Views: Communication No 17/2013*, UN Doc CRPD/C/22/D/17/2013 (30 August 2019) ('*Leo v Australia*') [2.4]; Committee on the Rights of Persons with Disabilities, *Views: Communication No 18/2013*, UN Doc CRPD/C/22/D/18/2013 (30 August 2019) ('*Doolan v Australia*') [2.4].

91   *Leo v Australia* [8.4], [8.10]; *Doolan v Australia* [8.4], [8.10].

92   *Leo v Australia* [8.13]; *Doolan v Australia* [8.13].

indefinite detention that led the Disabilities Committee to conclude that art 15 (the prohibition of cruel, inhuman and degrading treatment and punishment) had been violated.[93]

There are numerous reasons why the individual communication mechanism is not a satisfactory enforcement mechanism for the protection of imprisoned people in Australia. The first is that having to exhaust domestic remedies prior to making a communication adds to the expense and time taken for the process.

Second, although there is no requirement for parties to be legally represented to make a communication to committees, in practice, individuals may not be in a position to do so without such representation (particularly given the low educational levels among people in prison compared to the rest of the population, as discussed in Chapter 1, and the complex considerations surrounding admissibility of communications). Mr Noble, Mr Doolan and Mr Leo all required legal representation to bring their communications.

Third, the time taken for the TMBs to issue views on the merits is very lengthy. For example, in the Brough case, the complaint was made on 4 March 2003 and the decision was handed down on 17 March 2006. This was comparatively quick compared to the timeline for the communications to the Disabilities Committee. Mr Doolan and Mr Leo submitted their complaints on 19 September 2013 and the findings in both communications were published in October 2019.

Finally, and most importantly, there is the lack of enforceability of the views of the TMBs (detailed below). The general disregard for TMBs' views means that not only does the individual author not get redress, but a systemic change in policy or practice to prevent the same violation occurring in the future is also unlikely.

There is one positive example that goes against this general trend. This is the response to the communication concerning Tasmania's criminalisation of homosexual acts, with a penalty of 21 years imprisonment. Mr Toonen brought a communication to the HR Committee that 'alleged that the laws violated the right to privacy, distinguished between individuals in the exercise of the right to privacy on the basis of sexual activity or orientation, and amounted to the unequal treatment of homosexual men

---

93   *Leo v Australia* [8.10]; *Doolan v Australia* [8.10].

in Tasmania'.[94] The HR Committee held that the Tasmanian law violated the right to privacy in art 17 of the ICCPR.[95] The Australian Government responded by passing legislation to override the Tasmanian law, relying on the external affairs power.[96]

If the Australian Government were to adopt such an approach in response to communications concerning state and territory prison systems, it would lead to reform resulting from individual communications to TMB. However, this response to Mr Toonen's communication occurred in 1994 and it has been observed that '[s]ince *Toonen*, the Commonwealth Government has generally declined to intervene in what may be seen as rights-incompatible state laws'.[97]

Visits by Special Rapporteurs

In 2017, the Special Rapporteur on the rights of Indigenous peoples visited Australia and commented on the over-representation of Indigenous people in Australian prisons, referring to the rates as 'a major human rights concern'.[98] The Rapporteur went on to note that it was having 'devastating consequences for concerned individuals and communities' and that '[t]he focus urgently needs to move away from detention and punishment towards rehabilitation'.[99] This recommendation supports the third prerequisite in this book, to shift the focus on imprisonment to the goal of rehabilitation and restoration (see Chapter 6).

The Special Rapporteur on violence against women, its causes and consequences also visited Australia in 2017. Three pages of the Rapporteur's report were dedicated to '[v]iolence against women in detention and against indigenous and other women in prison', expressing concern about:

---

94   Paula Gerber and Joel Gory, 'The UN Human Rights Committee and LGBT Rights: What Is It Doing? What Could It Be Doing?' (2014) 14 *Human Rights Law Review* 403, 429.

95   Human Rights Committee, *Views: Communication No 488/1992*, UN Doc CCPR/C/50/D/488/1992 (4 April 1994) ('*Toonen v Australia*').

96   *Human Rights (Sexual Conduct) Act 1994* (Cth); Adam Fletcher, *Australia's Human Rights Scrutiny Regime. Democratic Masterstroke or Mere Window Dressing?* (Melbourne University Press, 2018) 37.

97   Ibid 38.

98   Human Rights Council, *Report of the Special Rapporteur on the Rights of Indigenous Peoples on Her Visit to Australia*, UN Doc A/HRC/36/46/Add.2 (8 August 2017) 12.

99   Ibid 14–15. These observations accord with many of the criticisms raised by the Royal Commission into Aboriginal Deaths in Custody, *National Report* (1991), which is discussed in detail in Chapter 3, as well as the Australian Law Reform Commission report, *Pathways to Justice—An Inquiry into the Incarceration Rate of Aboriginal and Torres Strait Islander Peoples*, Report No 133 (2017), which is discussed in detail in Chapter 4.

excessive incarceration, prison overcrowding, strip-searching, solitary confinement, lack of alternatives to custodial sentences, in particular for women with dependent children, inadequate access to health care (in particular mental health care) and inadequate re-entry programmes to prevent reoffending.[100]

The Rapporteur reiterated the points about the vulnerability of the female prison population made in Chapter 1 of this book, particularly the rates of mental and cognitive disability and experiences of victimisation.[101]

Australian Government Response to Treaty Monitoring Bodies

The Australian Government is not generally inclined to accept the views of TMBs as expressed in Concluding Observations or Comments, or in views on the merits following individual communications. As the only individual communications relating to imprisonment, it is significant that the Australian Government did not accept that there had been a violation of the ICCPR in response to the views of the HR Committee in *Brough*,[102] nor accept the findings of the Disabilities Committee in relation to the CRPD in *Noble*.[103] There has been no government response to the communications by Mr Doolan and Mr Leo.

---

100 Human Rights Council, *Report of the Special Rapporteur on Violence Against Women, Its Causes and Consequences on Her Mission to Australia*, UN Doc A/HRC/38/47/Add.1 (17 April 2018) 11.
101 Ibid 12–13. In 2010, the Special Rapporteur on the right of everyone to the enjoyment of the highest attainable standard of physical and mental health visited Australia and his report considered health care in prisons and the over-representation of Indigenous people in prisons in Australia. This report is not discussed here because it has been superseded by the observations of Special Rapporteurs who have visited more recently. See Human Rights Council, *Report of the Special Rapporteur on the Right of Everyone to the Enjoyment of the Highest Attainable Standard of Physical and Mental Health, Anand Grover*, UN DOC A/HRC/14/20/Add.4 (3 June 2010).
102 See *Response of the Australian Government to the Views of the Committee in Communication No 1184/2003 (Brough v Australia)*. Charlesworth has noted that Australia's initial delay in acceding to the First Optional Protocol to the ICCPR (allowing individual communications to be brought to the Human Right Committee) was due to state and territory concern about scrutiny of the treatment of people in prisons, which adds a historical context to the reluctance to accept the Human Rights Committee's views and Australia's response to this communication concerning imprisonment: Charlesworth, above n 81, 428–9.
103 *Response of the Australian Government to the Views of the Committee on the Rights of Persons with Disabilities in Communication No 7/2012 (Noble v Australia)*. Freckelton and Keyzer note that in the response the Australian Government 'repudiated each of the Committee's findings of violation of Noble's rights': Ian Freckelton and Patrick Keyzer, 'Fitness to Stand Trial and Disability Discrimination: An International Critique of Australia' (2017) 24(5) *Psychiatry, Psychology and Law* 770, 776. This response relating to the findings of TCID is critiqued in Chapter 7.

This is not atypical.[104] Remedy Australia provides comprehensive monitoring of the responses to individual communications to the HR Committee, including contacting the authors of the communications about the follow-up. In a report to the UN in October 2017, Remedy Australia summarised that of the 40 communications brought between 1994 and 2017 finding violations of the ICCPR against Australia, five have been fully remedied and 10 have been partially remedied. This leaves 25 (62 per cent) that have not been remedied.[105]

Given there are so few communications relating to conditions in Australian prisons, it is useful to examine the government's response to cases relating to another environment in which people are deprived of their liberty, immigration detention.

Australian governments, both Coalition and Labor, have been particularly dismissive of TMBs' criticisms of the rights incompatibility of the policy of mandatory immigration detention.[106] The HR Committee and CAT/C have both expressed concerns about this policy, and it has been considered in a number of individual communications.[107] The government's response to the HR Committee's views on the merits in *A v Australia* is typical of the government's views:

> [A]fter giving serious and careful consideration to the ... views of the Committee, the Government does not accept that the detention of Mr A was in contravention of the Covenant, nor

---

104 For a discussion of the government's response to communications concerning preventive detention of sex offenders see Darren O'Donovan and Patrick Keyzer, '"Visions of a Distant Millennium"? The Effectiveness of the UN Human Rights Petition System' in Patrick Keyzer et al (eds), *Access to International Justice* (Routledge, 2014).

105 Remedy Australia, *Follow-Up Report on Violations by Australia of ICCPR in Individual Communications (1994-2017)* (October 2017) 1. It should be noted that since this report was prepared, two of the individual communications referred to as 'unremedied' in it have been remedied by the legalisation of same-sex marriage in Australia in December 2017 (*Marriage Amendment (Definition and Religious Freedoms) Act 2017* (Cth)). These are: Human Rights Committee, *Views: Communication No 2216/2012*, 119th sess, UN Doc CCPR/C/119/D/2216/2012 (28 March 2017) ('*C v Australia*') and Human Rights Committee, *Views: Communication No 2172/2012*, 119th sess, UN Doc CCPR/C/119/D/2172/2012 (17 March 2017) ('*G v Australia*'). For further details about *C v Australia* and *G v Australia* see Oscar Roos and Anita Mackay, 'A Shift in the United Nations Human Rights Committee's Jurisprudence on Marriage Equality? An Analysis of Two Recent Communications from Australia' (2019) 42(2) *University of New South Wales Law Journal* 747.

106 See further Bronwyn Naylor, Julie Debeljak and Anita Mackay, 'A Strategic Framework for Implementing Human Rights in Closed Environments' (2015) 41 *Monash University Law Review* 218, 229–31.

107 Human Rights Committee, above n 69, 7–8; United Nations Committee against Torture, *Concluding Observations of the Committee against Torture: Australia*, UN Doc CAT/C/AUS/CO/3 (22 May 2008) [11], [22], [25].

that the provision for review of the lawfulness of that detention by Australian courts was inadequate. Consequently, the Government does not accept the view of the Committee that compensation should be paid to Mr A.

The Committee is not a court and does not render binding decisions or judgments. It provides views and opinions, and it is up to countries to decide whether they agree with those views and how they will respond to them.[108]

In fact, it is extremely rare for the Australian Government to respond to a TMB view on the merits with law reforms, and the main instances when this has occurred have been in relation to the protection of lesbian, gay, bisexual and transgender individuals.[109] Debeljak comments that this is 'despite the fact that the treaty-monitoring bodies consist of independent experts, that treaty-monitoring bodies are *the* authoritative voice on the application of the treaties, and that Australia voluntarily accepted the individual communication jurisdiction'.[110]

The HR Committee has noted the tendency for Australia to disregard its views. In Concluding Observations to Australia's recent periodic report, the HR Committee noted that they remain 'concerned (see CCPR/C/AUS/CO/5, para. 10) about the State party's repeated failure to implement its Views'.[111] The Committee had previously noted that 'a failure to give effect to its Views would call into question the State party's commitment to the First Optional Protocol'.[112]

---

108 Daryl Williams (Attorney-General) and Philip Ruddock (Minister for Immigration), 'Australian Government Responds to the United Nations Human Rights Committee' (Media Release, 17 December 1997).
109 Two communications were remedied by the legalisation of same-sex marriage in December 2017 (see above n 105), as was an earlier communication concerning Tasmania's legislation that criminalised consensual homosexual acts by adults when this legislation was repealed in 1997 by the *Criminal Code Amendment Act 1997* (Tas) (*Toonen v Australia*). However, Chiam observes that the legalisation of same-sex marriage was 'a result of domestic political imperatives', rather than an attempt to respond to the Human Rights Committee, further noting that 'Australia's response to the Committee in that claim was drafted in a way that did not accept any finding of violation on Australia's part': Chiam, above n 65, 241.
110 Julie Debeljak, 'Does Australia Need a Bill of Rights?' in Paula Gerber and Melissa Castan (eds), *Contemporary Perspectives on Human Rights Law in Australia* (Lawbook Co, 2013) 54 (emphasis in original).
111 Human Rights Committee, above n 69, 2.
112 Human Rights Committee, *Concluding Observations of the Human Rights Committee: Australia*, UN Doc CCPR/C/AUS/CO/5 (7 May 2009) [10]. In 2017, the Committee recommended: 'The State party should promptly and fully implement all pending Views adopted by the Committee so as to guarantee the right of victims to an effective remedy when there has been a violation of the Covenant, in accordance with article 2 (3) of the Covenant': ibid 2 [10]. For further discussion about the TMB's views of Australia's attitude towards them see Chiam, above n 65, 243–4.

In addition to this dismissive response following individual communications, the Australian Government has been equally dismissive of other TMB enforcement mechanisms. An example of this is the response to criticism by the Committee on the Elimination of Racial Discrimination concerning, among other things, amendments to the *Native Title Act 1993* (Cth).[113] In a response that in many ways mimics the response to the decision in *A v Australia* (see above)—that the committee is 'not giving binding decisions or judgments'—the then government 'rejected the views of the treaty-monitoring body in no uncertain terms'.[114]

In summary, while there are comprehensive human rights protections for imprisoned people at the international level, the lack of domestic incorporation, weak enforceability mechanisms and the Australian Government's reluctance to accept the views of TMBs mean there are major deficiencies in the *actual* protection of the human rights of Australian imprisoned people by international law.

Conclusion

International human rights law establishes that people in prison retain all their rights other than the right to liberty; prohibits 'torture, cruel, inhuman or degrading treatment or punishment'; requires that people 'be treated with humanity and with respect for the inherent dignity of the human person'; and specifies that the goal of imprisonment should be rehabilitation.

Although these are Australia's international legal obligations, there are no effective international enforcement mechanisms. Indeed, the Australian Government often ignores the expert views of TMBs in response to periodic reports and individual communications. While these are non-binding at the international level, for states committed to implementing their human rights obligations, they provide a useful mechanism for identifying areas that should be addressed to ensure human rights compliance.

---

113 Committee on the Elimination of Racial Discrimination, *Decision 2(54) on Australia: Concluding Observations/Comments*, UN Doc CERD/C/54/Misc.40/Rev.2 (1999) [6]–[8].
114 Debeljak, above n 110, 54. Other examples are provided by Eastman, above n 35.

Australia's recent ratification of the OPCAT may represent a renewed commitment to international human rights law compliance in Australian prisons, with the dual-level monitoring by the SPT and NPM. The significance of the OPCAT for monitoring is considered in the next chapter before the remaining chapters consider prerequisites for implementing the preventive focus of the OPCAT.

3

The OPCAT and the Changes It Will Impose to Prison Monitoring

Introduction

The *Optional Protocol to the Convention against Torture and Other Cruel, Inhuman or Degrading Treatment or Punishment* (OPCAT) is the most recent international law obligation entered into by Australia relevant to prisons.[1] Australia signed the OPCAT on 19 May 2009 and ratified it on 15 December 2017.[2] As outlined in Chapter 2, the OPCAT introduces a dual-level monitoring regime. Monitoring is conducted by both the international Subcommittee for the Prevention of Torture and Other Cruel, Inhuman or Degrading Treatment or Punishment (SPT), which is a United Nations (UN) committee of experts, and by the domestic National Preventive Mechanisms (NPMs) that signatories to the OPCAT are required to establish. Australia has determined that multiple bodies at the federal, state and territory level will form Australia's NPM (due to the

---

1   *Optional Protocol to the Convention against Torture*, adopted 18 December 1992, UN Doc A/RES/57/199 (entered into force 22 June 2006) ('OPCAT').
2   Minister for Foreign Affairs and Attorney-General (Cth), 'Ratification of OPCAT Caps Year of Significant Human Rights Achievements for Turnbull Government' (Media Release, 15 December 2017). For an analysis of the 'path' to ratification see Richard Harding, 'Australia's Circuitous Path Towards the Ratification of the OPCAT, 2002-2017: The Challenges of Implementation' (2019) 25(1) *Australian Journal of Human Rights* 4.

responsibility for places of detention being divided between different levels of government) and that the Commonwealth Ombudsman will perform the coordinating role[3] (a role that commenced from 1 July 2018[4]).

Australia currently has a wide variety of organisations that monitor, investigate and adjudicate what happens in prisons. These include courts, prison inspectorates, human rights commissions, Ombudsmen, Coroners and Royal Commissions. They provide scrutiny of prison operation in four main ways. First, courts and tribunals can adjudicate claims brought by people in prison. Second, people in prison may make complaints which complaint handling bodies can investigate. Third, investigatory/monitoring bodies can inspect prisons and prepare reports on the systematic conditions and treatment of imprisoned people. Such reports are usually made publicly available. Finally, Coroners scrutinise deaths in custody and make recommendations about how to avoid similar deaths occurring in the future.

The OPCAT will change prison monitoring in Australia in three significant ways. First, it will subject Australian prisons to international-level scrutiny by an expert committee (the SPT) that will assess Australia's compliance with the international law and standards outlined in Chapter 2. Second, it will shift the current predominantly reactive monitoring system to a preventive system—a system focused specifically on preventing torture, cruel, inhuman or degrading treatment or punishment in line with the *Convention against Torture and Other Cruel, Inhuman or Degrading Treatment or Punishment* (CAT) which the OPCAT falls under.[5] Third, it will require monitoring mechanisms to meet the six criteria in the OPCAT for NPM operation—criteria not currently met by Australian monitoring mechanisms.

This chapter will discuss each of these shifts in turn. It will also consider the recent work by the Victorian Ombudsman who undertook an OPCAT-compliant inspection of a women's prison in Victoria (the Dame

---

3   Australian Human Rights Commission, *OPCAT in Australia Consultation Paper* (May 2017) 7–8.
4   Australian Human Rights Commission, *OPCAT in Australia Consultation Paper: Stage 2* (June 2018) 5.
5   *Convention against Torture and Other Cruel, Inhuman or Degrading Treatment or Punishment*, opened for signature 10 December 1984, 1465 UNTS 85 (entered into force 26 June 1987) ('CAT'). Australia ratified the CAT on 10 December 1985. As noted in Chapter 2, other treaties also emphasise the prohibition of torture and cruel, inhuman or degrading treatment or punishment: see *International Covenant on Civil and Political Rights*, opened for signature 19 December 1966, 999 UNTS 171 (entered into force 23 March 1976) art 7 ('ICCPR'); *Convention on the Rights of Persons with Disabilities*, opened for signature 30 March 2007, 2515 UNTS 3 (entered into force 3 May 2008) art 15 ('CRPD').

Phyllis Frost Centre) to show the differences in approach that were required compared to the type of inspections the Ombudsman would typically carry out of prisons in Victoria.[6] This is a practical illustration of the difference the OPCAT may make to prison inspections in Australia nationally and it will be referred to throughout this chapter.

It will be obvious from this chapter that the matters either brought before the monitoring mechanisms (as litigation or complaints) or brought to light by the monitoring mechanism's investigatory functions paint a very bleak picture of the practices in Australian prisons. Therefore, in addition to explaining the differences that OPCAT will make to prison monitoring, the discussion below will also provide numerous justifications for the prerequisites for human rights compliance set out in the remaining chapters of this book.

The International Subcommittee for the Prevention of Torture

The SPT is comprised of 25 experts with varied backgrounds from countries that have ratified the OPCAT.[7] They carry out visits to places where people are deprived of their liberty in countries that have ratified the OPCAT. Such visits involve at least two members of the SPT and there are four types of visits: 'SPT country visits, SPT country follow-up visits, NPM advisory visits and OPCAT advisory visits'.[8] Following a visit, the SPT will provide a confidential report to the state party which is published only if the state party requests this.[9] The SPT has guiding principles to inform their overall approach as well as guidelines for their approach to country visits.[10]

---

6   Victorian Ombudsman, *Implementing OPCAT in Victoria: Report and Inspection of the Dame Phyllis Frost Centre* (2017).
7   'Members serve in their individual capacity and are drawn from a variety of different backgrounds relevant to its work, including lawyers, medical professionals and detention and inspection experts': United Nations Office of the High Commission, *Factfile on the SPT* <https://www.ohchr.org/EN/HRBodies/OPCAT/Pages/Factfile.aspx>.
8   United Nations Human Rights Office of the High Commissioner, *The SPT in Brief* <https://www.ohchr.org/en/hrbodies/opcat/pages/brief.aspx>.
9   OPCAT art 16.
10   SPT, *The Approach of the Subcommittee on Prevention of Torture to the Concept of Prevention of Torture and Other Cruel, Inhuman or Degrading Treatment or Punishment Under the Optional Protocol to the Convention Against Torture and Other Cruel, Inhuman or Degrading Treatment or Punishment*, CAT/OP/12/6 (30 December 2010); *Guidelines of the Subcommittee on Prevention of Torture and Other Cruel, Inhuman or Degrading Treatment or Punishment in Relation to Visits to States Parties Under Article 11 (a) of the Optional Protocol*, CAT/OP/5 (14 February 2015).

By the end of 2019, the OPCAT had been ratified by 90 state parties and signed by a further 13.[11] The SPT's capacity to visit individual state parties with any frequency is necessarily limited. The Australian Human Rights Commission anticipates that 'the SPT can be expected to conduct a visit to Australia once every seven to ten years'.[12]

The impact of SPT visits on Australia will not be known until they begin, but some insight may be drawn from New Zealand, which ratified the OPCAT in 2007 and was visited by the SPT in 2013. In summarising that experience, McGregor writes:

> The SPT after examining 35 places of detention in its 2013 visit to New Zealand said it 'did not encounter any consistent allegations of torture or physical ill treatment' … The visits are expected to serve as a deterrent to bad behaviour by staff and officials and also to put pressure on authorities to improve transparency and prison conditions.[13]

Hopefully the SPT will have a similar deterrent effect in Australia, and this may serve to counterbalance the lack of frequency of SPT visits. The NPM regime is crucial in this regard because there is a requirement that NPM visits are conducted regularly (as detailed later in this chapter under 'Evaluation of Monitoring Mechanisms in Australia').

Current Monitoring System in Australia

The major problem with current monitoring practices in Australia is that the system is predominantly reactive—that is, there needs to be a problem (death, harm or human rights violation) before investigation can be initiated (such as court proceedings, complaints investigations and major investigations such as coronial inquests and Royal Commissions). However, there are some proactive elements, such as the inspections carried out by prison inspectorates, Ombudsmen and human rights commissions.

---

11   United Nations Human Rights Office of the High Commissioner, *Status of Ratification Interactive Dashboard* <http://indicators.ohchr.org/>.
12   Australian Human Rights Commission, above n 4, 7.
13   Judy McGregor, 'The Challenges and Limitations of OPCAT National Preventive Mechanisms: Lessons From New Zealand' (2017) 23(3) *Australian Journal of Human Rights* 351, 357.

Courts and Tribunals

Courts form an integral part of the independent external monitoring system. Human rights legislation would be greatly devalued if redress from the courts was not available. As Nowak writes, '[t]he very notion of human rights implies that rights-holders must have some possibility to hold duty-bearers accountable for not living up to their legally binding human rights obligations'.[14] The problem in Australia is the absence of human rights legislation in jurisdictions other than the Australian Capital Territory (ACT), Victoria and Queensland. The operation of this legislation in the ACT and Victoria is considered here because these jurisdictions have had human rights legislation for several years. It is not yet possible to assess the impact of the Queensland legislation because it only commenced on 1 January 2020.

In all jurisdictions, there are considerable practical barriers facing imprisoned people seeking to litigate. These include accessing legal advice while in prison, the expense of legal proceedings and the challenges in accessing information when preparing for their hearing (particularly when self-represented). An example of the latter is the lack of access to computers, which has been the subject of (unsuccessful) litigation in New South Wales (NSW) and Victoria.[15] Moreover, many people are only in prison for a short sentence and, given the time taken for litigation, any relief granted by the court may not assist the individual during their incarceration.[16] Nevertheless, a decision of the court may lead to changes in prison operation that benefit other imprisoned people in similar circumstances.

Australian Capital Territory and Victoria

The ACT and Victoria have explicitly incorporated some of the international human rights protections contained in the *International Covenant on Civil and Political Rights* (ICCPR) into domestic legislation: the *Human Rights Act 2004* (ACT) ('*HRA*') and *Charter of Human Rights*

---

14   Manfred Nowak, 'The Need for a World Court of Human Rights' (2007) 7 *Human Rights Law Review* 251, 254.
15   *Liristis v New South Wales* [2018] NSWSC 39; *Knight v Deputy Commissioner, Corrections Victoria* [2012] VSC 506; *Brazel v Westin & Anor* [2013] VSC 527 (3 October 2013). See further Carolyn McKay, 'Digital Access to Justice from Prison: Is There a Right to Technology?' (2018) 42 *Criminal Law Journal* 303.
16   Anne Owers, 'Prison Inspection and the Protection of Prisoners' Rights' (2010) 30(5) *Pace Law Review* 1535, 1536.

and Responsibilities Act 2006 (Vic) ('*Charter*').[17] The details of the rights contained in this legislation are discussed in Chapter 5. This section provides an overview of some key litigation imprisoned people have brought under these Acts.

The approach to seeking a remedy for breach of the rights varies between jurisdictions. In the ACT, it is possible to bring a direct cause of action under the *HRA* when it is alleged that a public authority has breached their duty.[18] By contrast, in Victoria, under the *Charter*, the human rights claim has to be linked to another cause of action.[19] The cases discussed below will demonstrate that the enforcement mechanisms under both the *Charter* and *HRA* provide a relatively weak protection of human rights.

Australian Capital Territory

The most detailed consideration of the human rights of people in the Alexander Maconochie Centre (AMC) under the *HRA* has arisen in claims brought by Mr Isa Islam (self-represented). Mr Islam has made claims surrounding his right to:

- education without discrimination (s 27A)
- not to be treated or punished in a cruel, inhuman or degrading way (s 10(1))
- not to be discriminated against on the basis of religion (s 8(3))[20]
- adequate facilities to prepare a criminal appeal (s 22)[21]
- the provision of food consistent with his religious beliefs (s 14).[22]

All of Mr Islam's abovementioned claims have been unsuccessful. The decision relating to the provision of food will be discussed in Chapter 8 and the other claims will be discussed here.

---

17   Queensland has recently incorporated some ICCPR rights into domestic legislation in the *Human Rights Act 2019* (Qld).

18   *Human Rights Act 2004* (ACT) s40C(2) ('*HRA*').

19   *Charter of Human Rights and Responsibilities Act 2006* (Vic) s 39(1) ('*Charter*'). This makes the *Charter* remedy provision more difficult to rely on in practice compared to the provision in the *HRA*: see generally Mark Moshinsky, 'Charter Remedies' in Matthew Groves and Colin Campbell (eds), *Australian Charters of Rights a Decade On* (Federation Press, 2017).

20   *Islam v Director-General Justice and Community Safety Directorate (No 3)* [2016] ACTSC 27 (25 February 2016).

21   *Islam v Director-General, Justice and Community Safety Directorate* [2015] ACTCA 60 (16 December 2015).

22   *Islam v Director-General of the Department of Justice and Community Safety Directorate* [2018] ACTSC 322.

The ACT Supreme Court held that Mr Islam had had good access to education while imprisoned, having completed three Masters degrees (Mr Islam was also undertaking a doctorate),[23] and his complaints in relation to education concerned technical problems with the printer and the university's rules about contact with imprisoned people that meant, without Mr Islam giving written consent for AMC staff to liaise with the university, contact would be curtailed. In other words, the limits were due to the combination of university policy and Mr Islam's unwillingness to consent to staff contacting the university on his behalf.[24]

Mr Islam was unable to demonstrate that the allegations concerning cruel, inhuman or degrading treatment met the level of severity required[25] and unable to show that the 'frustrating and unpleasant' treatment he had been subjected to were causally linked to his religious beliefs.[26]

Mr Islam's claim relating to facilities to prepare for his self-represented sentencing appeal concerned access to a computer and the internet. Mr Islam had free access to a computer shared between 25–26 other imprisoned people, which equated to approximately two hours use per person per week.[27] He had the option to hire a computer for his sole use at a cost of $5 per week. In either case he would be permitted to access the *Austlii* online legal database for the purposes of legal research.[28] Walmsley AJ held that there had been no breach of s 22(2)(b) of the *HRA* because of these limits to computer access, given that the right is 'not absolute'.[29] It was further noted that Mr Islam had 'chosen to represent himself' for his appeal.[30]

---

23   *Islam v Director-General Justice and Community Safety Directorate (No 3)* [2016] ACTSC 27 (25 February 2016) [161], [121].
24   Ibid [118]–[123]. The following matter also dealt with the right to education and Mr Islam's concerns about printing: *Islam v Director-General of the Department of Justice and Community Safety Directorate* [2018] ACTSC 322.
25   Ibid [158].
26   Ibid [148].
27   *Islam v Director-General, Justice and Community Safety Directorate* [2015] ACTCA 60 (16 December 2015) [8]–[10].
28   Ibid [11]–[12].
29   Ibid [26].
30   Ibid [27]. See also the discussion of the decision by McKay, above n 15, 314.

Mr David Harold Eastman also brought some claims under the *HRA* prior to a retrial that led to him being released in November 2018.[31] Mr Eastman was transferred from a NSW prison to the AMC on 29 May 2009. He had been engaged in cleaning work while in the AMC but submitted that he wanted the opportunity to tutor other imprisoned people.[32]

There is no right to work provided for by the ICCPR. Article 8 precludes forced labour but provides an exception for forced hard labour that is part of a sentence of imprisonment. Work would generally be considered to be a component of rehabilitation as required by art 10(3) of the ICCPR. Although the *HRA* has not incorporated art 10(3), a number of provisions in the *Corrections Management Act 2007* (ACT) require rehabilitation.[33]

Refshauge J reviewed the international case law and concluded that people in prison do not have a right to work in the ACT, although he noted that an opportunity to work may be required under s 19(1) of the *HRA*, which is the right to humane treatment.[34] His Honour found there was no right for people in the AMC to *choose* what work they undertake *even if* there is the opportunity to work.[35]

Mr Eastman also claimed that on a number of occasions prison staff spoke to him in a way that contravened the right to be treated with humanity and respect for human dignity contained in s 19(1) of the *HRA*—for example, by calling him a 'murderer'.[36] However, the Court found that in some instances the conduct could not be proven, and in other

---

31   For an examination of the events that led to Mr Eastman's release see Jacqueline Fuller, 'The David Eastman Case: The Use of Inquiries to Investigate Miscarriages of Justice in Australia' (2020) 45(1) *Alternative Law Journal* 60.

32   *David Harold Eastman v Chief Executive Officer of the Department of Justice and Community Safety* [2010] ACTSC 4 (12 January 2010), [50], [54].

33   Paragraph 7(d) provides that an object of the CMA is 'promoting the rehabilitation of offenders and their reintegration into society'; Section 9, which is about the treatment of detainees generally, provides that '[f]unctions under this Act in relation to a detainee must be exercised as follows … (f) if the detainee is an offender—to promote, as far as practicable, the detainee's rehabilitation and reintegration into society'. For background on the history of the inclusion of these provisions in ACT law see Anita Mackay, 'The Road to the ACT's First Prison (the Alexander Maconochie Centre) was Paved with Rehabilitative Intentions' (2012) 11(1) *Canberra Law Review* 33.

34   *David Harold Eastman v Chief Executive Officer of the Department of Justice and Community Safety* [2010] ACTSC 4 (12 January 2010) [99].

35   Ibid [85]–[91] (emphasis added). Another decision relating to the provision of work in the AMC is *Islam v Director-General of the Justice and Community Safety Directorate* [2015] ACTSC 20.

36   *Eastman v Chief Executive of the Department of Justice and Community Safety* [2011] ACTSC 33 (4 March 2011) at [26]–[40].

instances that the conduct did not amount to a breach of the right.[37] Such reasoning arguably suggests that much of what imprisoned people might regard as demeaning treatment may be difficult to address through charters of rights.

Victoria

There have only been three successful cases brought in reliance on the Victorian *Charter* relating to adult imprisonment.[38] The first, decided in 2010, involved Ms Castles's challenge to a decision to deny her in-vitro fertilisation (IVF) treatment while in prison at a clinic outside the prison—*Castles v Secretary to the Department of Justice* ('*Castles*').[39] The second, decided in 2017, involved Mr Minogue's challenge to gain access to a book that had been mailed to him and then returned to sender in violation of his right to privacy and freedom of expression—*Minogue v Dougherty* ('*Minogue*').[40] The third, decided in 2018, involved Mr Haigh's challenge to gain access to Tarot cards for the purpose of his religious freedom—*Haigh v Ryan* ('*Haigh*').[41]

Ms Castles applied to have IVF treatment because she would be ineligible for it after her release due to her age. The Supreme Court held that Ms Castles was entitled to IVF treatment under s 47(1)(f) of the *Corrections Act 1986* (Vic) (*Corrections Act*) which provides a right to access medical care and treatment. Despite there being a number of human rights relevant to accessing IVF treatment,[42] Emerton J's decision was based primarily on an interpretation of s 47(1)(f) (which provides 'the right to have access to

---

37 Ibid [25], [29] and [40].
38 The Victorian Supreme Court has held that imprisoning minors in an adult prison breached the *Charter*: see *Certain Children v Minister for Families and Children & Ors* (No 2) [2017] VSC 251, but as this book does not examine juvenile detention this is not discussed here. For discussion of that decision see Judith Bessant and Rob Watts, 'Child Prisoners, Human Rights, and Human Rights Activism: Beyond "Emergency" and "Exceptionality"—An Australian Case Study' in Gabriel Blouin-Genest, Marie-Christine Doran and Sylvie Paquerot (eds), *Human Rights as Battlefields: Changing Practices and Contestations* (Springer Nature Switzerland, 2019).
39 *Castles v Secretary to the Department of Justice and Others* (2010) 28 VR 141.
40 *Minogue v Dougherty* [2017] VSC 724.
41 *Haigh v Ryan* [2018] VSC 474.
42 Such as the right to privacy against arbitrary interference with one's family contained in s 13(a) of the *Charter*. The equivalent right under the *European Convention for the Protection of Human Rights and Fundamental Freedoms* (ECHR) has been held by the European Court of Human Rights (ECtHR) to be violated by restrictions on access to in-vitro fertilisation (IVF) treatment for people in prison in the UK: *Dickson v UK* [2007] ECHR 1050. See Matthew Groves, 'Prisoners and the Victorian Charter' (2010) 34 *Criminal Law Journal* 217, 219.

reasonable medical care and treatment necessary for the preservation of health'), with the *Charter* 'serv[ing] to confirm the interpretation that had been arrived at in any event'.[43]

Emerton J held that s 47(1)(f) needed to be interpreted consistently with the *Charter* right of imprisoned people to be treated with humanity and respect for their human dignity (contained in s 22(1)).[44] In interpreting the right to medical care in the *Corrections Act* consistently with this *Charter* right, Emerton J went on to find that 'IVF treatment is treatment that is necessary for the preservation of Ms Castles' reproductive health'.[45] The interpretation of 'preservation of health' to include 'reproductive health' was not necessarily a self-evident one, nor one that had been reached in the many years that the right had been in the *Corrections Act* (enacted in 1986). It was an 'expansive reading' of the Act,[46] and one that has been described by Sifris as 'significant from a women's rights perspective.[47]

The Court did consider the application of the *Charter* to imprisoned people to an extent. The Court held that Ms Castles should not be denied rights other than her liberty,[48] and that '[l]ike other citizens, prisoners have a right to enjoyment of a variety of facilities, goods, services and conditions necessary for the realisation of a high standard of health. That is to say, the health of a prisoner is as important as the health of any other person'.[49] However, Emerton J emphasised that this right has to be balanced against the reality of deprivation of liberty. That is, imprisoned people are unable to leave the prison whenever they wish to access medical care. Her Honour opined that 'although prisoners do not forgo their

---

43   *Castles v Secretary to the Department of Justice and Others* (2010) 28 VR 141, 146. See also Groves, above n 42, 220. This contributes to Debeljak's conclusion that *Castles* is a 'Charter-inspired' decision, rather than a 'Charter-based' decision: Julie Debeljak, 'The Rights of Prisoners Under the Victorian Charter: A Critical Analysis of the Jurisprudence on the Treatment of Prisoners and Conditions of Detention' (2015) 38(4) *University of New South Wales Law Journal* 1332, 1349.
44   Ibid 173.
45   Ibid 174.
46   Matthew Groves, 'The Second Charters of Prisoners' Rights' in Matthew Groves and Colin Campbell (eds), *Australian Charters of Rights a Decade On* (Federation Press, 2017) 201.
47   Ronli Sifris, 'The Approach of the Victorian Charter to Women's Rights' in Matthew Groves and Colin Campbell (eds), *Australian Charters of Rights a Decade On* (Federation Press, 2017) 144.
48   Citing the Office of the High Commissioner for Human Rights General Comment in relation to Article 10 of the ICCPR: *Castles v Secretary to the Department of Justice and Others* (2010) 28 VR 141, 167. This accords with the common law 'residuum principle' discussed in Chapter 2 and Principle 5 of the United Nations *Basic Principles for the Treatment of Prisoners* cited in Chapter 2.
49   *Castles v Secretary to the Department of Justice and Others* (2010) 28 VR 141, 169.

human rights, their enjoyment of many rights and freedoms enjoyed by other citizens will necessarily be compromised by the fact that they have been deprived of their liberty'.[50]

In the *Minogue* case, Mr Minogue brought four claims relating to his ability to send and receive mail from Barwon prison. The Supreme Court considered the claims under both the *Corrections Act* and *Charter*;[51] however, the focus of this discussion will be on the *Charter* claims which rested on the rights to privacy and freedom of expression contained in ss 13 and 15(2) respectively. The relevant text of the provisions is as follows:

> A person has the right—(a) not to have his or her privacy, family, home or correspondence unlawfully or arbitrarily interfered with; and (b) not to have his or her reputation unlawfully attacked.

> Every person has the right to freedom of expression which includes the freedom to seek, receive and impart information and ideas of all kinds, whether within or outside Victoria and whether … (b) in writing; or (c) in print …

Only one of Mr Minogue's four claims was found to have breached the *Charter*. This related to a package containing a book that had been returned to sender by the prison's mail officer.[52] The officer admitted that she had failed to take into account Mr Minogue's *Charter* rights (as required by s 38 of the *Charter*, which imposes duties on public authorities) when making this decision and the Court declared that this was an 'unlawful' interference with Mr Minogue's correspondence and that the officer had not 'given proper consideration' to Mr Minogue's *Charter* rights.[53] This remedy was hardly helpful to Mr Minogue. He received a declaration that his *Charter* rights had not been properly considered but did not get access to the book that had been returned to the sender.

Mr Minogue's remaining claims related to three other incidents. First, a letter that was seized by the prison and not provided to Mr Minogue on the basis that it was 'unsolicited'. This claim was unsuccessful because

---

50   Ibid. For in-depth discussions of the *Castles* decision see Debeljak, above n 43, 1339–51; Groves, above n 46, 198–201; Sifris, above n 47, 141–4.
51   The relevant section of the *Corrections Act 1986* (Vic) provides: 'Every prisoner has the following rights - subject to section 47D, the right to send and receive other letters uncensored by prison staff': s 47(n). The dual claim stemmed from the requirement that all *Charter* claims be attached to another cause of action.
52   *Minogue v Dougherty* [2017] VSC 724 [36].
53   Ibid [83], [85], [96].

the prison had a 'reasonable belief' that the letter 'was a threat to prison security'. This was considered a reasonable limit in accordance with s 7 of the *Charter*.[54] Second, the prison's refusal to make 40 copies of an A3-sized newspaper article (relating to Mr Minogue's parole) that Mr Minogue wished to include with his Christmas letter. This claim was unsuccessful because the prison would have photocopied the article in a smaller size (A4) and the Court was of the view that 'there was no impediment' to Mr Minogue getting 'someone outside the prison' to perform 'this secretarial function for him'.[55] Therefore, the Court held there had not been an interference with Mr Minogue's right to freedom of expression.[56] Third, the prison's withholding of a letter containing a bank account statement and an email for investigation prior to their provision to Mr Minogue. This claim was unsuccessful, both because the delay in delivering the letter was held to be justified and because the claim had been brought against the wrong defendant.[57]

In the *Haigh* case, Mr Haigh had been denied four Tarot cards from the deck, which he argued breached his right to freedom of religion and freedom of expression protected by ss 14 and 15 of the *Charter* respectively. The claim also relied upon the right to practice a religion of choice protected by s 47(1)(i) of the *Corrections Act* (as the cause of action to which the *Charter* claim was attached).

There was no dispute that Mr Haigh's religion was Paganism (a religion recognised by Corrections Victoria), or that Tarot cards were one element of the practice of this religion.[58] The General Manager of the prison withheld the four cards that were the subject of the litigation because they displayed 'objectionable material'.[59] The Court found that there were reasonable grounds upon which such a conclusion could be reached, including that the cards might 'offend some prison staff' and be 'used

---

54   Ibid [3], [55], [79].
55   Ibid [21], [61].
56   Ibid [80].
57   Ibid [33]–[34], [66], [52]. For this reason no consideration to the *Charter* was given: ibid [82].
58   *Haigh v Ryan* [2018] VSC 474, [7]–[9]. Corrections Victoria therefore have an inclusive definition of religion for the purposes of the relevant Acts because the definition included Nature Religions: ibid [9]. Mr Haigh had previously been denied access to Tarot cards, but, following a complaint to the Victorian Equal Opportunity and Human Rights Commission, he was given access to Tarot cards excluding the four cards that were the subject of this litigation: ibid [22]–[23], [34].
59   Ibid [34].

to influence other prisoners' and that decisions about such matters fall within the responsibilities of the General Manager to ensure 'security and good order' in the prison.[60]

This aspect of the decision was similar to the *Minogue* case; namely, that the General Manager had failed to take into account Mr Haigh's *Charter* rights when deciding whether to allow Mr Haigh access to the Tarot cards—a fact that the General Manager admitted to the Court.[61] The Court made no finding on whether Mr Haigh was entitled to have access to the withheld Tarot cards and instead ordered that the General Manager remake the decision.[62] The Court emphasised its decision was limited to requiring that *Charter* rights be 'given proper consideration' when a request relating to religious practice is made.[63]

The reasoning in both the *Minogue* and *Haigh* cases imply that the *Charter* rights could have been properly considered and the limitation on those rights held to be justified (whether for the purposes of maintaining 'security and good order', or reasons relating to prison administration). If such, the result would be the same (denial of the book and Tarot cards). Both cases concerned important human rights of imprisoned people (privacy, freedom of religion and freedom of expression), yet both decisions gave considerable emphasis to the prison administrators' authority to control the prison and curtail human rights in the process of doing so. This is consistent with the long-held deference of courts to prison administrators. It may also be seen as an abdication of the Court's responsibility to protect the human rights that the Victorian Parliament has chosen to confer on all of its citizens. These are both matters that will be returned to below.

In other Victorian cases concerning prison conditions, the *Charter* has not been raised even when there was ample scope to argue that human rights were infringed. For example, in *Collins v the Queen*[64] ('*Collins*'), the *Charter* was not relied upon, despite the evidence that Mr Collins was locked in his cell for 23 hours per day in a high security unit and may have

---

60   Ibid [60]–[61].
61   Ibid [68]–[69] (in relation to s 14 of the *Charter*), [74]–[76] (in relation to s 15 of the *Charter*).
62   Ibid [98], [100].
63   Ibid [102].
64   [2012] VSCA 163, [12], [4], [7]. Mr Collins's counsel did not raise *Charter* arguments. The judgment states: 'during the hearing, the Court asked the appellant's counsel whether he was making any submissions based on the Charter of Human Rights and Responsibilities. Counsel expressly disavowed any reliance on the Charter. It is therefore unnecessary to consider whether the Charter has any effect on the legality of the continued detention of the appellant in the present conditions': at [12].

been subjected to such a regime for a number of years into the future. The international human rights law position is clear on the use of solitary confinement. As noted in Chapter 2, the Human Rights Committee has clarified that 'prolonged solitary confinement' may amount to 'torture, cruel, inhuman or degrading treatment or punishment' (as prohibited by art 7 of the ICCPR), which has been incorporated into Victorian law by s 10 of the *Charter*.[65] The UN *Standard Minimum Rules for the Treatment of Prisoners* (the Nelson Mandela Rules) Rule 44 provides definitions of 'solitary confinement' and 'prolonged solitary confinement' as follows: 'solitary confinement shall refer to the confinement of prisoners for 22 hours or more a day without meaningful human contact. Prolonged solitary confinement shall refer to solitary confinement for a time period in excess of 15 consecutive days'. Therefore, Mr Collins's treatment constitutes prolonged solitary confinement within the meaning of international law.[66] An analysis of *Collins* and other Victorian decisions led Debeljak to conclude that '[p]risoners have much to gain from the *Charter*, but surprisingly this is not borne out in the jurisprudence … the *Charter* "has generated far less litigation concerning prisoners" than comparative jurisdictions with rights instruments'.[67]

Concluding Remarks on the Australian Capital Territory and Victoria

Both the scarcity and outcomes of cases that have been brought in the ACT and Victoria illustrate the extremely limited success of imprisoned people in bringing actions under domestic human rights legislation. Mr Islam and Mr Eastman's claims under the *HRA* were unsuccessful. The *Castles* case reached an outcome that favoured the applicant (that is, the Court ordered that Ms Castles was entitled to IVF treatment), but the rights provided for in the *Charter* were not determinative of that outcome. In the *Minogue* case, only one of Mr Minogue's four claims succeeded. For both Mr Minogue and Mr Haigh, it is easy to envisage the decision being remade with proper consideration to *Charter* rights and

---

65 United Nations Human Rights Committee, *CCPR General Comment No. 20: Article 7 (Prohibition of Torture, or Other Cruel, Inhuman or Degrading Treatment or Punishment)* (10 March 1992) para 6.
66 Another case involving solitary confinement where possible *Charter* arguments were not raised is *Director of Public Prosecutions (Vic) v Foster* (Unreported, County Court of Victoria, Judge Gucciardo, 17 February 2014). Debeljak describes the *Collins* and *Foster* decisions as 'missed opportunities to avail prisoners of the benefit of rights jurisprudence': above n 43, 1372. Solitary confinement and the *Charter* are discussed in more detail in Chapter 7.
67 Debeljak, above n 43, 1333, citing Matthew Groves, 'Prisoners and the Victorian Charter' (2010) 34 *Criminal Law Journal* 217, 217.

the same conclusion being reached (as justifiable limitations of the human rights). It is also of concern that in other cases, including *Collins*, human rights claims have not been made where they may have been justified.[68]

Other Jurisdictions

International conventions do not give rise to domestic obligations in Australia unless they are incorporated into domestic law.[69] This has been confirmed by the High Court in numerous cases.[70] The practical effect of this is that imprisoned people in jurisdictions outside the ACT and Victoria cannot directly enforce rights under the Treaties detailed in Chapter 2. For example, in the cases of *Minogue v Williams*[71] and *Collins v State of South Australia*,[72] imprisoned people sought to rely on the ICCPR. In both instances, the courts confirmed the previously held position that the rights contained in the ICCPR cannot be enforced by individuals via litigation in domestic courts.[73] This was despite the fact that in *Collins v State of South Australia* the Court considered that arts 10(1) and 10(2)[74] of the ICCPR had indeed been violated.[75]

Notwithstanding this, there have been some decisions in jurisdictions that do not have human rights protections that have been relevant to the rights of imprisoned people, particularly the right not to be subjected to prolonged solitary confinement.

---

68   They were also not relied upon in *DPP v Foster & Ors* [2014] VCC 312 when Gucciardo J expressed concern about solitary confinement being imposed on a remandee for 22 or 23 hours per day for a period of 18 months in the Melbourne Remand Centre: at [50]–[53]. Nor were they relied upon in *Weaven v Secretary, Department of Justice* [2012] VSC 582. See the discussion of the Weaven decision by ibid 1151–2.

69   *Koowarta v Bjelke-Petersen* (1982) 153 CLR 168. The most well-known example of incorporation into domestic law is Commonwealth anti-discrimination legislation. For other examples see Julie Debeljak, 'Does Australia Need a Bill of Rights?' in Paula Gerber and Melissa Castan (eds), *Contemporary Perspectives on Human Rights Law in Australia* (Lawbook Co, 2013) 42.

70   See, eg, *Kioa v West* (1985) 159 CLR 550, 570–1; *Dietrich v The Queen* (1992) 177 CLR 292, [17].

71   *Minogue v Williams* (2000) 60 ALD 366.

72   *Collins v State of South Australia* [1999] SASC 257.

73   For a more detailed discussion of these cases see Bronwyn Naylor, 'Protecting the Human Rights of Prisoners in Australia' in Paula Gerber and Melissa Castan (eds), *Contemporary Perspectives on Human Rights Law in Australia* (Lawbook Co, 2013) 401–2. For a discussion of two earlier decisions where international human rights arguments were made, but were unsuccessful, see Matthew Groves, 'International Law and Australian Prisons' (2001) 24(1) *UNSW Law Journal* 17, 54–8 (discussing *Binse v Willians* [1998] 1 VR 381 and *R v Hollingshed and Rodgers* (1993) 112 FLR 109).

74   Article 10(1) requires treatment with humanity and with respect for the inherent dignity and art 10(2) requires unconvicted people to be separated from convicted people.

75   *Collins v State of South Australia* [1999] SASC 257, [30].

In Queensland (prior to the *Human Rights Act 2019* (Qld)), three Supreme Court decisions concerning the sentencing of three people convicted for contempt of court during a Crime and Misconduct Commission hearing resulted in reducing the sentences of imprisonment from six months to 28 or 42 days on the basis of Applegarth J's ruling that the people in question would be subject to a period of prolonged solitary confinement at the Woodford prison.[76] This is because all people in this prison are held in solitary confinement for 22 hours per day without access to sunlight during that period. The policy states, '[o]ut of cell time restricted to at least two daylight hours a day'.[77] Following a review of both international law and research evidence about solitary confinement,[78] Applegarth J concluded that 'a period of six weeks in solitary confinement is harsh punishment and carries a substantial risk of psychological harm'.[79] However, this remedy of a reduced sentence provided by direct reference to international law is an anomaly because other cases, such as *Minogue v Williams* and *Collins v State of South Australia*, where imprisoned people have sought to rely on rights under the ICCPR have been unsuccessful.

In Tasmania, the Tasmanian Supreme Court found that solitary confinement of 23 hours per day had breached the common law duty of care to ensure safety, as well as s 29(p) of the *Corrections Act 1997* (Tas) when read in conjunction with s 4 (the guiding principles of that Act).[80] Section 4(c) provides that 'services and procedures should be fair, equitable and have due regard to personal dignity and individuality, as far as is consistent with the need for appropriate levels of security and control'. Section 29(p) provides 'the right to be provided with information about the rules and conditions which will govern the prisoner's or detainee's behaviour in custody'.

---

76   Twenty-eight days in *Callanan v Attendee X* [2013] QSC 340 and *Callanan v Attendee Y* [2013] QSC 341, and 42 days in *Callanan v Attendee Z* [2013] QSC 342.
77   Cited by Applegarth J in *Callanan v Attendee Z* [2013] QSC 342, [27].
78   This included the ICCPR, United Nations *Standard Minimum Rules for the Treatment of Prisoners* (the Nelson Mandela Rules) and Istanbul Statement on the Use and Effects of Solitary Confinement, adopted on 9 December 2007 at the International Psychological Trauma Symposium: *Callanan v Attendee Z* [2013] QSC 342, [33]–[44].
79   Ibid [53].
80   *Pickett v The State of Tasmania* [2011] TASSC 907 (20 April 2011) [5], [6], [12]. A newspaper report suggested that Mr Pickett was confined as such for all but five months of his 14-year sentence, and he has been granted parole: David Killick, 'Troubled Prisoner Adrian Alwyn Pickett Freed After 14 Years' Jail, Almost All of which was Spent in Solitary Confinement', *The Mercury* (Tasmania), 25 February 2014.

There were two key features of Mr Pickett's incarceration that led to a finding that these provisions had been breached. The first was that for a period of two years he was not given information about the 'rules and conditions' governing his behaviour. There was a Behaviour Management Program in operation in the unit where he was being held, but he was not aware of the behaviour required to progress through the different stages. The second feature was that Mr Pickett was held in solitary confinement for very long periods on the 'most severe level of the program', which the Court held did not comply with the s 4(c) requirements that he be treated with 'due regard to personal dignity and individuality'.[81]

While this decision did not refer to any international human rights law in the same way as the Queensland Supreme Court decisions did, it is a rights-based decision due to the reference to 'personal dignity' in s 4, which resonates with art 10(1) of the ICCPR, and the reliance on s 29 which affords imprisoned people a number of rights.

Concluding Remarks on Prison Litigation in Australia

There are very few illustrations of successful prison litigation in Australia. This is partly because Australian courts appear reluctant to interfere in prison administration.[82] With very few exceptions, imprisoned people have not had the problem rectified or been compensated following bringing action in court. Courts have been open about their reluctance to interfere in prison administration, whether a matter is brought pursuant to corrections legislation or human rights legislation.

In relation to the former, the following decision is illustrative: '[p]rison legislation should ordinarily be interpreted so as to give full scope to the power of correctional authorities to carry out tasks of prison administration and management without undue influence from the Courts'.[83] There are many other examples of these types of comments by judges.[84] Groves has observed that '[t]he main rationale for this position was the fear that judicial intervention of any kind into prison administration would cause

---

81 *Pickett v The State of Tasmania* [2011] TASSC 907 (20 April 2011) [8]–[12].
82 It is worth noting that as recently as 1978 the High Court held that the doctrine of 'civil death'—where imprisonment led to the loss of the right to commence legal proceedings—was part of Australian law in *Dugan v Mirror Newspapers Ltd* (1978) 142 CLR 583. For a more detailed discussion of this history and how it stemmed from the United Kingdom see Groves, above n 46, 188.
83 *Anderson v Pavic* [2005] VSCA 244, [32] (Nettle JA).
84 For further illustrations see the discussion and footnotes in McKay, above n 15, 308–9.

chaos by unduly interfering with the functions of prison managers'.[85] Therefore, corrections legislation has not been a useful reactive mechanism for responding to human rights violations in prisons.

It is one thing if corrections legislation is not a useful mechanism for imprisoned people to achieve a court-based remedy. It is far more disappointing and puzzling when it continues in jurisdictions that have specifically chosen to incorporate human rights protections. This has occurred repeatedly in the Victorian Supreme Court, the authoritative interpreter of the *Charter*'s application to prisons. For example, in *Rich v Secretary of the Department of Justice*, the Court opined that '[d]etermining these allegations would convert the court into a prison regulator'.[86] Rush J subsequently held:

> It is not for judges, save in the most obvious of cases, to supervise or interfere with the administrative decisions of prison authorities concerning the conduct of prisons and prisoners. While acknowledging that prisoners are in a position of particular disadvantage and any abuse of power by prison authorities is unacceptable '... the Court must avoid becoming enmeshed in the merits of particular decisions. The management of prisons is a particularly difficult and sensitive task involving complex practical considerations and security implications with which the court is not familiar and it is difficult to understand or fully appreciate from the comfort of court surroundings'.[87]

It is precisely the role of judges to intervene when there is an abuse of power that constitutes a breach of the statutorily protected human rights protections. A more positive sentiment was recently expressed by the ACT Supreme Court, with McWilliam AsJ noting:

> There is nothing in the statutory regime which suggests a general principle that a Court's intervention in cases of human rights in prisons should be limited ... the opposite appears to be true, in that the particular vulnerability is recognised in the Act [the *HRA*] as being specifically worthy of protection. The prison context is of course relevant, but it features as part of the factual matrix by which the conduct is assessed under the Act.[88]

---

85 Groves, above n 73, 19.

86 *Rich v Secretary of the Department of Justice & Ors* [2010] VSC 390, [30]. This was in the context where Mr Rich was seeking facilities to prepare for his legal case, such as access to a computer.

87 *Knight v Shuard* [2014] VSC 475 at [33] citing *Fyfe v South Australia* [2000] SASC 84 at [18] (Martin J). See also *Castles v Secretary to the Department of Justice* [2010] VSC 310 (9 July 2010) [145], per Emerton J.

88 *Islam v Director-General of the Department of Justice and Community Safety Directorate* [2018] ACTSC 322, [34].

It should also be emphasised that the Court's response to the claim being made in the case in which McWilliam AsJ made these remarks was to find that there was a system in place for provision of special diets for imprisoned people to comply with their religious beliefs (in accordance with the protection of religious freedom under s 14 of the *HRA*) and, despite the fact that the system was not communicated to imprisoned people, the Court was not willing to direct prison management about how to discharge their statutory duty.[89] There was no finding that the *HRA* had been breached. Therefore, the decision itself did not involve any protection of the human rights of the claimant.

Imprisoned people—even in the jurisdictions that have specifically provided statutory human rights protections—do not seem to have the opportunity to 'hold duty-bearers accountable' (in the words of Nowak).[90] Given that courts have not proved a successful mechanism for the protection of the human rights of imprisoned people in Australia, it is necessary to look to other monitoring mechanisms to see if they perform better in this regard.

Prison Inspectorates

Several jurisdictions in Australia, the majority of which do not have human rights legislation, have introduced dedicated prisons-focused monitoring bodies known as 'inspectorates'. They are Western Australia (WA), NSW, Tasmania and the ACT. The ACT is the only one of these that has human rights legislation.

---

89   Ibid [119]–[122]. The prison was also found not to have breached Mr Islam's right to be treated with humanity and respect afforded in s 19(1) of the *HRA*: at [132]–[134]. The reasoning was rather circular. The Court noted that Mr Islam did not know about the procedure and the kitchen staff were entitled to rely on the incorrect information they had about his dietary requirements, as follows: '[t]he refusal to supply Mr Islam with a vegetarian roll on 2 July 2017, and the failure to supply food that Mr Islam has ordered on a regular basis, did not arise out of any lack of respect for Mr Islam's humanity or inherent dignity, or otherwise fail to give proper consideration to Mr Islam's human rights. It arose because of a non-compliance with a procedure, which meant that the AMC kitchen did not have on their system that a processed chicken roll was not appropriate for Mr Islam. This was not the fault of Mr Islam, given he did not know about the procedure, but nor was the failure or refusal a contravention of s 19(1) of the Act, given that the AMC kitchen staff were entitled to rely upon what was recorded on Mr Islam's electronic record as the registered dietary requirement': at [133].
90   Nowak, above n 14, 254.

WA was the first Australian jurisdiction to establish an inspectorate when it established the Office of the Inspector of Custodial Services (OICS) in 2003.[91] The OICS is modelled on Her Majesty's Inspectorate of Prisons (HMIP) in the United Kingdom. It conducts inspections with the self-declared intention of:

- improving public confidence in the justice system;
- ensuring the decent treatment of detained people; and
- ensuring the justice system provides value for money.[92]

Such inspections may be announced or unannounced and each prison is to be inspected every three years.[93] The Inspector has broad powers 'to do all things necessary or convenient to be done for or in connection with the performance of the Inspector's functions'.[94] The OICS is required to report to the Minister on findings of inspections it carries out.[95]

NSW became the second jurisdiction to establish an independent statutory-based inspectorate, with an Inspector appointed from 1 October 2013.[96] When introducing the legislation establishing the Inspectorate, the Hon David Clarke stated that:

> The inspector will be an independent statutory role that provides external scrutiny of the standards and operational practices of custodial services in New South Wales. The inspector will provide an independent mechanism for monitoring broader thematic and systemic issues arising out of inspections of adult and juvenile correctional facilities and services.[97]

---

91 Established by the *Inspector of Custodial Services Act 2003* (WA).
92 Government of Western Australia, Office of the Inspector of Custodial Services (OICS), *Vision and Mission* <http://www.oics.wa.gov.au/about-oics/vision-and-mission/>. An example of the final point—value for money—is an OICS report in which the Chief Inspector recommended that a 'master plan for the use of all existing custodial facilities, adult and juvenile, should be developed to better inform future investment decisions': OICS, *Directed Review into an Incident at Banksia Hill Detention Centre of 20 January 2013* (2013) x 'recommendation 33, xvi).
93 *Inspector of Custodial Services Act 2003* (WA) s 19.
94 Ibid s 27.
95 Ibid ss 20, 24.
96 Greg Smith MP (Attorney General and Minister for Justice) (NSW), 'Inspector of Custodial Services Appointed' (Media Release, 18 September 2013). NSW has had an Inspector-General of Custodial Services since 1999; established by s 213 of the Crimes (*Administration of Sentences*) Act 1999 (NSW) in response to a NSW Royal Commission.
97 New South Wales, *Parliamentary Debates*, Legislative Assembly, 23 May 2012, 11834 (the Hon David Clarke).

The NSW legislation requires prisons to be inspected once every five years and a report to Parliament on the findings of each inspection.[98] Although the requirement to inspect each prison is only every five years, the Inspector has the power to visit any prison at any time and can require staff to provide information and documents.[99] There is also a provision in the NSW Act similar to that in the WA Act, as follows: '[t]he Inspector has power to do all things necessary to be done for or in connection with, or reasonably incidental to, the exercise of the Inspector's functions'.[100]

Tasmania passed its *Custodial Inspector Act 2016* (Tas) in 2016 and appointed a Custodial Inspector in January 2017.[101] This implemented a recommendation made in 2011, following an independent inquiry into the Risdon prison in Tasmania.[102] Similarly to the OICS, the Tasmanian Office of the Custodial Inspector (TOCI) is required to inspect prisons every three years and report to the Minister on these inspections.[103] The Minister is then required to table the report in Parliament after 30 days of receipt (that is, there is an initial 30-day embargo period).[104]

The TOCI has a list of enumerated powers, as well as a similar catch-all provision to that found in the WA and NSW legislation: 'to do all things necessary or convenient to be done in connection with the performance and exercise of his or her functions and powers under this Act'.[105] The ACT also passed legislation establishing the Inspector of Correctional Services in 2017 (*Inspector of Correctional Services 2017* (ACT)) in response to the recommendation of an independent inquiry into a death in the AMC in 2016.[106] The Inspector was appointed in March 2018.[107]

---

98   *Inspector of Custodial Services Act 2012* (NSW) s 6.
99   Ibid s 7.
100 Ibid s 8.
101 Office of the Custodial Inspector Tasmania, *About Us* <https://www.custodialinspector.tas.gov.au/about_us>.
102 Mick Palmer, *Risdon Prison Complex Inquiry* (March 2011). Recommendation 2 was 'That Government establish an independent, competent, inspection authority to provide for the periodic inspection of custodial services and the publication of all inspection reports': at 12.
103 *Custodial Inspector Act 2016* (Tas) s 6(1).
104 Ibid s 15.
105 Ibid s 8(h). The enumerated powers are found in s 8.
106 Independent Inquiry into the Treatment in Custody of Mr Steven Freeman, *'So Much Sadness in Our Lives'* (2016); Minister for Corrections (ACT), 'New Oversight Agency Focused on Improving Care, Safety and Health of Detainees' (Media Release, 16 February 2017).
107 Minister for Corrections (ACT), 'ACT's First Inspector of Correctional Services Begins' (Media Release, 14 March 2018).

The media release announcing the appointment of the Inspector noted that '[t]he Inspector will take a whole of system focus, to identify areas for improvement and prevent poor practices'.[108]

The ACT is different to the other jurisdictions with inspectorates because there is only one adult prison, which accommodates both females and males, in the jurisdiction (the inspectorate is also responsible for oversight of the ACT's youth justice centre). Therefore, the legislation does not need to stipulate the regularity with which each prison should be visited. The legislation instead provides that the Inspector may enter the prison 'at any time', 'at the inspector's own initiative'.[109] Another unique feature of the ACT legislation is the requirement for the Inspector to review 'critical incidents', which are defined in the Act to include a death, escape, riot or assault leading to hospitalisation.[110] The Inspector reported on five critical incidents in 2018–19.[111]

The Inspector is required to report to Parliament within six months of carrying out a review and the legislation provides a detailed list of what this report is to include.[112] In particular, the report should include 'an assessment about whether the rights under *international* and territory law of detainees at a correctional centre subject to review are protected'.[113] This means that the Inspector may refer to international laws in addition to the human rights protections contained in the *HRA*.

Prison inspectorates tend to prepare three categories of report following their investigations. The first is inspection reports detailing the conditions in a particular prison (in response to the statutory requirement to carry out inspections). The second is reports about the treatment of individuals

---

108 Ibid.

109 *Inspector of Correctional Services 2017* (ACT) s 19(1).

110 *Inspector of Correctional Services 2017* (ACT) s 17. Reviews do occur in other jurisdictions. For example, there was an independent review of an incident in WA commissioned by the Director General of the Department of Justice in 2018: Jan Shuard, *Critical Incident Review into the Events at Greenough Regional Prison on 24-25 July 2018* (2018). There was also an independent review of the riot at a Victorian remand centre in 2015: Independent Investigation into the Metropolitan Remand Centre Riot, *Final Report* (December 2015).

111 ACT Inspector of Correctional Services, *Critical Incident Reviews* <https://www.ics.act.gov.au/reports-and-publications/critical-incident-reviews>.

112 *Inspector of Correctional Services 2017* (ACT) s 27(1)–(2).

113 *Inspector of Correctional Services 2017* (ACT) s 27(2)(c) (emphasis added).

(the least common type of report).[114] The third is thematic reports about a particular matter across numerous prisons in the jurisdiction. Examples of thematic reports include:

- investigations into funeral attendance by imprisoned people by OICS[115]
- a review of care and wellbeing in Tasmanian prisons by TOCI[116]
- a review of prison clothing and bedding by the NSW Inspector[117]
- a review of access to digital technology by OICS[118]
- a review of how 'radicalised' imprisoned people are managed in NSW prisons by the NSW Inspector.[119]

Human Rights and Anti-Discrimination Commissions

There is the (national) Australian Human Rights Commission (AHRC), as well as an equal opportunity or anti-discrimination commission in each of the states and territories. It might be reasonable to assume that human rights complaints could be taken to the AHRC. However, the AHRC only has Commonwealth jurisdiction, whereas the majority of people in prison are kept in state and territory prisons pursuant to state legislation. The AHRC consequently has no jurisdiction over imprisoned people in Australia.[120]

---

114 See, eg, OICS, *The Birth at Bandyup Women's Prison in March 2018* (2018).

115 OICS, *Access to Funerals and Other Compassionate Leave for People in Custody in Western Australia* (2017). This was a follow-up to the earlier review on this subject: OICS, *Funeral Attendances by Incarcerated People in Western Australia* (2013).

116 Tasmanian Custodial Inspector, *Inspection of Adult Custodial Services in Tasmania, 2017 Care and Wellbeing Inspection Report* (October 2018).

117 NSW Inspector of Custodial Services, *Prison Greens: The Clothing and Bedding of Inmates in NSW* (2017).

118 OICS, *The Digital Divide: Access to Digital Technology for People in Custody* (2018).

119 NSW Inspector of Custodial Services, *The Management of Radicalised Inmates in NSW* (2018).

120 Groves, above n 73, 40. This was also the subject of litigation in Victoria: *Craig William John Minogue v Human Rights and Equal Opportunity Commission* [1998] FCA 1283 (12 October 1998). One successful case decided under the *Disability Discrimination Act 1992* (Cth) by the Human Rights and Equal Opportunity Commission (HREOC) (the predecessor of the Australian Human Rights Commission) helped improve the treatment of HIV-positive people in West Australian prisons in 1996: *X & Y v State of Western Australia* [1996] HREOCA 32 (Unreported, The Hon Robert Nettlefield, 26 November 1996). For a discussion of that decision and detailed consideration of the HREOC jurisdiction see Groves, above n 73, 33–40.

In addition to receiving complaints from imprisoned people, state and territory human rights and anti-discrimination commissions conduct prison investigations from time to time.

Complaints

To make a complaint to a state or territory anti-discrimination commission, an imprisoned person must show that they were subject to differential treatment based on one of the prohibited grounds of discrimination, such as age, sexuality, race or religious belief.[121] It is difficult to get a sense about the number and types of complaints brought by people in prison because the majority of commissions report the numbers of complaints they receive by the *grounds* of discrimination, rather than the *place* in which the discrimination took place. Only the Victorian Equal Opportunity and Human Rights Commission regularly provides statistics about the number of enquiries received from persons in prisons. The total number of enquiries received in the three years from 2015–18 was 119.[122] Not all of these enquiries would necessarily have led to formal complaints.

There is also a scarcity of adjudicated determinations in the anti-discrimination arena.[123] This is because the legislation either imposes compulsory conciliation,[124] or encourages conciliation in the first instance.[125] It is usually only if conciliation is unsuccessful that matters are referred by the Commissioner to a tribunal for determination. There are also time limitations imposed on the receipt of complaints that may disadvantage imprisoned people who do not wish to make the complaint during their incarceration.[126]

---

121 See, eg, the *Anti-Discrimination Act 1991* (Qld) s 7. Other jurisdictions have parts of their legislation pertaining to the various attributes. See further *Anti-Discrimination Act 1998* (Tas).

122 Victorian Equal Opportunity and Human Rights Commission, *Annual Report 2017/18* (2018) 83. Comprising 28 enquiries in 2015–16, 66 enquiries in 2016–17 and 25 enquiries in 2017–18.

123 In relation to sex discrimination specifically, Thornton's research found that the less than 2 per cent of complaints are heard by a court: Margaret Thornton, 'Sex Discrimination, Courts and Corporate Power' (2008) 36 *Federal Law Review* 31, 34.

124 For example, conciliation is compulsory in the Australian Capital Territory (ACT) (*Human Rights Commission Act 2005* (ACT) s 59) and Victoria (*Victorian Civil and Administrative Tribunal Act 1998* (Vic) ss 83, 84).

125 This is the case in the Northern Territory (*Anti-Discrimination Act 1992* (NT) ss79, 80), NSW (*Anti-Discrimination Act 1977* (NSW) s 91A) and South Australia (*Equal Opportunity Act 1984* (SA) s 95(4)).

126 Usually 12 months (eg, *Equal Opportunity Act 1984* (WA) s 83; *Anti-Discrimination Act 1977* (NSW) s89(2)(b); *Anti-Discrimination Act 1991* (Qld) s 138), although in the Northern Territory the limit is six months: *Anti-Discrimination Act 1992* (NT) s 65. Most Acts do provide discretion to the Commissioner to extend these time limits.

The recent case law reveals the mixed success of imprisoned people making complaints under anti-discrimination legislation. There have been two successful claims about the lack of availability of fresh halal meat in Queensland prisons.[127] In contrast, a claim on behalf of an imprisoned person with gender identity disorder concerning denial of female hormone therapy was held not to be discriminatory because it was based on the Queensland Department of Corrective Services's policy in relation to transgender imprisoned people.[128] A disability discrimination complaint in Victoria claiming that prison cell and transport conditions failed to take into account a back injury was also held not to be unlawful discrimination.[129]

Investigation

In the same way that anti-discrimination commissions have not been a common avenue for imprisoned people to pursue complaints against prison authorities, they have also been an under-utilised mechanism of systemic review. There have been only four comprehensive systemic reviews about the treatment of women in prisons. They were conducted in the ACT (in 2014), Queensland (in 2006 and 2019) and Victoria (in 2013).[130]

---

127 *Mahommed v State of Queensland* [2006] QADT 21 (4 May 2006); *Ali v State of Queensland* [2013] QCAT 319 (6 August 2013). These are discussed in detail in Chapter 7.

128 *Sinden v State of Queensland* [2012] QCAT 284.

129 *Rainsford v Victoria* (2009) EOC ¶93–468. Two earlier cases dating from 1984 and 1986 are of little ongoing relevance given that the *Equal Opportunity Act 1977* (Vic) under which they were decided has since been repealed and replaced by the *Equal Opportunity Act 2010* (Vic). The cases were *Henderson v Victoria* (1984) EOC ¶92–027 concerning having a child accompany their parent in prison and *Clarkson v Governor of the Metropolitan Reception Prison & Anor* (1986) EOC ¶92–153 concerning the standard of food and accommodation in prison.

130 Australian Capital Territory Human Rights Commission, *Human Rights Audit on the Conditions of Detention of Women at the Alexander Maconochie Centre: A Report by the ACT Human Rights and Discrimination Commissioner* (2014). See the discussion of this review by Penelope Mathew, 'Taking Stock of the Audit Power' in Matthew Groves and Colin Campbell (eds), *Australian Charters of Rights a Decade On* (Federation Press, 2017) 63–6; Anti-Discrimination Commission Queensland, *Women in Prison 2019: A Human Rights Consultation Report* (2019); Anti-Discrimination Commission Queensland, *Women in Prison. A Report by the Anti-Discrimination Commission Queensland* (2006); Victorian Equal Opportunity and Human Rights Commission, *Unfinished Business. Koori Women and the Justice System* (2013).

Only the ACT anti-discrimination commission has conducted a review specifically about the systemic issues facing men in prisons, and this was prior to the AMC being built (ie, the review related to remand centres).[131] There have been reports by the NSW and Victorian commissions that have raised some concerns about prisons from an anti-discrimination perspective—such as discrimination on the basis of Hepatitis C—but these cannot be described as comprehensive systemic reviews.[132]

Ombudsmen

There is a Commonwealth Ombudsman which, as noted in the Introduction, has been designated as the coordinating organisation for Australia's NPM. There is also an Ombudsman in each of the states and territories. It becomes quite complicated to understand the jurisdiction of each of these organisations in relation to imprisoned people, not least for the people wishing to make a complaint. Similar to human rights and anti-discrimination commissions, Ombudsmen have both a complaints jurisdiction and an investigative function.[133]

Complaints

The Ombudsman in any particular jurisdiction provides a useful avenue for complaints of a general nature to be made by people in prison including, but not necessarily, complaints based on human rights. Ombudsmen receive a large number of complaints from people in prison annually. For example, in the 2017–18 financial year, the NSW Ombudsman received 5,144 complaints regarding adult correctional centres (12.6 per cent of a total of 40,687 complaints) and the Victorian Ombudsman 5,389 complaints, (35 per cent of all complaints).[134] The Western Australian Ombudsman received 415 complaints (34 per cent

---

131 ACT Human Rights Commission, *Human Rights Audit on the Operation of ACT Correctional Facilities Under Corrections Legislation* (2007). The ACT Health Services Commissioner reviewed the opioid replacement program in the single prison in the ACT: ACT Health Services Commissioner, *Review of the Opioid Replacement Program at the Alexander Maconochie Centre* (2018).

132 Anti-Discrimination Board of New South Wales, *C Change. Report of the Enquiry into Hepatitis C Related Discrimination* (2001) 66–74; Victorian Equal Opportunity and Human Rights Commission, *2013 Report on the Operation of the Charter of Human Rights and Responsibilities* (2014) 8–10.

133 These dual functions are what Groves has termed the 'fire fighting' (reactive) function of Ombudsman operations and the 'fire prevention' (proactive) function respectively: Matthew Groves, 'Ombudsmen's Jurisdiction in Prisons' in Marc Hertogh and Richard Kirkham (eds), *Research Handbook on the Ombudsman* (Edward Elgar Publishing, 2018) 328.

134 These were divided into formal (709) and informal (4,435) complaints: Ombudsman New South Wales, *Annual Report 2017-2018* (2018) 5; Victorian Ombudsman, *Annual Report 2018* (2018) 32.

of complaints concerning public agencies).[135] Most prisons have a free telephone service for people to use to contact the Ombudsman's office in their jurisdiction.[136] There are also legislative protections in place to ensure that correspondence with the Ombudsman remains confidential.[137]

Groves provides a useful example of an investigation by the WA Ombudsman following the receipt of complaints that ultimately led to positive reforms (though the investigation is not recent, dating from 2002). Complaints were made by females in WA prisons who had suffered pregnancy miscarriages due to the work they were undertaking. An investigation by the Ombudsman found widespread problems, particularly in the information provided to prison staff by medical staff. The result of the investigation was the revision of a number of procedures in WA prisons.[138]

In analysing the jurisdiction of the Ombudsman in relation to imprisoned people, Groves has more recently (in 2018) concluded that 'Ombudsman provide a free and accessible avenue for prisoners to raise complaints about almost every aspect of their treatment. This provides an important right to one of the most vulnerable groups in society'.[139] Of the two reactive mechanisms—litigation in court and making a complaint—it is possible that making a complaint is more effective. It is certainly the quicker and more cost-effective option and, therefore, more relevant and accessible for people in prison.

The alternative view is put forth by Harding and Morgan who note shortfalls in the approach of Ombudsmen to complaints by imprisoned people. They state that Ombudsmen around Australia 'have all chosen to some extent to devolve primary resolution of the bulk of prisoner complaints to the operational Department' and that 'Ombudsman offices (with the exception of NSW) have virtually abandoned the notion

---

135 Ombudsman Western Australia, *Annual Report 2017-18* (2018) 36.
136 Bronwyn Naylor and Lisa Harrison (with Inez Dussuyer and Rachel Kessel), 'Monitoring Closed Environments: The Role of Oversight Bodies' (Working Paper No 3, 'Applying Human Rights in Closed Environments: A Strategic Framework for Managing Compliance' project, ARC, May 2014) 13 ('Working Paper 3').
137 See, eg, the *Corrections Act 1986* (Vic) ss 47(j), 47(m)(iv); *Corrections Management Act 2007* (ACT) ss 12(1)(g), 12(1)(h) (latter to be read in conjunction with ss 50 and 51).
138 See discussion in Matthew Groves, 'Ombudsmen's Jurisdiction in Prisons' (2002) 28 *Monash University Law Review* 181, 189–90.
139 Groves, above n 133, 319.

of a visits-based process in relation to prisoner complaints'.[140] This substantiates Biles's earlier conclusion that Ombudsmen 'have not had the radical effect on correctional administration that was envisaged at the time when the positions were created'.[141]

Thus, while it is still likely that making a complaint to the Ombudsman is preferable to litigation, neither of these reactive mechanisms are reliable means of protecting the human rights of imprisoned people in Australia. Ratification of the OPCAT is therefore a welcome development.

Investigations

In jurisdictions that do not have a specific prison inspectorate, the Ombudsman can carry out 'own motion' investigations that focus on specific areas of concern.[142] These types of investigation may raise systemic concerns, such as the Victorian Ombudsman's investigation that found, among other things, that overcrowding is leading to increased violence in Victorian prisons and raised concerns about health care provision.[143] They also examine the impact of policies on the individuals who are subject to them, such as the South Australian investigation into restraint of people in hospital (discussed below).

Human rights concerns are sometimes identified by Ombudsmen. In the case of Victoria, the Ombudsman is required to take into account human rights under the *Charter* when carrying out investigations.[144] In the recent OPCAT-compliant investigation, the Ombudsman made extensive references to the Mandela Rules[145] and *Charter*.[146]

---

140 Australian Human Rights Commission, *Implementing the Optional Protocol to the Convention Against Torture: Options for Australia. A Report to the Australian Human Rights Commission by Professors Richard Harding and Neil Morgan (Centre for Law and Public Policy, The University of Western Australia)* (2008) 26 ('AHRC OPCAT report'). Ibid 36. Concern about Ombudsmen deferring to prison management's version of events was also expressed in interviews in Victorian and Western Australian prisons: Bronwyn Naylor, 'Human Rights and Respect in Prisons: The Prisoners' Perspective' in Bronwyn Naylor, Julie Debeljak and Anita Mackay (eds), *Human Rights in Closed Environments* (Federation Press, 2014) 120.
141 David Biles, 'Human Rights in Correctional Organisations in Australia and Asia: Some Criminological Observations' in Tom Campbell and Seumas Miller (eds), *Human Rights and the Moral Responsibilities of Corporate and Public Sector Organisations* (Kluwer Academic Publications, 2004) 198–9.
142 See, eg, *Ombudsman Act* (NT) s 14(1)(b); *Ombudsman Act 1973* (Vic) s 13A(2); *Ombudsman Act 1972* (SA) s 13(2); *Ombudsman Act 2001* (Qld) s 18.
143 Victorian Ombudsman, *Investigation into Deaths and Harms in Custody* (2014) 34.
144 *Ombudsman Act 1973* (Vic) s 13.
145 United Nations *Standard Minimum Rules for the Treatment of Prisoners* (the Nelson Mandela Rules), UN Doc A/RES/70/175 (17 December 2015) ('the Mandela Rules'). There were at least 29 references to the Rules in the report: Victorian Ombudsman, above n 6.
146 There are at least 24 references to the *Charter* in the report: ibid.

In some other jurisdictions, human rights may be considered even in the absence of human rights legislation, such as the South Australian Ombudsman's investigation into the shackling of imprisoned people while in hospital.[147] The report was prompted by 'Director's Instructions' issued by the Executive Director of Custodial Services requiring that all imprisoned people be restrained when in hospital receiving treatment regardless of their security classification or the risk of escape, including for end-of-life care and during childbirth.[148] The report allocated four pages to the consideration of the relevant human rights at the international and national level,[149] concluding that:

> the international and national standards and practice acknowledge that there are instances where the restraining of prisoners is necessary to protect the prisoner or the public. However, it is also universally accepted that in these instances prisoners must be restrained for the minimum time necessary, and with the least restrictive type of restraint possible.[150]

The recommendations included that use of restraints be based on the assessed risk of a person escaping, soft restraints be used instead of chains and pregnant women never be restrained during labour.[151]

There are more jurisdictions in Australia without human rights legislation than jurisdictions with such legislation. Ombudsmen perform an important role even in the absence of human rights legislation. There are nevertheless gaps in their coverage that will be discussed later in this chapter (under 'Evaluation of Monitoring Mechanisms in Australia').

Coronial Inquests

The role of the Coroner is to investigate deaths in certain circumstances prescribed by legislation. As in other areas of law in a federation such as Australia, there are variations in the precise terms of that legislation. Generally speaking, however, Coroners have jurisdiction over deaths that occur while an individual is in the custody of the state, such as

---

147 Ombudsman South Australia, *Ombudsman Investigation into the Department of Correctional Services in Relation to the Restraining and Shackling of Prisoners in Hospitals* (2012).
148 Ibid 1.
149 Ibid 12–15.
150 Ibid 16.
151 Recommendations 2, 3 and 5: ibid 3.

in police custody or in prison.[152] The role of the Coroner is to 'make recommendations which enhance public safety by learning from avoidable deaths' and to be 'an Ombudsman for the dead'.[153]

There have been numerous coronial inquests into deaths in prisons that could be discussed. A Victorian example has been chosen because it deals with the over-representation of people with mental illness in the prison population.[154] The inquest concerned the death of Mr Omerovic in the Melbourne Assessment Prison (MAP). Mr Omerovic had a history of severe mental illness and committed suicide by hanging himself in his cell.[155] The investigation focused on 'how those responsible for mental health services within MAP responded to his presentation and whether the systems in use reasonably identified the level of risk associated with that presentation'.[156] The concerns identified by the Coroner included the existence of hanging points in cells where people 'at risk' were accommodated, lack of resourcing of Forensicare (the organisation responsible for mental health services at the MAP) and failures of intake and assessment procedures for identifying and treating mental illness.[157] These findings are of grave concern at a systemic level in light of the number of imprisoned people with mental illness. Such concerns are also echoed in the Victorian Ombudsman's March 2014 report into an inquiry into deaths and harms in custody.[158]

Freckelton and Ranson have argued that human rights are becoming a 'new and important aspect of the infrastructure of the coronial role', particularly in relation to 'the deaths of vulnerable persons away from public gaze at the hands of the state or within institutions for which the state is responsible'.[159] Despite this observation, and despite having the *Charter*, the inquest referred to above does not refer to any breach of the human rights of the deceased.

---

152 See, eg, *Coroners Act 2008* (Vic) s 11 ('Obligation to report death of a person placed in custody or care'); *Coroners Act 2009* (NSW) s 23 ('Jurisdiction concerning deaths in custody or as a result of police operations'); *Coroners Act 2003* (Qld) ss 8, 10.

153 Ian Freckelton and David Ranson, 'Death Investigation and the Role of the Coroner' in Ian Freckelton and Kerry Peterson (eds), *Tensions and Traumas in Health Law* (Federation Press, 2017) 561.

154 Another recent example is the inquest into the death of an Aboriginal man in the Alexander Maconochie Centre in the Australian Capital Territory: *An Inquest into the Death of Steven Claude Freeman* [2018] ACTCD 7.

155 Peter White, *Inquest into the Death of Adam Sasha Omerovic*, Coroner's Court of Victoria, 24 January 2014.

156 Ibid 2.

157 Ibid 49, 53, 56.

158 Victorian Ombudsman, above n 143.

159 Freckelton and Ranson, above 153, 562.

This may be contrasted to the inquest into the death of Mr Ward in WA in a prison transport vehicle, the circumstances of which are discussed below. During the Coroner's inquest, submissions were made by the WA Human Rights and Equal Opportunity Commission about the relevance of the ICCPR to the treatment of Mr Ward.[160] Accordingly, the Coroner made the following observations:

> In the present case for the reasons outlined herein for determining that the quality of the supervision, treatment and care of the deceased in the hours before his death was disgracefully bad, I am satisfied that the deceased was subjected to degrading treatment and he was not treated with humanity and with respect for the inherent dignity of the human person. There has been, therefore, a breach of the *ICCPR*.[161]

There is no legal consequence from a finding by the WA Coroner that the ICCPR has been breached, but it does provide an additional source of criticism of the correctional administrator's actions. The changes that the WA Government has introduced since this inquest are discussed later in this chapter (under 'Evaluation of Monitoring Mechanisms in Australia').

Royal Commissions and Parliamentary Inquiries

In certain circumstances where there are widespread problems in the prison system, a broad inquiry may be required. This may be carried out either by a specially appointed Royal Commission of Inquiry or by an existing parliamentary committee.[162]

---

160 For other examples where human rights commissions have intervened in coronial inquests see Rebecca Scott Bray, 'Death Investigation, Coroners' Inquests and Human Rights' in Leanne Weber et al (eds), *The Routledge International Handbook of Criminology and Human Rights* (Routledge, 2017) 153.
161 A N Hope, *Inquest into Death of Ian Ward*, Western Australian Coroner's Court, 2009, 130.
162 There was also a 2017 inquiry by the Australian Law Reform Commission into the incarceration rate of Indigenous people that was referred to in Chapter 1: Australian Law Reform Commission, *Pathways to Justice—An Inquiry into the Incarceration Rate of Aboriginal and Torres Strait Islander Peoples*, Report No 133 (2017). This is not discussed in this section because it was an unusual inquiry for a Law Reform Commission. Law Reform Commissions typically inquire into the operation of a particular piece of legislation and make recommendations about how the operation of that legislation can be improved (eg, Australian Law Reform Commission, *Connection to Country: Review of the Native Title Act 1993 (Cth)*, Report No 126 (2015)) or inquire into a thematic area of law (eg, the encroachment of Commonwealth laws on 'traditional rights and freedoms': see Australian Law Reform Commission, *Traditional Rights and Freedoms—Encroachments by Commonwealth Laws*, Report No 129 (2016)). Therefore, they are not generally examining widespread problems in the prison system in the way that Royal Commissions and parliamentary committee inquiries do.

Federal Royal Commissions are established by the *Royal Commissions Act 1902* (Cth), and Royal Commissions can also be established by states and territories.[163] This legislation provides Royal Commissions with broad powers, such as the ability to compel witnesses to give evidence[164] and the power to gain search warrants.[165] There have been 136 Royal Commissions established at the federal level since 1902.[166]

There have been two significant Royal Commissions of relevance to adult imprisonment.[167] These were the Commonwealth Royal Commission into Aboriginal Deaths in Custody (RCIADIC) that reported in 1991, and the Royal Commission into NSW Prisons that reported in 1978.[168] The focus of this discussion will be on the RCIADIC because, despite it having concluded more than 25 years ago, there are continuing references to the failure of authorities to implement its recommendations,[169] including by international experts.[170]

163 States and territories have their own enabling legislation: see, eg, *Royal Commissions Act 1968* (WA); *Royal Commissions Act 1923* (NSW); *Inquiries Act 2014* (Vic); *Royal Commissions Act 1917* (SA).
164 *Royal Commissions Act 1902* (Cth) s 2. Such as arrest powers for failure to appear: *Royal Commissions Act 1902* (Cth) s 6B.
165 Ibid s 4.
166 Parliament of Australia, *Royal Commissions and Commissions of Inquiry* <http://www.aph.gov.au/About_Parliament/Parliamentary_Departments/Parliamentary_Library/Browse_by_Topic/law/royalcommissions>. The most recent Federal Royal Commission commenced is the Royal Commission into National Natural Disaster Arrangements that commenced on 20 February 2020.
167 There has been a Royal Commission concerning juvenile detention in the Northern Territory: see Commonwealth and Northern Territory, Royal Commission into the Protection and Detention of Children in the Northern Territory, *Final Report* (2017). See also the discussion in Taylah Cramp and Anita Mackay, 'Protecting Victims and Vulnerable Witnesses Participating in Royal Commissions: Lessons from the 2016–2017 Royal Commission into the Protection and Detention of Children in the Northern Territory' (2019) 29(1) *Journal of Judicial Administration* 3. There are two Royal Commissions currently underway that may consider prisons: Royal Commission into Victoria's Mental Health System (commenced February 2019) and Royal Commission into Violence, Abuse, Neglect and Exploitation of People with Disability (commenced April 2019).
168 Royal Commission into Aboriginal Deaths in Custody, *National Report* (1991); Justice Nagle, *Report of the Royal Commission into NSW Prisons* (Government Printer, 1978). Groves has described the Nagle Royal Commission as 'the most wide-ranging investigation of correctional services and the treatment of prisoners in Australian history': Groves, above n 133, 324.
169 See, eg, Elizabeth Grant, 'Approaches to the Design and Provision of Prison Accommodation and Facilities for Australian Indigenous Prisoners after the Royal Commission into Aboriginal Deaths in Custody' (2014) 17(1) *Australian Indigenous Law Review* 47; Victorian Ombudsman, above n 143, 6.
170 Human Rights Council, *Report of the Special Rapporteur on the Rights of Indigenous Peoples on Her Visit to Australia*, UN Doc A/HRC/36/46/Add.2 (8 August 2017) 12–13. Following an earlier visit by the UN Special Rapporteur for Indigenous People, the Rapporteur reported to the Human Rights Council that many of the recommendations of this Royal Commission had not been implemented, and recommended that they be 'fully implemented': United Nations Human Rights Council, *Report by the Special Rapporteur on the Situation of Human Rights and Fundamental Freedoms of Indigenous People, James Anaya, Addendum, Situation of Indigenous Peoples in Australia* (1 June 2010) 14, 22. The RCIADIC is also more recent than the Nagle Royal Commission and was national in focus (whereas the Nagle Royal Commission focused on NSW prisons).

The RCIADIC investigated the deaths of 99 Indigenous people in police custody or prison between 1 January 1980 and 31 May 1989. After an extensive inquiry, including public hearings relating to each of the 99 deaths in the location where the death occurred, the report made 339 recommendations.[171] Marchetti summarises the nature of the recommendations as follows:

> The 339 recommendations made by the RCIADIC focused primarily upon the adequacy of police and coronial investigations into deaths in custody; self-determination and empowerment; providing adequate social, educational, vocational and legal services for Indigenous youth; cultural diversity and the need for culturally sensitive practices to be incorporated in the dominant criminal and legal justice systems; managing alcohol and substance abuse; improving police relations with, and treatment of, Indigenous people; improving custodial care; conforming with international obligations; addressing land needs; and the continued recognition of the importance of reconciliation.[172]

Parliamentary inquiries are conducted by committees established to 'investigate specific matters of policy or government administration or performance'.[173] Similar to Royal Commissions, they may be conducted by either federal, state or territory committees. Such inquiries have been an under-utilised monitoring mechanism in the prison context in Australia. The only recent inquiries of relevance are the WA Community Development and Justice Standing Committee inquiry into 'the efficacy and effectiveness of prisoner education, training and employment strategies', which relates to rehabilitation; the NSW inquiry into the Parklea Correctional Centre; and the NSW inquiry into the increase in the prison population.[174]

---

171 Elena Marchetti, 'Critical Reflections upon Australia's Royal Commission into Aboriginal Deaths in Custody' (2005) 5 *Macquarie Law Journal* 103.
172 Ibid 110.
173 Parliament of Australia, *Infosheet 4 – Committees* <http://www.aph.gov.au/about_parliament/house _of_representatives/powers_practice_and_procedure/00_-_infosheets/infosheet_4_-_committees>.
174 Community Development and Justice Standing Committee (WA), *'Making Our Prisons Work': An Inquiry into the Efficiency and Effectiveness of Prisoner Education, Training and Employment Strategies* (2010); New South Wales, Parliament Legislative Council Portfolio Committee No. 4 – Legal Affairs, *Parklea Correctional Centre and Other Operational Issues* (2018); Select Committee on the Increase in Prisoner Population (NSW), *Final Report* (2001). There were some more proactive inquiries conducted in the ACT prior to the construction of a prison there, but these related to planning, rather than prison operation and management. See Standing Committee on Justice and Community Safety, ACT Legislative Assembly, *The Proposed ACT Prison Facility: Philosophy and Principles* (1999); Standing Committee on Justice and Community Safety, ACT Legislative Assembly, *Inquiry into the Establishment of an ACT Prison: Justification and Siting* (1999). There have also been earlier inquiries into prisons in particular states, such as: Parliament of Tasmania Legislative Council Select Committee, *Correctional Services and Sentencing in Tasmania* (1999) and Victorian Parliament Legislative Council, Select Committee of the Legislative Council upon the Victorian Prisons Service, *Interim Report* (1984).

Problems in prisons are occasionally identified indirectly during broader inquiries. For example, the Senate Committee inquiry into Justice Reinvestment raised concerns about the prison population being at an 'unacceptable level' and the consequent economic and social costs of this, including deterioration of the health of imprisoned people.[175] Another example is the Senate Select Committee on Regional and Remote Indigenous Communities broad inquiry into Indigenous communities. This inquiry prepared a discussion paper about the incarceration of Indigenous communities.[176]

Evaluation of Monitoring Mechanisms in Australia

There are six criteria for effective external monitoring under international law. These derive from the OPCAT specifications for the operation of an NPM. These six criteria will be used to evaluate existing mechanisms in Australia. In summary, they are: (1) independence; (2) expertise; (3) adequate resourcing; (4) regular visits with the aim of providing protection against torture and other cruel, inhuman or degrading treatment or punishment; (5) functions and powers; and (6) implementation of recommendations.

When writing about the appointment of the Commonwealth Ombudsman as the coordinating body for Australia's NPM, McMillan has argued that '[t]he designation of the Ombudsman points to the high esteem it has for independence, expertise, balance, efficiency and stakeholder respect'.[177] If this is accepted, it means that the first and second criteria may be achieved. However, it is important to bear in mind that Australia's NPM will be made up of many more organisations in addition to the Ombudsman, and that there are also other criteria that need to be met.

---

175 Senate Legal and Constitutional Affairs References Committee, *Value of a Justice Reinvestment Approach to Criminal Justice in Australia* (2013) 17, 25.
176 Senate Select Committee on Regional and Remote Indigenous Communities, *Indigenous Australians, Incarceration and the Criminal Justice System* (2010). See also Senate Community Affairs References Committee, *Indefinite Detention of People with Cognitive and Psychiatric Impairment in Australia* (2016).
177 John McMillan, 'The Ombudsman in Australia: Flourishing, Expanding, Diversifying, Innovating' in Marc Hertogh and Richard Kirkham (eds), *Research Handbook on the Ombudsman* (Edward Elgar Publishing, 2018) 443.

Independence

Article 18(1) of the OPCAT requires that 'State Parties shall guarantee the functional independence of the national preventive mechanisms as well as the independence of their personnel'. The independence criterion has three components, identified by Steinerte:[178] (1) functional independence, (2) independence of personnel and (3) perceived independence. The independence of NPMs is something that the SPT pays particular attention to when it visits countries, and the SPT will inevitably assess this when it visits Australia.[179]

Functional Independence

Functional independence has three sub-requirements. The first is that the NPM have 'a clear legislative basis' as stipulated in the SPT guidelines for NPMs.[180] Denmark and Hungary, both of which have constitutionally established Ombudsmen designated as their NPM, are good examples of what is intended here.[181]

The second is operational independence, meaning that 'an NPM cannot be subject to any orders or instructions by any State authority'.[182] An example of this is the NPM in the Netherlands which provides a report about investigations 'to the Secretary or Minister of State who has six weeks to send it to the Parliament' otherwise the NPM 'publishes the report itself'.[183]

The third is financial independence, which stems from the *Principles Relating to the Status of National Institutions (The Paris Principles)* rather than the OPCAT itself.[184] This criterion has two aspects. On the one hand is the level of resourcing required for independent operation, which has some overlap with the criterion of adequate resourcing, discussed below.

---

178 Elina Steinerte, 'The Jewel in the Crown and Its Three Guardians: Independence of National Preventive Mechanisms Under the Optional Protocol to the UN Torture Convention' (2014) 14 *Human Rights Law Review* 1.

179 Ibid 7, 25–6, including details of reports by the Subcommittee for the Prevention of Torture and Other Cruel, Inhuman or Degrading Treatment or Punishment (SPT) following visits to other countries where they have raised concerns about lack of independence.

180 Ibid 9.

181 Ibid 10.

182 Ibid 12.

183 Ibid 14.

184 Adopted by General Assembly resolution 48/134 of 20 December 1993. Steinerte, above n 178, 14. Steinerte notes that art 18(4) of the OPCAT refers to the Paris Principles: at 15.

This was a problem when Sweden initially signed the OPCAT, with 'the Parliamentary Ombudsman initially refusing the designation as NPM due to additional resources not being allocated to it to carry out the functions'.[185] On the other hand, the NPM needs to 'freely decide how its funding is to be utilised' without 'interference' by the Executive.[186]

Independence of Personnel

Independence of personnel can be achieved by having a transparent selection process,[187] ensuring that there is no potential conflict of interest and that the NPM has the necessary privileges and immunity (with the latter specified in art 35 of the OPCAT and the former contained in the NPM guidelines produced by the SPT).[188] In relation to this point, an example of non-compliance may be more enlightening than an example of compliance. The Cambodian NPM is made up of 'an inter-governmental committee, chaired by the Deputy Prime Minister and the Minister of the Interior'.[189] Thus, there is, by structural design, a lack of independence of personnel from government.

Perceived Independence

It is important that there is public confidence in NPMs, which is facilitated by the perception of independence from government and managers of places of detention.[190] This might also make people deprived of their liberty more likely to speak to NPM staff when they conduct investigations. Perceived independence can be fostered by the transparent selection process also required to achieve independence of personnel.[191] It is also fostered by publication about the work being carried out.[192] Indeed art 23 of the OPCAT requires that NPM annual reports be 'published and disseminated' by state parties.

---

185 Anita Mackay, 'Human Rights Law Compliance in Prisons: What Can Australia Learn From the Nordic Approach?' (2014) 20(1) *Australian Journal of Human Rights* 31, 49.
186 Steinerte, above n 178, 17.
187 As required by the NPM guidelines: ibid 18.
188 Ibid 19.
189 Ibid.
190 Ibid 19–20.
191 A note by the SPT, cited by ibid 20.
192 Ibid 21.

Australian Organisations

There should be no question about the Commonwealth Ombudsman's independence as the coordinating body for Australia's NPM under the OPCAT.[193] There have been some examples where Ombudsmen offices in Australia have had their independence compromised by being 'given roles that draw it into political or partisan controversy';[194] however, the Commonwealth Ombudsman has been monitoring immigration detention since 2005.[195] This has some obvious parallels with the role of inspecting prisons and is not an area where the office's independence has been called into question.

Prison inspectorates are obvious choices to be part of the state and territory NPM machinery. WA has announced that the OICS will be the NPM responsible for prisons in that state (as well as other justice system places of deprivation of liberty, such as police cells).[196] Prison inspectorates are established pursuant to legislation, have their own budget, operate completely separately from prison administrators and report directly to Parliament such that the reports are publicly available. The Commonwealth Ombudsman has deemed them all to have the functional independence required by the OPCAT.[197]

There is legislatively enshrined independence of inspectors. For example, s 7 of the *Custodial Inspector Act 2016* (Tas) provides that 'In performing his or her functions, the Inspector must act independently, impartially and in the public interest'. The ACT legislation also seeks to prevent conflict of interests by stipulating that '[t]he inspector must not (a) have

---

193 The Commonwealth Ombudsman reports that the Ombudsman's statutory appointment meets 'the OPCAT requirement for independence', the office has its own budget and can publish reports: Commonwealth Ombudsman, *Commonwealth Ombudsman Implementation of the Optional Protocol to the Convention Against Torture and Other Cruel, Inhuman or Degrading Treatment or Punishment (OPCAT) Baseline Assessment of Australia's OPCAT Readiness Report No. 3/2019* (September 2019) 21. Groves details the mechanisms that make Ombudsmen independent as follows: 'Ombudsmen are normally granted secure tenure, and may only be removed by a vote of Parliament. They are also granted immunity from civil liability for acts and conduct made in good faith in the discharge of their duties. Importantly, Ombudsmen are not subject to any form of ministerial direction': Groves, above n 138, 184. The Victorian Ombudsman's independence stems from the Constitution: Victorian Ombudsman, above n 6, 37.

194 McMillan, above n 177, 449. See illustrations provided by McMillan: at 449–52.

195 Ibid 441.

196 Commonwealth Ombudsman, above n 193.

197 Ibid 21 (ACT), 22 (NSW), 27 (Tasmania), 29 (Western Australia).

paid employment that is inconsistent with the inspector's functions; or (b) engage in any unpaid activity that is inconsistent with the inspector's functions'.[198]

However, there are also prison monitoring bodies that lack the requisite independence. For example, the Justice Assurance and Review Office (JARO) in Victoria and the Chief Inspector in Queensland are both located within the relevant government departments[199] and the Commonwealth Ombudsman's baseline assessment has found both to lack the functional independence required by the OPCAT.[200] Inspection reports conducted by these bodies are not made publicly available. A summary of the JARO's work is provided in the Victorian Department of Justice annual reports,[201] and the Queensland Chief Inspector provides a report to the Director-General of Corrective Services.[202]

The Queensland Government reportedly plans to establish an independent inspectorate with responsibility for both adult and juvenile facilities.[203] There have been a number of calls to establish an independent prison inspectorate in Victoria due to concerns about the Office of Correctional Services Review's (OCSR's) (JARO's predecessor) lack of independence and transparency.[204] For example, the Victorian Ombudsman has made such recommendations, noting that '[t]he Victorian community should have confidence that the prison system is subject to independent, robust and transparent oversight. By any measure,

---

198 *Inspector of Correctional Services Act 2017* (ACT) s 11. In relation to OICS's independence see Richard Harding and Neil Morgan, 'OPCAT in the Asia-Pacific and Australasia' (2010) 6(2) *Essex Human Rights Review* 99, 122.

199 Department of Justice and Regulation in Victoria and Queensland Corrective Services. Harding and Morgan have noted that the Queensland Inspectorate lacks 'functional independence': AHRC OPCAT report, above n 140, 27.

200 Commonwealth Ombudsman, above n 193, 24 (Queensland), 28 (Victoria).

201 See, eg, Department of Justice and Regulation, *Annual Report 2017–18* (2018) 205–7.

202 *Corrective Services Act 2006* (Qld) s 305. The Queensland Inspector has made some inspection reports from 2009–2013 available online: Queensland Government Queensland Corrective Services, *Healthy Prison Report* <https://corrections.qld.gov.au/documents/reviews-and-reports/healthy-prison-report/>.

203 Commonwealth Ombudsman, above n 193, 25.

204 The Office of Correctional Services Review became the Justice Assurance and Review Office when the office was given responsibility for youth justice in April 2017: Department of Justice and Regulation, above n 201, 205.

the OCSR does not achieve any of these objectives'.[205] The Human Rights Law Centre, Law Institute of Victoria and Jesuit Social Services have echoed this sentiment.[206]

Expertise

Article 18(2) of the OPCAT specifies that 'State Parties shall take the necessary measures to ensure that the experts of the national preventive mechanism have the required capabilities and professional knowledge. They shall strive for a gender balance and the adequate representation of ethnic and minority groups in the country'. Part of the reason for this requirement is that the OPCAT applies to varied places of detention. It may, for example, be appropriate to have personnel with military expertise when visiting military facilities and people with psychiatric expertise when visiting psychiatric institutions.[207]

Legislation establishing existing monitoring bodies in Australia is vague about the type of expertise required and, therefore, is unlikely to satisfy the OPCAT requirements. The *Inspector of Custodial Services Act 2003* (WA) provides that an 'appropriately qualified person' should fill the position of Inspector,[208] and the *Inspector of Correctional Services Act 2017* (ACT) notes that 'the Executive must not appoint a person as the inspector unless satisfied that the person has the experience or expertise necessary to exercise the inspector's functions'.[209] The NSW and Tasmanian legislation do not specify any particular qualifications.[210]

---

205 Victorian Ombudsman, above n 143, 135; Victorian Ombudsman, *The Death of Mr Carl Williams at HM Barwon Prison – Investigation into Corrections Victoria* (2012) 146.
206 ABC News Radio, 'Calls for Independent Prisons Monitor to Address Crisis in Vic System', *The World Today*, transcript of interview 26 November 2013, <http://www.abc.net.au/worldtoday/content/2013/s3899083.htm>; Law Institute, 'Calls for Independent Prisons Inspection Body' (2008) 82(6) *Law Institute Journal* 22; Jesuit Social Services, *All Alone. Young Adults in the Victorian Justice System* (2018) 38–9.
207 Rachel Murray et al, *The Optional Protocol to the UN Convention Against Torture* (Oxford University Press, 2011) 135.
208 *Inspector of Custodial Services Act 2003* (WA) s 6.
209 *Inspector of Correctional Services Act 2017* (ACT) s 9(3).
210 Section 4(1) of the *Inspector of Custodial Services Act 2012* (NSW) provides that '[t]he Governor may appoint an Inspector of Custodial Services'. Section 5 of the *Custodial Inspector Act 2016* (Tas) provides that 'The Governor may appoint a person as Custodial Inspector'.

Only one jurisdiction—the ACT—stipulates that there should be the transparent selection process detailed above required to achieve independence of personnel. The Act provides that '[t]he appointment must be made in accordance with an open and accountable selection process'.[211]

In relation to 'ethnic and minority groups' representation required by OPCAT, it will be essential for organisations inspecting prisons in Australia to have Indigenous representation in light of the proportion of the prison population that is Indigenous (as documented in Chapter 1). This point was highlighted by the Victorian Ombudsman in their OPCAT-compliant inspection of the Dame Phyllis Frost Centre in Victoria, despite the fact that it was not possible for the inspection team to include an Aboriginal person for that particular inspection.[212] The team instead sought advice from several Aboriginal people and organisations.[213]

Given the high proportion of people with cognitive disability in prisons (discussed in Chapter 1), consideration should also be given to ensuring Australian organisations that form part of the NPM are what Weller has termed 'disability aware', which may include having people with lived experience form part of monitoring teams.[214]

Where inspections are being carried out by a dedicated prison inspectorate, it is likely that staff will develop suitable expertise. This may also be the case in the JARO, which is dedicated to prison monitoring. Suitable attention will need to be given to the requirements for gender balance and diversity.

Appropriate expertise is less likely to be found in non-specialist monitoring bodies, such as generalist Ombudsmen that cover a range of public service organisations and, therefore, are unlikely to have particular expertise relating to prisons. This is particularly the case in smaller jurisdictions, such as the Northern Territory and Queensland (discussed below), and when inspections are rare.

---

211 *Inspector of Correctional Services Act 2017* (ACT) s 9(2).
212 Victorian Ombudsman, above n 6, 46.
213 Ibid 48.
214 Penelope Weller, 'OPCAT Monitoring and the Convention on the Rights of Persons with Disabilities' (2019) 25(1) *Australian Journal of Human Rights* 130, 143.

Adequate Resourcing

Article 18(3) of the OPCAT stipulates that 'State Parties undertake to make available the necessary resources for the functioning of the national preventive mechanisms'. This is essential for the independence of the organisation. This connection is provided for by Principle 2 of the *Principles Relating to the Status of National Institutions (The Paris Principles)* as follows:

> The national institution shall have an infrastructure which is suited to the smooth conduct of its activities, in particular adequate funding. The purpose of this funding should be to enable it to have its own staff and premises, in order to be independent of the Government and not subject to financial control which might affect its independence.

The reality in Australia is that while monitoring bodies may have the statutory responsibility to monitor prison conditions, they lack the resources to do so in practice. A survey of organisations responsible for monitoring closed environments across Australia found that 59 per cent considered their current resources to be 'inadequate'.[215]

The ACT Human Rights Commission's submission to the AHRC consultation on OPCAT noted that:

> while several entities are empowered to address systemic issues through various audit powers, own motion powers, annual reporting processes, or informal engagement with authorities, these bodies are not sufficiently resourced to use these powers with the regularity and consistency required of a NPM.[216]

The Commission has previously noted that lack of resources has specifically prevented them from conducting a comprehensive audit of the AMC, and they instead opted to audit the treatment of women only.[217]

---

215 Working Paper 3, above n 136, 22.

216 ACT Human Rights Commission, *Response to the Australian Human Rights Commission's May 2017 'OPCAT in Australia Consultation Paper'* (21 July 2017) 3.

217 The report states 'there are not sufficient resources to conduct a comprehensive Human Rights Audit of all detainees' conditions of detention': ACT Human Rights Commission, *Annual Report 2012–2013* (2013) 7. See also ACT Human Rights Commission, *Annual Report 2011/12* (2012) 13. The audit of the treatment of women is by the Australian Capital Territory Human Rights Commission, above n 130. The report made 61 recommendations about ways to improve the treatment of, and services provided to, women in the Alexander Maconochie Centre.

The OICS has also expressed concern that budget cuts are restricting the office's ability to carry out their statutory functions. New prisons have been opened, yet the OICS's budget has been cut. The most recent annual report noted that 'budget constraints make it increasingly difficult for us to meet our statutory responsibilities and to provide advice that reduces risk and maximises opportunities'.[218]

State and territory governments around Australia are implementing 'tough on crime' policies that are causing prison populations to increase (as demonstrated by the statistics outlined in Chapter 1). This is very expensive, given that it costs on average $391.18 per day to keep someone in prison.[219] The resources required for independent external monitoring are, by comparison, a fraction of this. For example, the OICS budget is 'just 0.4 of one per cent of the corrections budget' in WA.[220] This is comparable with other jurisdictions with established OPCAT-compliant inspectorates. Harding writes that:

> the Correctional Investigator Canada, an OPCAT-compliant inspectorate that oversights the federal prison system, costs about 0.15 of 1% of the cost of the operational Department. The UK Inspector of Prisons comes in at about 0.4 of 1% of the cost of carrying out the inspect[ion] activities.[221]

It is not unreasonable to expect governments to increase budgetary allocations for external oversight as they increase their prison populations. Allocating resources to monitoring should be seen as an investment. Preventing human rights abuses has a value that cannot be quantified in economic terms for the lives of imprisoned people. However, even if this is set aside, preventing human rights abuses can save governments money by avoiding litigation and compensation pay-outs when violations do occur. For example, following the death of Mr Ward (discussed further below), the WA Government paid his family members $3.2 million in compensation.[222] In the Tasmanian case of *Pickett v State of Tasmania*, the government was ordered to pay $30,000 in legal costs.[223]

---

218 OICS, *Annual Report 2017–18* (2018) 13.
219 Australian Institute of Criminology, *How Much Does Prison Really Cost? Comparing the Costs of Imprisonment with Community Corrections* (Research Report No 5, 2018) x.
220 OICS, above n 218, 13.
221 Harding, above n 2, 18.
222 Chalpat Sonti, 'Multimillion-Dollar Payout to Mr Ward's Family After Prison Van Death', *WA News* (Western Australia), 29 July 2010.
223 *Pickett v The State of Tasmania* [2011] TASSC 907 (20 April 2011).

Allocating money to OPCAT-compliant monitoring may avoid the need for a Royal Commission,[224] coronial inquest or parliamentary committee inquiry, all of which are very expensive. For example, the 2016–2017 Royal Commission into the Protection and Detention of Children in the Northern Territory which was required to investigate problems in two juvenile detention centres (as well as child protection) had a budget of $54 million (paid for jointly by the federal and Northern Territory governments), plus the Northern Territory reportedly spent a further $16 million for legal and staffing costs.[225] By contrast, the Victorian Ombudsman's OPCAT-compliant inspection of the Dame Phyllis Frost Centre in Victoria cost $105,000.[226] Given an OPCAT inspection has the aim of preventing human rights abuses of multiple imprisoned people, this is by any definition better value for money.

Regular Visits to Ensure Protection From Torture and Other Cruel, Inhuman or Degrading Treatment or Punishment

Article 19(a) of the OPCAT requires that 'at a minimum' NPMS should have the power to 'regularly examine the treatment of the persons deprived of their liberty … with a view to strengthening, if necessary, their protection against torture and other cruel, inhuman or degrading treatment or punishment'. There are two elements to this criterion. The first concerns the regularity of visits. The second concerns the purpose of the visits, which is to protect against torture and other cruel, inhuman or degrading treatment or punishment (TCID).

Regularity

Deitch has made the following observations about the role of regular monitoring:

---

224 As noted by the Victorian Ombudsman, above n 6, 5.
225 Tom Maddocks, 'Royal Commission into Child Detention and Protection Costs NT Government More Than $40 Million', *ABC News* (Australia), 28 November 2017.
226 Victorian Ombudsman, above n 6, 38. Harding suggests this may be an under-estimate because it did not include the costs of running the office. He instead gives an estimate of $150,000: Harding, above n 2, 18.

> Regular monitoring helps keep the quality of correctional services
> high, because the staff's knowledge that an inspector could arrive
> at any time acts as a means of informal control over staff behavior.
> In other words, it 'keeps staff on their toes' and helps them avoid
> complacency, even when everything is going well.[227]

Regular visits should be required by legislation in the way that three-yearly visits are specified in the WA legislation establishing the OICS and the Tasmanian legislation establishing the TOCI. Five-yearly visits are specified in the equivalent NSW legislation (as previously detailed in this chapter under 'Current Monitoring System in Australia'). While there is no inspection interval specified in the ACT legislation, the ACT Inspector has conducted one inspection, produced one thematic review (on the treatment of remandees) and reported on five critical incidents in the first two years of operation.[228]

In the absence of legislation requiring regular visits, inspections occur on an ad hoc basis. This is particularly the case in jurisdictions without inspectorates. In a survey conducted of oversight agencies with responsibilities for closed environments in Australia,[229] it was found that the power to conduct systemic reviews was used 'rarely' by 48 per cent of organisations who had the power. Similarly, the power to conduct thematic reviews was used 'rarely' by 46 per cent and never by a further 12 per cent. Moreover, the power to conduct own motion investigations was used 'rarely' in 57 per cent of cases and never in a further four per cent.[230] These results indicate a widespread absence of regular inspection by monitoring bodies nationally.

Ombudsmen in some jurisdictions do opt to investigate prisons regularly using their 'own motion' powers. The South Australian Ombudsman is probably the most active prison inspector in Australia other than the designated prison inspectors that have a statutory mandate to inspect prisons at set intervals. The South Australian Ombudsman has conducted prison investigations in 2010 and 2011; two in 2012; 2013 and 2014;

---

227 Michele Deitch, 'Distinguishing the Various Functions of Effective Prison Oversight' (2010) 30 *Pace Law Review* 1438, 1443. For a discussion of how 'regular' has been interpreted by NPMs in Europe see Nick Hardwick and Rachel Murray, 'Regularity of OPCAT Visits by NPMs in Europe' (2019) 25(1) *Australian Journal of Human Rights* 66.

228 ACT Inspector of Correctional Services, *Our Reports* <https://www.ics.act.gov.au/reports-and-publications>.

229 That is, organisations including, but not limited to, prisons.

230 Working Paper 3, above n 136, 12.

three in 2016 and 2017; and two in 2018 and 2019.[231] The Victorian Ombudsman is also dedicated to prison inspections and has been conducting prison-focused investigations with increasing frequency.[232] This is entirely at the initiative of the particular Ombudsmen.

The situation is different in other jurisdictions. It is particularly concerning that investigations have not been carried out for years at a time in the Northern Territory, given that the Northern Territory has the fastest growing prison population in the country (as discussed in Chapter 1) and does not have a prison inspectorate. In the Northern Territory, the Ombudsman has not investigated male prison conditions since 2008. It has produced two reports about women's imprisonment in that timeframe (in 2008 and 2017).[233] The Commonwealth Ombudsman has reported that there 'is not a fully independent, regular preventive prison inspection system' in the Northern Territory and that the Ombudsman's inspections 'occur on an ad hoc basis'.[234]

---

231 All of the following reports are by the Ombudsman South Australia: *Department for Correctional Services – Port Augusta Prison Disturbance* (2010), *Department for Correctional Services – Prisoner Amenities Levy* (2011), *Department for Correctional Services – Continuing Separation of a Prisoner* (2012), *Ombudsman Investigation into the Department of Correctional Services in Relation to the Restraining and Shackling of Prisoners in Hospitals* (2012), *Department for Correctional Services – Treatment of a Prisoner* (2013), *Department for Correctional Services – Restraint of a Prisoner* (2014), *Department for Correctional Services – Shackling of a Prisoner in Hospital* (2016), *Department for Correctional Services – Unreasonable Shackling of a Prisoner in Hospital* (2016), *Department for Correctional Services – Prohibition of Correspondence* (2016), *Department for Correctional Services – Unjust and Oppressive Separation of a Prisoner* (2017), *Department for Correctional Services – Failure to Ensure that a Prisoner Understood the Induction Process* (2017), *Department for Correctional Services – Failure to Induct Prisoner* (2017), *Department for Correctional Services – Failure to Amend Record of Gender Media Release* (2018), *Department for Correctional Services – Handling of a Prisoner's Diabetes* (2018), *Department for Correctional Services – Handling of a Physical Altercation* (2019) and *Restraint of Prisoner During Hospitalisation – Compliance with Standard Operating Procedures in Relation to Checking of Restraints* (2019).
232 The Victorian Ombudsman has produced the following reports between 2005 and 2018: *Investigation into the Handling, Storage and Transfer of Prisoner Property in Victorian Prisons* (2005); *Conditions for Persons in Custody* (2006) (produced in conjunction with the Office of Police Integrity); *Investigation into Contraband Entering a Prison and Related Issues* (2008); *Investigation into Prisoner Access to Health Care* (2011); *The Death of Mr Carl Williams at HM Barwon Prison – Investigation into Corrections Victoria* (2012); *Investigation into Children Transferred from the Youth Justice System to the Adult Prison System* (2013); *Investigation into Deaths and Harms in Custody* (2014); *Investigation into the Rehabilitation and Reintegration of Prisoners in Victoria* (2015); *Implementing OPCAT in Victoria: Report and Inspection of the Dame Phyllis Frost Centre* (2017); and *Investigation into the Imprisonment of a Woman Found Unfit to Stand Trial* (2018).
233 Ombudsman for the Northern Territory, *Women in Prison Northern Territory. Report of the Investigation into Complaints from Women Prisoners at Darwin Correctional Centre* (2008); Ombudsman NT, *Ombudsman NT Investigation Report. Women in Prison II - Alice Springs Women's Correctional Facility* (2017).
234 Commonwealth Ombudsman, above n 193, 23–4.

There is also an absence of prisons monitoring in Queensland—another jurisdiction without a prison inspectorate. The Queensland Ombudsman has only prepared one report about male prisons and two reports about women's prisons since 2006.[235] The Anti-Discrimination Commission has prepared two reports about women's prisons.[236]

Based on this overview, 'regular', or at least not infrequent, inspections are carried out in the four jurisdictions with inspectorates (WA, NSW, ACT and Tasmania) and the two jurisdictions with proactive Ombudsmen (South Australia and Victoria). This leaves the Northern Territory and Queensland with an absence of regular preventive monitoring. This should be addressed when the NPM is operational, provided the NPM satisfies the OPCAT criterion of regular inspections.

Criteria Targeted at Protection

The importance of the standards for monitoring being both human rights based and preventive focused should not be underestimated. The way this should operate in practice is articulated by Lawson:

> Publication of the basic expectations ... can serve to inform those responsible for places of detention of *how* relevant monitoring bodies consider that detainees 'ought to be treated'. It can thus help to drive up standards – a process underpinned by inspection visits and dialogue.[237]

Compliance with this criterion is mixed throughout Australia. All jurisdictions with prison inspectorates have published criteria or standards. While the Victorian Ombudsman carries out their prison inspections by reference to the *Charter* and used TCID as the framework for the OPCAT inspection in 2017, this is not the same as having standards for monitoring.[238]

---

235 Queensland Ombudsman, *The Classification and Movement of Prisoners Report. An Investigation of Queensland Corrective Services' Process for the Classification, Placement and Transfer of Prisoners* (2009); Queensland Ombudsman, *Strip Searching of Female Prisoners Report* (2014); Queensland Ombudsman, *Overcrowding at Brisbane Women's Correctional Centre Report* (2016).
236 Anti-Discrimination Commission Queensland, *Women in Prison 2019*, above n 130; Anti-Discrimination Commission Queensland, *Women in Prison*, above n 130. NSW Ombudsman investigation reports about prisons may also be described as rare. The last report by this office was in 2012: Ombudsman New South Wales, *Managing Use of Force in Prisons: The Need for Better Policy and Practice* (2012). This may be due to the appointment of the Inspector of Custodial Services in 2013.
237 Anna Lawson, 'Disability, Equality, Reasonable Accommodation and the Avoidance of Ill-Treatment in Places of Detention: The Role of Supranational Monitoring and Inspection Bodies' (2012) 16(6) *The International Journal of Human Rights* 845, 860 (emphasis added).
238 The South Australian Ombudsman also frequently refers to international human rights law in reports. See, eg, the finding that 'the complainant was kept separated from other prisoners for a period well in excess of the maximum period identified by the Special Rapporteur and established by the Mandela Rules': Ombudsman South Australia, *Department for Correctional Services – Unjust and Oppressive Separation of a Prisoner* (2017) 29.

The OICS in WA publishes three sets of detailed Codes of Inspection—one for adults, one for Indigenous imprisoned people and one for young people in detention.[239] In an interview, it has been suggested that the OICS standards are 'based' on human rights, and that 'the … absence of specific human rights legislation in WA has not hindered the work of this office'.[240] The code makes some specific references to cruel treatment and also refers to the relevant 1955 UN *Standard Minimum Rules for the Treatment of Prisoners* that preceded the Mandela Rules (because the Mandela Rules were released after the inspection standards) throughout.[241]

The NSW inspection standards, published in 2014, are organised around five categories: (1) custody, (2) care and wellbeing, (3) rehabilitation, (4) reparation and (5) resources and systems.[242] There is explicit reference to the human rights foundation of the NSW inspection standards that is not in evidence in the WA Code. The introduction describes the standards as 'founded on an approach which is considerably broader than an inevitably limited human rights-based approach' and '[t]he basis of the Inspection Standards lies in the principles of independent inspection, accountability, prevention, purposeful and rehabilitative imprisonment, and the protection of human rights'.[243]

The Tasmanian legislation requires the TOCI 'to prepare and publish guidelines and standards in relation to the conduct of inspections', which the TOCI did in November 2018.[244] The Tasmanian standards note that they 'draw significantly on the NSW standards, and were developed with the assistance of the WA OICS'.[245] They are organised under similar headings to the NSW standards, except that 'rehabilitation and reintegration' is one heading and there is no separate category for reparation. The Tasmanian standards also explicitly refer to the protection of human rights, noting, '[t]he observance of human rights is integral

---

239 OICS, *How We Inspect* <http://www.oics.wa.gov.au/how-we-inspect/>.
240 Working Paper 3, above n 136, 36.
241 For example, in noting that segregation may constitute 'cruel and unusual punishment': OICS, *Code of Inspection Standards for Adult Custodial Services, Version 1* (19 April 2007) 32. See also pages 6, 7, 32.
242 NSW Inspector of Custodial Services, *Inspection Standards for Adult Custodial Services in New South Wales* (2014).
243 Ibid 5–6.
244 *Custodial Inspector Act 2016* (Tas) s 6(1)(c); Office of the Custodial Inspector Tasmania, *Inspection Standards for Adult Custodial Services in Tasmania* (2018). The office has separate 'inspection standards' for young people, published in July 2018.
245 Ibid Foreword.

to good prison management and the most effective and safest way of managing prisons. A prisoner's fundamental human rights are not forfeited because of their imprisonment and are limited only in so far as is necessitated by the fact of imprisonment'.[246]

Both the NSW and Tasmanian standards make numerous references to human rights, the 1955 UN *Standard Minimum Rules for the Treatment of Prisoners* that preceded the Mandela Rules (because the Mandela Rules were released after the inspection standards, so the standards need to be updated to reflect changes to these Rules), as well as the UN *Rules for the Treatment of Women Prisoners and Non-Custodial Measures for Women Offenders* ('the Bangkok Rules').[247] Both of these standards include provisions that are both preventive in focus and human rights compliant, such as:

> Staff should be consistently fair and firm in their dealings with inmates and model respectful relations at all times.[248]

> Prolonged solitary confinement, corporal punishment, punishment by placement in a dark cell, reduction of diet, sensory deprivation and all cruel, inhumane or degrading punishments must not be used.[249]

> Instruments of restraint should be:

> * used only where the restraint of an inmate is strictly necessary to maintain the security of the inmate or prevent injury to any person;
> * of the least restrictive type appropriate;
> * applied for the minimum time necessary to control the inmate; and
> * removed during medical tests and procedures, provided this meets security and management requirements.[250]

---

246 Ibid.

247 United Nations *Rules for the Treatment of Women Prisoners and Non-Custodial Measures for Women Offenders*, UN Doc A/RES/65/229 (adopted by the General Assembly on 21 December 2010) ('the Bangkok Rules').

248 NSW Inspector of Custodial Services, above n 242, 57, standard 67.1; Office of the Custodial Inspector Tasmania, above n 244, 53, standard 66.1.

249 NSW Inspector of Custodial Services, above n 242, 45, standard 52.5. The wording of the Tasmanian standard is identical except for the final sentence that says 'should not be used' (rather than 'must not'): Office of the Custodial Inspector Tasmania, above n 244, 41, standard 53.4.

250 NSW Inspector of Custodial Services, above n 242, 47, standard 55.1; Office of the Custodial Inspector Tasmania, above n 244, 44, standard 56.1.

The ACT Standards are the most recent to have been published (in 2019) and they specifically refer to both the Mandela Rules and OPCAT:

> These ACT Standards were prepared with the OPCAT's preventive approach to oversight in mind to provide a relevant standard against which this oversight of adult corrections can occur once the relevant provisions of the OPCAT are operational in the ACT.[251]

Similarly to the inspection criteria used by HMIP (known as *Expectations*), the ACT Standards are based on the four pillars of the 'healthy prison' test by the World Health Organization:

- **Safety**: detainees, particularly the most vulnerable, are held safely and staff and visitors feel and are safe;
- **Respect**: all persons are treated with respect for their human dignity;
- **Purposeful activity**: detainees engage in activity that is likely to benefit them;
- **Rehabilitation and preparation for release**: detainees are supported to connect with their family and the community; supported to rehabilitate; and prepared for release back into the community.[252]

For each pillar there are standards, indicators and evidence detailed for the purposes of inspections. This led to an extremely comprehensive inspection of the AMC in late 2019, resulting in a 164-page report.[253] The ACT Standards provide significantly more detail on some of the matters referred to above in relation to the NSW and Tasmanian standards. For example, there is more detailed guidance about use of restraints, including absolute prohibition in certain circumstances. Restraints are 'never' to be used 'for disciplinary action' (indicator 14.3), 'on women during labour, childbirth and immediately after childbirth' (indicator 14.6), or if they are 'inherently painful or degrading' (indicator 14.2). When they are used, they are 'only applied by staff who are appropriately trained' (indicator 14.7) and use is to be 'always in accordance with law, appropriately recorded, used in the least restrictive manner possible, and in a way that is mindful of detainee dignity' (indicator 14.1).[254]

---

251 ACT Inspector of Correctional Services, *ACT Standards for Adult Correctional Services* (2019) 7.
252 Ibid 5 (emphasis in original).
253 ACT Inspector of Correctional Services, *Report of a Review of a Correctional Centre by the ACT Inspector of Correctional Services: Healthy Prison Review of the Alexander Maconochie Centre* (2019).
254 Ibid 23.

The ACT inspection standards offer the best example of human rights–based prison inspection criteria for prison monitoring in Australia. They are aligned with both the Mandela Rules and the preventive focus of the OPCAT and have drawn on the experience of HMIP that was established in 1982 and has been using the 'healthy prison' test as a basis for inspections for over a decade.[255]

Functions and Powers

Article 20 of the OPCAT specifies that NPMs should have the power to choose the places of detention they visit, full access to such places, and private interviews with people who are detained and other relevant individuals. These powers are important for the monitoring body to be able to objectively assess the daily practices in the individual prison. This reflects the role envisaged for NPMs by the OPCAT. They are intended to 'provide local and regular scrutiny of the day-to-day reality of detention and of the risk of ill-treatment than [sic] would otherwise be possible'.[256]

Most Australian monitoring organisations have adequate functions and powers, so this is a criterion against which they perform well.[257] As previously outlined in this chapter, the prison inspectorates have broad powers provided for by legislation—in particular, the ACT Inspector, who is required to review critical incidents. Other relevant legislative provisions make it an offence to obstruct the activities of the Inspectors.[258] Additionally, in NSW and the ACT, it is an offence to seek retribution against a person who has provided information to the Inspector as part of their investigations. For example, s 20 of the *Inspector of Custodial Services Act 2012* (NSW) provides:

---

255 The expectations based on the 'healthy prison' were well established by 2006: Anne Owers, 'The Protection of Prisoners' Rights in England and Wales' (2006) 12 *European Journal on Criminal Policy and Research* 85, 88.

256 Statement by Mr Malcolm Evans, Chairperson of the SPT, 23 October 2012, cited by Steinerte, above n 178, 6.

257 A summary of the powers of oversight bodies surveyed for the purposes of the Australian Research Council project 'Applying Human Rights in Closed Environments: A Strategic Framework for Managing Compliance' is provided in Working Paper 3, above n 136, 11.

258 See, eg, *Inspector of Custodial Services Act 2012* (NSW) s 19; *Inspector of Custodial Services Act 2003* (WA) s 32; *Custodial Inspector Act 2016* (Tas) ss 9, 25.

> A person must not take or threaten to take detrimental action against another person because that other person or any other person provides, or proposes to provide, information, documents or evidence to the Inspector or a member of staff of the Inspector in the exercise of functions under this Act.[259]

Ombudsman legislation ordinarily provides the power to enter premises[260] and to have people appear before them voluntarily and involuntarily.[261] It is also typically an offence to obstruct Ombudsman investigations.[262] These legislative provisions can be seen to support independence of personnel, as discussed above.

The AHRC is also consulting stakeholders on how suitable legislation might be drafted to give suitable functions and powers to all organisations that comprise the NPM. Their 2018 consultation paper posed the question, '[w]hat are the core principles that need to be set out in relevant legislation to ensure that each body fulfilling the NPM function has unfettered, unrestricted access to places of detention in accordance with OPCAT?'[263]

This legislation could certainly draw on the legislation establishing prison inspectorates in WA, NSW, Tasmania and the ACT. The ACT is arguably the most OPCAT-compliant legislation, which is unsurprising given it is the most recent inspectorate Act passed in Australia and the *HRA* requires that all legislation be accompanied by a statement of compatibility with the *HRA* when it is introduced into Parliament.[264] One addition to the ACT legislation that is required in jurisdictions with more than one prison is a requirement for regular inspections, such as the requirement for three-yearly inspections contained in the WA and Tasmanian Acts.[265]

---

259 See also *Inspector of Correctional Services 2017* (ACT) s 26.
260 *Ombudsman Act 1974* (NSW) s 20; *Ombudsman Act 2001* (Qld) s 34; *Ombudsman Act 1972* (SA) s 23; *Ombudsman Act 1978* (Tas) s 25; *Ombudsman Act 1973* (Vic) s 21.
261 *Ombudsman Act 1974* (NSW) s 19; *Ombudsman Act 2001* (Qld) ss 25, 29, 36; *Ombudsman Act 1978* (Tas) s 24.
262 *Ombudsman Act 1972* (SA) s 24; *Ombudsman Act 1978* (Tas) s 27; *Ombudsman Act 1973* (Vic) s 22.
263 Australian Human Rights Commission, above n 4, 7 (consultation question 4).
264 *HRA* s 37.
265 *Inspector of Custodial Services Act 2012* (WA) s 19; *Custodial Inspector Act 2016* (Tas) s 6(1). This is preferable to the five-yearly intervals prescribed by the NSW Act because this is too long between inspections (*Inspector of Custodial Services Act 2012* (NSW) s 6).

Implementation of Recommendations

It is critical for the independence of monitoring bodies that they be separate from government. However, this means that they are not empowered to implement or enforce their recommendations. Acceptance and implementation of recommendations remains the responsibility of the relevant government.[266] The main mechanism Australian external monitoring bodies have for encouraging compliance with their recommendations is publication of their reports, which may attract media attention.[267]

Articles 19(b) and 22 of the OPCAT are relevant to this final criterion. Article 19(b) provides that NPMs have the power to 'make recommendations to the relevant authorities with the aim of improving the treatment and the conditions of the persons deprived of liberty'. Article 22 provides that 'authorities of the State Party concerned shall examine the recommendations of the national preventive mechanism and enter into a dialogue with it on possible implementation measures'.

Failure of governments to implement the recommendations of monitoring organisations is arguably the biggest weakness of the external monitoring landscape in Australia. There are numerous examples of this failure across Australia, but four of significance will suffice to illustrate the point here.[268]

The first example is the widespread failure of jurisdictions to respond to the recommendations made by the RCIADIC. The UN Special Rapporteur for Indigenous People noted in 2017 that many of the recommendations of the RCIADIC have not been implemented, drawing particular attention to the failure to address the growth in Indigenous over-representation, address deaths in custody and implement 'custody notification services'.[269]

---

266 Murray et al, above n 207, 133.
267 For example, 'Woman Gave Birth Alone in Perth Prison Cell in "Degrading" Conditions, Report Finds', *The Guardian* (Australia), 12 December 2018; Calla Wahlquist, 'Tasmanian Prisons Report Uncovers "Degrading" Conditions – and One Plague of Rabbits', *The Guardian* (Australia), 1 December 2018; Richard Willingham, 'Prison Death Risks Rising: Ombudsman George Brouwer Warns on Overcrowding', *The Age* (Victoria), 26 March 2014; Michael Owen, 'Shackling Prisoners "is Illegal"', *The Australian* (Australia), 5 September 2012.
268 Other examples are provided elsewhere in this book, such as the South Australian Government's refusal to change the policy relating to shackling of imprisoned people receiving medical treatment (including end-of-life care and women in labour) that has been heavily criticised by the South Australian Ombudsman (see Chapter 7).
269 Human Rights Council, above n 170, 12–13.

The Northern Territory's response is relevant here, given this jurisdiction has the highest proportion of the prison population that is Indigenous in Australia.[270] In a 2012 update on the implementation of recommendations, Bartels highlights that the Northern Territory has done little in response to the recommendations.[271] There is also the failure to remove hanging points in cells in a number of jurisdictions, again including the Northern Territory, as repeatedly raised in coronial inquests. A Coroner noted in 2017, 'it beggars belief that a prison designed and constructed in the 21st century has such classic hanging points with no mitigation of that risk'.[272] In 2014, it was found that 38 per cent of Victorian prison cells still have hanging points[273] and the South Australian Coroner has repeatedly raised concerns about hanging points in that jurisdiction.[274]

The second example is the death of Mr Ward in WA (mentioned in relation to the coronial inquest). This could have been prevented if the WA Government had followed earlier recommendations of the OICS. Mr Ward, an Aboriginal elder, died in the back of a prison transport van while being transported 360 km in WA to face minor charges in court—a journey taking almost four hours. Mr Ward died of heatstroke because of the extremely hot temperature in the van, where no air-conditioning was provided. The temperature in the van was found by the Coroner to be over 50 degrees Celsius and Mr Ward had third degree burns on his body where his skin had come into contact with the metal floor.[275] The two drivers of the van were criticised by the Coroner for, among other things, failing to check that the air-conditioning was working in the back of the van before setting out, failing to provide Mr Ward with cold drinking water during the journey (he was only provided with a 600 ml bottle of water at the start of the journey), and not stopping to check Mr Ward's welfare throughout the entire journey, or to see if he needed to use a toilet.[276]

---

270 83.4 per cent: Australian Bureau of Statistics, *Prisoners in Australia 2019* (5 December 2019) Table 14.

271 Lorana Bartels, 'Twenty Years On: Indigenous Deaths in Police Custody and Lessons from the Frontline' in Isabelle Bartkowiak-Théron and Nicole Asquith (eds), *Policing Vulnerabilities* (Federation Press, 2012) 190–1.

272 *Inquest into the Death of Roy Melbourne* [2017] NTLC 017 [47]. See also *Inquest into the Death of Vernon Bonson* [2018] NTLC 006; *Inquest into the Death of Bird* [2011] NTMC 050.

273 Victorian Ombudsman, above n 143, 6.

274 Elizabeth Grant, 'Approaches to the Design and Provision of Prison Accommodation and Facilities for Australian Indigenous Prisoners after the Royal Commission into Aboriginal Deaths in Custody' (2014) 17(1) *Australian Indigenous Law Review* 47, 48.

275 Hope, above n 161, 34, 8–9.

276 Ibid 63, 65, 82–3.

The OICS had provided two reports to the WA Government (in 2004 and 2007) containing advice about the dangers of using the outdated prison transport vans in operation in WA.[277] The OICS had specifically recommended significant enhancements, including '[r]obust climate control for staff and passengers, adjustable in each zone'.[278] The Coroner concluded, '[i]n my view all of the above observations made by the OICS were accurate and should have been acted upon as a matter of urgency'.[279]

The WA Government has made some significant changes to transport arrangements and services since the death of Mr Ward and the subsequent coronial inquest. These include the use of planes and coaches for transport over long distances; use of alternatives to travelling to court, such as audio-visual links; engaging a different service provider to operate prison transport services; and greater emphasis on both the duty of care owed by staff when transporting imprisoned people and appropriate training for staff.[280]

A third example is the problems in the Risdon prison in Tasmania. Successive reports have highlighted serious concerns with prison conditions and management, including failure to prevent self-harm and suicide of people in prison.[281] In 2001, the Tasmanian Ombudsman observed, '[n]o prison is a pleasant place, but the Risdon Prison is a particularly unpleasant place. It is bleak, cold and grey and, even if a

---

277 OICS, *Report of an Announced Inspection of Adult Prisoner Transport Services* (2004); OICS, *Thematic Review of Custodial Transport Services in Western Australia* (2007).

278 See OICS, *Thematic Review of Custodial Transport Services in Western Australia* (2007) 90–1, Recommendation 27.

279 Hope, above n 161, 89. Another more recent example of the WA Government's refusal to implement recommendations is the response to the report about strip searching in WA prisons. The WA Government does not support key recommendations, including phasing out 'routine strip searching' (recommendation 8) and using technology to 'reduce reliance on strip searching' (recommendation 10): OICS, *Strip Searching Practices in Western Australian Prisons* (2019) 32–3.

280 Government of Western Australia Department of Corrective Services, *Annual Report 2010/11. Contract for the Provision of Court Security and Custodial Services* (2011) 4–5. OICS conducted an audit of transportation, but the focus of the report is empirical data, rather than treatment of people during transport: OICS, *Prisoner/Detainee Transportation 1 July 2011 – 31 December 2011* (2012).

281 There was a coronial inquest into five deaths in Risdon prison that occurred between August 1999 and January 2000: Magistrates Court of Tasmania, *Findings. Deaths in Custody Inquest* (2001); Two Ombudsman reports on an inquiry carried out in 2001: Ombudsman Tasmania, *Report on an Inquiry into Risdon Prison. The Risdon Prison Complex* (2001) and Ombudsman Tasmania, *Report on an Inquiry into Risdon Prison. Risdon Prison Hospital & Forensic Mental Health Service* (2001); a 2010 Ombudsman inquiry: Ombudsman Tasmania, *Risdon Prison Complex Tamar Unit and Behaviour Management Program. Investigation Report June 2010* (2010); and an independent inquiry conducted by Mick Palmer commissioned by the Minister for Corrections in 2010, which reported in 2011. The latter report and the government's response are available at Tasmania, Department of Justice, Corrective Services, *Inquiry into the Risdon Prison Complex* <http://www.justice.tas.gov.au/correctiveservices/risdonprisoninquiry>. It was the 2011 report that led to the eventual establishment of the Tasmanian Custodial Inspector.

very large amount of money were to be spent on the facility, it is unlikely that it could ever conform to contemporary prison standards'.[282] In 2010, the Ombudsman, writing about the Tamar Unit within Risdon, observed, 'as long as Tamar continues to operate as it has been, there is cause to be concerned for the mental and emotional wellbeing of the prisoners accommodated there'.[283] It was the Tamar Unit that was the subject of the *Pickett* litigation in 2011 (discussed earlier in this chapter) where the practice of solitary confinement was found to breach both a common law duty of care and the *Corrections Act 1997* (Tas).[284]

Three years later, in 2014, there were media reports suggesting that people were still being held in solitary confinement for 23 hours per day in Risdon Prison.[285] A 2018 report by the TOCI found that all Tasmanian prisons were overcrowded and that this was leading to people having to spend more time in their cells in 'lock downs'.[286]

The fourth and final example is the Victorian Government's failure to support the 2017 recommendation made by the Victorian Ombudsman that *routine* strip searching of women in the Dame Phyllis Frost Centre (that is, upon arrival and after all visits by non-professionals, such as family members[287]) cease and be replaced with 'a *Charter*-compliant practice of strip searching based on intelligence and risk assessment'.[288] The Ombudsman noted that the searches were generally not leading to the identification of contraband and that alternatives could be used, such as body scanning.[289] This would be consistent with Rule 20 of the Bangkok Rules, which provides that 'alternative screening methods, such as scans, shall be developed to replace strip searches and invasive body searches, in order to avoid the harmful psychological and possible physical impact of invasive body searches'.

---

282 Ombudsman Tasmania, *Report on an Inquiry into Risdon Prison. The Risdon Prison Complex* (2001) 3.
283 Ombudsman Tasmania, *Risdon Prison Complex Tamar Unit and Behaviour Management Program. Investigation Report June 2010* (2010) 4.
284 *Pickett v The State of Tasmania* [2011] TASSC 907 (20 April 2011).
285 Matt Smith, 'Solitary Life for Risdon Prison Inmates', *The Mercury* (Tasmania), 14 June 2014.
286 Tasmanian Custodial Inspector, *Annual Report 2017-18* (2018) 11.
287 Victorian Ombudsman, above n 6, 57.
288 Ibid 103, Recommendation 5.
289 Ibid 59.

The Department of Justice and Regulation's response to this recommendation was:

> While the General Manager of Dame Phyllis Frost Centre acknowledges the need to improve record keeping with respect to strip searching, the department does not consider that current practice with respect to observation and supervision of women changing into overalls before contact visits amounts to 'strip searching'. The department is also of the view that current supervision, observation and strip searching is Charter compliant.[290]

The Ombudsman provided the following response to this response:

> I am disappointed that the department has not accepted that this practice should stop unless justified by intelligence and risk. The claim that the women simply 'undress' prior to visits is at best misguided: they do so in the presence of two guards wearing latex gloves, consistent with a strip search.[291]

There are undoubtedly instances where monitoring bodies' recommendations do lead to positive changes in prisons because of the implementation of their recommendations. For instance, 18 of the 19 recommendations made by the Victorian Ombudsman about the Dame Phyllis Frost Centre were accepted by the department.[292]

However, there are far too many serious consequences arising from the failure to implement recommendations. A useful reform would be to introduce a legislative requirement for the responsible government to respond to the recommendations made by the organisations that form part of the NPM, and to do so within a specific timeframe. Precedents for this exist in Victoria. The Victorian Government is required to respond to coronial inquest recommendations within three months and to Joint Investigatory Committees of the Parliament's recommendations within six months.[293] These are legislative requirements to *respond*, not necessarily to support, but they at least work to ensure that governments have turned their minds to the content of the recommendations and risks associated with ignoring them. Further, it would also be helpful if the

---

290 Ibid 103.
291 Ibid 5.
292 Ibid 102–6.
293 *Coroners Act 2008* (Vic) s 52(6); *Parliamentary Committees Act 2003* (Vic) s 36.

monitoring organisation kept track of the implementation of their own recommendations (in the way that the Victorian Ombudsman does).[294] Alternatively, a specific organisation could be given the responsibility to monitor the implementation of the recommendations of these bodies.[295]

Concluding Remarks

It is difficult to identify an Australian jurisdiction with external monitoring mechanisms that meet all of the OPCAT criteria. This is because even when there is regular, independent and expert-led monitoring leading to comprehensive and relevant recommendations made by monitoring organisations, the majority of jurisdictions have a poor record of implementing the recommendations.[296]

A second priority area for improvement—to meet the OPCAT criteria— is to ensure monitoring bodies are adequately resourced to carry out their important functions. The reasons for this are self-evident.

Jurisdictions without prison inspectorates and proactive Ombudsmen (particularly the Northern Territory and Queensland) have the most work to do to meet the OPCAT criteria for NPM. If they do not wish to create a new body (such as a prison inspectorate), it is likely that these organisations would designate their Ombudsman or anti-discrimination commissions as the organisation responsible for prison monitoring as part of the NPM with responsibility for monitoring prisons. Either way, they will need to draw on the experience of other jurisdictions that are further advanced in this area. There are some examples of good practice to draw on, such as the *Inspector of Custodial Services Act 2017* (ACT) and the detailed standards published by the Inspector in 2019.

The path ahead for all Australian jurisdictions may also be further informed by the OPCAT-compliant inspection of a Victorian prison that has been conducted by the Victorian Ombudsman. The Ombudsman's

---

294 Victorian Ombudsman, *Ombudsman's Recommendations. Third Report on Their Implementation* (Report for Parliament, 19 February 2014).
295 For example, the Victorian Inspector-General for Emergency Management is tasked with reporting on the implementation of the recommendations made by the Victorian Bushfires Royal Commission.
296 It is too early to assess how the ACT Government will respond to recommendations by the ACT Inspector of Custodial Services, but at the national level, the record of implementation of recommendations by prison monitoring bodies is poor.

office developed practical tools, including a detailed survey for imprisoned people and staff, and an aide memoire for inspection staff, which are appended to the report.[297]

Summary and Conclusion

At first glance, it may seem that the OPCAT has nothing to add to the multitude of monitoring bodies involved in prison oversight in Australia—courts, inspectorates, Ombudsmen, human rights and anti-discrimination commissions, Coroners, Royal Commissions and parliamentary committees. But a closer examination reveals that the existing monitoring and investigatory regime has not been sufficient to protect the human rights of imprisoned people. The many concerning practices documented in this chapter make clear that these existing oversight organisations have not, despite numerous sensible recommendations, been able to rectify violations of rights, much less prevent them from occurring in the first place.

There are three problems facing Australia in relation to prison monitoring at present. First, it occurs at the domestic level only, without insight or involvement from international human rights monitoring experts. Second, it is predominantly reactive, rather than preventive in focus (although this has improved with growing numbers of jurisdictions introducing dedicated prison inspectorates). Third, there are serious deficiencies in meeting the six criteria for NPMs set out in the OPCAT. When those criteria are not met—particularly implementation of recommendations—the consequences are not merely repeated human rights violations in Australian prisons. These violations include deaths and significant harms to people in Australian prisons.

Ratification of the OPCAT is a distinct opportunity for this situation to be rectified. It has the potential to solve all three problems currently faced. First, it introduces international monitoring by the SPT, which is a UN committee of experts that will inspect Australian prisons and 'advise and assist' Australia with the establishment of its NPM.[298] Second, it will shift

---

297 Victorian Ombudsman, above n 6, 107–32 (Appendix 1 'Prisoner Survey'; Appendix 2 'Staff Survey'; Appendix 3 'Aide Memoire (Health and Wellbeing)').
298 OPCAT art 11. Bearing in mind the limitations of this mechanism stemming from the infrequency of visits.

the focus on monitoring at the national level by the NPM to preventive issues, in accordance with the OPCAT. Third, it will require that the NPM meet the six criteria specified in the OPCAT: (1) independence; (2) expertise; (3) adequate resourcing; (4) regular visits with the aim of providing protection against torture and other cruel, inhuman or degrading treatment or punishment; (5) functions and powers; and (6) implementation of recommendations.

In this way, the OPCAT has the potential to revolutionise the prison monitoring landscape in Australia. It is appropriate to conclude with the aptly written words of the Victorian Ombudsman in their report on the OPCAT-compliant inspection of a Victorian prison:

> The ratification of OPCAT is an important symbol of Australia's commitment to human rights. Its implementation, through setting up, resourcing or empowering independent agencies, is equally important in ensuring that commitment is not merely symbolic.[299]

---

299 Victorian Ombudsman, above n 6, 5.

Part 2: Macro-level Prerequisites

4

The First Prerequisite: Reduce Reliance on Imprisonment

Introduction

When the United Nations (UN) Human Rights Committee (HR Committee) provided its Concluding Observations in its periodic report on Australia in December 2017, the first concern it listed about imprisonment was overcrowding.[1] The first of the HR Committee's six recommendations was that Australia '[e]liminate overcrowding in places of detention, including by increasing resort to non-custodial alternative measures to detention'.[2] Therefore, it is appropriate that the first prerequisite in this book is to reduce reliance on imprisonment, which is the best way to reduce overcrowding.

An alternative method for addressing overcrowding would, of course, be to continue to expand the number of prisons so that there is plenty of space for more people to be imprisoned. However, even if governments were willing to allocate the necessary expenditure to such an endeavour, which they have not been to date, this is hardly desirable. It would not accord with the strong emphasis international human rights law places on the prohibition of torture or cruel, inhuman or degrading treatment

---

1   Human Rights Committee, *Concluding Observations on the Sixth Periodic Report of Australia*, UN Doc CCPR/C/AUS/CO/6 (1 December 2017) 8.
2   Ibid [42](a).

or punishment.[3] Australia's 2017 ratification of the *Optional Protocol to the Convention against Torture and Other Cruel, Inhuman or Degrading Treatment or Punishment* (OPCAT), which sets in place mechanisms for preventing the occurrence of practices falling within this definition in prisons, gives further weight to this argument.[4] Given the nature of prisons as 'total institutions' and the 'pains of imprisonment' outlined in Chapter 1, the best way to prevent people potentially being subjected to such practices is to keep them out of prison. This is recognised by the Subcommittee for the Prevention of Torture and Other Cruel, Inhuman or Degrading Treatment or Punishment (SPT) (the UN expert committee established by the OPCAT) in its guiding principles, which note that 'detention conditions … in some circumstances can also be a means of torture'.[5] This has led some scholars to argue that prisons should be abolished entirely.[6]

The human rights violations that are more likely to occur in overcrowded prisons are detailed in this chapter (under 'Prison Overcrowding and Human Rights Violations') and clearly demonstrate that reducing reliance on imprisonment is essential as a prerequisite for human rights compliance in Australian prisons. This chapter then turns to three strategies for achieving this goal. The first is prison abolition, and is dealt with relatively briefly here given the overwhelming political challenges it presents. A discussion of two other, more politically feasible strategies—justice reinvestment and a reductionist prison policy—follows.

---

3   *International Covenant on Civil and Political Rights*, opened for signature 19 December 1966, 999 UNTS 171 (entered into force 23 March 1976) art 7 ('ICCPR'); *Convention against Torture and Other Cruel, Inhuman or Degrading Treatment or Punishment*, opened for signature 10 December 1984, 1465 UNTS 85 (entered into force 26 June 1987) ('CAT'); *Convention on the Rights of Persons with Disabilities*, opened for signature 30 March 2007, 2515 UNTS 3 (entered into force 3 May 2008) art 15 ('CRPD').

4   *Optional Protocol to the Convention against Torture*, adopted 18 December 1992, UN Doc A/RES/57/199 (entered into force 22 June 2006) ('OPCAT'). The OPCAT also applies to other places of detention: see art 4(2).

5   Subcommittee for the Prevention of Torture and Other Cruel, Inhuman or Degrading Treatment or Punishment, *The Approach of the Subcommittee on Prevention of Torture to the Concept of Prevention of Torture and Other Cruel, Inhuman or Degrading Treatment or Punishment Under the Optional Protocol to the Convention Against Torture and Other Cruel, Inhuman or Degrading Treatment or Punishment*, CAT/OP/12/6 (30 December 2010) 5(d).

6   See, eg, Angela Davis, *Are Prisons Obsolete?* (Seven Stories Press, 2003); Thomas Mathieson, 'The Politics of Abolition' (1986) 10 *Contemporary Crises* 81.

Justice reinvestment was recommended by the Australian Law Reform Commission (ALRC) as a useful strategy for dealing with over-imprisonment of Indigenous Australians in 2017.[7] A reductionist prison policy is a response that is contained within the criminal justice system itself and does not require the wholesale social change that both prison abolition and justice reinvestment would necessitate. It is the most feasible of the three strategies. Therefore, the way that a reductionist prison policy could be implemented in Australia is the final topic of this chapter (under 'Application of a Reductionist Policy in Australia').

Prison Overcrowding and Human Rights Violations

The Australian prison population is growing, and this growth is consistent across all jurisdictions (as outlined in Chapter 1). In 2018 alone, male imprisonment rose by 4 per cent and female imprisonment rose by 10 per cent.[8] Most Australian jurisdictions are expanding their prison capacity. New South Wales (NSW) has recently opened two 'rapid build' prisons that house imprisoned people in dormitories, adding 1,044 beds in the 2017–18 financial year.[9] Victoria opened a new 1,000-bed prison in 2017.[10] Western Australia (WA) has built two new prisons.[11] The Australian Capital Territory (ACT) has added 120 beds to the Alexander Maconochie Centre (the sole adult prison in the ACT, which accommodates both men and women).[12] Despite these expansion efforts, prison infrastructure has at times failed to keep pace with the growth in prison population. The Queensland Productivity Commission estimated that it would cost $3.6 billion dollars by 2025 to increase the capacity of the Queensland prison system to meet the current shortfall.[13]

---

7   Australian Law Reform Commission (ALRC), *Pathways to Justice—An Inquiry into the Incarceration Rate of Aboriginal and Torres Strait Islander Peoples*, Report No 133 (2017) 137–8, Recommendations 4-1, 4-2.
8   Australian Bureau of Statistics, *Prisoners in Australia 2018* (6 December 2018). For a longer-term perspective see Don Weatherburn, 'Australian Imprisonment 2002-2016: Crime, Policing and Penal Policy' (2018) 51(4) *Australian & New Zealand Journal of Criminology* 537.
9   NSW Government, *Department of Justice Annual Report 2017-18* (2018) 52–3.
10   Minister for Corrections, 'Ravenhall Correctional Centre Officially Opened' (Media Release, 12 October 2017).
11   Office of the Inspector of Custodial Services (OICS), *Western Australia's Prison Capacity* (2016) i.
12   Lorana Bartels, 'The ACT Prison: Human Rights Rhetoric Versus Crowded and Bored Reality' (2015) 9 *Court of Conscience* 13, 16.
13   Queensland Productivity Commission, *Inquiry into Imprisonment and Recidivism. Final Report* (2019) x.

Despite prison capacity expansion, prisons are exceeding the number of people they are designed to house. They are overcrowded. The Productivity Commission reported in 2018 that secure facilities were operating at 121.2 per cent of capacity in 2016–17 (the most recent year for which a reliable national rate is available),[14] with West Australian secure prisons operating at 132.8 per cent capacity in 2018–19.[15]

Overcrowding has led some jurisdictions to use shipping containers to cope with their expanding prison populations. This has occurred in South Australia, WA and Victoria.[16]

A good overview of the multitude of problems associated with overcrowding is provided by the NSW Inspector of Custodial Services inspection standards:

> Overcrowding can have significant detrimental effects on the standard of living, regime and safety within a correctional centre. An overcrowded correctional centre may entail cramped and unhygienic accommodation, a constant lack of privacy, reduced out of cell activities, demand outstripping the capacity of staff and facilities, overburdened health care services, increased tension and potentially increased levels of violence.[17]

The major implication of overcrowding is people having to share cells that are not designed to accommodate the number of people placed in them. For instance, in WA, there have been situations where two people have had to share cells designed for one person, and of cells designed for three people accommodating four to six people.[18] Moreover, triple bunking has

---

14　Steering Committee for the Review of Government Service Provision, *Report on Government Services 2018, Volume C: Justice* (Commonwealth of Australia, 2018) 8.14, Table 8A.13. The figure is 115.6 per cent for 2017–2018 but Victoria, New South Wales (NSW) and South Australia did not provide data and, given Victoria and NSW operate two of the larger prison systems in Australia, this skews the data: Steering Committee for the Review of Government Service Provision, *Report on Government Services 2019, Part C: Justice* (Commonwealth of Australia, 2019) 8.17.

15　Steering Committee for the Review of Government Service Provision, *Report on Government Services 2020, Volume C: Justice* (Commonwealth of Australia, 2020) Table 8A.13.

16　Elizabeth Grant, '"Pack 'em, Rack 'em and Stack 'em": The Appropriateness of the Use and Reuse of Shipping Containers for Prison Accommodation' (2013) 13(2) *Australasian Journal of Construction Economics and Building* 35, 37–8 (in relation to SA), 36 (in relation to WA); Jane Lee, 'Prisoners Moved into Shipping Containers', *The Age* (Victoria), 6 January 2014; Margaret Paul, 'More Shipping Containers Cells Purchased to Accommodate Growing Prisoner Population', *ABC News* (Australia), 9 April 2014.

17　NSW Inspector of Custodial Services, *Inspection Standards for Adult Custodial Services in New South Wales* (2014) 27, Standard 21.1.

18　OICS, *Report of an Announced Inspection of Greenough Regional Prison* (2013) 26.

occurred in Victorian prisons.[19] In NSW, where imprisoned people are housed in dormitories in two new prisons, all of the same concerns apply and are amplified.

Sharing cells is contrary to Rule 12 of the UN *Standard Minimum Rules for the Treatment of Prisoners* (the Nelson Mandela Rules) ('the Mandela Rules'), which stipulates:

> [w]here sleeping accommodation is in individual cells or rooms, each prisoner shall occupy by night a cell or room by himself or herself. If for special reasons, such as temporary overcrowding, it becomes necessary for the central prison administration to make an exception to this rule, it is not desirable to have two prisoners in a cell or room.[20]

The Mandela Rules do not specify how much space each person is to be provided with in prison and nor do the 2018 *Guiding Principles for Corrections in Australia* ('Guiding Principles'). The superseded 2012 *Standard Guidelines for Corrections in Australia* ('Guidelines') referred to the cell size being consistent with the 'Standard Guidelines for Prison Facilities in Australia and New Zealand (1990)'.[21] The Office of the Inspector of Custodial Services (OICS) in WA summarises these requirements as follows:

> The Standard Guidelines for Prison Facilities in Australia and New Zealand 1990 (Australasian Standard Guidelines 1990) provide that a single person cell without ablution facilities (toilet, shower, and basin) should be a minimum of 7.5 m² ('dry cells'). An additional 1.25 m² is required for cells that include ablution facilities ('wet cells'). If a cell is to be shared, a further 4.0 m² is required for each additional person.[22]

---

19   Victorian Auditor-General, *Prison Capacity Planning* (2012) 15.
20   United Nations *Standard Minimum Rules for the Treatment of Prisoners* (the Nelson Mandela Rules), UN Doc A/RES/70/175 (17 December 2015) ('the Mandela Rules').
21   The Corrective Services Ministers' Conference (Cth), *Standard Guidelines for Corrections in Australia* (3rd ed, 2004) 2, Guideline 2.3 ('Guidelines').
22   OICS, above n 11, 10.

Following an assessment of prison cells in WA, the OICS concluded that 'only one third of prisoners can be held in conditions that comply with Australasian Standard Guidelines for Corrections for cell size ... the practice of routinely double bunking single cells is in breach of the "Mandela Rules"'.[23]

Cell sharing raises a number of concerns. First, people have far less than the recommended seven square metres of space each. This is particularly problematic when imprisoned people spend as much time in their cells as they do in Australian prisons. The national average of time spent *out* of cells is nine hours per day and, in some jurisdictions, it is less (eg, 7.2 hours per day in NSW and 7.7 hours in Tasmania and SA).[24]

Second, overcrowding in cells leads to the violation of the right to be treated with humanity and respect, and the prohibition of torture, cruel, inhuman and degrading treatment or punishment. This is clear from individual communications to the HR Committee. Part of the responsibility of the HR Committee is to consider whether the circumstances complained of in individual communications constitute violations of arts 7 and 10(1) of the *International Covenant on Civil and Political Rights* (ICCPR) by state parties.[25] As there have been no communications to the HR Committee concerning overcrowding in Australian prisons, some examples from other countries are illustrative.

In a prison in the Philippines, a complainant was accommodated in a dormitory with over 200 others where violence was 'acquiesced in by the prison authorities'. This, in the view of the HR Committee, amounted to violations of both articles.[26] Similarly, a complaint concerning conditions in a prison in the Dominican Republic saw the HR Committee find that both articles had been violated due to the following circumstances:[27]

---

23   Ibid v, 10–15.

24   These figures are for secure prisons. Steering Committee for the Review of Government Service Provision, above n 15, Table 8A.13.

25   The prohibition of 'torture, cruel, inhuman or degrading treatment or punishment' (art 7) and the requirement that '[a]ll persons deprived of their liberty shall be treated with humanity and with respect for the inherent dignity of the human person' (art 10(1)).

26   Human Rights Committee, *Views: Communication No 868/99*, UN Doc CCPR/C/79/D/868/1999 (30 October 2003) ('*Wilson v The Philippines*') [2.4]–[2.5], [7.3].

27   Human Rights Committee, *Views: Communication No 188/84*, UN Doc CCPR/C/31/D/188/1984 (5 November 1987) ('*Portorreal v Dominican Republic*') [11].

Later the same day, the author was allegedly separated from the other political opposition leaders and transferred to another cell (known as the 'Viet Nam cell'), measuring 20 by 5 metres, where approximately 125 persons accused of common crimes were being held. Conditions were allegedly inhuman in this overcrowded cell, the heat was unbearable, the cell extremely dirty and owing to lack of space some detainees had to sit on excrement.[28]

In the Australian context, concerns about these rights have been referred to in reports by monitoring bodies such as the OICS: '[t]oilets in shared cells are unscreened and there is no dignified way to use them in front of another person. This presents particular problems at night when prisoners are locked in cells for 12.5 hours or more'.[29] These matters are discussed further in Chapter 7.

Third, there is an increased risk of intimidation, bullying and violence. This was reflected in the now superseded 2012 Guidelines, which stipulated the following requirements in relation to sharing of cells to protect against such risks: 'Where prisoners are accommodated in multiple occupancy cells or rooms, the prisoners are to be carefully assessed and selected as being suitable to associate with one another in those conditions. Particular care should be taken to avoid prisoners being subjected to intimidation or bullying'.[30]

It was difficult to establish whether this policy is being followed in practice because there was no reporting requirement stipulated in the Guidelines. While the 2018 Guiding Principles contain 40 principles relating to 'safety and security', none of these specifically refer to the potential risk of intimidation, bullying and violence caused by cell sharing in the way that the 2012 Guidelines did.[31] There is a very broad principle pursuant to which this risk might be taken into account by prison managers: 'Prisoners are assessed and allocated to accommodation compatible with their assessed risks and needs to ensure their safety and security and the good order of the facility'.[32]

---

28   Ibid [2.2].
29   OICS, above n 11, 15.
30   Guidelines, above n 21, 24.
31   Corrective Services Administrators' Conference (Cth), *Guiding Principles for Corrections in Australia* (2018) 15–19.
32   Ibid 18, Principle 3.3.2.

In light of the high levels of violence in prisons generally (irrespective of cell sharing) (as outlined in Chapter 1), combined with Steels and Goulding's finding that shared cells are one of the places in prisons where the risk of sexual assault is highest, it seems more likely than not that 'intimidation or bullying', or worse, is occurring.[33]

While the NSW dormitory prisons have not been in operation for long, there were concerns expressed about safety during a recent parliamentary committee inquiry:

> Inmates were strongly opposed to the dormitory style accommodation, in which older and quieter inmates must co-reside with younger, more troublesome inmates. For some, there is a fear of being attacked or assaulted in their sleep, especially as there is a no transfer policy between pods, such that 'there is no escaping the threats and abuse'.[34]

Overcrowding raises some other concerns, in addition to those raised by cell sharing. There is evidence from Victorian prisons that as the prison population has increased the rate of assaults and self-harm has also increased.[35] The Victorian Auditor-General has documented this as follows:

> The increase in prisoner numbers and overcrowding within prisons and management cells has coincided with an increase in prisoner incidents over the past six years. The rate of serious incidents per prisoner, such as assaults, attempted suicides and self-mutilation, has almost doubled over this time.[36]

Overcrowding puts pressure on services for imprisoned people, including medical care, means of communicating with family members (such as telephones), education and programs to facilitate their rehabilitation (such as drug and alcohol programs). The difficulty of providing health

---

33 Protection units contain a high concentration of people convicted of sex offences because they need protection from those in mainstream units and they may victimise others in the protection unit: Brian Steels and Dot Goulding, *Predator or Prey? An Exploration of the Impact and Incidence of Sexual Assault in West Australian Prisons* (November 2009) 50–1.

34 New South Wales, Parliament Legislative Council Portfolio Committee No. 4 – Legal Affairs, *Parklea Correctional Centre and Other Operational Issues* (2018) 80. The Committee also heard evidence about problems with dormitory-style prison accommodation overseas and in juvenile detention centres in Australia: ibid 85–6.

35 By 40 per cent in the last 10 years: Sentencing Advisory Council, *Victoria's Prison Population 2002-2012* (2013).

36 Victorian Auditor-General, above n 19, xii.

care in overcrowded prisons has been recognised by the Australian Institute of Health and Welfare. The Institute has noted that, in response to overcrowding, imprisoned people are frequently being transferred between facilities, action that makes 'continuing health care more difficult'.[37] Overcrowding has had an impact on the operation of Victoria's residential drug program[38] and there has been pressure put on telephone services in NSW prisons, with the NSW Inspector of Custodial Services giving the illustration of a prison with one telephone shared between 48 imprisoned people.[39]

The dangers to prison health care services that can result from overcrowding should not be underestimated and are starkly illustrated by a decision of the United States Supreme Court in 2011. Severe overcrowding in Californian prisons had resulted in people with mental illness not receiving adequate treatment. The situation was so dire that there were 68 preventable deaths in a year. People were waiting for 12 months to receive mental health treatment and some mentally ill people were held in cages while awaiting treatment.[40] The Supreme Court held that this violated the *United States Constitution* Eighth Amendment (prohibition of cruel and unusual punishment).[41]

Overcrowding can increase the risk of riots, which pose obvious risks to the safety of all people imprisoned (as well as staff) at the time of the riot. Overcrowding was described as a 'contributing factor' in an independent investigation of the causes of a riot in a Victorian prison that occurred in 2015.[42] The OICS noted this as a risk of overcrowding in a 2016 report and referred to riots in WA prisons in 2013, 1998 and 1988.[43]

---

37   Australian Institute of Health and Welfare, *The Health of Australian Prisoners 2018* (2019) 7.
38   Victorian Ombudsman, *Investigation into the Rehabilitation and Reintegration of Prisoners in Victoria* (2015) 59.
39   NSW Inspector of Custodial Services, *Full House: The Growth of the Inmate Population in NSW* (2015) 12. See also OICS, above n 11, 19. Lack of access to telephones is also a problem in the Alexander Maconochie Centre in the ACT and in Western Australian prisons: ACT Inspector of Correctional Services, *Review into the Treatment and Care of Remandees at the Alexander Maconochie Centre* (2018) 54–5; OICS, *Contact with Family and Friends While in Custody* (2018).
40   Alicia Bower, 'Unconstitutionally Crowded: Brown v Plata and How the Supreme Court Pushed Back to Keep Prison Reform Litigation Alive' (2012) 45 *Loyola of Los Angeles Law Review* 555, 556–7.
41   *Brown v Plata*, unreported, Supreme Court of the United States, 23 May 2011. See also Ian Freckelton, 'Cruel and Unusual Punishment of Prisoners with Mental Illnesses: From Oates to Plata' (2011) 18(3) *Psychiatry, Psychology and Law* 329, 329.
42   Independent Investigation into the Metropolitan Remand Centre Riot, *Final Report* (December 2015) 7. The introduction of a smoking ban in Victorian prisons was another contributing factor, as noted in Chapter 1.
43   OICS, above n 11, 20.

It is clear that overcrowded prisons lead to human rights violations of imprisoned people. They also exacerbate the 'pains of imprisonment', as outlined in Chapter 1.

Strategies to Reduce Reliance on Imprisonment

The most radical strategy for resolving the problems outlined above is to abolish prisons. Given this response is unlikely to be pursued, alternative responses need to be explored. Justice reinvestment and a reductionist prison policy instead focus on minimising the use of imprisonment to the greatest extent possible. These three strategies are discussed below.

Prison Abolition

The prison abolition literature suggests that prisons would not be needed if society was transformed in such a way that alternative mechanisms were used to deal with vulnerabilities such as mental illness. In a similar vein to other abolition movements (eg, the abolition of slavery), prison abolitionists have developed a vision of society without prisons and with much lower crime rates. Scott describes this as an 'abolitionist real utopia'.[44] This vision involves large-scale social changes, including:

- greater investment in schools as they provide 'the most powerful alternative to jails'[45]

- decriminalisation of drug use, with community-based drug treatment made freely available on a voluntary basis[46]

- providing adequate mental health services in the community, so that people with mental illness are not imprisoned[47]

- where sanctions are required, basing them on 'reparation and reconciliation rather than retribution and vengeance'.[48]

---

44   David Scott, 'Unequalled in Pain' in David Scott (ed), *Why Prison?* (Cambridge University Press, 2013) 323.
45   Angela Davis, *Are Prisons Obsolete?* (Seven Stories Press, 2003) 108.
46   Ibid 108–9.
47   Ibid 108.
48   Ibid 107, 114–15.

The changes required are large scale and broader than changes to the criminal justice system. The changes would build the sense of community, specifically the interdependency a person has with their society, including such things as their 'relationships of loyalty, trust and concern'.[49] When these relationships break down, a person is more likely to commit crime. Therefore, social changes that rebuild these relationships should reduce the incidence of crime. However, it must be recognised that these changes would require a significant investment of resources, only some of which could reliably be obtained from the savings made by not operating existing prisons.

While in many ways an attractive approach to the problems caused by imprisonment, prison abolition is not a very realistic solution. Abolition scholarship has been criticised for posing a solution that may only be workable 'in an environment that bears practically no resemblance with modern social and political order'[50] and for only being potentially workable in small countries like Norway.[51] There is also a very real risk that abolition would not be accompanied by the necessary social changes. A parallel example is the abolition of mental health institutions in the 1960s and 1970s which were supposed to be replaced by community care for mentally ill people. This has never been properly resourced and people do not get the support they need.[52] This is a contributing factor to the large number of mentally ill people in Australian prisons.[53]

However, it would be foolish to dismiss these arguments in their entirety. First, however unrealistic prison abolition may be for the general community, the types of social change identified by the prison abolition movement are essential if the harm caused by imprisonment to vulnerable segments of the population is to be addressed. Second, the prison abolition movement has both middle- and long-term aims. The long-term aim—a society without prisons—is arguably unrealistic. The middle-term aim—to minimise the expansion of prisons and 'shrink the scope

---

49   Rob White and Fiona Haines, *Crime and Criminology* (Oxford University Press, 4th ed, 2008) 168.
50   Sebastian Scheerer, 'Towards Abolitionism' (1986) 10 *Contemporary Crises* 5, 15.
51   Ibid 18. Norway is where prominent abolitionist Mathieson is from.
52   See, eg, Sebastian Rosenberg et al, 'National Mental Health Reform: Less Talk, More Action' (2009) 190(4) *Medical Journal of Australia* 193.
53   See, eg, Paul White and Harvey Whiteford, 'Prisons: Mental Health Institutions of the 21st Century?' (2006) 185(6) *Medical Journal of Australia* 302.

of criminal law to the absolutely necessary core'—is more realistic.[54] It is an argument that has been made in relation to women's imprisonment in Australia (discussed below).

Mathieson puts forward eight arguments against building more prisons— arguments for achieving the middle-term aim:[55]

1. Prisons do not lead to individuals being less likely to commit crime upon their release. In other words, they are ineffectual at achieving the often-declared aim of individual crime prevention[56]

2. There is evidence that prisons do not have a general deterrent effect[57]

3. Overcrowding can be addressed by changing sentencing laws, releasing people earlier from prison and lowering the limit for parole eligibility[58]

4. Once a prison is built, it will be used for a long period of time. That is, a prison has an 'irreversible character'[59]

5. The prison system has an 'expansionist character'. This means individual prisons will always be full and there will always be a need to build more unless a conscious decision is made to reduce the prison population[60]

6. Prisons are inhumane and involve numerous 'pains' (see Chapter 1)[61]

7. Building more prisons 'solidified the prison solution in our society'. This is a cultural problem because it suggests that it is a 'good' solution, despite the fact that building prisons 'emphasizes violence and degradation as a method of solving inter-human conflicts'[62]

8. There are huge costs associated with building and operating prisons, and the money could be better spent. Mathieson describes this last as a supporting argument to his main points, rather than a standalone argument.[63]

---

54 Scheerer, above n 50, 19.
55 Many of these arguments are supported by the more recent abolitionist movement launched in the United States of America (USA) in the 1990s: see, eg, Julia Oparah, 'Why No Prisons?' in David Scott (ed), *Why Prison?* (Cambridge University Press, 2013) 298–300; Scott, above n 44, 320.
56 Thomas Mathieson, 'The Politics of Abolition' (1986) 10 *Contemporary Crises* 81, 89.
57 Ibid.
58 Ibid 90. These are 'front door' and 'back door' strategies and are discussed further in 'Reductionist Prison Policy' below.
59 Ibid 90–1.
60 Ibid 91.
61 Ibid.
62 Ibid 92.
63 Ibid.

Mathieson writes that these arguments constitute 'a forceful basis for advocating a policy of a permanent international ban on prison building'.[64]

In addition to supporting the abolitionist middle-term option, they are each worth considering in their own right. They are also consistent with the reductionist prison policy that is advocated later in this chapter. Indeed, they have had some impact on discussion about women's imprisonment.

Prison Abolition in Australia

There is potentially more political saleability to the argument that imprisonment should be abolished—or at the very least minimised—for women than there is for imprisonment overall. This is because women are predominantly sentenced for less serious criminal offences and shorter terms of imprisonment. They also frequently have a history of victimisation. There is also the need to take into account the impact that imprisonment has on the dependent children of these women (as referred to in Chapter 1). The combination of these factors has led the Law Council of Australia to suggest that most women could 'safely serve their sentences within the community'.[65]

A summary of the profile of different offences committed by men and women in Victoria provided by the Victorian Sentencing Advisory Council in 2010 is pertinent here and illustrative of national trends:

> Men predominate in offences such as assault (11.8% of men versus 7.5% of women), sex offences (18.5% versus 3.5%) and unlawful entry with intent (burglary) (11.0% versus 6.0%), while women most commonly appear in prison with property offences (including theft) (21% of women versus 6.1% of men) and deception offences (10.0% versus 3.1%).[66]

When women do commit violent offences, it has been observed that '[m]ost violent offences by women are one-off events and few women are repeat violent offenders'.[67] The OICS in WA has found that women—particularly Indigenous women—are over-represented among people in prison for fine default.[68]

---

64   Ibid 88.
65   Cited by Anna Kerr and Rita Shackel, 'Equality with a Vengeance: The Over-Incarceration of Women' (2018) 147 *Precedent* 20, 24.
66   Sentencing Advisory Council, *Gender Differences in Sentencing Outcomes* (2010) 60.
67   Mary Stathopoulos, 'Addressing Women's Victimisation in Custodial Settings' (ACSSA Issues No 13, Australian Institute of Family Studies, Australian Centre for the Study of Sexual Assault, 2012) 7.
68   OICS, *Fine Defaulters in the Western Australian Prison System* (2016) v.

Women tend to be imprisoned for short sentences and the Victorian Sentencing Advisory Council has noted 'an increase in the number of women sentenced to short terms of imprisonment (less than one month)'.[69] This is particularly the case for Indigenous women, and Stathopoulos has observed that 'Indigenous women serve shorter sentences, meaning they are imprisoned for very minor offences—such as driving infringements and non-payment of fines—and that they are more likely than non-Indigenous women to be on remand'.[70]

There have been calls to stop building more women's prisons, commencing with a NSW Task Force in 1985. Stubbs and Baldry summarise that:

> [a]t the time, the number of women in prison in NSW had more than doubled in just two years ... The Task Force adopted a critical approach and a strong reductionist stance ... [and] concluded that building a new prison for women would 'in all probability be counter-productive'.[71]

This was followed by another NSW report in the late 1990s recommending 'a moratorium on expanding the number of places for women in prison aligned with a focus on prison reduction', but despite this, 'within 20 minutes of the Committee's report being tabled, the government announced that the new women's prison would go ahead'.[72]

While these reports are not recent, and they have not stemmed the tide of continuous growth in the female prison population in Australia (with Stubbs and Baldry describing them as 'long forgotten'[73]), it is worth noting that there are sound justifications for considering alternatives to imprisonment for the majority of women and that these justifications have been seen as sensible in recent history. Reasonable alternatives are outlined by McCausland and Baldry as including:

---

69   Sentencing Advisory Council, above n 66, 56.
70   Stathopoulos, above n 67, 3. This is supported by the recent ALRC inquiry: ALRC, above n 7, 356, 371.
71   Julie Stubbs and Eileen Baldry, 'In Pursuit of Fundamental Change Within the Australian Penal Landscape. Taking Inspiration from the Corston Report' in Linda Moore et al (eds), *Women's Imprisonment and the Case for Abolition: Critical Reflections on Corston Ten Years On* (Routledge, 2017) 134.
72   Ibid 136. This is another illustration of the government failing to implement the recommendations of monitoring bodies, as detailed in Chapter 3.
73   Ibid 143.

- early intervention and diversionary programmes, e.g. police cautioning schemes; bail housing that diverts women from escalating contact with the criminal justice system; [and]
- sentencing alternatives, e.g. home detention, community-based orders with adequate support to meet parole conditions and avoid incarceration.[74]

Justice Reinvestment

Justice reinvestment involves redirecting resources from prison infrastructure towards those communities from which a large proportion of the prison population is drawn. The rationale is that if people from these communities are provided with sufficient services and support, they will be less likely to commit crimes that result in imprisonment. As is the case with prison abolition, justice reinvestment requires social change. However, the changes required to implement justice reinvestment are less radical than those required to achieve prison abolition. It nevertheless still recognises both the vulnerability of most imprisoned people and the need to reduce society's reliance on prisons.

Justice reinvestment is a relatively recent approach that seeks to respond to a number of important research findings.[75] It has been shown that the majority of the prison population is drawn from certain localities.[76] These localities can be identified using a process termed 'justice mapping' and have high rates of social disadvantage. In addition, recidivism studies show that imprisoning high numbers of people increases crime, rather than reducing it.[77] Also, as previously detailed, imprisonment is expensive, and the higher the rate of imprisonment, the higher the cost to society.[78] This, arguably, involves misuse of public money when it does not result in crime reduction.

---

74   Ruth McCausland and Eileen Baldry, 'Understanding Women Offenders in Prison' in Jane Ireland et al (eds), *The Routledge International Handbook of Forensic Psychology in Secure Settings* (Routledge, 2017) 37.
75   The term 'justice reinvestment' was first used by Tucker and Cadora in 2003: David Brown et al, *Justice Reinvestment. Winding Back Imprisonment* (Palgrave Studies in Prisons and Penology, 2016) 18.
76   Some examples of Australian localities were provided in Chapter 1.
77   Sentencing Advisory Council, *Does Imprisonment Deter? A Review of the Evidence* (2011) 17; Lorana Bartels, 'Criminal Justice Reform Challenges for the Future: It's Time to Curb Australia's Prison Addiction' in Ron Levy et al (eds), *New Directions for Law in Australia: Essays in Contemporary Law Reform* (ANU Press, 2017) 124.
78   It costs on average $391.18 per day to keep someone in prison: Australian Institute of Criminology (AIC), *How Much Does Prison Really Cost? Comparing the Costs of Imprisonment with Community Corrections* (Research Report No 5, 2018) x. The costs of building new prisons in Australia is referred to in 'Concluding Remarks on Justice Reinvestment' below.

The justice reinvestment response to these findings is to propose two courses of action: (1) that resources should be reallocated away from prisons and (2) that resources should be invested in the localities where the majority of imprisoned people come from. The first proposal entails not building new prisons and reducing the population of existing prisons. The second requires justice mapping, both to identify the target communities and to assess what services are already available in these localities.[79] Investment would be in infrastructure and programs that would benefit the community, such as public housing, substance abuse and mental health treatment programs, education and employment assistance.[80] Justice reinvestment has been argued to be 'Preventative financing, through which policymakers shift funds away from dealing with problems "downstream" (policing, prisons) and towards tackling them "upstream" (family breakdown, poverty, mental illness, drug and alcohol dependency)'.[81]

Justice reinvestment has been implemented in over half the states in the United States of America (USA)[82] and has also been used in the United Kingdom (UK) to a lesser extent.[83] In the USA, the annual prison budget exceeds US$53 billion.[84] Economic pressures have led to 32 states trialling justice reinvestment, with 18 of those having embedded it in legislation.[85] There was also federal legislation passed in 2009.[86] The Australian Senate Legal and Constitutional Affairs References Committee (Senate Committee) summarised the success of justice reinvestment in Texas, USA, as follows:

> Texas recorded savings of $443.9 million in 2008-09 including savings from the cancellation of plans to build new prison units. Savings were reinvested in treatment and diversion programs including $241 million to expand the capacity of substance abuse, mental health, and intermediate sanctions facilities and programs.[87]

---

79   David Brown, Melanie Schwartz and Laura Boseley, 'The Promise of Justice Reinvestment' (2012) 37(2) *Alternative Law Journal* 96, 97.
80   Ibid 96.
81   Lanning et al cited by ibid 97.
82   Australian Institute of Crimonology, *Justice Reinvestment in Australia: A Review of the Literature* (Research Report No 9, 2018) vii.
83   See ibid 24–5.
84   These are 2013 figures, based on US$47 billion used by states and US$6.7 billion at the federal level: Brown et al, above n 75, 29.
85   Senate Legal and Constitutional Affairs References Committee, *Value of a Justice Reinvestment Approach to Criminal Justice in Australia* (2013) 48–61, 49.
86   *Criminal Justice Reinvestment Act 2009*: AIC, above n 82, 11.
87   Senate Legal and Constitutional Affairs References Committee, above n 85, 51.

The Australian Institute of Criminology adds to this that 'as opposed to the projected increase in the prison population of 5,141 people, actual growth in the prison population was only 529 people between January 2007 and December 2008'.[88]

There is growing interest in this approach in Australia—particularly for addressing Indigenous over-imprisonment—and it is already being trialled in some communities.

Support for Justice Reinvestment in Australia

Recent support for justice reinvestment has been expressed at the national level by the ALRC in the context of a report into Indigenous incarceration in 2017, as well as by the Queensland Productivity Commission (QPC) in 2019. The ALRC's report recommended an 'independent justice reinvestment body' and 'trials initiated in partnership with Aboriginal and Torres Strait Islander communities'.[89] The QPC also recommended that the government 'prioritise projects aimed at reducing Indigenous offending' in considering justice reinvestment.[90]

This builds on the continuous support for justice reinvestment for addressing Indigenous over-imprisonment that has been expressed by Aboriginal and Torres Strait Islander Social Justice Commissioners since 2009.[91] The reasons for this include the high levels of disadvantage in Indigenous communities from which many imprisoned people come.[92] They also include the 'democratic nature of decision making in the JR [justice reinvestment] methodology', which involves a high level of participation from the communities in the development of solutions.[93]

---

88   AIC, above n 82, 21.

89   ALRC, above n 7, 137–8, Recommendations 4-1, 4-2.

90   Queensland Productivity Commission, above n 13, 151, Recommendation 30.

91   Brown, Schwartz and Boseley, above n 79, 99. See also recommendation 40 of the House of Representatives Standing Committee on Aboriginal and Torres Strait Islander Affairs report on incarceration of Indigenous youth and young adults (*Doing Time – Time for Doing. Indigenous Youth in the Criminal Justice System* (2011)) and recommendation 9 of the Senate Legal and Constitutional Affairs References Committee, above n 85. This support is also summarised by the ALRC, above n 7, 138–9.

92   For example, Indigenous Australians fare much worse than non-Indigenous Australians in the areas of educational attainment, employment and health indicators, and there are more Indigenous people living in overcrowded housing and with children in out-of-home care: Melanie Schwartz, 'Building Communities, Not Prisons: Justice Reinvestment and Indigenous Overimprisonment' (2010) 14(1) *Australian Indigenous Law Review* 2, 9. This was also documented by the ALRC, above n 7, 61–81.

93   Brown, Schwartz and Boseley, above n 79, 100; ALRC, above n 7, 141.

Additionally, there is the economic irrationality of the amount of money being spent on Indigenous incarceration. The ALRC estimated that this cost was $3.9 billion in 2016.[94] This irrationality is more acute when it is broken down to the level of particular communities. Schwartz gives the illustration of the town of Papunya, Northern Territory, where 72 out of 308 adults (23 per cent) were in prison during 2007–2008, at a cost of $3,468,960 per year.[95] One does not need to be an economist to imagine what this funding could achieve if it was instead spent on social services for the total Papunya population of 379 adults and children.

This is purely the economic costs. There is also the separate issue of the long-term social costs to individuals and communities of incarceration that are more difficult to measure.[96]

Justice Reinvestment Trials

The ACT had a four-year justice reinvestment strategy that applied from 2014–18 and included a goal of 'reducing recidivism by 25% by 2025'.[97] It also involved two trials, both tailored to Indigenous people. One provided bail support and the other was for families with 'complex needs'.[98] The ACT Government announced in February 2019 that they were expanding their commitment to justice reinvestment as part of a new 'Building Communities Not Prisons' strategy, and that as part of this strategy, additional funding has been provided to one of the trials.[99]

One of the earliest justice reinvestment trials to commence in Australia was in the NSW town of Bourke. The town had the following demographic characteristics at the time of the trial: '[t]here are 2,465 people living in the Bourke Shire of which 762 people are Aboriginal and Torres Strait Islander (approximately 30.9%). The median age of Bourke's Indigenous population is 25 years, approximately 33.7% of which are children aged

---

94   ALRC, above n 7, 127.
95   Schwartz, above n 92, 4–5.
96   See, eg, the quotation from the submission from Jesuit Social Services to the ALRC, above n 7, 128.
97   ACT Justice and Community Safety Directorate, *Reducing Recidivism* <https://www.justice.act. gov.au/justice-programs-and-initiatives/reducing-recidivism>.
98   ALRC, above n 7, 135. ACT Government, 'Family-Focused Justice Reinvestment Trial to Help Reduce Over-Representation of Aboriginal and Torres Strait Islanders in Justice System' (Media Release, 26 April 2017).
99   Jordan Hayne and Niki Burnside, 'Canberra's Only Jail is Running Out of Cells, But the Government Wants to "Build Communities Not Prisons"', *ABC News* (Australia), 15 February 2019.

0 to 14 years'.[100] The ALRC noted that '[i]t was estimated that the direct costs of Aboriginal juvenile and young adult involvement with the justice system was approximately $4 million per year'.[101]

The development phases of the trial commenced in 2012 by the community in partnership with an organisation called 'Just Reinvest NSW' and the Australian Human Rights Commission,[102] and it was later funded by an Australian Research Council project.[103] Implementation commenced from 2016 and it is known as the 'Maranguka Justice Reinvestment Project'.[104] It is too soon for there to be any formal evaluations of the project, but Just Reinvest NSW released some positive statistics in October 2018:

> Newly released statistics demonstrate the following changes in Bourke between 2015 and 2017:
>
> - 18% reduction in the number of major offences reported
> - 34% reduction in the number of non-domestic violence related assaults reported
> - 39% reduction in the number of domestic violence related assaults reported
> - 39% reduction in the number of people proceeded against for drug offences
> - 35% reduction in the number of people proceeded against for driving offences.[105]

The ALRC's report notes that there were also trials being conducted in the Northern Territory, Queensland and South Australia.[106]

---

100 Just Reinvest NSW, *Justice Reinvestment in Bourke* <http://www.justreinvest.org.au/justice-reinvestment-in-bourke/>.
101 ALRC, above n 7, 136. A report was also produced about the changes that occurred in Bourke in 2017 as a result of the project: KPMG, *Maranguka Justice Reinvestment Project Impact Assessment* (2018).
102 Brown et al, above n 75, 134–5.
103 ALRC, above n 7, 135.
104 Ibid 136–7. See also AIC, above n 82, 32–5.
105 Just Reinvest NSW, *New Evidence From Bourke* <http://www.justreinvest.org.au/new-evidence-from-bourke/>.
106 ALRC, above n 7, 136. There is more detail about some of these contained in AIC, above n 82, 35–40. The Queensland Productivity Commission reports that a trial may be conducted in Cherbourg, Queensland, but the details of the proposed trial were not available: above n 13, 140.

Challenges Posed by Justice Reinvestment

There are some reasons to be cautious about the justice reinvestment approach and several challenges to its implementation were recognised by the Senate Committee and other reports, including:

- lack of clarity about what the strategy means and encompasses[107]

- need for multi-partisan support, because funding within communities would need to be maintained for longer than election cycles for it to be effective[108]

- jurisdictional split of responsibility between federal and state and territory governments for the wide-ranging types of community services that would be required (a whole of government approach would be necessary)[109]

- probability that the level of economic savings would be less in Australia compared to countries with larger populations[110]

- lack of availability of data, which would impact on the mapping and evaluation stages.[111]

Another reason to be cautious of this approach is that it may result in a 'disinvestment' in prison-based services and programs justified under the guise of justice reinvestment. This is a particular danger in 'a cost cutting environment'.[112] Justice reinvestment is intended to divert resources away from building new prisons and expanding prison capacity, without abolishing prisons entirely. However, because the core concern of the strategy is using resources in a manner that benefits the community and reduces the commission of crime, disinvestment in services for the smaller number of people who are incarcerated may be inconsistent with the aims of justice reinvestment.

---

107 Senate Legal and Constitutional Affairs References Committee, above n 85, 83–4. See also Brown, Schwartz and Boseley, above n 79, 101.

108 Ibid 85–6. See also Brown, Schwartz and Boseley, above n 79, 101–2.

109 Ibid 86–8. Guthrie et al note that local government would also need to be involved: Jill Guthrie, Michael Levy and Cressida Forde, 'Investment in Prisons: An Investment in Social Exclusion?' (2013) 1(2) *Griffith Journal of Human Dignity* 254, 261.

110 Ibid 89–91.

111 Ibid 94–9. See also Brown et al, above n 75, 156–7; ALRC, above n 7, 144–5.

112 David Brown, 'Prison Rates, Social Democracy, Neoliberalism and Justice Reinvestment' in Kerry Carrington et al, *Crime, Justice and Social Democracy: International Perspectives* (Palgrave Macmillan, 2012) 80. Supported by Chris Cunneen et al, *Penal Culture and Hyperincarceration. The Revival of the Prison* (Ashgate, 2013) 173.

Concluding Remarks on Justice Reinvestment

There is no doubt that a hard-headed economic analysis favours justice reinvestment over current expenditure on the expansion of the prison system. As previously detailed, the expenditure on the prison infrastructure expansion is enormous. For example, the Ravenhall prison in Victoria (opened in 2017) reportedly cost $670 million to build,[113] and Victoria has allocated another $689.5 million to build another prison (construction commencing in 2019).[114] Further, once prisons are built imprisoning people is very expensive, costing a total of $3.8 billion each year nationally.[115]

As the imprisonment rate continues to grow (as detailed in Chapter 1), without any evidence that it is reducing the crime rate, such expenditure is increasingly recognised to be an unwise use of public funds.[116] In addition to curbing the growth of the prison population, justice reinvestment has the added advantage of reducing many societal problems that lead to vulnerable people being over-represented in the prison population.

Notwithstanding the significant advantages of justice reinvestment and the positive indications from the early trials in Australia, there are some challenges posed to implementing it in a federation where imprisonment is the responsibility of the states and territories. The ALRC's recommended national body is designed to address this.[117]

There is also no denying that this approach requires a major shift of resources and significant social change, with the ALRC noting that 'justice reinvestment involves a holistic approach to the drivers of incarceration, which extend beyond justice-related factors to community and social determinants of crime and incarceration'.[118] An alternative approach that requires changes confined to the criminal justice sphere may be preferable and is considered next.

---

113 Tom Cowie, 'Inside Victoria's Newest Prison, at Ravenhall, and the Room Where You Don't Want to End Up', *The Age* (Victoria), 5 July 2017.
114 'Vic Prison Secures Almost $690m in Budget', *SBS News* (Australia), 24 April 2018.
115 Bartels, above n 77, 123.
116 The overall crime rate is reducing for unrelated reasons: see, eg, David Brown, 'The Limited Benefit of Prison in Controlling Crime' (2010) 22(1) *Current Issues in Criminal Justice* 137. For NSW-specific data see Lily Trimboli, *NSW Trends in the Age-Specific Rates of Offending, 1995 – 2018* (Issues Paper No 143, NSW Bureau of Crime Statistics and Research, 2019).
117 ALRC, above n 7, 139.
118 Ibid.

Reductionist Prison Policy

Prison abolition and justice reinvestment are long-term strategies aimed at shifting the function of imprisonment away from social control towards either minimal use, or if radical social change is achieved, eliminating it entirely. Given that justice reinvestment in Australia is still being debated, and the radical longer-term social change required for prison abolition is not being actively pursued, a relatively short-term solution to reduce the extent to which prison is relied on in Australia is required. A reductionist prison policy is confined to the criminal justice sphere and involves measures such as shortening prison sentences and using alternative sanctions wherever possible. It has the advantage over both the prison abolition and justice reinvestment approaches in that it does not require sweeping social change—something that is both difficult to achieve and unlikely to occur in the current socio-political environment in Australia.

The term 'reductionist' in this context was identified by Rutherford, writing in the 1980s, who categorised approaches of countries to imprisonment as falling into the following three categories:

1. Expansionist—characterised by consistent growth in the prison population and concomitant building of more prisons, expanding existing prisons and recruiting more staff. An example of the application of this approach can be found in the USA since the 1970s.[119]

2. Standstill—characterised by the use of alternative sanctions to replace some prison sentences, replacement of outdated buildings rather than increasing prison capacity, placing a cap on the prison population, and maintaining current operations rather than questioning the fundamental purpose of imprisonment. An example of the application of this approach may be found in the UK in the 1970s–1980s.[120]

3. Reductionist—characterised by reducing the capacity of the system (eg, by closing prisons), early release mechanisms, sentencing focused on lesser sanctions (alternatives to imprisonment), mechanisms to avoid overcrowding and narrowing the scope of the criminal law.[121] Rutherford gives the examples of Japan and the Netherlands during the period of 1950–75.[122]

---

119 Andrew Rutherford, *Prisons and the Process of Justice: The Reductionist Challenge* (Heinemann, 1984) 48–9.
120 Ibid 52–5.
121 Ibid 175–6.
122 Ibid Chapter 6.

A reductionist approach requires the employment of 'front door' and 'back door' strategies. 'Front door' strategies include using prison as the penalty of 'last resort' in the sentencing regime. 'Back door' strategies include giving people shorter prison sentences and having automatic release on parole after a certain proportion of the sentence has been served. These strategies reflect what Clear and Austin term the 'iron law of prison populations', which is that 'the total number of prisoners behind bars is purely and simply a result of two factors: *the number of people put there* and *how long they stay*'.[123]

Application of a Reductionist Policy in Australia

The following sections discuss the changes that would be required for Australia to implement a reductionist policy (both philosophically and practically) and the obstacles to implementing such a policy.

Philosophical-Level Changes

Implementation of a reductionist policy in Australia would involve a major shift from the existing trends that are causing the prison population to increase and prisons to be overcrowded. This section will outline existing philosophical-level trends, then consider what might trigger a change at this level.

Existing Trends

Australia is subject to what Garland has termed the 'culture of control'[124] and Pratt has termed the 'new punitiveness'.[125] The term 'new punitiveness' refers to what is often colloquially termed 'law and order' or 'tough on crime' political agendas. In short, this involves a political climate that prioritises retribution at the expense of rehabilitation (this is discussed further in Chapter 6). Tubex et al have documented increasing punitiveness since the 1980s in four Australian states: NSW, Victoria, South Australia and WA.[126]

---

123 Todd Clear and James Austin, 'Reducing Mass Incarceration: Implications of the Iron Law of Prison Populations' (2009) 3 *Harvard Law & Policy Review* 307, 308 (emphasis in original).
124 David Garland, *The Culture of Control: Crime and Social Order in Contemporary Society* (Oxford University Press, 2001).
125 John Pratt et al, *The New Punitiveness: Trends, Theories, Perspectives* (Willan Publishing, 2005).
126 Hilde Tubex et al, 'Penal Diversity Within Australia' (2015) 17(3) *Punishment & Society* 345.

Features of this philosophy include reliance on public opinion, particularly victims and the lobby groups they form, in support of reforms, rather than experts and evidence. This is known as 'penal populism'. Garland describes this trend as, '[t]he importance of research and criminological knowledge is downgraded and in its place is a new deference to the voice of "experience", of "common sense", of "what everyone knows"'.[127]

There are numerous examples of Australian governments' failure to rely on evidence and expertise. Two examples from Victoria and Queensland will be provided. The Victorian example, from 2010, is provided by Tubex et al:

> the [newly elected] government conducted a public opinion survey in conjunction with the state's tabloid newspaper (the *Herald Sun*), the aim of which was to seek public opinion on the appropriate sentence for a range of offences. At the same time, the survey evidence collected by the state's expert advisory body, the Sentencing Advisory Council, was released, showing that Victorians are more accepting of alternatives to imprisonment than might be expected on the basis of political rhetoric and media headlines. The research undertaken by the Council, however, was dismissed as flawed.[128]

In Queensland, the Sentencing Advisory Council was issued terms of reference on minimum standard non-parole periods. The Council's 2011 report stated that the majority of members were against the introduction of such a scheme and concluded that '[t]he absence of strong evidence that minimum standard non-parole period schemes are effective, and achieve better sentencing outcomes than existing approaches, has led the Council to question the merits of introducing a minimum standard non-parole period scheme in this State'.[129] Despite this expert body's opinion, the Queensland Government has introduced a non-parole period of 25 years for murdering a police officer and a requirement that at least 80 per cent of the term of drug trafficking sentences must be served. These reforms were passed in conjunction with the abolition of the Queensland Sentencing Advisory Council.[130] The abolition of an expert advisory body is an extreme reaction to unwanted advice.[131]

---

127 Garland, above n 124, 13. See also John Pratt, 'Penal Populism and the Contemporary Role of Punishment' in Thalia Anthony and Chris Cunneen (eds), *The Critical Criminology Companion* (Hawkins Press, 2008) 268.
128 Tubex et al, above n 126, 355.
129 Sentencing Advisory Council, *Minimum Standard Non-Parole Periods. Final Report* (2011) x, xv.
130 Andrew Trotter and Harry Hobbs, 'The Great Leap Backward: Criminal Law Reform with the Hon Jarrod Bleijie' (2014) 36(1) *Sydney Law Review* 1, 15.
131 Queensland re-established the Sentencing Advisory Council in 2016: Queensland Sentencing Advisory Council, *Governance* <https://www.sentencingcouncil.qld.gov.au/about-us/governance>.

A further review of minimum standard parole periods in Queensland in 2016 recommended that judges should 'have the discretion to depart from that mandatory period' in certain circumstances (Recommendation 7).[132] This recommendation was not supported by the government, with the response to the review noting, '[i]n our view the potential risk to community safety by implementing Recommendation 7 outweighs the benefits it could bring to the new parole system and as such, it is not intended to remove mandatory non-parole periods at this point in time'.[133] Freiberg et al note that '[t]his is particularly striking, given that NSW and South Australia … do incorporate "special circumstances" provisions'.[134]

As will be seen further in the discussion of practical strategies for applying a reductionist prison strategy (under 'Practical Strategies for Change in Custodial Sentencing Policies'), evidence-based legislative reform informed by organisations such as Sentencing Advisory Councils will need to be undertaken across Australia if a reductionist policy is to have any hope of being achieved.

Potential Triggers for Change

An economic argument may be employed to achieve philosophical-level change and is likely to be the strongest impetus for change. Given that the costs of imprisonment are spiralling, and given that recidivism rates are high, imprisonment may be construed as a misuse of public funds. It is helpful when organisations such as Productivity Commissions highlight that investing in prisons does not help to make the community safer. For example, the Queensland Productivity Commission has recently reported that 'the costs of imprisonment are likely to outweigh the benefits, with increasing imprisonment working to reduce community safety over time'.[135]

The economic argument is part of the attraction of justice reinvestment and has received support from conservative politicians in the USA as a result, especially in times of financial crisis.[136] Justice reinvestment is likely to be a longer-term goal due to the investment in social services

132 Walter Sofronoff, *Queensland Parole System Review, Final Report* (Department of Justice and Attorney-General, 2016) 105–6.
133 Queensland Government, *Response to Queensland Parole System Review Recommendations* (2017) <https://parolereview.premiers.qld.gov.au/assets/government-response-to-qpsr-recommendations.pdf>.
134 Arie Freiberg et al, 'Parole, Politics and Penal Policy' (2018) 18(1) *QUT Law Review* 191, 202.
135 Queensland Productivity Commission, above n 13, x.
136 Brown, Schwartz and Boseley, above n 79, 98.

required and the complexity of implementing this change in a federation (as previously discussed in this chapter, under 'Justice Reinvestment'). However, the economic argument is certainly also worth employing as a strategy to combat overcrowding and to work towards a reductionist prison policy.[137]

Compliance with international human rights law, particularly art 10(3) of the ICCPR requiring the purpose of imprisonment to be rehabilitation and social reformation, is a potential lever for arguing that a change in philosophy is required. However, it is not a strong lever, given that Australia has a tendency to disagree with, or ignore, the Concluding Observations or Comments of UN treaty monitoring bodies (as discussed in Chapter 2). Moreover, Australia does not have national human rights legislation, nor state and territory statutory human rights protections across all states and territories (only Victoria, the ACT and Queensland have such statutes) (detailed in Chapter 5). The ratification of the OPCAT, and the monitoring regime this will introduce, offers the most potential for a shift towards human rights compliance, but this may not result in a broad enough philosophical-level shift in the approach to criminal justice.

Another possibility is that there will be a crisis in one or more prisons that precipitates change.[138] For example, violence by prison staff towards imprisoned people in the Bathurst prison in NSW in the early 1970s culminated in a riot in 1974. A number of people were injured (including by guns being fired from the towers) and a section of the prison was destroyed.[139] This led to a Royal Commission headed by Justice Nagle of the NSW Supreme Court[140] which 'essentially verified prisoners' accounts of events at Bathurst'.[141] This led to a number of improvements in the NSW prison system, including a shift away from an entrenched culture of use of systematic violence by prison staff,[142] and legislative changes across

---

137 See, eg, the 2006 study that found that to reduce the NSW burglary rate by 10 per cent would require a 34 per cent increase in the number of burglars imprisoned, at a cost of $26 million per year: Don Weatherburn, Jiuzhao Hua and Steve Moffatt, 'How Much Crime Does Prison Stop? The Incapacitation Effect of Prison on Burglary', *Crime and Justice Bulletin* (NSW Bureau of Crime Statistics and Research, 2006).
138 A United Kingdom example is riots in 1990 that led to a major inquiry headed by Lord Woolf: Andrew Coyle, *The Prisons We Deserve* (Harper Collins Publishers, 1994) 5, 156–60.
139 David Brown, 'The Nagle Royal Commission 25 Years On. Gaining Perspective on Two and a Half Decades of NSW Prison Reform' (2004) 29(3) *Alternative Law Journal* 135, 135.
140 Justice Nagle, *Report of the Royal Commission into NSW Prisons* (Government Printer, 1978).
141 Brown, above n 139, 136.
142 Ibid 137.

other Australian jurisdictions.[143] However, a proactive rather than reactive change in philosophy will avoid the tragic human cost of a crisis. The aim of the OPCAT is preventive, as discussed in detail in Chapter 3, and this approach is preferable. In short, the required changes at the philosophical level are difficult to envisage occurring in the short term in Australia. Nevertheless, they are necessary to reduce reliance on imprisonment.

Practical Strategies for Change in Custodial Sentencing Policies

A number of practical strategies would also need to be employed to implement a reductionist prison policy in Australia. These include amendments to state and territory sentencing legislation and generating support from the general public.[144]

Sentencing Law Reform

The changes to sentencing laws needed to implement a reductionist policy would be sweeping, given that, as noted above, the trend since the 1980s has been for criminal sanctions to get 'tougher'.[145] Another challenge is that there are sentencing laws at the federal, state and territory level.[146] Moreover, nine different governments would have to undertake a legislative reform program to achieve national-level implementation.

A cataloguing of the sentencing law changes that would be required is beyond the scope of this book. Rather, this section considers four trends in sentencing reform that illustrate the types of sentencing laws that need to be countered because they are in direct opposition to a reductionist policy:

---

143 These are summarised by Matthew Groves, 'Ombudsmen's Jurisdiction in Prisons' in Marc Hertogh and Richard Kirkham (eds), *Research Handbook on the Ombudsman* (Edward Elgar Publishing, 2018) 324–5 n 24.

144 Another major area that could be addressed is bail laws because bail law reforms are increasing the number of people remanded in custody before they have been sentenced (33 per cent of the Australian prison population is unsentenced: Australian Bureau of Statistics, *Prisoners in Australia 2019* (5 December 2019) Table 1). For a discussion of the contribution of bail to prison numbers see Weatherburn, above n 8. One of the strategies for reducing overcrowding in prisons recommended by the United Nations Office on Drugs and Crime is 'reducing pretrial detention': United Nations Office on Drugs and Crime, *Handbook on Strategies to Reduce Overcrowding in Prisons* (United Nations, 2013) Chapter E. However, consideration of bail laws is outside the scope of this book. For an up-to-date catalogue of recent reforms see Lorana Bartels et al, 'Bail, Risk and Law Reform: A Review of Bail Legislation Across Australia' (2018) 42 *Criminal Law Journal* 91.

145 Tubex et al, above n 126.

146 Federal sentencing laws cover approximately 10 per cent of crime: Geraldine Mackenzie, Nigel Stobbs and Jodie O'Leary, *Principles of Sentencing* (Federation Press, 2010) 14.

(1) 'particularism', (2) abolishing alternatives to prison, (3) restricting parole (including imposing mandatory sentences) and (4) introducing terrorism or organised crime offences.

It is worth briefly noting that Bagaric has proposed uniform national sentencing laws, arguing this would lead to less use of imprisonment.[147] If this suggestion were adopted, it might 'assist to depoliticise the process of sentencing reform' and allow for the laws to become more evidence-based.[148] This is because it reduces the need for politicians to introduce sentencing reforms directly responding to the demands of their constituents by relocating reform to the national level. However, there is no guarantee that federal politicians will not become caught up in similar pressures. As will be seen shortly, there are mandatory minimum sentences for Commonwealth terrorism offences. There are also significant challenges associated with the legislative harmonisation, even in areas of law that are less politicised than sentencing law.[149]

Australian jurisdictions have been enacting additional particular offences, often in situations where there are already criminal laws in place, to deal with the behaviour in question. Loughnan terms this trend 'particularism', which she defines as 'a phenomenon in the drafting of offences where the particular wording of offences provides "the definitional detail that merely exemplifies rather than delimits wrongdoing"'.[150] An example of this is the 2008 NSW offence of rock throwing to counteract behaviour such as throwing rocks from freeway overpasses onto the cars passing below.[151]

---

147 Mirko Bagaric, 'An Argument for Uniform Australian Sentencing Law' (2013) 37(1) *Australian Bar Review* 40, 41.

148 Ibid 50–1.

149 Harmonisation has not been achieved in evidence law, despite the fact that discussions about the desirability of harmonisation commenced in 1979 with an ALRC inquiry that produced draft legislation in 1985: ALRC and New South Wales Law Reform Commission, *Uniform Evidence Law* (2006) [1.3]. For an overview of the history of uniform evidence law in Australia see ibid Chapter 1. For a discussion of the current situation see Stephen Odgers, 'Uniform Evidence Law at 21' (2017) 28(3) *Current Issues in Criminal Justice* 311; Andrew Roberts and Jeremy Gans (eds), *Critical Perspectives on the Uniform Evidence Law* (The Federation Press, 2017). Harmonisation of legislation across Australia has been considered in relation to criminal responsibility with the drafting of a Model Criminal Code in the 1990s; see further Arlie Loughnan, '"The Very Foundations of Any System of Criminal Justice": Criminal Responsibility in the Australian Model Criminal Code' (2017) 6(3) *International Journal for Crime, Justice and Social Democracy* 8.

150 Arlie Loughnan, 'Drink Spiking and Rock Throwing. The Creation and Construction of Criminal Offences in the Current Era' (2010) 35(1) *Alternative Law Journal* 18, 20.

151 Another example is Queensland's 'anti-hooning' legislation: Andrew Trotter and Harry Hobbs, 'The Great Leap Backward: Criminal Law Reform with the Hon Jarrod Bleijie' (2014) 36(1) *Sydney Law Review* 1, 15.

The NSW Attorney-General recognised that there were other offences (such as assault) that could be employed to deal with such behaviour.[152] However, the NSW Government insisted on introducing an offence that Loughnan argues is not 'morally' but rather merely 'factually distinct' from existing offences. In addition to expanding the scope of the criminal law, she argues that this reduces the 'internal logic and order of the criminal law'.[153] This trend towards particularism should be reversed.

Australian jurisdictions have been abolishing alternative sanctions to prison.[154] For example, the Victorian Government abolished home detention in 2012 because 'it was perceived (particularly in the media) as a "soft punishment" and not a substitute for jail'.[155] Between 2011 and 2014, the Victorian Government phased out suspended sentences[156] and they were abolished in NSW in 2017.[157]

It has been observed that in South Australia:

> no major party parliamentarian debates non-custodial alternatives, lest they be seen to be 'soft on crime'. The only debates are about what sort of expansions to prison capacity should be considered, not whether there needs to be an expansion to capacity, or how much longer a new penalty of imprisonment will be for a certain offence rather than whether a non-custodial alternative is more effective.[158]

Some Australian jurisdictions have tightened eligibility for parole, and many have introduced minimum non-parole periods (also known as mandatory sentencing because the prescribed non-parole period is

---

152 Loughnan, above n 150, 20.

153 Ibid 20–1.

154 This is inconsistent with one of the strategies for reducing overcrowding in prisons recommended by the United Nations Office on Drugs and Crime, 'introducing alternatives to imprisonment': United Nations Office on Drugs and Crime, above n 144, Chapter B Section 6.

155 Michelle McDonnell and James Farrell, 'Tough, Tougher, Toughest? A New Government's Approach to Sentencing Laws in Victoria' (2012) 37(3) *Alternative Law Journal* 238, 239.

156 Sentencing Advisory Council, *Abolished Sentencing Orders* <https://www.sentencingcouncil. vic.gov.au/about-sentencing/abolished-sentencing-orders>. For a history of their use in Victoria see Arie Freiberg, 'Suspended Sentences in Australia: Uncertain, Unstable, Unpopular, and Unnecessary Alternatives to Imprisonment' (2019) 82(1) *Law and Contemporary Problems* 81, 86–8.

157 Freiberg explains that this type of sentence 'is generally regarded as a sentence of imprisonment that is imposed but not immediately executed … It may or may not have conditions attached and can vary in length from maximum periods of two years to indefinitely': Freiberg, above n 156, 83. In 2019, the Queensland Productivity Commission recommended that home detention be 'established' and non-custodial sentences be 'encouraged': above n 13, Recommendation 9.

158 Tubex et al, above n 126, 359.

the amount of time the person must spend in prison).[159] Mandatory sentencing legislation severely restricts the discretion that traditionally characterises sentencing decisions in Australia.[160] In particular, it has been shown to have a disproportionate impact on Indigenous people.[161] Examples identified by Freiberg et al[162] include:

- Terrorism offences under Commonwealth legislation[163]
- Murder (with a higher sentence if the victim was a police officer),[164] firearms offences[165] and for members of 'criminal organisations' in Queensland[166]
- Murder[167] and sex offences in the Northern Territory[168]
- Offences involving 'gross violence' and specific victims, such as 'emergency workers or custodial officers on duty unless "special circumstances" exist' in Victoria.[169]

Many of the legislative changes to parole stem from inquiries, such as the inquiry that followed the rape and murder of Jill Meagher by Adrian Bayley while on parole while in September 2012 in Victoria, a crime that gained a particularly high profile.[170] Former High Court Judge Callinan was asked to review the operations of the Victorian Adult Parole Board. His report reflected the view that people who commit crimes forfeit their rights, with

---

159 Freiberg et al note that '[t]here are two ways in which such schemes can be created. One is a defined scheme, under which the non-parole period is specifically prescribed in legislation ... The other is to set a percentage of the head sentence that must be served before the offender is eligible for parole': Freiberg et al, above n 134, 198–9. This is inconsistent with one of the strategies for reducing overcrowding in prisons recommended by the United Nations Office on Drugs and Crime, 'removing mandatory minimum sentencing provisions': United Nations Office on Drugs and Crime, above n 144, Chapter B Section 3.

160 Mackenzie, Stobbs and O'Leary, above n 146, 1. This was noted by the Queensland Productivity Commission in recommending a review by the Queensland Sentencing Advisory Council (within 24 months) of legislated limits on judicial discretion to 'to ensure they are serving their intended purpose': Queensland Productivity Commission, above n 13, 299, 303, Recommendation 12.

161 Freiberg et al, above n 134, 201–2.

162 Ibid 200–1.

163 *Crimes Act 1914* (Cth) s 19AG; *Criminal Code 1995* (Cth) ss 80, 91.

164 *Criminal Code Act 1899* (Qld) ss 305(1)–(2).

165 *Weapons and Other Legislation Amendment Act 2012* (Qld).

166 *Criminal Law (Criminal Organisations Disruption) Amendment Act 2013* (Qld).

167 *Sentencing Act 1995* (NT) ss 54(1)–(2).

168 Ibid s 55.

169 Freiberg et al, above n 134, 201. See *Crimes Act 1958* (Vic) ss15A, 15B. The Australian Capital Territory is the exception and has been resisting the introduction of mandatory sentences: Bartels, above n 77, 126.

170 Freiberg et al, above n 134, 194–5. See also Monique Moffa, Greg Stratton and Michele Ruyters, 'Parole Populism: The Politicisation of Parole in Victoria' (2019) 31(1) *Current Issues in Criminal Justice* 75.

the report noting that 'convicted criminals are intentionally denied rights. It is an important object of the justice system that they are so denied'.[171] The report went on to recommend that the Board continue to be exempt from the *Charter of Human Rights and Responsibilities Act 2006* (Vic).[172]

Another illustration of laws that reduce eligibility for parole are the so-called 'no body, no parole laws'.[173] As the name suggests, '[t]hese laws require a parole authority to take into account an offender's cooperation with, or assistance to, authorities with respect to disclosing the whereabouts of the deceased's body'.[174] They have been introduced in South Australia, Victoria and the Northern Territory.[175] Freiberg et al note that '[t]he "no body, no parole law" have the effect of superseding the judge's original decision and possibly extending the offender's sentence by many years'.[176]

These types of parole reforms will contribute to the maintenance of an overcrowded prison system, among other problems. If this trend continues, it will undoubtedly thwart the realisation of a reductionist policy in Australia.

The final trend to note is that, according to McGarrity, 'extraordinary measures' introduced to address the 'extraordinary threat of terrorism' have become 'normalised' since 9/11, and are expanding into general criminal law.[177] An example is legislation intended to control motorcycle clubs. This legislation violates the fundamental human rights of people impacted by it—particularly, the right to freedom of association and right not to have one's liberty restricted unless a court has made a determination of guilt.[178]

---

171 Ian Callinan, *Review of the Parole System in Victoria* (2013) 69. See also the discussion in Freiberg et al, above n 134, 196.

172 Ibid 91, Measure 8. This recommendation was adopted: 'Regulation 5(a) of the *Charter of Human Rights and Responsibilities (Public Authorities) Regulations 2013* declares that the Board is not a public authority for the purposes of the Charter of Human Rights and Responsibilities. This has the effect of excluding the Board from the operation of the Charter. In particular, this means that the Board is not subject to the prohibitions against acting in a way that is incompatible with a human right or against failing to give proper consideration to a relevant human right in making a decision': Adult Parole Board Victoria, *Parole Manual Adult Parole Board of Victoria* (Adult Parole Board of Victoria, 2018) 9.

173 Freiberg et al, above n 134, 212.

174 Ibid.

175 See discussion by ibid 212–13.

176 Ibid 213.

177 Nicola McGarrity, 'From Terrorism to Bikies. Control Orders in Australia' (2012) 37(3) *Alternative Law Journal* 166, 169.

178 Ibid 168. See also Nicola McGarrity and Jessie Blackbourn, 'Anti-Terrorism Laws and Human Rights' in Leanne Weber et al (eds), *The Routledge International Handbook of Criminology and Human Rights* (Routledge, 2016).

McGarrity summarises the operation of the legislation as follows:

> First an organisation may be declared to be a serious organised
> crime organisation … the making of a declaration enlivens the
> second stage of the process. That is, a control order may be
> issued by a court in relation to a member or former member of
> the declared organisation … The purpose of a control order is
> to impose limits on a person's liberty so as to prevent them from
> being a threat to the community … It is a criminal offence for
> a person to breach the terms of a control order.[179]

This type of legislation has been in force in South Australia since 2008,
and in NSW, the Northern Territory and Queensland since 2009.[180]
Western Australia also passed such legislation in 2012, and NSW revised
theirs in 2012.[181]

These are just a few examples of the trends that would need to be countered
to achieve a reductionist policy in Australia. The task is substantial, to say
the least.

Generate Public Support

In addition to these changes to legislation and the policymaking process,
the general public needs to come to understand the need for, and support,
a reduction in imprisonment.[182] It is first necessary to consider what
public attitudes to the use of imprisonment are. The wide divergence
that can occur on this subject is aptly shown by some research about
the difference in attitudes about the use of imprisonment between Finns
(Finland's imprisonment rate is one of the lowest in the world, at 51 per
100,000) and Texans in the USA (where the national imprisonment rate
is the highest in the world, at 655 per 100,000).[183] Houseman gives the
following example:

---

179 McGarrity, above n 177, 166.
180 *Serious and Organised Crime (Control) Act 2008* (SA); *Crimes (Criminal Organisations Control) Act 2009* (NSW); *Serious Crime Control Act 2009* (NT); *Criminal Organisation Act 2009* (Qld). A number of jurisdictions amended their legislation following a High Court challenge to the Queensland legislation that found it to be constitutionally valid: *Assistant Commissioner Condon v Pompano Pty Ltd* (2013) 252 CLR 38. See discussion by Luke McNamara and Julia Quilter, 'High Court Constitutional Challenges to Criminal Law and Procedure Legislation in Australia' (2018) *University of New South Wales Law Journal* 1047, 1070–1.
181 *Criminal Organisations Control Act 2012* (WA); *Crimes (Criminal Organisations Control) Act 2012* (NSW).
182 One of the strategies for reducing overcrowding in prisons recommended by the United Nations Office on Drugs and Crime is 'gaining public support': United Nations Office on Drugs and Crime, above n 144, Chapter A Section 4.
183 International Centre for Prison Studies, *World Prison Brief* <http://www.prisonstudies.org/world-prison-brief>.

Individuals were questioned about an appropriate sentence for a repeat burglar who is twenty-one years of age. In Finland, seventeen-and-a-half percent of those surveyed were in favour of imprisonment. In contrast, fifty-six percent of Americans favoured imprisonment for the hypothetical offender.[184]

In Australia, there have been numerous studies of public opinions about sentencing and levels of punitiveness at the national level and in specific states and territories. In brief, this research has found that there are not large differences in public attitudes across jurisdictions (despite legal differences around Australia).[185] People are more likely to consider leniency when it is a person's first time offence.[186] They also believe that imprisonment is best reserved for serious offences, with non-custodial options available for other types of crimes.[187]

In one Victorian study, the respondents were aware of the high cost of imprisonment. Bartels et al summarise the findings as follows:

> Specifically, 51 percent of respondents agreed that 'we need to find alternatives to prison to reduce the high cost to the community of keeping people in prison' was 'very important', while 69 percent said it was 'very important' that 'taxpayer money should be used on programs that reduce crime in the first place rather than on prison'.[188]

Based on these public attitudes, there are two themes that can be harnessed to support a reduction in imprisonment. The first is the general support for reserving imprisonment for the most serious offences and exploring non-custodial alternatives for other types of criminal offences. This runs counter to the abolition of these non-custodial sanctions by legislatures around the country. The second is to emphasise the high cost

184 Lilith Houseman, 'Reducing Reliance on Incarceration in Texas: Does Finland Hold Answers?' (2010) 46 *Texas International Law Journal* 209, 228.
185 Lorana Bartels, Robin Fitzgerald and Arie Freiberg, 'Public Opinion on Sentencing and Parole in Australia' (2018) 65(3) *Probation Journal* 269, 272.
186 For example, a Victorian study found, '[f]or first-time burglars, respondents were most likely to nominate rehabilitation as the most important sentencing purpose for both young (62 percent) and adult (50 percent) offenders, followed by punishment (13 percent and 23 percent respectively). For repeat burglars, by contrast, the most important purpose was punishment for both young and adult offenders (40 percent and 51 percent), followed by rehabilitation for young offenders (26 percent) and incapacitation for adult offenders (20 percent)': ibid 273.
187 Ibid. Based on a NSW study.
188 Ibid 272.

of imprisonment and that this does not necessarily represent good value for money. This is something that has helped justice reinvestment to gain some traction in other countries.[189]

Bartels has argued that it is important to educate the public on the facts that 'prison is not a particularly effective crime reduction tool ... [and] that crime is decreasing, and has been doing so for some time'.[190] The Northern Territory Ombudsman has also recommended shifting the focus of public debate surrounding imprisonment away from punishment and towards rehabilitation, with particular emphasis on the fact that rehabilitation is more likely to make the community safer. The Ombudsman observed that the government has a responsibility 'to convince members of the public that change can also bring benefits in terms [of] assisting individuals to play a more constructive role in society and at the same time minimise crime in the future'.[191]

Another aspect of a campaign to garner public support, advocated by Scott, could be to increase public awareness about the harm suffered by people in prison. For example, by providing people who have been incarcerated with an opportunity to speak about their experiences.[192] The media attention given to the reports of monitoring bodies referred to in Chapter 3 may assist with this endeavour. Implementation of the OPCAT will improve the transparency of monitoring in Australia, as well as opening up Australia to the scrutiny of the SPT.

In summary, if the public are better educated, and a level of public empathy for imprisoned people can be generated, the public may be more likely to support reforms intended to reduce the use of imprisonment as a sanction.[193]

---

189 It is also one of Houseman's two 'prongs' of a public education campaign when suggesting what Texas may learn from Finland: see Houseman, above n 184, 229–30.

190 Bartels, above n 77, 127.

191 Ombudsman Northern Territory, *Ombudsman NT Investigation Report. Women in Prison II - Alice Springs Women's Correctional Facility* (2017) vol 1, 45.

192 Scott, above n 44, 316–17.

193 Bartels notes that '[r]esearch from both Australia and overseas demonstrates that the more educated people are about crime, the less punitive they become': Bartels, above n 77, 128.

Conclusion

The prison population in Australia is undergoing unmitigated growth and, while jurisdictions are investing in new prisons, capacity has not kept pace with this growth. Australia has reached the point where even shipping containers and 'rapid build' prisons with dormitory accommodation are not keeping pace with the growth in prison population. Bartels describes this as an 'addiction to prisons'.[194]

The corollary of this growth is significant overcrowding. Human rights violations in overcrowded prisons are not risks, they are guaranteed. There is evidence that sharing prison cells leads to increased intimidation; bullying; violence and potential for torture or cruel, inhuman or degrading treatment or punishment. This will be of interest to the SPT when it visits Australia. Overcrowded prisons also cannot provide adequate services and there are increased risks of riots.

There are three potential strategies for reducing Australia's reliance on imprisonment. The first—prison abolition—has long-term and middle-term aims and it has been argued that the latter *may* receive some traction in relation to women's imprisonment. The second—justice reinvestment—is already being trialled in some communities and has particular advantages as a strategy for addressing the over-imprisonment of Indigenous Australians. However, it is not without practical challenges when it comes to implementation. Both of these strategies involve wholesale social change of a scale that Australia may not be ready for.

This chapter has therefore argued that a reductionist prison policy should be implemented in Australia because it is the most realistic option for reducing reliance on imprisonment as a prerequisite to human rights compliance. Such a policy is unlikely to achieve changes quickly. It will involve incremental change over a number of years, particularly to achieve the philosophical changes and generate the public support that will need to accompany the substantial legislative reform agenda that will be required across all jurisdictions. Perhaps the implementation of the monitoring requirements under the OPCAT will provide an incentive for the necessary changes?

---

194 Ibid 119.

5

The Second Prerequisite: Align Domestic Legislation with Australia's International Human Rights Law Obligations

Introduction

The second prerequisite for human rights compliance in Australian prisons is legislation that aligns with Australia's international human rights law obligations. The need for such a legislative framework arises from the international law requirements contained in the Treaties that Australia has chosen to sign, which oblige state parties to implement the rights domestically.[1] For example, both the *International Covenant on Civil and Political Rights* (ICCPR) and *Convention on the Rights of Persons with Disabilities* (CRPD) require states 'to adopt such laws or other measures

---

1   This is not an enforceable requirement, as outlined in Chapter 2. The international committees responsible for overseeing the Treaties regularly comment on Australia's failure to do so, but there is no other 'sanction'. For example, in December 2017, the Human Rights Committee made the following recommendation in their periodic review of Australia's compliance with the *International Covenant on Civil and Political Rights*: 'The Committee reiterates its recommendation (see CCPR/C/ AUS/CO/5, para. 8) that the State party should adopt comprehensive federal legislation giving full legal effect to all Covenant provisions across all state and territory jurisdictions': Human Rights Committee, *Concluding Observations on the Sixth Periodic Report of Australia*, UN Doc CCPR/C/ AUS/CO/6 (1 December 2017) 2.

as may be necessary to give effect to the rights recognized in the present Covenant/Convention', and the ICCPR further requires that there be 'effective' remedies provided.[2]

The particular rights that are to be recognised at the domestic level were outlined in Chapter 2. A central focus for three of the Treaties Australia has signed—the aforementioned ICCPR and CRPD, as well as the *Convention against Torture and Other Cruel, Inhuman or Degrading Treatment or Punishment* (CAT)[3] in particular—is the prohibition of torture or cruel, inhuman or degrading treatment or punishment (TCID).[4] This has to be given particular attention now that Australia has ratified the *Optional Protocol to the Convention against Torture and Other Cruel, Inhuman or Degrading Treatment or Punishment* (OPCAT)[5] and the consequent National Preventive Mechanisms (NPMs) that state parties are required to establish with the purpose of *preventing* TCID in prisons (as discussed in detail in Chapter 3).

There are existing human rights protections in Australia under the Constitution, in common law and in legislation. This includes explicit human rights legislation in the Australian Capital Territory (ACT), Victoria and Queensland and corrections legislation. How well Australia's current domestic legislation aligns with Australia's international human rights law obligations, however, is debatable and needs to be analysed in each state and territory separately. The reforms necessary to achieve compliance with this prerequisite then become more readily apparent.

---

2   *International Covenant on Civil and Political Rights*, opened for signature 19 December 1966, 999 UNTS 171 (entered into force 23 March 1976) art 2 ('ICCPR'); *Convention on the Rights of Persons with Disabilities*, opened for signature 30 March 2007, 2515 UNTS 3 (entered into force 3 May 2008) art 4 ('CRPD').

3   *Convention against Torture and Other Cruel, Inhuman or Degrading Treatment or Punishment*, opened for signature 10 December 1984, 1465 UNTS 85 (entered into force 26 June 1987) ('CAT').

4   ICCPR art 7; CRPD art 15.

5   *Optional Protocol to the Convention against Torture*, adopted 18 December 1992, UN Doc A/RES/57/199 (entered into force 22 June 2006) ('OPCAT').

Human Rights Protections in Australia

Australia does not have a culture of human rights protection and some authors have suggested there is a 'deep seated' 'reluctance about rights in Australia'[6] that is longstanding.[7] Nowhere is this more evident than in relation to imprisoned people, where historically people suffered a 'civil death' upon incarceration. There are attitudes held by some in the community that committing a crime means a person forfeits their rights.[8] These attitudes are not confined to members of the public and are sometimes expressed by experts, such as the former High Court judge who was reviewing the parole system in Victoria.[9] There is also a gap between the obligations imposed on Australia by international law and the current legal protections, such as they are, for imprisoned people.

Domestic Implications of International Law

International conventions do not give rise to domestic obligations in Australia unless they are incorporated into domestic law.[10] The High Court has confirmed this point many times.[11] Australia has not enacted national human rights legislation incorporating the rights contained in the international treaties to which we are a signatory (a matter that will be returned to later in this chapter, under 'Assessment of Alignment of Domestic Legislation with International Human Rights Law Obligations').

---

6   Adam Fletcher, *Australia's Human Rights Scrutiny Regime. Democratic Masterstroke or Mere Window Dressing?* (Melbourne University Press, 2018) 9.

7   Hilary Charlesworth, 'The Australian Reluctance About Rights' (1993) 31(1) *Osgoode Hall Law Journal* 195. In 2003, Charlesworth et al described a 'negative view of international law' as 'part of mainstream politics': Hilary Charlesworth et al, 'Deep Anxieties: Australia and the International Legal Order' (2003) 25 *Sydney Law Review* 423, 464. The general lack of a culture of human rights protection was also documented by the National Human Rights Consultation, *National Human Rights Consultation Report* (September 2009).

8   Tony Ward and Astrid Birgden, 'Human Rights and Clinical Correctional Practice' (2007) 12(6) *Aggression and Violent Behaviour* 628, 635.

9   Callinan wrote that 'convicted criminals are intentionally denied rights. It is an important object of the justice system that they are so denied': Ian Callinan, *Review of the Parole System in Victoria* (2013) 196.

10   *Koowarta v Bjelke-Petersen* (1982) 153 CLR 168. The most well-known example of incorporation into domestic law is Commonwealth anti-discrimination legislation. For other examples see Julie Debeljak, 'Does Australia Need a Bill of Rights?' in Paula Gerber and Melissa Castan (eds), *Contemporary Perspectives on Human Rights Law in Australia* (Lawbook Co, 2013) 42. This position was modified by the High Court's decision in *Minister for Immigration and Ethnic Affairs v Teoh* (1995) 183 CLR 273, a decision that Charlesworth et al describe as creating 'considerable political anxiety': Charlesworth et al, above n 7, 437 (see also the discussion at 449–50).

11   See, eg, *Kioa v West* (1985) 159 CLR 550, 570–1; *Dietrich v The Queen* (1992) 177 CLR 292, [17].

The practical effect of this is that imprisoned people cannot directly enforce rights under the treaties in the domestic setting, except to the extent that they are reflected in domestic human rights legislation in the ACT, Victoria and Queensland (discussed below). For example, as noted in Chapter 3, in *Minogue v Williams*[12] and *Collins v State of South Australia*[13] ('*Collins*'), people in prison sought to rely on the ICCPR. In each case, the courts confirmed the position that the rights contained in the ICCPR cannot be enforced by individuals via litigation in domestic courts.[14] This was despite the fact that in *Collins* the Court considered that arts 10(1) and 10(2) of the ICCPR had indeed been violated.[15]

The Constitution

The *Commonwealth of Australia Constitution Act 1900* ('*Constitution*') does not contain a Bill of Rights and 'does *not* provide comprehensive protection of human rights'.[16] There are only three express rights that Debeljak considers 'can be categorised as human rights proper':[17]

- s 80 that provides the right to a jury trial for trial on indictment
- s 116 that protects the free exercise of any religion
- s 117 that provides for the right to be free of discrimination for choosing a particular state of residence.[18]

The *Constitution* has been found to contain some *implied* rights, such as the implied freedom of political communication.[19] Most relevantly, the *Constitution* has been found to provide limited protection of electoral

---

12   *Minogue v Williams* (2000) 60 ALD 366.
13   *Collins v State of South Australia* [1999] SASC 257.
14   For a more detailed discussion of these cases see Bronwyn Naylor, 'Protecting the Human Rights of Prisoners in Australia' in Paula Gerber and Melissa Castan (eds), *Contemporary Perspectives on Human Rights Law in Australia* (Lawbook Co, 2013) 401–2.
15   *Collins v State of South Australia* [1999] SASC 257, [30]. Article 10(1) requires treatment with humanity and with respect for the inherent dignity and art 10(2) requires unconvicted people to be separated from convicted people.
16   Debeljak, above n 10, 41 (emphasis in original).
17   Ibid 39.
18   For a discussion of the interpretation of these provisions see Rosalind Dixon, 'An Australian (Partial) Bill of Rights' (2016) 14(1) *International Journal of Constitutional Law* 80, 87–90.
19   In relation to the implied right to freedom of political communication see *Lange v Australian Broadcasting Corporation* (1997) 189 CLR 520. Dixon argues there are three or four implied rights: ibid 86. After a hiatus in discovering additional implied rights, however, the High Court recognised some protections for voting rights of imprisoned people in *Roach v Electoral Commissioner* (2007) 233 CLR 162.

participation for some imprisoned people. The franchise for imprisoned people was the subject of High Court litigation when the Federal Government introduced legislation in 2006 to amend the *Commonwealth Electoral Act 1918* to ban all people serving prison sentences from voting.[20] Previously, only those sentenced to three years or more were prohibited from voting. The majority of the High Court in *Roach v Electoral Commissioner* held that the ban was a disproportionate limit on the constitutional provisions pertaining to Parliament being 'directly chosen by the people'.[21] However, the previous position of a ban applying only to people sentenced to more than three years in prison was held to be valid.[22]

Orr and Williams argue that the decision in *Roach* 'amounts only to a very modest protection' and 'represents a partial shield against any federal legislative attempts to roll back well-established aspects of the federal franchise'.[23] By way of comparison, in jurisdictions that have an express constitutional protection of the right to vote—such as Canada and New Zealand—both blanket bans on imprisoned people voting and restrictions applying to those serving sentences of two years or more have been held to be unconstitutional.[24]

---

20   *Electoral and Referendum Amendment (Electoral Integrity and Other Measures) Act 2006* (Cth). The 'doctrine of legal equality' suggested in *Leeth v Commonwealth* (1992) 174 CLR 455 had some potential for protecting the interests of people in Australian prisons. That case concerned differential treatment of people convicted under Commonwealth legislation who are kept in state and territory prisons. Deane and Toohey JJ opined: '[t]he conditions of imprisonment may vary from State to State and, to that extent, a person imprisoned in one State for an offence against a law of the Commonwealth may be more harshly treated than a person imprisoned for the same offence in another State. If the Constitution's doctrine of equality would otherwise preclude such different treatment, it must be modified to permit it at least to the extent that it is a necessary concomitant of the use of State prisons to punish Commonwealth offenders': at [490]. However, the doctrine has been rejected in later cases (including in *Kruger v Commonwealth (Stolen Generations Case)* (1997) 190 CLR 1): George Williams, Sean Brennan and Andrew Lynch, *Blackshield & Williams Australian Constitutional Law & Theory: Commentary & Materials* (The Federation Press, 6th ed, 2014) 627. Therefore, this does not currently provide an avenue of protection for the rights of imprisoned people.
21   Sections 7 and 24. See *Roach v Electoral Commissioner* (2007) 233 CLR 162, 182 [24]–[25], 202 [95] per Gleeson CJ, Gummow, Kirby and Crennan JJ (Hayne and Heydon JJ dissenting).
22   *Roach v Electoral Commissioner* (2007) 233 CLR 162, 179–80 [19], 204 [102].
23   Graeme Orr and George Williams, 'The People's Choice: The Prisoner Franchise and the Constitutional Protection of Voting Rights in Australia' (2009) 8(2) *Election Law Journal* 123, 138.
24   Ibid 129. The relevant Canadian cases are *Sauvé v Canada (Attorney-General)* [1993] 2 SCR 438 and *Sauvé v Canada (Chief Electoral Officer)* [2002] SCR 519. In relation to New Zealand see *Attorney-General v Taylor* [2018] NZSC 104.

International human rights law has influenced statutory interpretation by the High Court in other ways, although none of these have been applied in cases relating to prisons.[25] It is clear that when there is a legislative intention to override 'common law rights or liberties, or human rights', the High Court cannot protect these.[26]

Common Law Position

Historically, imprisonment led to what was known as 'civil death'. That is, a person who was sentenced to imprisonment 'lost all civil rights such as the right to inherit, to own or deal with property and the right to sue'.[27] This position shifted in the late twentieth century and was replaced with the 'residuum principle'.[28] This principle is that a person sentenced to imprisonment retains all their rights other than those unavoidably lost by virtue of their imprisonment, such as liberty.[29]

The common law residuum principle, prima facie, complies with the core feature of international human rights law in relation to prisons, which is that people who are incarcerated do not lose any of their human rights other than the right to liberty.[30] However, the reality is complicated by numerous factors, including corrections legislation allowing for limits on rights based on security concerns (discussed later in this chapter, under 'Corrections Legislation'); courts being reluctant to interfere in prison

---

25   Debeljak, above n 10, 48.

26   Dixon, above n 18, 85.

27   Melinda Ridley-Smith and Ronnit Redman, 'Prisoners and the Right to Vote' in David Brown and Meredith Wilkie (eds), *Prisoners as Citizens* (Federation Press, 2002) 284. As recently as 1978, the High Court held that the doctrine of 'civil death' was part of Australian law, in *Dugan v Mirror Newspapers Ltd* (1978) 142 CLR 583. For a more detailed discussion of this history and how it stemmed from the United Kingdom see Matthew Groves, 'The Second Charters of Prisoners' Rights' in Matthew Groves and Colin Campbell (eds), *Australian Charters of Rights a Decade On* (Federation Press, 2017) 188.

28   *Raymond v Honey* [1983] 1 AC 1, 10 (Lord Wilberforce).

29   Naylor, above n 14, 396. This has been described as the basis for the *Crimes (Administration of Sentences) Act 1999* (NSW) by Basten JA in *Clark v Commissioner for Corrective Services* [2016] NSWCA 186, [8].

30   As required under Principle 5 of the United Nations *Basic Principles for the Treatment of Prisoners* (1990), which stipulates: 'Except for those limitations that are demonstrably necessitated by the fact of incarceration, all prisoners shall retain the human rights and fundamental freedoms set out in the Universal Declaration of Human Rights, and, where the State concerned is a party, the International Covenant on Economic, Social and Cultural Rights, and the International Covenant on Civil and Political Rights and the Optional Protocol thereto, as well as such other rights as are set out in other United Nations covenants'.

administration (discussed in Chapter 3); and legislation that specifically limits imprisoned people's rights, such as electoral legislation that precludes certain categories of imprisoned people from voting (discussed above).

As Brown has argued, '"civil death" and a variety of practices it spawned, are clearly evident in relation to prisoners'.[31] The denial of the franchise for all people sentenced to imprisonment for three years or more is an example of this. This historical background is crucial for understanding the rights of imprisoned people at present.

Human Rights Legislation

The ACT's *Human Rights Act 2004* ('*HRA*') commenced on 1 July 2004 and Victoria's *Charter of Human Rights and Responsibilities Act 2006* ('*Charter*') commenced on 1 January 2007.[32] The *Human Rights Act 2019* (Qld) ('*QHRA*') was passed on 27 February 2019 and commenced on 1 January 2020.[33] The recency of this Act's assent means that the provisions of the *QHRA* are referred to in this discussion, but no comments may be made about their operation. There are several key components of the *HRA*, *Charter* and *QHRA*, which will be discussed in turn. These are: (1) the rights and permissible limitations, (2) legislative scrutiny provisions, (3) the interpretation and declaration of incompatibility powers of the courts and (4) the duties imposed on public authorities. A discussion of each is followed by a summary of the judicial interpretation of the *HRA* and *Charter*.

It is important to note that all three Acts fall within the 'dialogue' model of human rights protection. That is, the Executive, Parliament and Judiciary all have particular roles set out under the Acts such that none have a monopoly over the protection of human rights.[34] This model does

---

31   David Brown, 'Prisoners as Citizens' in David Brown and Meredith Wilkie (eds), *Prisoners as Citizens* (Federation Press, 2002) 310.

32   With the exception of divs 3 and 4 of pt 3 which commenced on 1 January 2008.

33   Queensland Government, *Human Rights* <https://www.qld.gov.au/law/your-rights/human-rights>.

34   Debeljak, above n 10, 59. See also George Williams and Daniel Reynolds, *A Charter of Rights for Australia* (UNSW Press, 4th ed, 2017) 77. For an evaluation of whether the Victorian *Charter of Human Rights and Responsibilities Act 2006* (Vic) ('*Charter*') has been successful in creating such 'dialogue' see Janina Boughey, 'The Victorian Charter: A Slow Start or Fundamentally Flawed?' in Matthew Groves, Janina Boughey and Dan Meagher (eds), *The Legal Protection of Rights in Australia* (Bloomsbury Publishing, 2019) Part III, 222–7.

not require the three branches of government to agree; rather, it 'exposes each arm of government to the diverse perspectives on rights of those with different institutional strengths, motivations and forms of reasoning'.[35]

The Rights and Permissible Limitations

The Acts guarantee a set of human rights, which in essence reflect the rights contained in the ICCPR.[36] Importantly, for the purposes of complying with the OPCAT, all Acts prohibit TCID.[37] They also require that people deprived of their liberty be 'treated with humanity and with respect for the inherent dignity of the human person' in accordance with art 10(1) of the ICCPR.[38] The third major requirement under the ICCPR—that the aim of the prison system be 'reformation and social rehabilitation' as set out in art 10(3)—has not been incorporated into any of the Acts. None of the jurisdictions provide adequate justification for this omission, and this will be discussed further in Chapter 6 where it is argued that the third prerequisite for human rights compliance for prisons in Australia should be to shift the focus of imprisonment to the goal of rehabilitation in accordance with this international law requirement.

Rights of special importance to imprisoned people provided in the Acts include the right to life,[39] the right to security of the person,[40] the right to privacy[41] and the specification that a person can only be deprived of liberty according to legal procedures.[42]

Other rights that are also relevant include (but are not limited to) the right to equality before the law and not to be discriminated against;[43] the right to protection of family and children;[44] the right to peaceful assembly and

---

35   Julie Debeljak, 'Rights Dialogue Where There is Disagreement Under the Victorian Charter' in Julie Debeljak and Laura Grenfell (eds), *Law Making and Human Rights: Executive and Parliamentary Scrutiny Across Australian Jurisdictions* (Lawbook Co, 2020) 275. Debeljak's chapter provides detailed case studies of the interplay between the judicial and executive branches of government in Victoria: at 282–320.

36   *Human Rights Act 2004* (ACT) pt 3 ('*HRA*'); *Charter* pt 2; *Human Rights Act 2019* (Qld) pt 2 div 2 ('*QHRA*').

37   *HRA* s 10; *Charter* s 10; *QHRA* s 17.

38   *HRA* s 19; *Charter* s 22; *QHRA* s 30.

39   *HRA* s 9; *Charter* s 9; *QHRA* s 16.

40   *HRA* s 18; *Charter* s 21; *QHRA* s 29.

41   *HRA* s 12; *Charter* s 13; *QHRA* s 25.

42   *HRA* s 18; *Charter* s 21; *QHRA* s 29(3).

43   *HRA* s 8; *Charter* s 8; *QHRA* 15.

44   *HRA* s 11; *Charter* s 17; *QHRA* s 26.

freedom of association;[45] the right to freedom of thought, belief and religion;[46] and the right to culture and religion.[47] The *QHRA* also contains a 'right to access health services without discrimination', which is a right from the *International Covenant on Economic, Social and Cultural Rights*.[48]

All of these rights can be subject to limitations pursuant to s 7(2) of the *Charter*, s 28 of the *HRA* and s 13 of the *QHRA*.[49] Specifically, these limitations are to be 'reasonable' and 'demonstrably justified in a free and democratic society'.[50] Whether there is a limit on rights, and whether it is reasonable and 'demonstrably justified', will be a matter the court determines based on the facts and evidence in the particular case.[51] In the ACT and Victoria, the courts have held that the government bears the burden of satisfying the court that the limit is justified.[52] A great deal of confusion has been created about the operation of these provisions resulting from a 3:3 split in the High Court's interpretation of the *Charter* provisions on an appeal (in a decision that Boughey describes as a 'train wreck').[53]

A particularly pertinent example of a limitation in the prison context is the need to maintain security.[54] This potential limitation was clear in Queensland. The Bill that led to the *QHRA* also made amendments to the Queensland corrections legislation to make it explicit that when taking into consideration the human rights protected by the *QHRA*, it is not a breach of the *QHRA* for corrections managers to also consider 'the security and good management of corrective services facilities'.[55] This is an additional limitation that may be taken into account when interpreting the

---

45   *HRA* s 15; *Charter* s 16; *QHRA* s 22.

46   *HRA* s 14; *Charter* s 14; *QHRA* s 20.

47   *HRA* s 27; *Charter* s 19; *QHRA* s 27. The *QHRA* also provides protection of Aboriginal and Torres Strait Islander cultural rights in s 28.

48   *QHRA* s 37; *International Covenant on Economic, Social and Cultural Rights*, opened for signature 16 December 1966, 999 UNTS 3 (entered into force 3 January 1976) art 12.

49   For an overview of the differences between the Queensland and Victorian provisions see Bruce Chen, 'The *Human Rights Act 2019* (Qld): Some Perspectives from Victoria' (2020) 45(1) *Alternative Law Journal* 1, 2.

50   In accordance with the *HRA* s 28, *Charter* s 7 and *QHRA* s 13.

51   Christopher Tran, 'Facts and Evidence in Litigation Under the *Charter of Human Rights and Responsibilities Act 2006* (Vic) and the *Human Rights Act 2004* (ACT)' (2012) 36 *Melbourne University Law Review* 287, 289.

52   Ibid 309, 316.

53   The High Court's decision is *Momcilovic v The Queen* (2011) 280 ALR 221. Boughey, above n 34, 210. See discussion in Williams and Reynolds, above n 34, 79; Will Bateman and James Stellios, 'Chapter III of the Constitution, Federal Jurisdiction and Dialogue Charters of Rights' (2012) 36 *Melbourne University Law Review* 1.

54   Naylor, above n 14, 414.

55   *QHRA* s 126 inserting new section 5A into the *Corrective Services Act 2006* (Qld).

rights protected in the *QHRA* and poses a serious limitation to the right to humane treatment, particularly when deprived of liberty under s 30. Chen surmises that it may have the effect of exempting prison managers from the obligation to comply with this right, representing a 'marked abdication of human rights responsibilities in closed environments'.[56] He further notes that this concern was raised during the inquiry about the provisions of the Bill, but given that no change was made to the proposed provision, its operation will need to be considered as part of the first review of the *QHRA*.[57]

Corrections legislation is replete with examples of situations where rights can be overridden by security concerns, such as provisions to deny or terminate visits for security reasons,[58] provisions to keep a person in solitary confinement for security purposes,[59] and limitation or denial of access to religious or cultural services if they would 'undermine security or good order at a correctional centre'.[60] As Owers points out, emphasis on security is a legitimate concern for prison managers. However, the danger is that 'security can come to have the quality of the parental "because I say so"; the trump card, the excuse rather than the reason'.[61] Thus, there is a need to balance the competing concerns of maintaining security and ensuring limitations on the human rights of imprisoned people are reasonable and demonstrably justified. Every occasion of such a balancing exercise must be articulated according to the legislative criteria in an open and transparent way.

Legislative Scrutiny Provisions

Since the *HRA* and *Charter* have been in operation, new legislation introduced into Parliament has been subject to a two-stage scrutiny process. The *QHRA* introduces a similar scrutiny process. The first stage is for the Bill to be accompanied by a statement of compatibility with human rights when it is introduced into the relevant Parliament.[62]

---

56 Chen, above n 49, 6.
57 Ibid 6–7.
58 *Corrections Act 1986* (Vic) s 43.
59 *Correctional Services Act 1982* (SA) s 36(2)(d).
60 *Corrections Management Act 2007* (ACT) s 55(3)(a) ('*CMA*').
61 Anne Owers, 'Prison Inspection and the Protection of Human Rights' (2004) 2 *European Human Rights Law Review* 107, 109.
62 *HRA* s 37; *Charter* s 28; *QHRA* s 38. Note that the *Charter* requirement applies to any member of Parliament introducing a Bill, whereas the *HRA* requirement only applies to Bills introduced by a Minister and requires the Attorney-General to prepare the compatibility statement.

This process is intended to ensure that human rights are at the forefront of policymakers' and politicians' minds when new legislation is being developed and enacted.

In the context of the *Charter*, Debeljak has described how this fits into the dialogue model as follows: '[s]ection 28 statements allow the executive to identify *its* understanding of the open-textured rights because an assessment of whether a right is limited by legislation contains information about the executive's assessment of the scope of the right'.[63] Victorian statements of compatibility have been observed to be of variable quality.[64] Also, in the context of Victoria, Debeljak has noted that the statements may simply note an incompatibility without detailing what this is (such as which right is infringed or limited, and how).[65] Thus, this mechanism does not stop rights-infringing legislation from being introduced and passed. What it does do is make this occurrence slightly more transparent.

The second stage is for the Bill to be considered by a parliamentary committee that provides a report to Parliament about any human rights issues it may raise.[66] In the ACT, it is the relevant standing committee of the Legislative Assembly that provides Scrutiny Reports. In Victoria, it is a specialised scrutiny committee—the Scrutiny of Acts and Regulations Committee (SARC)—that produces reports in an Alerts Digest. In Queensland, similar to the ACT, Bills will be referred to '[t]he portfolio committee', rather than a standalone scrutiny committee.[67]

---

63   Julie Debeljak, 'Parliamentary Sovereignty and Dialogue Under the Victorian *Charter of Human Rights and Responsibilities*: Drawing the Line Between Judicial Interpretation and Judicial Law-Making' (2007) 33(1) *Monash University Law Review* 9, 28 (emphasis in original).
64   Boughey, above n 34, 222.
65   Julie Debeljak, 'Rights Dialogue Under the Victorian Charter: The Potential and the Pitfalls' in Ron Levy et al (eds), *New Directions for Law in Australia: Essays in Contemporary Law Reform* (ANU Press, 2017) 415. For a detailed discussion of statements of compatibility in Victoria see Chris Humphreys, Jessica Cleaver and Catherine Roberts, 'Considering Human Rights in the Development of Legislation in Victoria' in Julie Debeljak and Laura Grenfell (eds), *Law Making and Human Rights: Executive and Parliamentary Scrutiny Across Australian Jurisdictions* (Lawbook Co, 2020).
66   *Charter* s 30; *HRA* s 38; *QHRA* s 39. There is also a Commonwealth scrutiny committee (the Joint Committee on Human Rights), but this is not discussed here because states and territories are responsible for legislation governing imprisonment. For information about the operation of the Commonwealth committee see Fletcher, above n 6.
67   *QHRA* s 39. For a discussion of scrutiny in Queensland prior to the passage of the *QHRA* see Charles Sampford, 'Queensland Scrutiny in Context' in Julie Debeljak and Laura Grenfell (eds), *Law Making and Human Rights: Executive and Parliamentary Scrutiny Across Australian Jurisdictions* (Lawbook Co, 2020).

This also fits into the dialogue model. To again cite Debeljak, in relation to Victoria, 'the SARC report, the parliamentary debate, and the final legislation similarly indicate to the executive and the judiciary what *parliament's* understanding of the rights are, whether the legislation limits rights, and whether the limits are justified under s 7(2)'.[68]

This mechanism sounds better on paper as a rights-protection mechanism than it is in practice, particularly in Victoria. There have been examples of Victorian Bills where debate has concluded before the SARC has prepared a report.[69] This occurs in a context where the SARC is also generally unable to report on all of the Bills in the timeframe it is given (two weeks or less).[70] The frequency of references to SARC reports in parliamentary debates has declined over the years that the *Charter* has been in operation.[71] Even when the SARC does produce a report raising human rights concerns about a Bill this, in the words of a Chair of the SARC, 'has had little influence over the content of legislation'.[72]

The impact of legislative scrutiny in the ACT has been better. In 2014, there were 100 amendments to Bills in response to Committee reports.[73] One example of an ACT Bill that was amended as a result of this scrutiny process is summarised as follows:

> In 2008, for example, the Scrutiny of Bills Committee made comments in relation to the ACT Civil and Administrative Tribunal Bill recommending that the Bill be amended to include notes explicitly preserving the privilege against self-incrimination in the new Tribunal. The government agreed to the amendment.[74]

---

68 Debeljak, above n 10, 66.
69 Debeljak, above n 65, 411.
70 Ibid 415. See also George Williams and Daniel Reynolds, 'A Human Rights Act for Queensland? Lessons From Recent Australian Experience' (2016) 41(2) *Alternative Law Journal* 81, 83 and the case studies provided in Sharon Mo, 'Parliamentary Deliberation in the Operation of the Victorian Human Rights Charter' in Julie Debeljak and Laura Grenfell (eds), *Law Making and Human Rights: Executive and Parliamentary Scrutiny Across Australian Jurisdictions* (Lawbook Co, 2020).
71 Boughey, above n 34, 222–3.
72 Carlo Carli MP, cited by Debeljak, above n 65, 415.
73 Williams and Reynolds, above n 70, 84.
74 Helen Watchirs and Gabrielle McKinnon, 'Five Years' Experience with the *Human Rights Act 2004* (ACT): Insights for Human Rights Protection in Australia' (2010) 33(1) *UNSW Law Journal* 136, 144.

From 2015–2018, there have been amendments to seven ACT Bills in response to the Scrutiny Committee's recommendations and it has been noted that the 'unicameral Assembly, with its preponderance of minority governments' may explain why the ACT's scrutiny process has been more successful than Victoria's.[75]

Interpretation and Declaration of Incompatibility Powers of the Courts

Another way the legislation protects human rights is by requiring that the court interpret all laws in a manner that is compatible with human rights 'as far as it is possible to do so' consistently with their purpose.[76] This provision applies even when there is no ambiguity about the relevant provision, and applies to all legislation, rather than just legislation impacting the relationship between government and individuals.[77] All of the Acts allow the court to refer to international law and the judgments of international courts when conducting this interpretation.[78]

The interpretation of legislation in a rights-compatible manner may provide a remedy in some instances—'that is, a rights-compatible interpretation of a law is a complete remedy for a person whose rights would have otherwise been violated had the law been interpreted rights-*in*compatibly'.[79] However, there have been several instances in Victoria where a court has adopted a rights-compatible interpretation of legislation and the legislature has then responded by amending the legislature to ensure this

---

75   Helen Watchirs, Sean Costello and Renuka Thilagaratnam, 'Human Rights Scrutiny Under the Human Rights Act 2004 (ACT)' in Julie Debeljak and Laura Grenfell (eds), *Law Making and Human Rights: Executive and Parliamentary Scrutiny Across Australian Jurisdictions* (Lawbook Co, 2020) 186. On the role of the ACT Committee generally see their discussion from 183–6.

76   *HRA* s 30; *Charter* s 32; *QHRA* s 48.

77   Simon Evans and Carolyn Evans, 'Legal Redress Under the Victorian Charter of Human Rights and Responsibilities' (2006) 17 *Public Law Review* 264, 267, 269.

78   *HRA* s 31; *Charter* s 32(2); *QHRA* s 48(3).

79   Debeljak, above n 10, 65 (emphasis in original). In relation to the *Charter*, Boughey has observed that '[i]n the early years of the *Charter*, there was a view among some judges and scholars that s 32 permitted courts to adopt a "remedial" approach to interpreting legislation', similar to the UK. However, Boughey goes on to explain that since the High Court's decision in *Momcilovic v The Queen* (2011) 245 CLR 1, 'Victorian courts have taken the view that s 32 simply codifies the common law principle known in Australia as the "principle of legality" and extends its application to a wider range of rights': Boughey, above n 34, 210.

rights-compatible interpretation is not possible in future.[80] Such changes show the limitations of a rights-compatible interpretation—they may be precluded by a 'rights-incompatible' statutory amendment.

If it is not possible for the court to interpret the law in a manner compatible with human rights, the court has the power to make a declaration of 'incompatibility' (ACT and Queensland[81]) or 'inconsistent interpretation' (Victoria).[82] Such a declaration does not affect the validity or operation of the legislation in any jurisdiction.[83] Debeljak explains that it is 'simply a warning to the executive and parliament that legislation is inconsistent with the *judiciary's understanding* of the protected rights'.[84] It is up to the responsible Minister in Victoria and Queensland, and the Attorney-General in the ACT, to respond to the declaration in Parliament.[85] In all three jurisdictions, there is a six-month timeframe imposed for such a response.[86]

Declarations complete the dialogue between the three arms of government. The Judiciary makes its interpretation clear, and the Executive and Parliament are then required to respond to this interpretation, although such a response may not necessarily be a change to the law.[87] The response may be to defend the existing legislative provisions, despite the Judiciary's declaration that they are inconsistent with human rights.

There has only been one declaration made in the ACT and Victoria to date.[88] The Victorian declaration was the subject of a High Court appeal that has created uncertainty about how courts should use these provisions, leading Williams and Reynolds (writing before the introduction of the Queensland legislation) to argue that if Queensland goes ahead with the

---

80 Debeljak gives two illustrations of this, one of which is the interpretation of the *Serious Sex Offender Monitoring Act 2005* (Vic) in *RJE v Secretary to the Department of Justice* [2008] VSCA 265 that was overturned by amendments passed in the next sitting of Parliament. See Debeljak, above n 65, 409–10.
81 *HRA* s 32; *QHRA* s 53.
82 *Charter* s 36. The interpretation of this provision is somewhat unclear since the High Court decision in *Momcilovic v The Queen* (2011) 280 ALR 221, where the court was split as to whether a 'weaker' or 'stronger' remedial approach was to be taken: Debeljak, above n 10, 66.
83 *HRA* s 32(3); *Charter* s 36(5); *QHRA* s 54.
84 Debeljak, above n 10, 64 (emphasis in original).
85 *HRA* s33; *Charter* s 37; *QHRA* s 56.
86 *HRA* s 33; *Charter* s 37; *QHRA* s 56(1).
87 Debeljak, above n 10, 67.
88 Williams and Reynolds, above n 70, 82. For a discussion of the ACT declaration made *In the Matter of an Application for Bail by Isa Islam* [2010] ACTSC 147 see Watchirs, Costello and Thilagaratnam, above n 75, 192–3.

introduction of human rights legislation, they should adopt a different legislative provision for this purpose.[89] The Queensland interpretative provision is worded slightly differently to the Victorian one considered by the High Court, but it remains unclear whether these small differences will lead Queensland courts to adopt a different approach.[90]

Duties Imposed on Public Authorities

The final way the legislation provides protection of human rights is by imposing a duty on public authorities/entities. 'Public authorities' are defined by the ACT and Victorian Acts to include the police, government ministers and public officials (among others).[91] This definition clearly covers the Alexander Maconochie Centre (AMC) as a publicly run prison, as well as Victorian public prisons. It is a more complicated position for the three privately managed prisons in Victoria.[92] In addition to purely public bodies, the *Charter* applies to private entities that carry out public functions. Section 4 gives a privately managed prison as an example of an entity that is considered to carry out 'correctional services', and this is generally considered to be a government function. Therefore, Victoria's private prisons are also considered public authorities for the purposes of the *Charter*. However, they only have human rights obligations when carrying out their public functions.

The *QHRA* uses the term 'public entity', rather than 'authority', which is defined to include entities carrying out 'functions of a public nature' and, therefore, includes public prisons.[93] Privately managed prisons come within the meaning of what is described in the explanatory notes to the Human Rights Bill 2018 as a 'functional public entity'.[94] The *QHRA* lists operating a 'correctional services facility' as a public function,[95] then the explanatory statement helpfully clarifies that 'a private company managing a prison' is an example of such a public entity.[96]

---

89   Williams and Reynolds, above n 70, 84. The High Court decision was *Momcilovic v The Queen* (2011) 245 CLR 1.
90   The wording of the provision could have been improved further: see the discussion by Williams and Reynolds, above n 70, 85. For a discussion of the differences between the *Charter* and *QHRA* interpretive provisions see Chen, above n 49, 3–5.
91   *HRA* s 40; *Charter* s 4.
92   Fulham Correctional Centre, Port Phillip Prison and Ravenhall Correctional Centre.
93   *QHRA* s 9(1)(h).
94   This refers to s 10 of the *QHRA* that concerns entities that are carrying out functions that are 'of a public nature'.
95   *QHRA* s 10(3)(a).
96   Explanatory Notes, Human Rights Bill 2018, 15.

The duty imposed on public authorities/entities has two components. First, it is unlawful for public authorities/entities to act or decide inconsistently with the human rights protected by the legislation. Second, when making decisions, 'proper consideration' must be given to these rights.[97] These may be described as the 'substantive' and 'procedural' obligations, respectively.[98] The introduction of these requirements led Victoria to conduct an audit of policies to ensure rights consistency with *Charter* rights in Victoria prior to the commencement of the *Charter*.[99]

There is an exemption to this duty in all three Acts for situations where it is not possible for the public authority to have made a different decision or acted in a different way.[100] This would occur where, for example, the legislation is not compatible with human rights.[101]

If an imprisoned person considers that a prison authority has breached their human rights obligations as a public authority/entity, the remedy available is different in the ACT on the one hand, and in Victoria and Queensland on the other. In the ACT, the person may bring an action in the Supreme Court directly—the breach being a breach of a statutory duty, and the *HRA* being the statute so breached (s 40C(2)). In the first application made to the Supreme Court under s 40C of the *HRA*, the Court developed seven questions that need to be considered when an application is made under the provision.[102] These questions surround identifying the act or decision, identifying the human right, assessing whether the entity is a public authority, assessing whether the act or decision is inconsistent with the right, determining if there is a limitation and whether it is reasonable and demonstrably justifiable, assessing whether the decision-maker gave enough consideration to the right, and assessing whether there is a discretion that may be exercised consistently with the right.[103]

---

97   *HRA* s 40B; *Charter* s 38; *QHRA* s 58.
98   Explanatory Notes, Human Rights Bill 2018, 34.
99   The audit is detailed in Victorian Government, Submission 324 to Scrutiny of Acts and Regulations Committee, *Review of the Charter of Human Rights and Responsibilities Act 2006*, 2011, [7]–[17].
100 *HRA* s 40B(2); *Charter* s 38(2); *QHRA* s 58(2).
101 There are exceptions provided for religious bodies in Victoria and Queensland, which is not relevant to this discussion: *Charter* s 38(1); *QHRA* s 58(3).
102 *Hakimi v Legal Aid Commission (ACT)* (2009) ACTLR 127.
103 Ibid [137].

The ACT Supreme Court can grant any type of relief with the exception of damages.[104] It has been argued that the unavailability of damages has limited litigation to enforce the duties imposed on public authorities, because it 'removes an incentive for private law firms to take on human rights cases for impecunious litigants on a pro bono or "no win, no fee basis"'.[105]

In Victoria and Queensland, an action can only be brought if the person has another cause of action.[106] The human rights claim must be linked to that other cause of action, in tort law for example, or for judicial review of an administrative decision.[107] Both Acts specifically provide that damages cannot be awarded for a breach of human rights; however, damages may be available for the other cause of action to which the human rights claim is attached.[108]

The requirement to attach a claim to another cause of action has been described as 'convoluted and counter-productive'.[109] When the Queensland Bill was under consideration, human rights experts strongly recommended that Queensland follow the ACT approach of providing a standalone cause of action, rather than the much more convoluted Victorian approach.[110] Queensland did not follow this advice and Chen argues that this is a 'missed opportunity' and that '[l]itigants will undoubtedly be similarly hamstrung in their ability to obtain an effective relief or remedy for a breach of the Qld HRA in court and tribunal proceedings'.[111] The requirement to attach the human rights claim to another cause of action adds an additional hurdle to imprisoned people

---

104 *HRA* s 40C(4).
105 Watchirs and McKinnon, above n 74, 158–9.
106 *Charter* s 39(1); *QHRA* s 59(1).
107 In relation to the *Charter* see Julie Debeljak, 'Human Rights Responsibilities of Public Authorities Under the *Charter* of Rights' (Paper presented at the Law Institute of Victoria *Charter* of Rights Conference, Melbourne, 18 May 2007) 12. The second example is mentioned in s 39(2) of the *Charter*.
108 *Charter* s 39(3); *QHRA* ss 59(3), 59(6). In relation to the *Charter* see Bronwyn Naylor, Julie Debeljak and Anita Mackay, 'A Strategic Framework for Implementing Human Rights in Closed Environments' (2015) 41 *Monash University Law Review* 218, 240. Also in relation to the *Charter*, Boughey provides a number of references for the academic critique of s 39 and notes that is has been 'recommended that it be repealed or redrafted': Boughey, above n 34, 219.
109 Williams and Reynolds, above n 70, 83.
110 Ibid. Submissions were made recommending that the Queensland Civil and Administrative Tribunal have jurisdiction under the *QHRA*: Louis Schetzer, 'Queensland's Human Rights Act: Perhaps Not Such a Great Step Forward' (2020) (Advance) *Alternative Law Journal* 1, 4.
111 Chen, above n 49, 7–8.

who already face numerous barriers to taking legal action (including, getting legal representation and practical facilities such as computers to access online legal materials).[112]

The Victorian Supreme Court, like its ACT counterpart, has also developed a guide for assessing whether a public authority has given proper consideration to *Charter* rights (which Dixon J refers to as a 'road map').[113] There are five questions, including whether there is a relevant human right, whether it has been limited, if the limit is reasonable and whether proper consideration was given to the right.[114]

Finally, it is worth noting that the courts' interpretive power interacts with the obligation of public authorities. For example, if a public authority claims the s 38(2) exception under the *Charter*, s 32 of the *Charter* may operate as a remedy, as Debeljak explains:

> Once the law is given a rights-compatible interpretation, the potential violation of human rights will be avoided. The rights-compatible interpretation, in effect, becomes your remedy – the law is re-interpreted to be rights-compatible, the public authority has obligations under s 38(1), and the s 38(2) exceptions to unlawfulness do not apply.[115]

Judicial Interpretation

Chapter 3 analysed some of the claims brought by imprisoned people under the *Charter* and *HRA* and concluded these claims met limited success. In summary, the general position is that, irrespective of human rights legislation, judges are reluctant to interfere with the discretion of corrections administrators. More specifically, where human rights are afforded by legislation, in some cases people have been unable to prove their claims. For example, in several ACT cases brought by Mr Islam and Mr Eastman in reliance on a variety of rights protected by the *HRA*,

---

112 Naylor, Debeljak and Mackay, above n 108, 240. See the detailed discussion of cases concerning access to computers from a variety of jurisdictions in Carolyn McKay, 'Digital Access to Justice from Prison: Is There a Right to Technology?' (2018) 42 *Criminal Law Journal* 303.

113 These were submitted by the Victorian Equal Opportunity and Human Rights Commission as intervener, and accepted by the Court in *Certain Children v Minister for Families and Children & Ors* (No 2) [2017] VSC 251 [174], and Dixon J referred to them as a 'road map' in *Minogue v Dougherty* [2017] VSC 724 [74].

114 *Minogue v Dougherty* [2017] VSC 724 [74].

115 Debeljak, above n 107, 19.

the ACT Supreme Court either found that the conduct could not be proven to have occurred, or did not accept that the conduct amounted to breaches of the *HRA*.[116]

In Victoria, Ms Castles did get the outcome she wanted (that is, an order that she was entitled to in-vitro fertilisation (IVF) treatment), but the rights provided for in the *Charter* were not determinative of that outcome.[117] Mr Minogue and Mr Haigh both successfully showed that their *Charter* rights had been breached when a book addressed to Mr Minogue was returned to sender and when Mr Haigh was denied certain Tarot cards that he required for the practice of his religion. Both cases were notable for admissions by the relevant decision-makers in the prison that they had failed to consider *Charter* rights when making the particular decisions.[118] There were other cases where *Charter* claims could have been made but were not.[119]

Summary

The enforcement mechanisms under the *Charter* and *QHRA*, and to a lesser extent the *HRA*, provide a relatively weak protection of human rights. For instance, it is entirely possible for rights to be limited in the initial drafting stages and justified throughout the scrutiny process. If a court reaches a rights-compatible interpretation, the legislature may quickly amend the legislation to clarify that they intended it to be rights incompatible. Even if the Judiciary holds that the legislation is incompatible with human rights, the Parliament may respond that such incompatibility is justified, willing to risk the political consequences this may entail.

Further, in Victoria and Queensland, a breach of duty by public authorities/entities cannot give rise to an independent cause of action and it may be difficult to reach the threshold for other causes of action to

---

116 *Islam v Director-General of the Department of Justice and Community Safety Directorate* [2018] ACTSC 322; *Islam v Director-General Justice and Community Safety Directorate (No 3)* [2016] ACTSC 27 (25 February 2016); *Islam v Director-General, Justice and Community Safety Directorate* [2015] ACTCA 60 (16 December 2015); *Eastman v Chief Executive of the Department of Justice and Community Safety* [2011] ACTSC 33 (4 March 2011); *David Harold Eastman v Chief Executive Officer of the Department of Justice and Community Safety* [2010] ACTSC 4 (12 January 2010).
117 *Castles v Secretary to the Department of Justice* [2010] VSC 310 (9 July 2010).
118 *Minogue v Dougherty* [2017] VSC 724 [36], [83], [85]; *Haigh v Ryan* [2018] VSC 474 [68]–[69].
119 *Collins v The Queen* [2012] VSCA 163; *DPP v Foster & Ors* [2014] VCC 312; *Weaven v Secretary, Department of Justice* [2012] VSC 582. See further Julie Debeljak, 'The Rights of Prisoners Under the Victorian Charter: A Critical Analysis of the Jurisprudence on the Treatment of Prisoners and Conditions of Detention' (2015) 38(4) *University of New South Wales Law Journal* 1332.

which a *Charter* or *QHRA* claim may be added. Accordingly, the *Charter* has not generated very much prison-related litigation.[120] While it is easier to bring an action under the *HRA*, imprisoned people face substantial barriers to litigating and the litigation to date has not led to substantive rights enforcement. It remains to be seen how the *QHRA* will be relied upon in litigation and interpreted by courts.

Corrections Legislation

In Victoria, Tasmania and the ACT, corrections legislation affords imprisoned people additional rights. The ACT provisions are far more detailed than the Victorian and Tasmanian provisions. This is because the ACT corrections legislation was introduced after the *HRA* was in operation, whereas the Victorian corrections legislation is from 1986 and has not been updated since the introduction of the *Charter*.[121] The Tasmanian Corrections legislation will be discussed in the same section as Victoria because the rights contained therein (introduced in 1997) were modelled on the Victorian provisions. The corrections legislation of other Australian jurisdictions is then discussed, and it will be seen that rights protection is scant, entirely lacking or, in fact, rights infringing.

Corrections Management Act 2007 (ACT)

Despite the fact that the *HRA* does not incorporate art 10(3) of the ICCPR, there are a number of provisions in the *Corrections Management Act 2007* (ACT) (*CMA*) stating that the goal of the AMC is to rehabilitate people. Section 7(d) provides that an object of the *CMA* is 'promoting the rehabilitation of offenders and their reintegration into society'. Section 9(f) of the *CMA*, which is about the treatment of detainees generally, provides that '[f]unctions under this Act in relation to a detainee must be exercised as follows ... (f) if the detainee is an offender—to promote, as far as practicable, the detainee's rehabilitation and reintegration into society'. There is a further reference to rehabilitation in s 52 of the *CMA* concerning case management plans. As detailed elsewhere, the intention behind the ACT building a prison was rehabilitation focused.[122]

---

120 Matthew Groves, 'Prisoners and the Victorian Charter' (2010) 34 *Criminal Law Journal* 217, 217.
121 The *CMA* commenced on 1 August 2007; *Corrections Act 1986* (Vic).
122 Anita Mackay, 'The Road to the ACT's First Prison (the Alexander Maconochie Centre) was Paved with Rehabilitative Intentions' (2012) 11(1) *Canberra Law Review* 33.

The objects of the *CMA* include a requirement that functions under the Act be exercised in a manner that ensures prison management 'respect and protect the detainee's human rights' (s 9(a)), and promote 'the detainee's rehabilitation and reintegration into society' (s 9(f)). The objects also reinforce the provisions in the *HRA* about treating people in a humane and respectful way (in accordance with art 10(1) of the ICCPR). Section 7(c) provides that one object of the Act is 'ensuring that detainees are treated in a decent, humane and just way'.

There are some provisions prohibiting TCID that operate at the overarching level. For example, s 9(c) (concerning the treatment of detainees generally) provides that '[f]unctions under this Act in relation to a detainee must be exercised … to preclude torture or cruel, inhuman or degrading treatment'.

Section 12 prescribes the minimum living conditions for detainees that the Director-General 'must ensure, as far as practicable'.[123] Examples include 'suitable accommodation and bedding for sleeping in reasonable privacy and comfort';[124] 'reasonable access to the open air and exercise' (at least one hour per day);[125] reasonable opportunity to have visitors;[126] confidential communication with a lawyer;[127] access to health services;[128] and opportunities for religious, spiritual and cultural observance.[129]

The *CMA* makes a distinction between these minimum living conditions on the one hand, and privileges on the other. Section 154 of the *CMA* defines 'privileges' as 'any amenity, facility or opportunity the detainee may have the benefit of in detention'. That provision also gives examples that include 'participating in activities other than those forming part of a detainee's case management plan' and 'pursuing hobbies and crafts'. The importance of this distinction is that privileges can be removed for disciplinary purposes. They may be withdrawn if, for example, an imprisoned person has committed a disciplinary breach,

---

123 This section is to be read in conjunction with Chapter 6 of the *CMA*, which imposes concomitant requirements on the Director-General.
124 *CMA* ss 12(d), 43.
125 Ibid ss 12(e), 45.
126 Ibid ss 12(g), 49.
127 Ibid ss 12(h), 50, 51.
128 Ibid ss 12(j), 53, 54.
129 Ibid ss 12(k), 55.

such as assaulting someone.[130] The living conditions, on the other hand, are designated as 'entitlements'.[131] These cannot be removed for disciplinary purposes.

Significantly, the *CMA* requires that imprisoned people be provided with medical care of an equivalent standard to people in the community.[132] This is in accordance with Principle 9 of the United Nations Basic Principles which provides that '[p]risoners shall have access to the health services available in the country without discrimination on the grounds of their legal situation'.[133]

These provisions are comprehensive and the ACT has the most rights-compliant corrections legislation in Australia. However, there is no enforcement mechanism for failure to comply with them. For this reason, the few cases that have been brought since the AMC commenced operations have instead relied upon the right to bring a case before the Supreme Court under s 40C(2) of the *HRA*. When this has occurred, and the Supreme Court has had to consider the interaction between a right protected by the *HRA* and the provisions of the *CMA*, it has sometimes led to a narrow interpretation of the right. For example, in one case the Supreme Court held that the interference with the applicant's right to privacy was not 'arbitrary' because it was conducted in accordance with the search and seizure provisions contained in the *CMA*.[134] This is an illustration of security concerns limiting a right.

Victorian and Tasmanian Corrections Acts

The Victorian and Tasmanian corrections legislation both afford imprisoned people a number of rights.[135] The Victorian provisions were considered progressive when they were introduced in 1986, and in 1991

---

130 'Disciplinary breach' is defined in s 152 of ibid.

131 Ibid s 154.

132 Ibid s 53(1)(a).

133 See also Rule 24 of the United Nations *Standard Minimum Rules for the Treatment of Prisoners* (the Nelson Mandela Rules), UN Doc A/RES/70/175 (17 December 2015) ('the Mandela Rules').

134 *R v Cringle* [2013] ACTSC 34 (5 March 2013). Another example is *Miles v Director-General of the Justice and Community Safety Directorate* [2016] ACTSC 70 where the Court was asked to determine the 'adequacy' of contact between Mr Miles and another person detained in the AMC (referred to as CU) where CU was Mr Miles' chosen 'advisor' under s 22(2)(b) of the *HRA* (the right to 'communicate with lawyers or advisors chosen by him or her' when preparing a defence to criminal charges). The Court held that it would not interfere with the AMC management's decision that contact by mail was 'adequate': at [40]–[41].

135 *Corrections Act 1986* (Vic) s 47; *Corrections Act 1997* (Tas) s 29.

the Royal Commission into Aboriginal Deaths in Custody recommended that similar provisions be introduced at the national level.[136] Only Tasmania followed suit, in 1997.

The rights contained in both of these Acts include:

- the right to reasonable access to the open air and exercise (at least one hour per day)[137]
- opportunity to communicate with, and receive visits from, family members and friends[138]
- access to medical treatment and health care[139]
- opportunity to communicate with lawyers and complaints handling bodies such as human rights commissions, Official Visitors and Ombudsmen,[140] and in Tasmania more recently, the Custodial Inspector.[141]

Some of these rights do align with some international human rights law protections. For example, the rights to communication with family members and to correspond with family members and lawyers and complaint handling bodies. These are consistent with art 17 of the ICCPR which prohibits 'arbitrary interference' with 'privacy, family, home or correspondence', and art 14(3)(b) of the ICCPR which protects the right of persons 'charged with a criminal offence' '[t]o communicate with counsel of his [sic] own choosing'. However, the absence of the prohibition of TCID and the requirement that imprisoned people be treated with humanity and respect is significant.

In theory, these rights offer useful protections. However, in practice, there are at least two problems with them, aptly summed up by Groves: '[t]he imprecise nature of the rights contained in these statutory charters, coupled with the absence of any means by which those rights may be enforced, detracts significantly from their value for prisoners'.[142]

---

136 Groves, above n 27, 192.
137 *Corrections Act 1986* (Vic) s 47(1)(a); *Corrections Act 1997* (Tas) s 29(1)(a).
138 *Corrections Act 1986* (Vic) ss 47(1)(k), 37; *Corrections Act 1997* (Tas) ss 29(1)(j), 29(1)(k), 29(1)(m). This is consistent with the protection of families provided for by s 17 of the *Charter* and the right to privacy provided for by s 13 of the *Charter*.
139 *Corrections Act 1986* (Vic) s 47(1)(f); *Corrections Act 1997* (Tas) s 29(1)(f).
140 *Corrections Act 1986* (Vic) ss 47(1)(j), 47(1)(m), 40; *Corrections Act 1997* (Tas) ss 29(1)(l), 29(1)(o).
141 *Corrections Act 1997* (Tas) s 29(1)(l).
142 Groves, above n 27, 194.

First, the 'imprecise' nature of the rights and other limitations of the way they are drafted. Some are vague, such as, the 'right to take part in educational programmes' contained in s 47(1)(o) of the Victorian Act. Naylor has noted that this does not provide any 'detail about the standard of programme, or the regularity or quality of teaching'.[143] Others are contingent on certain preconditions—such as (in s 29(1)(a) of the Tasmanian Act), 'the right to be in the open air for at least an hour each day *if the facilities of the prison are suitable* for allowing the prisoner or detainee to be in the open air'.[144] Others leave it up to management to determine whether the right is available, with security representing a 'trump card'.[145] An example is 'the right to practise a religion of the prisoner's choice and, *if consistent with prison security and good prison management* to join with other prisoners in practising that religion and to possess such articles as are necessary for the practice of that religion'.[146] These are all ways in which the protections are weakened.

Second, there is the lack of an enforcement mechanism, or provision for remedies should they be breached. Groves gives the example of the entitlement to food contained in s 47(1)(c) of the *Corrections Act 1986* (Vic), which provides 'the right to be provided with special dietary food where the Governor is satisfied that such food is necessary for medical reasons or on account of the prisoner's religious beliefs or because the prisoner is a vegetarian'. When Mr Weaven sought to rely on this provision because he was not being provided with an adequate yeast-free diet, the Judge opined, '[i]t is not my function, in any general sense, to adjudicate on the daily machinations of prison culture' and 'I am not satisfied that the Secretary is currently refusing to discharge her duty'.[147]

There have been only four successful cases relying on the provisions since their enactment in 1986 in Victoria and 1997 in Tasmania. These are the Tasmanian Supreme Court ruling concerning a breach of the right to be provided with information about rules governing behaviour under s 29(p) of the *Corrections Act 1997* (Tas),[148] and the Victorian Supreme Court decisions concerning (1) Ms Castles's entitlement to IVF treatment under s 47(1)(f)

---

143 Naylor, above n 14, 404.
144 Emphasis added.
145 Owers, above n 61, 109.
146 *Corrections Act 1986* (Vic), s 47(1)(i) (emphasis added).
147 *Weaven v Secretary, Department of Justice* [2012] VSC 582, [35], [36]. See Groves, above n 27, 194.
148 *Pickett v The State of Tasmania* [2011] TASSC 907 (20 April 2011). Section 29(p) protects 'the right to be provided with information about the rules and conditions which will govern the prisoner's or detainee's behaviour in custody'.

of the *Corrections Act 1986* (Vic), which provides a right to access medical care and treatment;[149] (2) the breach of Mr Minogue's right to receive mail under s 47(1)(n);[150] and (3) Mr Haigh's being denied access to certain Tarot cards he required to practise the Pagan religion under s 47(1)(i).[151] The latter two cases were unlikely to have succeeded without reliance on the *Charter* rights because they hinged on admissions by prison staff that they had failed to take into account *Charter* rights when making the decisions in question. All of these cases were discussed in detail in Chapter 3.

Corrections Legislation in Other Jurisdictions

There are limited references in corrections legislation to respectful treatment of imprisoned people as an object of the legislation. For example, s 3(3)(a) of the *Corrective Services Act 2006* (Qld) stipulates, '[t]his Act also recognises—the need to respect an offender's dignity'.

Corrections legislation in other jurisdictions does not provide imprisoned people with any rights. There are some examples of specific entitlements, such as:

- 'prisoners are entitled to receive and send letters' in South Australia[152]
- an entitlement to be visited every two weeks in South Australia[153]
- an entitlement to access legal aid in South Australia[154]
- an entitlement to private correspondence with organisations such as the Ombudsman and, in Western Australia, the Office of the Inspector of Custodial Services[155]
- in NSW, '[e]ach inmate (other than one who is confined to cell under s 53 or s 56 of the Act) is to be allowed at least 2 hours each day for exercise in the open air'.[156]

---

149 *Castles v Secretary to the Department of Justice* [2010] VSC 310 (9 July 2010). Section 47(1)(f) protects 'the right to have access to reasonable medical care and treatment necessary for the preservation of health'.

150 *Minogue v Dougherty* [2017] VSC 724. Section 47(1)(n) protects the 'right to send and receive other letters uncensored by prison staff'.

151 *Haigh v Ryan* [2018] VSC 474. Section 47(1)(i) provides 'the right to practise a religion of the prisoner's choice and, if consistent with prison security and good prison management to join with other prisoners in practising that religion and to possess such articles as are necessary for the practice of that religion'.

152 *Correctional Services Act 1982* (SA) s 33(1)(a).

153 Ibid s 34(1).

154 Ibid s 35.

155 *Prisons Act 1981* (WA) s 67.

156 *Crimes (Administration of Sentences) Regulations 2008* (NSW) Reg 50. This entitlement is somewhat weak given that it is found in regulations rather than an Act of Parliament.

There are also some examples of provisions that are expressed using the language 'may', which is a weak form of entitlement because it is quite easy for correctional administrators to deny these. For example, in the Northern Territory, '[a] prisoner may send and receive mail' or 'make and receive telephone calls', 'in accordance with the Commissioner's Directions'.[157]

The *Corrective Services Act 2006* (Qld) also contains as an object that entitlements should not be taken away, except to the extent necessitated by imprisonment. For example, 'an offender's entitlements, other than those that are necessarily diminished because of imprisonment or another court sentence, should be safeguarded'.[158]

In corrections legislation in some jurisdictions, not only do imprisoned people have no rights, they are specifically denied basic rights, such as the right to consent to medical treatment. For example, the *Corrective Services Act 2006* (Qld) s 21(1) provides that '[a] prisoner *must* submit to a medical examination or treatment by a doctor if the doctor considers the prisoner requires medical attention' (emphasis added). The section goes on to state, '[i]f a prisoner does not submit to an examination or treatment as required under this section, the doctor and anyone acting at the doctor's direction may use the force that is reasonably necessary to carry out the examination or treatment'.[159] Section 51 of the *Correctional Services Act* (NT) provides:

1. A prisoner *must* submit to a prescribed alcohol/drug test if directed by the General Manager to do so.

2. If the prisoner does not submit to the test as required under section 195(2):

   (a) the prescribed sampler may take the required sample *without the prisoner's consent*.[160]

---

157 *Correctional Services Act* (NT) ss 106(1), 104(1).

158 *Corrective Services Act 2006* (Qld) s 3(2). This echoes the 'residuum principle' recognised at common law by *Raymond v Honey* [1983] 1 AC 1, 10 (Lord Wilberforce).

159 *Corrective Services Act 2006* (Qld) s 21(8). See also the similar provision in Western Australia: *Prisons Act 1981* (WA) s 95D.

160 Emphasis added. See also *Crimes (Administration of Sentences) Act 1999* (NSW) s 73.

In summary, corrections legislation does not provide a source of rights outside the ACT, Victoria and Tasmania, and in these jurisdictions the rights have not (with limited exceptions) been enforceable in practice. Thus, the majority of jurisdictions have neither human rights legislation, nor enforceable rights in corrections legislation. In short, there is no effective legislative protection of human rights for imprisoned people.

Non-Legislative Regulation of Prisons

In addition to the human rights legislation in the ACT and Victoria and corrections legislation outlined above, there are two main types of non-legislative regulation of Australian prisons.

The first is the *Guiding Principles for Corrections in Australia* ('Guiding Principles') discussed in Chapter 2.[161] These operate at the national level, are non-binding and—despite being published after the United Nations updated the *Standard Minimum Rules for the Treatment of Prisoners* in 2015 (when they became known as the Mandela Rules)—are significantly out of alignment with the Mandela Rules.

The second is the inspection codes and standards used by the prison inspectorates in the states and territories with prison inspectorates discussed in Chapter 3. These operate in the ACT, WA, NSW and Tasmania. The ACT Standards are aligned with the Mandela Rules, but the other jurisdictions' inspection codes and standards all refer to the 1955 United Nations Rules, rather than the Mandela Rules.

Neither of these constitute domestic incorporation of the treaty obligations into *law*, as required by international law. They are unenforceable in court and generally provide a poor substitute for legislation. However, it will be seen in the state- and territory-based assessment of Australian law below that in some states and territories only these non-legislative regulations are in place.

---

161 Corrective Services Administrators' Conference (Cth), *Guiding Principles for Corrections in Australia* (2018).

Assessment of Alignment of Domestic Legislation with International Human Rights Law Obligations

As the above discussion suggests, there is considerable variation between jurisdictions in Australia in the extent to which their prison-relevant legislation meets international treaty obligations. These can be ranked from 'most aligned' to 'least aligned'. This process can suggest to individual jurisdictions both areas for improvement and models to draw from. Four broad areas for reform can also be identified.

State- and Territory-Based Assessment

The ACT's legislation governing the operations of the AMC is currently the most closely aligned with Australia's international obligations of all the jurisdictions. The *HRA* protects most of the relevant human rights (the only key ICCPR article it does not incorporate is the goal of imprisonment as rehabilitation) and provides people with direct access to the court when they consider a right has been breached.

The *CMA* is the most up to date corrections legislation in Australia and was passed pursuant to the *HRA*'s scrutiny requirements. The objects and overarching provisions of the *CMA* refer to rehabilitation, the right to humane and respectful treatment and the prohibition of TCID. The *CMA* also prescribes minimum living conditions, which is unique in Australian corrections legislation.

When considering the combined effect of the *HRA* and *CMA*, Bartels and Boland have concluded that '[t]ogether, they cover a lot of ground, and, in many respects, provide a template – if not the beginnings of an entirely new model – for the administrative and legal protection of prisoners' human rights'.[162] This is a conclusion to be endorsed.

As outlined in Chapter 3, the ACT has also recently established an Inspector of Correctional Services who published inspections standards in 2019 that align with the Mandela Rules and have taken into account

---

162 Lorana Bartels and Jeremy Boland, 'Human Rights and Prison. A Case Study from the Australian Capital Territory' in Leanne Weber et al (eds), *The Routledge International Handbook of Criminology and Human Rights* (Routledge, 2017) 560.

the OPCAT.[163] The Inspector may refer to the *Human Rights Principles for ACT Correctional Centres*, which provide some additional detail to that contained in the *HRA* and *CMA* that may assist the Inspector assessing compliance.[164] For example, s 53(1)(b) of the *CMA* requires that medical care be 'appropriate'. There are eight principles about health care that refer to matters such as access to an 'interdisciplinary health team', 'harm minimisation' for people going through drug withdrawal, 'Indigenous-specific health services' and appropriate health care for 'all detainees, including those who are female, transgender or intersex'.[165] This is a level of detail that may assist the inspector with assessing compliance with the provisions of the *CMA*, as will other principles.

The Inspector's reports to the Legislative Assembly are required to include 'an assessment about whether the rights under international and territory law of detainees at a correctional centre subject to review are protected'.[166] Therefore, the Inspector will be specifically required to assess compliance with the rights contained in the *HRA* and *CMA*.

Victoria is the next best jurisdiction for the legislative protection of the rights of imprisoned people. There are key rights protected by the *Charter*, including the prohibition of TCID and a requirement that people deprived of their liberty be treated humanely and with respect. The problem with the *Charter* is that claims for breaches of rights must be attached to other legal claims. The *Corrections Act 1986* (Vic) contains a number of rights, notwithstanding the limitations noted with their drafting and lack of enforceability.[167]

Queensland, having recently incorporated ICCPR rights into domestic legislation via the *QHRA*, ranks next. Importantly for OPCAT compliance, this includes the prohibition of TCID. It is also positive that it requires that people deprived of their liberty be treated humanely and with respect. How this may affect or assist imprisoned people in practice is another matter. The *QHRA* is likely to suffer the same problem as the *Charter* in relation to enforcement because there is no option to bring a standalone claim for its breach.

---

163 ACT Inspector of Correctional Services, *ACT Standards for Adult Correctional Services* (2019) 7. The Standards are required by the *Inspector of Correctional Services 2017* (ACT) s 20.
164 ACT Government, Justice and Community Safety, *Human Rights Principles for ACT Correctional Centres* (January 2019).
165 Principles 10.2, 10.5, 10.7 and 10.8 respectively: ibid 10.
166 *Inspector of Correctional Services 2017* (ACT) s 27(1)(c).
167 *Corrections Act 1986* (Vic) s 47.

Tasmania has a number of rights contained in the *Corrections Act 1997* (Tas).[168] Some of these align with rights contained in the ICCPR, but there is no prohibition of TCID in Tasmania, nor a requirement that people deprived of their liberty be treated humanely and with respect. These are very significant omissions. The rights contained in the *Corrections Act* have been relied upon once, successfully, with the Supreme Court making a ruling concerning a breach of the right to be provided with information about rules governing behaviour under s 29(p).[169]

Tasmania also has a new Custodial Inspector and the standards used for inspection of adult prisons that refer to the 1955 United Nations Rules (as detailed in Chapter 3).[170] Therefore, they need to be updated to reflect the changes introduced by the Mandela Rules.

Both WA and NSW have inspectors (both called the Inspector of Custodial Services). Both inspectors have standards that have the advantage of being specific to prisons and, similar to Tasmania, both refer to the 1955 United Nations Rules (as detailed in Chapter 3).[171] Therefore, these also need to be updated to reflect the changes introduced by the Mandela Rules. However, having human rights protections in non-binding inspection standards is insufficient to meet the prerequisite of *legislative* protection of human rights. Nevertheless, it is better than a complete absence of recognition of the existence of human rights.

Finally, there is the Northern Territory and South Australia. Both have corrections legislation only—legislation that cannot be said to provide rights protections. They also have the Guiding Principles, but these are non-binding and not aligned with the Mandela Rules. These jurisdictions need to seriously consider legislative reform to achieve compliance with this prerequisite.

---

168 *Corrections Act 1997* (Tas) s 29.

169 *Pickett v The State of Tasmania* [2011] TASSC 907 (20 April 2011).

170 Office of the Custodial Inspector Tasmania, *Inspection Standards for Adult Custodial Services in Tasmania* (2018).

171 Office of the Inspector of Custodial Services, *Code of Inspection Standards for Adult Custodial Services, Version 1* (19 April 2007); NSW Inspector of Custodial Services, *Inspection Standards for Adult Custodial Services in New South Wales* (2014).

Legislative and Regulatory Reform Options

It has been demonstrated that most Australian jurisdictions do not have legislation that aligns with the international human rights law obligations that apply to prisons. There are three options for addressing this. The first is to introduce a national Human Rights Act that prohibits TCID nationally. The second would be for the states and territories to individually introduce legislative human rights protections, either in specific human rights legislation for all people (in all jurisdictions other than the ACT, Victoria and Queensland), or as amendments to their corrections legislation, applying only to imprisoned people. Finally, the regulatory framework could be updated. This should be in addition to legislative amendment and would be where additional detail could be located.

A National Human Rights Act

A national Human Rights Act would implement an oft-made recommendation by United Nations treaty monitoring bodies. For example, the Human Rights Committee, in 'Concluding Observations' in December 2017 on Australia's periodic report, wrote, 'The Committee reiterates its recommendation (see CCPR/C/AUS/CO/5, para. 8) that the State party should adopt comprehensive federal legislation giving full legal effect to all Covenant provisions across all state and territory jurisdictions'.[172] While it should be recognised at the outset that a national Human Rights Act (assuming it was based on the *HRA/Charter* model) would not necessarily introduce a dialogue model in relation to prison legislation (because this is the responsibility of state and territory governments), it would clarify that TCID is prohibited nationally and protect the rights of imprisoned people consistently across all jurisdictions.

There has been consideration of introducing statutory human rights protection at the national level dating back to the 1970s and 1980s, with Bills introduced that did not pass.[173] More recently, the National Human Rights Consultation in 2009 found that 87 per cent of submissions supported a national Human Rights Act and recommended to the government that such an Act be adopted modelled on the *Charter* and

---

172 Human Rights Committee, *Concluding Observations on the Sixth Periodic Report of Australia*, UN Doc CCPR/C/AUS/CO/6 (1 December 2017) 2.
173 Williams and Reynolds, above n 70, 81.

HRA.[174] Despite this, the government did not accept the recommendation. Instead, on 21 April 2010, it released a Human Rights Framework with the centrepiece being the Joint Committee on Human Rights that scrutinises Commonwealth legislation.[175]

There has been no indication since that a national Act will be introduced. In a 2016 report to the Human Rights Committee, the Australian Government provided the following statement: 'Australia notes that there is no requirement for a single national law to implement the ICCPR and notes that this would be inappropriate for Australia's federal system of government'.[176] In 2018, Fletcher concluded that 'the prospects for an Australian Human Rights Act seem no brighter than in the past'.[177]

State and Territory Human Rights Acts

Tasmania is the only state currently giving any consideration to a state-based Human Rights Act, and even this is only in the form of a petition.[178]

There were consultation processes about human rights legislation conducted in both Tasmania and Western Australia in 2007.[179] Despite recommendations supporting human rights legislation in both cases, these processes were stalled while awaiting the outcome of the National Consultation, and were then shelved when the National Consultation failed to lead to the introduction of national-level human rights legislation. Fletcher notes that seven of the eight states and territories have considered human rights legislation since 1998, with only South Australia not having officially considered such legislation within that timeframe.[180]

---

174 National Human Rights Consultation, above n 7; Phillip Lynch, 'Australia's Human Rights Framework: Can There be Action Without Accountability?' in Paula Gerber and Melissa Castan (eds), *Contemporary Perspectives on Human Rights Law in Australia* (Lawbook Co, 2013) 20–1.

175 For discussion of the framework see Fletcher, above n 6, Chapter 2; Williams and Reynolds, above n 34, Chapter 5. For a discussion of the impact of this Committee see Fletcher, above n 6, Chapters 4 and 5.

176 Human Rights Committee, *Consideration of Reports Submitted by States Parties Under Article 40 of the Covenant Sixth Periodic Reports of States Parties Due in 2013 Australia*, UN Doc CCPR/C/AUS/6 (2 June 2016) 2.

177 Fletcher, above n 6, 53.

178 Tasmanian Human Rights Act Campaign, <https://www.tashumanrightsact.org/>.

179 Tasmania Law Reform Institute, *A Charter of Rights for Tasmania*, Report No 10 (2007) discussed by Rose Mackie and Anja Hilkemeijer, 'Tasmania: Time to Move Beyond the Smoke and Mirrors' in Julie Debeljak and Laura Grenfell (eds), *Law Making and Human Rights: Executive and Parliamentary Scrutiny Across Australian Jurisdictions* (Lawbook Co, 2020) 533; *A WA Human Rights Act: Report of the Consultation Committee for a Proposed WA Human Rights Act*, (2007). For a discussion of consideration of Human Rights Acts prior to this see Williams and Reynolds, above n 34, 66–7.

180 Fletcher, above n 6, 34.

There is no reason at this point in time to be optimistic that additional states and territories (beyond Victoria, the ACT and Queensland) will introduce Human Rights Acts.

Amending Corrections Legislation

Corrections legislation in many Australian jurisdictions dates from the 1980s and does not reflect Australia's international human rights obligations in relation to imprisoned people.[181] The exception is the *CMA*, which is the most recent corrections Act passed, having been passed in 2007. The *CMA* undoubtedly provides the best example of human rights–compliant corrections legislation in Australia. However, jurisdictions that do not have a Human Rights Act would need to carefully consider the connections between the *HRA* and *CMA* if they wished to pass a standalone corrections Act based on the *CMA*.

Updates to corrections legislation in the states and territories also seem unlikely in the foreseeable future. To take Victoria as an example, the *Charter* has been in operation for over a decade, yet the government has not shown any signs of updating the *Corrections Act 1986* (Vic) to ensure consistency with the *Charter*. This is because the majority of jurisdictions are pursuing a 'tough on crime' agenda, which is leading to longer prison sentences, overcrowded prison conditions (as outlined in Chapters 1 and 4) and, consequently, harsher prison conditions and exacerbation of the pains of imprisonment (also discussed in Chapter 1).[182] Introducing human rights protections in corrections legislation would counter these trends.

Updating the Regulatory Framework

Another option is for Australia to address non-legislative regulations to ensure that there are nation-wide standards. These could then be used by organisations comprising the NPM in conducting OPCAT inspections. This is also where a lot of the detail that cannot be included in legislation may be located.

---

181 For example, *Corrections Act 1986* (Vic), *Correctional Services Act 1982* (SA) and *Prisons Act 1981* (WA).

182 See, eg, Michelle McDonnell and James Farrell, 'Tough, Tougher, Toughest? A New Government's Approach to Sentencing Laws in Victoria' (2012) 37(3) *Alternative Law Journal* 238; Andrew Trotter and Harry Hobbs, 'The Great Leap Backward: Criminal Law Reform with the Hon Jarrod Bleijie' (2014) 36(1) *Sydney Law Review* 1. See also the discussion of sentencing law reforms in Chapter 4.

There are two ways of doing this. The first would be for Corrections Ministers to overhaul the Guiding Principles to properly align them with the 2015 Mandela Rules.[183] This seems unlikely, given that the Guiding Principles were updated recently (in 2018) and three years after the Mandela Rules.

The second is to introduce national-level prison inspection standards. The ACT Standards would provide a useful starting point for this because they are comprehensive and draw on the extensive experience of Her Majesty's Inspectorate of Prisons.

The latter may be preferable because Australia needs to ensure the NPM meets all of the six criteria stipulated in the OPCAT and, as noted in Chapter 3, one of those is regular visits with the aim of providing protection against TCID, requiring clear inspection standards.[184] The standards are also more detailed and practical in focus than the Guiding Principles; therefore, they have more scope for direct application.

Conclusion

The legislation governing the administration of prisons in Australia is predominantly out of alignment with Australia's international human rights law obligations. This means Australia is in breach of the Treaty obligation to incorporate human rights into domestic legislation.

There is one positive exception, the ACT, which has both statutory human rights protections (the *HRA*) and human rights–compliant corrections legislation (the *CMA*). This model is a useful one for other jurisdictions that wish to improve their legislation.

This is necessary to achieve this second prerequisite for human rights compliance in Australian prisons. It is significant for Australia's implementation of the OPCAT because TCID needs to be prohibited in domestic legislation. As it stands, only the ACT, Victoria and Queensland have done so.

---

183 See further Anita Mackay, 'Human rights guidance for Australian prisons: Complementing implementation of the OPCAT' (2020) (Online Advance) *Alternative Law Journal*.
184 OPCAT art 19(a).

This chapter has outlined several ways that Australia may achieve this prerequisite, including by introducing a national Human Rights Act; state and territory Human Rights Acts in all states and territories other than the ACT, Victoria and Queensland; and/or amendments to corrections legislation. These are not mutually exclusive. However, there is not much reason for optimism that any of these reform options will be pursued soon. The main reason for optimism is the ratification of the OPCAT, which will result in visits by the Subcommittee for the Prevention of Torture and Other Cruel, Inhuman or Degrading Treatment or Punishment (SPT), as well as the requirement for an NPM to conduct inspections using standards that prevent TCID.

Changes to legislation are also necessary to achieve other prerequisites put forward in this book. The prerequisite of shifting the focus of imprisonment to the goal of rehabilitation discussed in Chapter 6 will require legislative change in all jurisdictions, including the ACT, because the *HRA* does not incorporate art 10(3) of the ICCPR. Legislation should also mandate that prison staff treat people in a human rights–consistent manner (the fourth prerequisite, discussed in Chapter 7) and establish objective benchmarks for ensuring decent physical conditions in all prisons (the fifth prerequisite, discussed in Chapter 8).

It would be naïve to suggest that domestic legislative protection of the human rights of imprisoned people in Australia guarantees good prison conditions in practice. It is a necessary, but not sufficient, requirement for achieving human rights compliance. This is because, without legislating a commitment to protecting specific rights and supplementing this with detailed regulation, it is difficult to articulate how rights will be protected and enforced domestically.[185]

---

185 Naylor, Debeljak and Mackay include domestic legislation as part of the regulatory framework that forms one of the three pillars of the strategic framework for protecting human rights in closed environments: Naylor, Debeljak and Mackay, above n 108, 224–48. The other two pillars are external monitoring and culture change.

6

The Third Prerequisite: Shift the Focus of Imprisonment to the Goal of Rehabilitation and Restoration

Introduction

International human rights law requires the goal of the prison system to be 'rehabilitation and social reformation'. The full wording of art 10(3) of the *International Covenant on Civil and Political Rights* (ICCPR) is, '[t]he penitentiary system shall comprise treatment of prisoners the *essential aim* of which shall be their reformation and social rehabilitation' (emphasis added).[1] This obligation poses three problems, all of which need to be addressed if Australia is to comply with this requirement.

First, international human rights law provides inadequate guidance as to how the goal of rehabilitation and social reformation is to be achieved in practice. In the absence of more detailed guidance from the United Nations Human Rights Committee (HR Committee), 'it is generally perceived that states have broad discretion in how they approach the Article 10(3) obligation'.[2]

---

1   *International Covenant on Civil and Political Rights*, opened for signature 19 December 1966, 999 UNTS 171 (entered into force 23 March 1976) ('ICCPR').
2   Sarah Joseph and Melissa Castan, *The International Covenant on Civil and Political Rights. Cases, Materials, and Commentary* (Oxford University Press, 3rd ed, 2013) 325; Sarah Joseph, Katie Mitchell and Linda Gyorki, *Seeking Remedies for Torture Victims. A Handbook on the Individual Complaint Procedures of the UN Treaty Bodies* (World Organisation Against Torture, 2006) 203.

Three clauses in General Comment 21 (which is mainly about art 10(1) of the ICCPR) issued by the HR Committee refer to the obligations under art 10(3). These refer to 'assistance after release', the availability of 'teaching, education and re-education, vocational guidance and training and also concerning work programmes for prisoners' and contact with the 'outside world' while imprisoned.[3] Naylor and Winford have concluded that this General Comment indicates that 'prison-based correctional rehabilitation is generally considered to consist of "programmes" offered to offenders'.[4]

There have been very few individual communications to the HR Committee brought under art 10(3). The few from Australia usefully illustrate how communications shed little light on the challenges states parties to the ICCPR face with complying with art 10(3).

One communication where it was found that Australia was violating art 10(3) was that involving Mr Brough, the circumstances of which were discussed in Chapter 2. The HR Committee's findings provide little guidance about how broader compliance is to be achieved across the entire prison system.[5] In another communication from Australia, from Mr Jensen in Western Australia (WA), Mr Jensen claimed:

> while in prison he has followed intensive therapy and that the psychological reports show that he is unlikely to re-offend. The author argues that further imprisonment, after he was ready to be rehabilitated and reintegrated in society, for offences that happened ten years ago, is detrimental to his rehabilitation and has led to heavy emotional and psychological stress. He thus claims a violation of article 10, paragraph 3, of the Covenant.[6]

---

3   United Nations Human Rights Committee, *CCPR General Comment No. 21: Article 10 (Humane Treatment of Persons Deprived of Their Liberty)* (10 April 1992) [10]–[12].
4   Bronwyn Naylor and Stan Winford, 'Implementing the OPCAT Through Prison Monitoring: The Relevance of Rehabilitation' (2019) 25(1) *Australian Journal of Human Rights* 113, 116.
5   Human Rights Committee, *Views: Communication No 1184/2003*, UN Doc CCPR/C/86/D/1184/2003 (17 March 2006) ('*Brough v Australia*') [9.4]. For another communication where a violation of art 10(3) has been upheld see Human Rights Committee, *Views: Communication No 878/99*, UN Doc CCPR/C/78/D/878/1999 (15 July 2003) ('*Kang v Republic of Korea*'). Similarly, the Committee on the Rights of Persons with Disabilities guidance on the right to 'habitation and rehabilitation' contained in art 26 of the *Convention of the Rights of Persons with Disabilities* in the context of Australian prisons is vague. The Committee's views in response to two recent communications concerning Australia found that the authors of the communication and the state party (Australia) provided different information about the services provided and that 'the information provided does not enable it to conclude' that art 26 had been violated: Committee on the Rights of Persons with Disabilities, *Views: Communication No 17/2013*, UN Doc CRPD/C/22/D/17/2013 (30 August 2019) ('*Leo v Australia*') [8.12]; Committee on the Rights of Persons with Disabilities, *Views: Communication No 18/2013*, UN Doc CRPD/C/22/D/18/2013 (30 August 2019) ('*Doolan v Australia*') [8.10].
6   Human Rights Committee, *Views: Communication No 762/1997*, UN Doc CCPR/C/71/D/762/1997 (22 March 2001) ('*Jensen v Australia*') [3.5].

The HR Committee found that Mr Jensen had failed to substantiate his claims and held it was inadmissible.[7]

Second, the Australian criminal justice system seeks to achieve many goals other than rehabilitation, such as deterrence and retribution, *in addition* to rehabilitation. In other words, rehabilitation is *one* goal within a matrix. Moreover, as noted in Chapter 5, the Australian Capital Territory (ACT), Victoria and Queensland have not incorporated art 10(3) of the ICCPR into their human rights legislation. Therefore, the article does not form part of domestic law even in the three jurisdictions that afford imprisoned people domestic human rights protections.

Third, the ICCPR was drafted and adopted in 1966 during a time when 'penal welfarism' was the dominant paradigm. This era was followed by a loss of faith in rehabilitation among criminologists, known as the 'decline of the rehabilitative ideal'.[8] Due to these shifts, Joseph and Castan speculate that '[i]t is possible that the "rehabilitation" aspect of article 10(3) has been treated by States Parties as an anachronism'.[9]

Despite these problems, Australia still has an obligation to comply with art 10(3) of the ICCPR. Consequently, there is a need for practical strategies for achieving this goal at the level of daily prison operations. A way forward may be to develop a rights-based approach to rehabilitation as restoration in Australian prisons. A discussion of the advantages and barriers to such an approach being implemented in Australia concludes this chapter.[10]

---

7   Ibid [9.4]. The claim under art 10(3) in relation to imprisoned people on death row was also held to be inadmissible in Human Rights Committee, *Views: Communication No 748/1997*, UN Doc CCPR/C/67/D/748/1997 (3 June 1998) ('*McTaggart v Jamaica*').
8   These developments are outlined in more detail in Anita Mackay, 'The Road to the ACT's First Prison (the Alexander Maconochie Centre) was Paved with Rehabilitative Intentions' (2012) 11(1) *Canberra Law Review* 33, 48–52.
9   Joseph and Castan, above n 2, 325. By point of comparison, the European Court of Human Rights imposed a positive obligation on European countries to achieve rehabilitation in 2016 in the decision of *Murray v The Netherlands* [2016] ECHR 10511/10. For a discussion see Sonja Meijer, 'Rehabilitation as a Positive Obligation' (2017) 25 *European Journal of Crime, Criminal Law and Criminal Justice* 145.
10   The scope of this book is, as much as possible, confined to what occurs *within* prisons, as opposed to how people end up in prison and what occurs after their release. It is not entirely possible to exclude a discussion about what occurs once a person returns to the community when dealing with the requirement of prisons to rehabilitate. However, this chapter in no way attempts to comprehensively deal with the broad range of criminological research and debates about re-entry/reintegration/desistance/resettlement and other similar concepts, nor with the measurement of recidivism. An explanation of the relationship between the relevant concepts is provided by Shadd Maruna, Russ Immarigeon and Thomas LeBel, 'Ex-Offender Reintegration: Theory and Practice' in Shadd Maruna and Russ Immarigeon (eds), *After Crime and Punishment. Pathways to Offender Reintegration* (Willan Publishing, 2004).

Rehabilitation in the Matrix of the Goals of Australian Prisons

Because of the federal system, there is neither horizontal nor vertical uniformity across Australian prisons. Goals are not set at the national level because the responsibility for imprisonment lies with the states and territories. States and territories specify different goals in their legislation. Nor is there a single type of legislation in which to locate the goals of the prison system. Information pertaining to goals can be found in both corrections legislation and sentencing legislation.

Sentencing legislation and corrections legislation have different aims. Sentencing legislation concerns the imposition of an appropriate sanction on someone who has committed a criminal offence by reference to various goals (detailed below). Imprisonment is one such sanction, and it is usually specified to be the sanction of 'last resort'. Corrections legislation is narrower in focus. It concerns the administration of prisons and community corrections, and is mostly administrative.

A detailed analysis of both types of legislation across jurisdictions reveals that there are many goals of the Australian prison system, including deterrence and retribution. Rehabilitation is *sometimes* one of these goals, but the situation is by no means uniform.

Corrections Legislation

In three out of eight Australian jurisdictions, corrections legislation identifies rehabilitation as one explicit object of the corrections system. These are the ACT, New South Wales (NSW) and Queensland.[11] Some other jurisdictions do not contain objects provisions in their corrections legislation (WA, Northern Territory, South Australia[12]), and the other jurisdictions (Victoria and Tasmania[13]) contain objects provisions that do not feature rehabilitation.

---

11 *Corrections Management Act 2007* (ACT) s 7(d); *Crimes (Administration of Sentences) Act 1999* (NSW) s 1(d); *Corrective Services Act 2006* (Qld) s 3(1).
12 *Prisons Act 1981* (WA); *Correctional Services Act* (NT); *Correctional Services Act 1982* (SA).
13 *Corrections Act 1986* (Vic) s 1; *Corrections Act 1997* (Tas) s 4.

In the three jurisdictions that include rehabilitation as a goal, none prioritise it above other goals. Further, in all cases, public safety and the maintenance of security in prisons are the priorities. For example, s 3(1) of the *Corrective Services Act 2006* (Qld) provides that '[t]he purpose of corrective services is community safety and crime prevention through the humane containment, supervision and rehabilitation of offenders'.[14]

As outlined in Chapter 5, security is used to justify limitations on human rights contained in human rights legislation. Rehabilitation is given the lowest priority in the three jurisdictions that include it as a goal within corrections legislation. It is more often the case than not that, in practice, security considerations outweigh it.

Sentencing Legislation

Sentencing legislation also incorporates several goals. An example from NSW is extracted below. While in theory sentencing goals are designed to be equal, as Freiberg observes, '[a]ll these purposes cannot, in logic, coexist'.[15] Therefore, it usually falls to the sentencing judge to strike a balance between the goals when deciding whether to impose a prison sentence. Imprisonment is the harshest penalty available to sentencing judges and is deemed by legislation around the country to be appropriate only after other options have been ruled out—it is intended to be a 'last resort'.[16] As discussed in Chapters 1 and 4, the growth of the prison population, over-reliance on prison as a sanction and consequent overcrowding of Australian prisons reveals that prison as a 'last resort' is far from the reality.

Rehabilitation as a goal features in the sentencing legislation of six out of eight Australian jurisdictions—all except WA and Tasmania.[17] Therefore, in the absence of reference to rehabilitation in corrections legislation, WA and Tasmania have no reference at all to rehabilitation in either corrections or sentencing legislation.

---

14   See also *Crimes (Administration of Sentences) Act 1999* (NSW) s 2A; *Correctional Management Act 2007* (ACT) s 7.

15   Arie Freiberg, *Fox & Freiberg's Sentencing: State and Federal Law in Victoria* (Lawbook Co, 3rd ed, 2014) 235.

16   See, eg, *Crimes (Sentencing) Act 2005* (ACT) s 10(2); *Penalties and Sentences Act 1992* (Qld) s 9(2)(a); *Sentencing Act 1997* (Tas) s 12; *Crimes (Sentencing Procedure) Act 1999* (NSW) s 5(1). This also reflects the common law position: ibid 729. The 'matters that the courts have said to point to imprisonment' are outlined by ibid 731.

17   Lesley Hardcastle, Terry Bartholomew and Joe Graffam, 'Legislative and Community Support for Offender Reintegration in Victoria' (2011) 16(1) *Deakin Law Review* 111, 114.

In the six jurisdictions that include rehabilitation, the goals against which rehabilitation must be balanced are numerous. An example of the goals that are to be balanced when a person is being sentenced can be found in s 3A of the NSW *Crimes (Sentencing Procedure) Act 1999*, as follows:

> The purposes for which a court may impose a sentence on an offender are as follows:
>
> (a) to ensure that the offender is adequately punished for the offence,
>
> (b) to prevent crime by deterring the offender and other persons from committing similar offences,
>
> (c) to protect the community from the offender,
>
> (d) to promote the *rehabilitation of the offender*,
>
> (e) to make the offender accountable for his or her actions,
>
> (f) to denounce the conduct of the offender,
>
> (g) to recognise the harm done to the victim of the crime and the community.[18]

These goals are diverse. Some, such as deterring the offender from committing further crimes and rehabilitating them, are forward looking.[19] Others, such as those concerned with retribution/punishment and holding the offender accountable, and those considering the harm inflicted upon the victim and the community, look back at the criminal action.[20] Moreover, some are targeted at the individual offender (their punishment, rehabilitation and accountability), while others focus on the interests of the community (the need for protection and deterring other people from committing similar offences).

Many of these goals have origins in broader theories about the organisation of society.[21] For example, the principle of general deterrence (that is, that imprisoning one person will deter others from committing the same crime) is based on Bentham's theory of utilitarianism, being the greatest good for the greatest number.[22] As Cavadino and Dignan succinctly explain:

18 Emphasis added. Other state and territory legislation is similar. See, eg, *Crimes (Sentencing) Act 2005* (ACT) s 7; *Sentencing Act 1991* (Vic) s 5; *Penalties and Sentences Act 1992* (Qld) s 9.
19 Simon Bronitt and Bernadette McSherry, *Principles of Criminal Law* (Lawbook Co, 3rd ed, 2010) 21.
20 Ibid 19.
21 Although the way in which the goals are translated into practice in the current system does not necessarily adhere entirely to these theories.
22 See, eg, Jeremy Bentham, *A Fragment on Government* (Clarendon Press, 1891); Jeremy Bentham, *Introduction to the Principles of Morals and Legislation* (Clarendon Press, 1789). Another example is the goal of denunciation stemming from the work of Durkheim: Michael Cavadino and James Dignan, *The Penal System. An Introduction* (SAGE, 2007) 47.

> If punishment does indeed reduce the future incidence of crime, then the pain and unhappiness caused to the offender may be outweighed by the unpleasantness to other people in the future which is prevented – thus making punishment morally right from a utilitarian point of view.[23]

Rehabilitation is clearly not the prime statutory goal of sentencing in Australia. Consequently, the more serious the offence, the less likely it is that priority will be given to rehabilitation when sentencing decisions are being made. As Freiberg argues, '[i]t will become part of the instinctive synthesis and will be subjugated to other sentencing principles if the offence is particularly serious'.[24]

Legal Position of Rehabilitation as a Goal

It is clear from the above that rehabilitation as a goal of imprisonment is not given the primacy required by art 10(3) of the ICCPR. In two jurisdictions (WA and Tasmania), it is noticeable only for its absence in legislation. In the jurisdictions that do include it, the legislation has been described as giving it mere 'lip service'.[25] Competing goals, such as maintaining security within prisons or general deterrence, are higher priorities. Even if rehabilitation features as a rhetorical goal, this does not necessarily translate into reality.[26]

It seems unlikely that this situation will change in the near future. For example, the ACT, Victoria and Queensland have not incorporated art 10(3) into their human rights legislation. The Explanatory Statement for the Human Rights Bill 2003 (ACT) justifies the omission of certain articles of the ICCPR as follows: '[i]n some instances a right has been omitted because it is not appropriate to the ACT as a territory under the authority of the Commonwealth'. However, given the ACT Government

---

23 Cavadino and Dignan, above n 22, 37.
24 Freiberg, above n 15, 258.
25 Rick Sarre, 'Beyond "What Works?" A 25-Year Jubilee Retrospective of Robert Martinson's Famous Article' (2001) 34(1) *Australian and New Zealand Journal of Criminology* 38, 42. See also Karen Heseltine, Andrew Day and Rick Sarre, *Prison-Based Correctional Offender Rehabilitation Programs: The 2009 National Picture in Australia* (Australian Institute of Criminology Reports Research and Public Policy Series 112, 2011) 12. Naylor and Winford have observed that the 'lack of legislative guidance' contributes to the 'ill-defined' nature of rehabilitation in Australia: Naylor and Winford, above n 4, 115.
26 This argument has been made in relation to Queensland: Tamara Walsh, 'Is Corrections Correcting? An Examination of Prisoner Rehabilitation Policy and Practice in Queensland' (2006) 39(1) *Australian and New Zealand Journal of Criminology* 109, 111.

has responsibility for corrections in the territory under s 37 and sch 4 of the *Australian Capital Territory (Self-Government) Act 1988* (Cth), this does not provide an adequate explanation as to why art 10(3) has been omitted from the *Human Rights Act 2004* (ACT).

In the Victorian Government's submission to a review of the *Charter of Human Rights and Responsibilities Act 2006* (Vic) by the Victorian Scrutiny of Acts and Regulations Committee, it was stated that the reason for the omission of art 10(3) in Victoria was because 'the prison system may have other aims and that this was a matter for public debate'.[27]

In Chapter 5, it was argued that states and territories need to undertake legislative reform to achieve the second prerequisite (alignment of domestic legislation with Australia's international human rights law obligations). This is particularly the case now that Australia has ratified the *Optional Protocol to the Convention against Torture and Other Cruel, Inhuman or Degrading Treatment or Punishment* (OPCAT).[28] It was argued that states and territories other than the ACT, Victoria and Queensland might consider introducing a specific Human Rights Act. If they did so, this could incorporate art 10(3) and the ACT, Victoria and Queensland could also make this change. Alternatively, or additionally, corrections legislation could be amended to protect human rights and this could include adding rehabilitation as an aim in the jurisdictions that currently do not include it.

In the meantime, however, having concluded that rehabilitation is either a non-existent or non-prominent goal in corrections, sentencing and human rights legislation, it is necessary to explore non-legislative mechanisms by which rehabilitation might still be given appropriate importance.

---

27 Victorian Government, Submission 324 to Scrutiny of Acts and Regulations Committee, *Review of the Charter of Human Rights and Responsibilities Act 2006*, 2011, 70.

28 *Optional Protocol to the Convention against Torture*, adopted 18 December 1992, UN Doc A/RES/57/199 (entered into force 22 June 2006) ('OPCAT').

Rights-Based Model of Rehabilitation and Practical Strategies for Implementation

There is more than one way of approaching the issue of rehabilitation. A 'rights-based model', with particular emphasis on the conceptualisation of rehabilitation as 'restoration', is one with much to recommend it. From it can be formulated a strategy to move beyond the fact that rehabilitation is not given precedence in Australian legislation, towards compliance with art 10(3) at a practical level. Such a strategy also serves to give meaning to art 10(3) at the level of day-to-day prison operations and go some way towards overcoming the lack of guidance provided by the HR Committee.

Rights-Based Model of Rehabilitation

Critique has been levelled at the treatment-based model of rehabilitation. This is a model that considers individuals as needing to be 'treated' for the benefit of society—to make society safer.[29] A problem with this conceptualisation is that it denies the role of social disadvantage in leading people to commit crime.[30] An alternative approach was developed in response to this inadequacy. According to Raynor and Robinson, it 'rests on a version of social contract theory: the moral legitimacy of the State's demand that people refrain from offending is maintained if the State fulfils its duty to ensure people's basic needs are met'.[31] In addition to imposing a responsibility on the state, this conceptualisation views people who have committed an offence as capable of learning new skills, rather than needing to be 'treated'.[32]

This alternative approach is the rights-based model of rehabilitation. It contains four key components. The first is that people have a 'right' to rehabilitation, particularly when they are incarcerated.[33] Rotman defines the right as one 'of the offenders to certain minimum services from the correctional authorities. The purpose of such a right is to offer

---

29 Peter Raynor and Gwen Robinson, *Rehabilitation, Crime and Justice* (Palgrave Macmillan, 2005) 24–5.
30 Ibid 25.
31 Ibid 27. See also Sam Lewis, 'Rehabilitation: Headline or Footnote in the New Penal Policy?' (2005) 52(2) *Probation Journal* 119, 124–5.
32 Peter Raynor and Gwen Robinson, 'Why Help Offenders? Arguments for Rehabilitation as a Penal Strategy' (2009) 1(1) *European Journal of Probation* 3, 14.
33 Lewis, above n 31, 124.

each offender an opportunity to reintegrate into society as a useful human being'.[34] Rotman makes clear that this imposes both positive and negative duties on the state. The positive ones include the duty of correctional authorities to offer education and training. The negative duties include ensuring that people are not being subjected to the physical and mental harm that flows from incarceration, because this makes it difficult for people to adapt back into society.[35]

These negative aspects lead to the second component of the rights-based model of rehabilitation—that prison should remain a 'last resort'.[36] While not specified by Rotman in precisely these terms, his argument alludes to reasons why there should be reduced reliance on imprisonment, including the need to avoid the 'pains of imprisonment' and the risks of 'prisonisation'.[37]

Third, sentencing should be disconnected from considerations about rehabilitation and focus instead on culpability for the crime committed.[38] This is to overcome one of the critiques of rehabilitation that arose during the decline of the rehabilitative ideal—that sentences based on the (indeterminate) time it may take to rehabilitate a person were perceived to be bringing the justice system into disrepute. Overly harsh sentences also infringe the right to rehabilitation.[39]

Finally, rehabilitation should be voluntary, rather than coerced.[40] This is a complex issue, especially in the context of court-ordered rehabilitation and incarceration. However, at the very least, people 'should have some choice about how to utilize rehabilitative opportunities in order to respect their right to autonomy and self-determination'.[41]

---

34   Edgardo Rotman, *Beyond Punishment. A New View on the Rehabilitation of Criminal Offenders* (Greenwood Press, 1990) 6.
35   Ibid.
36   Lewis, above n 31; ibid 15.
37   Rotman, above n 34, 143–4. The 'pains of imprisonment' were discussed in Chapter 1. 'Prisonisation' refers to the process whereby people become conditioned by prison rules, procedures and routines, making them less likely to be able to function as law-abiding citizens upon their return to the community. The longer people spend in prison, the more likely they are to be negatively affected by that environment. This is also known as 'institutionalisation'.
38   Lewis, above n 31, 124.
39   Ibid.
40   Ibid.
41   Ibid 125 (noting that 'how this might be achieved in practice should be the subject of lengthy and earnest debate').

This rights-based conceptualisation of rehabilitation accords with international human rights law—particularly, by aiming to ensure that prison remains a sanction of last resort. This aligns with the first prerequisite for human rights compliance in this book. This conceptualisation also attempts to overcome the concerns that led to the decline of the rehabilitative ideal.

Implementing the Rights-Based Model

There are two main approaches to implementing the rights-based model of rehabilitation. These are the Good Lives Model of Offender Rehabilitation (GLM) and the restorative justice approach to rehabilitation. A short summary of both is provided here, though a preliminary comment is appropriate.

First, and most importantly, the GLM is a framework for therapeutic intervention by clinical practitioners. In contrast, restorative justice may be used as an overarching philosophy for prison operation such that *all* prison staff are required to assist imprisoned people with their preparation for returning to the community. The restorative justice framework, which involves all prison staff, is preferable in Australian prisons where there is clear demarcation between custodial staff on the one hand, and professional staff who would be implementing the GLM on the other. It is also preferable given that art 10(3) relates to the 'essential aim' of imprisonment, which extends beyond the aim of therapeutic interventions.

Good Lives Model of Offender Rehabilitation

The GLM was first proposed by Ward and Stewart in 2003 and developed to complement the Risk-Need-Responsivity model (RNR model).[42] The GLM is described as a 'rehabilitation framework', within which various specific treatment methods (such as cognitive behavioural therapy) can be used by practitioners.[43] Fortune, Ward and Willis have described the GLM as:

---

42   Clare-Ann Fortune, Tony Ward and Gwenda Willis, 'The Rehabilitation of Offenders: Reducing Risk and Promoting Better Lives' (2012) 19(5) *Psychiatry, Psychology and Law* 646, 653; Chi Meng Chu, Tony Ward and Gwenda Willis, 'Practising the Good Lives Model (GLM)' in Ioan Durnescu and Fergus McNeill, *Understanding Penal Practice* (Taylor and Francis, 2013) 206.
43   Fortune, Ward and Willis, above n 42, 656.

a strength-based rehabilitation theory as it is responsive to offenders' particular interests, abilities, and aspirations and directs practitioners to develop intervention plans which assist offenders in acquiring the capabilities and accessing the relevant internal and external resources to achieve goals which are personally meaningful.[44]

The individual agency of individuals is the first assumption on which the GLM is based, because it is grounded in the concept of human dignity.[45] Another assumption on which the GLM is based is that 'offenders, like all individuals, are goal directed and attempt to seek primary human goods'.[46] There are 11 of these 'primary goods', including knowledge, life (including good health) and relatedness.[47] Therapeutic intervention under the GLM aims to assist individuals to access these goods without engaging in illegal behaviour.[48]

Because of the emphasis on human dignity and helping people learn, the GLM is arguably a useful way to achieve a rights-based approach to rehabilitation. However, for the reasons outlined above, rehabilitation as restoration is a better suited, more comprehensive way of achieving the third prerequisite in Australia.

Restorative Justice Approach

Defining Restorative Justice

It is difficult to define restorative justice comprehensively because it has become an 'umbrella term' used to refer to a wide range of strategies to address both criminal and non-criminal behaviour (eg, anti-bullying programs in schools).[49] However, a commonly adopted definition, espoused by Marshall, is that '[r]estorative justice is a process whereby all the parties with a stake in a particular offence come together to resolve collectively how to deal with the aftermath of the offence and its implications for the

---

44   Ibid 654.
45   Ibid.
46   Chu, Ward and Willis, above n 42, 207.
47   Ibid 207.
48   Fortune, Ward and Willis, above n 42, 10. This is done in a five phase process, outlined by Chu, Ward and Willis, above n 42, 209–10.
49   John Pratt, 'Beyond Evangelical Criminology: The Meaning and Significance of Restorative Justice' in Ivo Aertsen, Tom Daems and Luc Robert (eds), *Institutionalizing Restorative Justice* (Willan Publishing, 2006) 44.

future'.[50] When Marshall refers to those with 'a stake' in the offence, this includes the victim and the community, but it also necessarily includes the person who committed the offence. Restorative justice shifts the emphasis from the state vis-à-vis the person who committed the offence, to that person vis-à-vis the victim and the community.

At the broad level, within a restorative justice framework, the person who committed the offence is required to acknowledge the harm they have caused to the victim and the community and, 'as much as possible', make amends for that harm.[51] The community then has a responsibility to support the person's reintegration.[52]

Relationship Between Restorative Justice, Rights and Rehabilitation

Connections between restorative justice and rehabilitation are not immediately obvious and there are commentators who argue they should be kept separate.[53] This may be because the two have often been juxtaposed,[54] with restorative justice presented as an alternative goal of criminal justice—that is, an alternative to rehabilitation, retribution, deterrence and other goals.[55] It may also be because rehabilitation focuses on the person who committed the offence, whereas restorative justice has been presented as extending the focus to victims and other stakeholders.[56] The latter is not necessarily an accurate portrayal of restorative justice, especially in light of recent literature exploring the capacity of restorative justice to promote desistance from criminal offending.[57]

However, it is difficult to sustain a strict demarcation between restorative justice and rehabilitation. The origin of the word 'rehabilitation' tends to support an overlap between 'rehabilitation' and 'restoration'. Mathieson explains its etymology as follows:

---

50   Cited by John Braithwaite, *Restorative Justice and Responsive Regulation* (Oxford University Press, 2002) 11.
51   Howard Zehr and Harry Mika, 'Fundamental Concepts of Restorative Justice' (1997) 1(1) *Contemporary Justice Review* 47, 48.
52   Ibid 49.
53   Tony Ward and Robyn Langlands, 'Repairing the Rupture: Restorative Justice and the Rehabilitation of Offenders' (2009) 14 *Aggression and Violent Behavior* 205.
54   Raynor and Robinson, above n 29, 136.
55   Braithwaite cited by ibid 136.
56   Raynor and Robinson, above n 29, 136.
57   Ibid 137. An example of this is Tony Ward, Kathryn Fox and Melissa Garber, 'Restorative Justice, Offender Rehabilitation and Desistance' (2014) 2(1) *Restorative Justice: An International Journal* 24.

> 'Rehabilitation' is a combined French and Latin word, coming from the French *re*, which means 'return' or 'repetition', and the Latin *habilis*, which means 'competent'. Originally, the word thus denoted 'return to competence'. Today the word denotes in a broad sense the process of bringing something back to functioning order.[58]

Mathieson goes on to consider how the term is applied in the prison context, which also connects the term to 'restoration': 'What about the prisoner? The shades of meaning mentioned are also relevant to him or her. The prisoner is to be restored to his or her old form, notably the form before the crime'.[59]

There are several commentators who argue that restorative justice is connected to rehabilitation. Zedner, for instance, argues that restorative justice is being 'seen as an attempt to revive rehabilitation for a new political era'.[60] Raynor and Robinson have argued that restorative justice is a method of rights-based rehabilitation because of 'the fact that offenders involved in restorative procedures are meant to learn a social lesson which will influence their future behaviour'.[61] This aligns with the learning model of rehabilitation, as opposed to the largely discredited treatment model. Further, Dhami et al have suggested that 'RJ [restorative justice] and imprisonment are seemingly compatible when the goal of both is to rehabilitate'.[62] Significantly for this prerequisite, Wallace and Wylie argue that restorative justice is useful in achieving compliance with art 10(3) of the ICCPR.[63]

---

58   Thomas Mathieson, *Prison on Trial* (Waterside Press, 3rd ed, 2006) 27 (emphasis in original).
59   Ibid.
60   Lucia Zedner, 'Dangers and Dystopias in Penal Theory' (2002) 22(2) *Oxford Journal of Legal Studies* 341, 356.
61   Raynor and Robinson, above n 32, 13. See also Raynor and Robinson referring to the work of Bazemore: Raynor and Robinson, above n 29, 138.
62   Mandeep Dhami, Greg Mantle and Darrell Fox, 'Restorative Justice in Prisons' (2009) 12(4) *Contemporary Justice Review* 433, 435.
63   Rebecca Wallace and Karen Wylie, 'Changing on the Inside: Restorative Justice in Prisons: A Literature Review' (2013) 19 *Journal of Bahamian Studies* 57, 66.

Rehabilitation and Restoration in Australia

What are the implications of these theoretical and practical developments for Australia? The above discussion suggests that restorative justice as a rights-based approach to rehabilitation offers significant potential to overcome some of the problems with rehabilitation identified in the criminological literature. Therefore, it could be very helpful as a strategy to assist Australia in meeting its obligations to comply with art 10(3) of the ICCPR. More specifically, restorative prisons offer practical strategies to overcome the lack of focus on rehabilitation in Australian corrections and sentencing legislation—a necessary first step for compliance. Therefore, there are a number of good reasons for considering the adoption of restorative justice in Australian prisons. There are also many barriers that would need to be overcome.

Arguments for the Restorative Approach to Rehabilitation

Three reasons may be used to support the restorative approach to rehabilitation for the purposes of improving compliance with art 10(3) of the ICCPR in Australian prisons.

Established Nature of Restorative Justice

The main advantage of this approach is that there are already well-established restorative justice processes in operation in Australia and a consequent level of expertise. Australia and New Zealand are considered world leaders in the use of restorative justice conferencing, especially for juveniles.[64] Conferencing began in New Zealand in 1989 and the New Zealand model has been adopted by a number of Australian jurisdictions. South Australia was the first state to introduce legislation to implement conferencing, and every jurisdiction uses conferencing for juveniles[65] (with some authors arguing it has been institutionalised and that this is

---

64   Gabrielle Maxwell and Hennessey Hayes, 'Section F Pacific' of 'Regional Reviews' in Gerry Johnstone and Daniel Van Ness (eds), *Handbook of Restorative Justice* (Willan Publishing, 2003) 524; Hilde Tubex and Roger Houchin, 'Opportunities for Restorative Justice in the Contemporary Penal Climate' (2009) 11(2) *Journal of Police Studies* 173, 174.
65   Ibid 522, 524–5; Freiberg, above n 15, 266.

problematic[66]). There are also restorative justice-based problem-solving courts, such as drug courts and Indigenous sentencing courts.[67] Naylor argues that the latter are 'the closest in Australia to offering a "rehabilitative ritual"'.[68] Restorative justice was the model used for a major taskforce established to respond to sexual offending and abuse in the defence forces (the Defence Abuse Response Taskforce).[69]

Although Australia has not adopted restorative justice as the overarching philosophy in prisons, there are nevertheless some restorative justice programs operating in Australian prisons. An example is the 'Sycamore Tree' program.[70] Goulding et al argue that this program, operating in the Acacia prison in WA, includes one of the elements of restorative prisons—'establishing an awareness of the impact of crime on victims through direct mediation'.[71] These initiatives constitute a baseline from which it would be possible to move more broadly towards what may be termed 'restorative prisons'.[72]

Broad Appeal to Victims and the Community

Restorative justice-based approaches may appeal to the community because of their emphasis on making amends to the victims of crime, and also because the community work done by imprisoned people may improve community perceptions of incarcerated people. In relation

---

66   See Masahiro Suzuki and William Wood, 'Co-Option, Coercion and Compromise: Challenges of Restorative Justice in Victoria, Australia' (2017) 20(2) *Contemporary Justice Review* 274.

67   Arie Freiberg et al, *Drug and Specialist Courts Review* (Department of Justice and Attorney-General, Queensland, 2016); Elena Marchetti, 'Indigenous Sentencing Courts in Australia' in Antje Deckert and Rick Sarre (eds), *The Palgrave Handbook of Australian and New Zealand Criminology, Crime and Justice* (Palgrave, 2017).

68   Bronwyn Naylor, 'Criminal Records and Rehabilitation in Australia' (2011) 3(1) *European Journal of Probation* 79, 93.

69   See further Alikki Vernon, 'The Ethics of Appropriate Justice Approaches: Lessons From a Restorative Response to Institutional Abuse' (2017) 35(1) *Law in Context* 139.

70   Dot Goulding, Guy Hall and Brian Steels, 'Restorative Prisons: Towards Radical Prison Reform' (2008) 20(2) *Current Issues in Criminal Justice* 231, 236, 239–40. The authors note that it would be preferable to have a secular program because the Sycamore Tree is a Christian faith-based program: ibid 239. More recently, the program has been redesigned in a way that has 'minimised' (but not 'excluded') the faith-based elements: see Jane Anderson, 'Introducing and Theorising an In-Prison Restorative Justice Programme: the Second-Generation Sycamore Tree Project' (2018) 1(2) *International Journal of Restorative Justice* 210, 214.

71   Goulding, Hall and Steels, above n 70, 240.

72   From 2000–04, the International Centre for Prison Studies had a project with the aim of considering 'the extent to which restorative principles could be used in the prison setting as a means of assisting prisoners to resettle into their communities after release'. Further information and research findings may be found at *Restorative Prison Project* <https://www.prisonstudies.org/resources/restorative-prison-project-0>.

to victims, it has been argued that 'the process attempts to restore the emotional (and sometimes financial) losses of the victim(s), as well as to redevelop their sense of security'.[73] This emphasis given to the victim contrasts with traditional criminal justice processes, such as court hearings, that are essentially a matter between the state and the person who committed the offence. This often leaves the victim feeling sidelined.[74] Members of the community can see that imprisoned people are making a contribution to society. This may go some way towards counteracting negative perceptions of people in prisons.

Barriers to the Restorative Approach to Rehabilitation

There are at least five barriers to compliance with art 10(3) of the ICCPR based on the restorative approach to rehabilitation.

The Lack of a Legislative Mandate for Rehabilitation and Restoration

As outlined earlier in this chapter (under 'Rehabilitation in the Matrix of the Goals of Australian Prisons'), rehabilitation is only one goal among many referred to in Australian sentencing and corrections legislation, and even then, not in all jurisdictions. Restoration is generally not referred to, with the general position summarised by Freiberg as: 'there is little formal recognition in sentencing statutes of the growing importance of other forms of reparation or restoration such as restorative justice'.[75]

There are some references made to restoration as one of the many goals to be balanced when a sentence is being imposed. For example, s 7(1)(g) of the *Crimes (Sentencing) Act 2005* (ACT) stipulates that one purpose of sentencing be 'to recognise the harm done to the victim of the crime and the community'.[76] In Chapter 5, it was argued that human rights legislation at the national level or in all states and territories is required to achieve human rights compliance in prisons (the second prerequisite). Similarly, it will be difficult for a restorative justice-based approach to

---

73   The Quaker Council for European Affairs, *The Social Reintegration of Ex-Prisoners in Council of Europe Member States* (Quaker Council for European Affairs, 2011) 108.
74   See further Jo-Anne Wemmers, 'Where Do They Belong? Giving Victims a Place in the Criminal Justice Process' (2009) 20 *Criminal Law Forum* 395.
75   Freiberg, above n 15, 266.
76   Note that this is similar to s 3A(g) of the *Crimes (Sentencing Procedure) Act 1999* (NSW), cited in above n 16.

be implemented in Australian prisons in the absence of prioritisation of this goal in human rights, sentencing and corrections legislation in all jurisdictions (that is, in the absence of parliamentary endorsement).

Overcrowding and Lack of Resources Allocated to Rehabilitation in Australian Prisons

Overcrowding presents a significant challenge to achieving rehabilitation, as it does to achieving many of the other prerequisites proposed in this book. This is because resources are not necessarily increased as the prison population rises and restorative justice processes are resource intensive (eg, they require the specialist mediators to be engaged). Further, overcrowding often results in greater use of 'lock downs', such that people cannot attend the programs that are already in place. This development must be considered in the light of current practice that results in imprisoned people already spending an average of 15 hours per day in their cells even before 'lock downs' are taken into account.[77] It significantly undermines the 'restorative prison' if people spend long hours in their cells and are therefore unable to attend mediation, work and courses. They also have their autonomy overridden in a security-focused environment.

Imprisonment of People a Long Distance Away From Their Community of Origin

Restorative prison processes rely on imprisoned people having mediation conferences with their victim/s (when appropriate), doing work for the community in which the crime was committed and building trusting relationships with that community. In Australia, particularly in geographically large jurisdictions such as WA and Queensland, people may be imprisoned many hundreds of kilometres away from the victim/s and that community. This makes the logistics of restorative prisons quite challenging.

The Questionable Connection Imprisoned People may have had with the Community Prior to Their Incarceration

Restorative prisons presume a *re*-establishment of connection with the community. This is problematic when the prison population is made up of predominantly marginalised individuals (as detailed in Chapter 1) who

---

77 Based on the national average of nine hours per day spent out of cells in secure prisons: Steering Committee for the Review of Government Service Provision, *Report on Government Services 2020, Volume C: Justice* (Commonwealth of Australia, 2020) Table 8A.13.

may not have been part of the community in any real sense prior to their incarceration.[78] For instance, family support has been found to be crucial for people to successfully stay out of prison after their release, but it has also been observed that 'this group is often marginalised upon release, with limited family and friend networks'.[79] It is also difficult when the socio-economic conditions people face upon release are similar to those they came from (as detailed in Chapter 1)—that is, characterised by poverty, unemployment and homelessness.[80]

Another possibility is that people may have been integrated into a particular subset of the community that supported the commission of crime prior to their imprisonment and returning to this subset will hinder law-abiding behaviour. These are what Cohen terms 'subcultures' that support and justify 'deviance' both before and after incarceration.[81] This is not the broader community with which restorative prisons seek to connect imprisoned people.

The Need for the Community to Support People Upon Their Return to Society

Restorative prisons rely on the imprisoned person building relationships with the community so that the public improve their perception of imprisoned people, ready for their return after release. Detailed analysis of public perceptions in Australia is beyond the scope of this book. However, it may be noted that studies of the connection with 'reintegration' (defined as 'social inclusion, or productive membership of the community'[82]) have found that the Australian community is generally not very supportive of people following their imprisonment and many members of the public express 'anxiety about personal interaction with ex-offenders'.[83]

---

78   Carlen argues that 'the bulk of those presently filling the prisons … have never had anything to be rehabilitated to': Pat Carlen, 'Against Rehabilitation; For Reparative Justice' in Kerry Carrington et al (eds), *Crime, Justice and Social Democracy: International Perspectives* (Palgrave Macmillan, 2012) 102.
79   Alison Shinkfield and Joseph Graffam, 'Community Reintegration of Ex-Prisoners' (2009) 53(1) *International Journal of Offender Therapy and Comparative Criminology* 29, 30–1.
80   Carlen, above n 78, 91.
81   Stanley Cohen, *Visions of Social Control: Crime, Punishment and Classification* (Polity Press, 1985) 122.
82   Hardcastle, Bartholomew and Graffam, above n 17, 112–13.
83   Georgina Heydon and Bronwyn Naylor, 'Criminal Record Checking and Employment: The Importance of Policy and Proximity' (2018) 51(3) *Australian & New Zealand Journal of Criminology* 372, 384.

A specific area where negative public perception is evident is employment, with an unwillingness on behalf of employers to 'hire ex-prisoners', as well as a structure in place—criminal record checks—that leads to stigmatisation.[84] The importance of employment to connectedness with one's community has been noted by Heydon and Naylor as follows: '[f]ulfilling employment is clearly linked to reducing reoffending and increasing social participation of ex-offenders'.[85]

Linkages

There is a clear connection between these barriers. People who are marginalised prior to their imprisonment face further marginalisation and stigmatisation following their imprisonment. Both of these hinder their ability to achieve connection with the community (a connection they may not have had prior to their incarceration). This is especially the case when the community may be hostile to their presence. Restorative justice initiatives aim to reduce this hostility, but its ability to do so when people are imprisoned a long way from the community where they normally reside, or within which they had problematic relations, is questionable. It is also difficult to overcome when there are legislative barriers to the employment of people with criminal records.

Concluding Remarks

Unfortunately, the balance of supporting arguments and barriers discussed here clearly favours the barriers. When writing about the possibility of restorative prisons in Australia, Goulding et al refer to it as requiring a 'radical transformation'.[86] The barriers exist because of the vast difference between restorative prisons and Australian prisons as they currently operate.

This does not affect the claim here that restorative prisons would be an appropriate way to achieve compliance with art 10(3) of the ICCPR. Moreover, it is certainly possible that some restorative justice processes could be implemented more widely in prisons, given that they are already present in some programs. This remains true even if it is very unlikely

---

84 Hardcastle, Bartholomew and Graffam, above n 17, 128. In relation to criminal record checks see Heydon and Naylor, above n 83, 373.
85 Heydon and Naylor, above n 83, 373.
86 Goulding, Hall and Steels, above n 70, 240. This is similar to the observations made about justice reinvestment that is being trialled in some communities around Australia, as detailed in Chapter 4.

that all Australian jurisdictions will change their legislation to prioritise rehabilitation as required by international human rights law. This may help to tilt the balance back, even if only a little, against the weight of the barriers.

Summary and Conclusion

The goals of rehabilitation and social reformation are a prerequisite for human rights compliance in Australian prisons because of the requirement in art 10(3) of the ICCPR. This chapter outlined three problems that needed to be addressed if compliance with art 10(3) is to be achieved in Australian prisons. The first of these was that there is inadequate guidance issued by the HR Committee about how rehabilitation is to be achieved in practice. This problem has been addressed by reference to 'restorative prisons' which provide practical processes for achieving rehabilitation.

The second was that a detailed analysis of corrections and sentencing legislation reveals that rehabilitation does not feature as a goal in all Australian jurisdictions. In the jurisdictions where it does feature, it is one goal among many. Moreover, it is a goal that is not given prominence compared to other goals that, in the current punitive political climate, are considered to be more important. The emphasis on security in corrections legislation also precludes emphasis on rehabilitation. This *may* change if states and territories amend their legislation to comply with the second prerequisite (domestic legislative reform), particularly as a result of Australia's ratification of the OPCAT. Regardless of if or when this occurs, the practical processes offered in this chapter mean that rehabilitation could be pursued, even if it does not become the explicit and overarching goal of the prison system.

The third was that art 10(3) was drafted in an era when rehabilitation was given primacy in the way that it is not currently. This can be overcome by the rights-based model that aims to shifts the focus of rehabilitation to learning new skills, rather than involving 'treatment'. This is a more modern conceptualisation of rehabilitation. Within the rights-based model, rehabilitation can be 'restorative'. Although the GLM would be a possible strategy for implementing a restorative conception of rehabilitation in relation to therapeutic interventions, restorative justice-based approaches are preferred because of their broader application.

In addition to assisting in the achievement of compliance with art 10(3) of the ICCPR, a restorative justice approach to rights-based rehabilitation is also consistent with other prerequisites for human rights compliance in prisons proposed in this book. Under this model, prison should remain a 'last resort' in accordance with the first prerequisite (Chapter 4), and staff have a duty to treat imprisoned people consistently with human rights in accordance with the fifth prerequisite (Chapter 7).

Significant barriers to compliance with this prerequisite in Australian prisons have been identified. These remain, despite the effort taken to identify an approach that overcomes the three major problems with it. This is where the advantages of restorative prisons may play a role. Quite apart from the contribution this model makes to achieving compliance with art 10(3), the processes may have appeal to victims, giving them a role that they do not currently have in the criminal justice system, and to the community more broadly. Restorative justice is also a well-established process in Australia, which may contribute to acceptance of its expansion into the penal domain. Changes of this nature are clearly required, given that rehabilitation as one of the goals of the Australian prison system is being overshadowed by other, counterproductive goals, precluding compliance with art 10(3) and other international human rights law requirements.

Part 3: Micro-level Prerequisites

7

The Fourth Prerequisite: Support Prison Staff to Treat Imprisoned People in a Human Rights–Consistent Manner

Introduction

Prison staff have daily interactions with imprisoned people and international human rights law seeks to regulate these interactions in two important ways. The first is by requiring that imprisoned people are *not* 'subjected to torture or to cruel, inhuman or degrading treatment or punishment' (TCID).[1] This will be referred to as the prohibition against TCID. The second is by requiring that '[a]ll persons deprived of their

---

1   *Convention against Torture and Other Cruel, Inhuman or Degrading Treatment or Punishment*, opened for signature 10 December 1984, 1465 UNTS 85 (entered into force 26 June 1987) ('CAT'); *International Covenant on Civil and Political Rights*, opened for signature 19 December 1966, 999 UNTS 171 (entered into force 23 March 1976) art 7 ('ICCPR'); *Convention on the Rights of Persons with Disabilities*, opened for signature 30 March 2007, 2515 UNTS 3 (entered into force 3 May 2008) art 15 ('CRPD'). This requirement has been incorporated directly into Victorian, Australian Capital Territory (ACT) and Queensland law by s 10 of the *Charter of Human Rights and Responsibilities Act 2006* (Vic) s 10 ('*Charter*'), *Human Rights Act 2004* (ACT) s 10 ('*HRA*') and *Human Rights Act 2019* (Qld) s 17, respectively. See also *Corrections Management Act 2007* (ACT) s 9(c) ('*CMA*') (discussed in more detail in Chapter 5).

liberty shall be treated with humanity and with respect for the inherent dignity of the human person'.[2] This will be referred to as the requirement that people be treated with humanity and respect.

These obligations may be described as two sides of the same coin, with one requirement being positive and the other negative. One way of precluding TCID is to ensure that people are treated with humanity and respect. If that happens, there is little likelihood of TCID. The *prevention* of TCID will be the focus of the international and domestic monitoring bodies that inspect prisons now that Australia has ratified the *Optional Protocol to the Convention against Torture and Other Cruel, Inhuman or Degrading Treatment or Punishment* (OPCAT).[3] This adds a level of urgency to compliance with this prerequisite.

From the perspective of imprisoned people, this is a prerequisite that can make a major difference in their experience of imprisonment. In qualitative research about people's experiences of imprisonment, people will commonly refer to the absence of respectful treatment as one of the most challenging aspects of their incarceration, and this may cause distress, anxiety and depression.[4] Extensive empirical research conducted in prisons in the United Kingdom (UK) has led Liebling to characterise the importance of respect as follows: '[t]he absence of respect and fairness is experienced as psychologically painful. Being treated disrespectfully or without dignity generates negative emotions such as anger, tension, indignation, depression and rage'.[5]

It is recognised at the outset that there are several challenges to achieving these obligations in practice. These include the fact that they are abstract and require further explanation about the types of practices and behaviour that are consistent with, or run counter to, compliance with them. There is also the fact that prisons are coercive and hierarchical environments— 'total institutions' as outlined in Chapter 1. It was noted in Chapter 4 that 'detention conditions ... in some circumstances can also be a means

---

2   ICCPR art 10(1). This requirement has been incorporated into Victorian, ACT and Queensland law by the *Charter* s 22, *HRA* s 19 and *Human Rights Act 2019* (Qld) s 30, respectively. See also *CMA* ss7(c), 9(a) (discussed in more detail in Chapter 5).
3   *Optional Protocol to the Convention against Torture*, adopted 18 December 1992, UN Doc A/RES/57/199 (entered into force 22 June 2006) ('OPCAT').
4   Bronwyn Naylor, 'Human Rights and Respect in Prisons: The Prisoners' Perspective' in Bronwyn Naylor, Julie Debeljak and Anita Mackay (eds), *Human Rights in Closed Environments* (Federation Press, 2014); Alison Liebling, 'Moral Performance, Inhuman and Degrading Treatment and Prison Pain' (2011) 13(5) *Punishment & Society* 530; Karin Beijersbergen et al, 'Procedural Justice and Prisoners' Mental Health Problems: A Longitudinal Study' (2014) 24 *Criminal Behaviour and Mental Health* 100, 101.
5   Liebling, above n 4, 534.

of torture'.[6] That is, simply being in a prison may constitute TCID. The hierarchical environment also means that there is always going to be a power imbalance between staff and imprisoned people, and it can be difficult to get those in power to behave in a respectful manner towards those in their custody.[7]

International Guidance on the International Law Requirements and Their Interpretation

There are three main sources of international law: treaties, 'soft' law, and General Comments issued by treaty monitoring bodies (TMBs). The treaty requirements were detailed in Chapter 2, so the next section in this chapter will consider the remaining international law requirements. The TMBs' views expressed in response to individual communications are important for understanding how the treaty obligations are to be interpreted and will be considered in the following section.

Rules, Principles and General Comments

This section aims to draw out as much detail as possible from soft law and TMBs to clarify the prohibition against TCID and the requirement that people be treated with humanity and respect.

The three most relevant 'soft' law requirements relating to imprisonment are the United Nations (UN) *Standard Minimum Rules for the Treatment of Prisoners* (the Nelson Mandela Rules) ('the Mandela Rules'), UN *Rules for the Treatment of Women Prisoners and Non-Custodial Measures for Women Offenders* ('the Bangkok Rules') and UN *Body of Principles for the Protection of All Persons under Any Form of Detention or Imprisonment* ('Body of Principles').[8] Some examples of these were provided in Chapter 2.

---

6   Subcommittee for the Prevention of Torture and Other Cruel, Inhuman or Degrading Treatment or Punishment, *The Approach of the Subcommittee on Prevention of Torture to the Concept of Prevention of Torture and Other Cruel, Inhuman or Degrading Treatment or Punishment Under the Optional Protocol to the Convention Against Torture and Other Cruel, Inhuman or Degrading Treatment or Punishment*, CAT/OP/12/6 (30 December 2010) 5(d).
7   Crewe notes 'there are always difficulties in sustaining positive staff-prisoner relationships in an environment that is ultimately coercive': Ben Crewe, 'Soft Power in Prison: Implications for Staff-Prisoner Relationships, Liberty and Legitimacy' (2011) 8(6) *European Journal of Criminology* 455, 463.
8   United Nations *Standard Minimum Rules for the Treatment of Prisoners* (the Nelson Mandela Rules), UN Doc A/RES/70/175 (17 December 2015) ('the Mandela Rules'); United Nations *Rules for the Treatment of Women Prisoners and Non-Custodial Measures for Women Offenders*, UN Doc A/RES/65/229 (adopted by the General Assembly on 21 December 2010) ('the Bangkok Rules').

Extracts of some of the relevant rules, categorised according to the two treaty obligations, are provided in Tables 7.1 (Rules relating to the prohibition of TCID), 7.2 (the Mandela Rules relating to treatment with humanity and respect) and 7.3 (the Bangkok Rules relating to treatment with humanity and respect). There is also an additional rule that does not relate to either treaty obligation, but is relevant to the appropriateness of the prison setting for some people. This is Mandela Rule 109, which provides that:

> persons who are found to be not criminally responsible, or who are later diagnosed with severe mental disabilities and/or health conditions, for whom staying in prison would mean an exacerbation of their condition, shall not be detained in prisons, and arrangements shall be made to transfer them to mental health facilities as soon as possible.

A separate table (Table 7.4) is provided for the Body of Principles because most of these relate to the prohibition against TCID (only Principle 1 is relevant to treatment with humanity and respect).

Table 7.1: The Mandela Rules Relating to the Prohibition of 'Torture and Other Cruel, Inhuman or Degrading Treatment or Punishment'

The Mandela Rules	The Bangkok Rules
Rule 44 (Solitary confinement) For the purpose of these rules, solitary confinement shall refer to the confinement of prisoners for 22 hours or more a day without meaningful human contact. Prolonged solitary confinement shall refer to solitary confinement for a time period in excess of 15 consecutive days. Rule 45 (Solitary confinement) 1. Solitary confinement shall be used only in exceptional cases as a last resort, for as short a time as possible and subject to independent review, and only pursuant to the authorization by a competent authority. It shall not be imposed by virtue of a prisoner's sentence. 2. The imposition of solitary confinement should be prohibited in the case of prisoners with mental or physical disabilities when their conditions would be exacerbated by such measures. The prohibition of the use of solitary confinement and similar measures in cases involving women and children, as referred to in other United Nations standards and norms in crime prevention and criminal justice, continues to apply.	**Rule 22 (Confinement)** Punishment by close confinement or disciplinary segregation shall not be applied to pregnant women, women with infants and breastfeeding mothers in prison.

The Mandela Rules	The Bangkok Rules
Rule 47 (Use of restraint) 1. The use of chains, irons or other instruments of restraint which are inherently degrading or painful shall be prohibited. 2. Other instruments of restraint shall only be used when authorized by law and in the following circumstances: 　(a) As a precaution against escape during a transfer, provided that they are removed when the prisoner appears before a judicial or administrative authority; 　(b) By order of the prison director, if other methods of control fail, in order to prevent a prisoner from injuring himself or herself or others or from damaging property; in such instances, the director shall immediately alert the physician or other qualified health-care professionals and report to the higher administrative authority.	**Rule 24 (Restraint)** Instruments of restraint shall never be used on women during labour, during birth and immediately after birth.

Table 7.2: The Mandela Rules Relating to Treatment with Humanity and Respect

Rule 5(1) (Normality) The prison regime should seek to minimize any differences between prison life and life at liberty that tend to lessen the responsibility of the prisoners or the respect due to their dignity as human beings.
Rule 50 (Searches) The laws and regulations governing searches of prisoners and cells shall be in accordance with obligations under international law and shall take into account international standards and norms, keeping in mind the need to ensure security in the prison. Searches shall be conducted in a manner that is respectful of the inherent human dignity and privacy of the individual being searched, as well as the principles of proportionality, legality and necessity.
Rule 74 (Staff recruitment) The prison administration shall provide for the careful selection of every grade of the personnel, since it is on their integrity, humanity, professional capacity and personal suitability for the work that the proper administration of prisons depends.

Table 7.3: The Bangkok Rules Relating to Treatment with Humanity and Respect

Rule 5 (Personal hygiene) The accommodation of women prisoners shall have facilities and materials required to meet women's specific hygiene needs, including sanitary towels provided free of charge and a regular supply of water to be made available for the personal care of children and women, in particular women involved in cooking and those who are pregnant, breastfeeding or menstruating.
Rule 8 (Medical privacy) The right of women prisoners to medical confidentiality, including specifically the right not to share information and not to undergo screening in relation to their reproductive health history, shall be respected at all times.

Rule 10 (Gender-specific health care)
1. Gender-specific health-care services at least equivalent to those available in the community shall be provided to women prisoners.
2. If a woman prisoner requests that she be examined or treated by a woman physician or nurse, a woman physician or nurse shall be made available to the extent possible, except for situations requiring urgent medical intervention. If a male medical practitioner undertakes the examination contrary to the wishes of the woman prisoner, a woman staff member shall be present during the examination.

Rule 11 (Gender-specific health care)
1. Only medical staff shall be present during medical examinations unless the doctor is of the view that exceptional circumstances exist or the doctor requests a member of the prison staff to be present for security reasons or the woman prisoner specifically requests the presence of a member of staff as indicated in rule 10, paragraph 2 above.
2. If it is necessary for non-medical prison staff to be present during medical examinations, such staff should be women and examinations shall be carried out in a manner that safeguards privacy, dignity and confidentiality.

Table 7.4: Body of Principles

Principle 1
All persons under any form of detention or imprisonment shall be treated in a humane manner and with respect for the inherent dignity of the human person.

Principle 6
No person under any form of detention or imprisonment shall be subjected to torture or to cruel, inhuman or degrading treatment or punishment.* No circumstance whatever may be invoked as a justification for torture or other cruel, inhuman or degrading treatment or punishment.
* The term 'cruel, inhuman or degrading treatment or punishment' should be interpreted so as to extend the widest possible protection against abuses, whether physical or mental, including the holding of a detained or imprisoned person in conditions which deprive him [sic], temporarily or permanently, of the use of any of his [sic] natural senses, such as sight or hearing, or of his [sic] awareness of place and the passing of time.

Principle 21
1. It shall be prohibited to take undue advantage of the situation of a detained or imprisoned person for the purpose of compelling him [sic] to confess, to incriminate himself [sic] otherwise or to testify against any other person.
2. No detained person while being interrogated shall be subject to violence, threats or methods of interrogation which impair his [sic] capacity of decision or his [sic] judgement.

Principle 22
No detained or imprisoned person shall, even with his [sic] consent, be subjected to any medical or scientific experimentation which may be detrimental to his [sic] health.

Principle 33
1. A detained or imprisoned person or his [sic] counsel shall have the right to make a request or complaint regarding his [sic] treatment, in particular in case of torture or other cruel, inhuman or degrading treatment, to the authorities responsible for the administration of the place of detention and to higher authorities and, when necessary, to appropriate authorities vested with reviewing or remedial powers.

One of the most helpful pieces of guidance comes from General Comment 21 (GC 21), relating to art 10(1) of the *International Covenant on Civil and Political Rights* (ICCPR), issued by the Human Rights Committee (HR Committee) (the TMB responsible for interpreting the ICCPR). GC 21 outlines the interrelationship of the prohibition against TCID contained in art 7 of the ICCPR and the requirement that people be treated with humanity and respect contained in art 10(1) of the ICCPR. The HR Committee states:

> Article 10, paragraph 1, imposes on States parties a positive obligation towards persons who are particularly vulnerable because of their status as persons deprived of liberty, and complements for them the ban on torture or other cruel, inhuman or degrading treatment or punishment contained in article 7 of the Covenant. Thus, not only may persons deprived of their liberty not be subjected to treatment that is contrary to article 7, including medical or scientific experimentation, but neither may they be subjected to any hardship or constraint other than that resulting from the deprivation of liberty; respect for the dignity of such persons must be guaranteed under the same conditions as for that of free persons.[9]

GC 21 also clarifies that a lack of resources is not a justification for failing to treat people with humanity and respect.[10] This reasoning precludes Australia from arguing that the growth of the prison population and failure of prison infrastructure and staffing to keep pace with this growth are an excuse for lack of compliance.[11]

General Comment 20 (GC 20) relates to art 7 of the ICCPR. This clarifies that TCID includes treatment that causes either physical pain or mental suffering.[12] It notes that 'prolonged solitary confinement' may constitute TCID and that states parties must undertake a variety of measures to prevent TCID, including 'States parties should inform the Committee of the legislative, administrative, judicial and other measures they take to prevent and punish acts of torture and cruel, inhuman and degrading treatment in any territory under their jurisdiction'.[13]

---

9   United Nations Human Rights Committee, *CCPR General Comment No. 21: Article 10 (Humane Treatment of Persons Deprived of Their Liberty)* (10 April 1992) [3].

10   'Treating all persons deprived of their liberty with humanity and with respect for their dignity is a fundamental and universally applicable rule. Consequently, the application of this rule, as a minimum, cannot be dependent on the material resources available in the State party': ibid [4].

11   This growth and concomitant pressure on infrastructure was detailed in Chapters 1 and 4.

12   United Nations Human Rights Committee, *CCPR General Comment No. 20: Article 7 (Prohibition of Torture, or Other Cruel, Inhuman or Degrading Treatment or Punishment)* (10 March 1992) [5].

13   Ibid [6], [8].

Views of Treaty Monitoring Bodies

The views of TMBs are instructive. There are some general points to be made before the views in some specific instances are outlined. The first is that the HR Committee has found situations that violate either art 7 or art 10(1) of the ICCPR, or both articles. Shah has helpfully explained that a violation of art 10(1) might occur when there are 'attacks on dignity that do not reach the severity of suffering threshold required by Article 7'.[14]

The second point to note is that in all instances the HR Committee will take a holistic view of the circumstances in the matter before them. The HR Committee looks at matters such as 'the nature and context of the treatment, its duration, its physical and mental effects and, in some instances, the sex, age, state of health or other status of the victim'.[15] Even though there is a lower threshold for a violation of art 10(1) to occur compared to a violation of art 7, there is still a 'minimum level of severity that must be reached'.[16]

The third point is that the obligations are non-derogable, which means that they cannot be suspended even in a 'time of public emergency'.[17] Article 7 is specifically listed as a non-derogable Treaty provision in art 4(2) of the ICCPR, and the information about the non-derogability of art 10(1) comes from a General Comment from the HR Committee:

> In those provisions of the Covenant that are not listed in article 4, paragraph 2, there are elements that in the Committee's opinion cannot be made subject to lawful derogation under article 4. Some illustrative examples are presented below.
>
> (a) All persons deprived of their liberty shall be treated with humanity and with respect for the inherent dignity of the human person. Although this right, prescribed in article 10 of the Covenant, is not separately mentioned in the list of non-derogable rights in article 4, paragraph 2, the Committee believes that here the Covenant expresses a norm of general international law not

---

14 Sangeeta Shah, 'Detention and Trial' in Daniel Moeckli et al (eds), *International Human Rights Law* (Oxford University Press, 2014) 259.

15 Human Rights Committee, *Views: Communication No 1184/2003*, UN Doc CCPR/C/86/D/1184/2003 (17 March 2006) ('*Brough v Australia*') [9.2].

16 Anita Mackay, 'Article 10(1) of the International Covenant on Civil and Political Rights (ICCPR) and Australian Prisons' (2017) 23(3) *Australian Journal of Human Rights* 368, 370.

17 ICCPR art 4(1).

subject to derogation. This is supported by the reference to the inherent dignity of the human person in the preamble to the Covenant and by the close connection between articles 7 and 10.[18]

The fact that art 10(1) is the first example provided by the HR Committee is indicative of the importance of this Article. It also reinforces the interrelationship between the two articles.

There are some communications considered by the HR Committee and other TMBs that are especially relevant to the problematic practices in Australian prisons, that will be discussed later in this chapter (under 'Problematic Practices in Australian Prisons').

Solitary confinement has been a consistent theme in communications involving violations. The Committee against Torture (CAT/C) (the TMB responsible for interpreting the *Convention against Torture and Other Cruel, Inhuman or Degrading Treatment or Punishment* (CAT)) considered a particularly egregious case of solitary confinement relating to Tunisia in 2017. The complainant had been held in solitary confinement for a period of four years in one prison and a period of five months in another. For 30 months, he had one leg and one arm chained to the wall. He was also kept in a cell without windows and not allowed to leave the cell even to shower.[19] He was also subjected to repeated sessions where the 'guards beat his entire body with batons, plastic pipes and kicks' and other types of abuse.[20] The CAT/C found that the complainant had been subjected to torture and was continuing to suffer 'severe physical and psychological after-effects'.[21]

The HR Committee has also found violations of art 7 of the ICCPR in a complaint involving solitary confinement in Uzbekistan.[22] The complainant was held in solitary confinement for 112 days, in contravention of the local laws that prohibited solitary confinement for

18   United Nations Human Rights Committee, *General Comment 29, States of Emergency (Article 4)*, UN Doc CCPR/C/21/Rev.1/Add.11 (2001) [13].
19   Committee against Torture, *Views: Communication No 654/2015*, UN Doc CAT/C/61/D/654/2015 (11 August 2017) ('*Jaïdane v Tunisia*') [2.11], [2/17].
20   Ibid [2.13].
21   Ibid [3.2], [3.5].
22   Human Rights Committee, *Views: Communication No 2234/2013*, UN Doc CCPR/C/114/D/2234/2013 (23 July 2015) ('*M.T. v Uzbekistan*') [7.1]–[7.4]. For an example of a communication concerning solitary confinement that led to a finding that both arts 7 and 10(1) had been violated following six months of solitary confinement see Human Rights Committee, *Views: Communication No 123/1982*, UN Doc CCPR/C/21/D/123/1982 (25 March 1983) ('*Lluberas v Uruguay*').

more than 15 days. The complainant submitted that on some occasions she was released for a couple of hours after 15 days, before being put back in isolation.[23]

Access to medical care is an important matter considered by TMBs and there are two different aspects to this, both of which are problematic in Australia. The first is provision of adequate medical care and the second is where prison is an inappropriate environment because of either mental illness or disability.

Adequate Medical Care

There have not been any HR Committee cases concerning the provision of medical care in Australian prisons. However, there have been complaints concerning the development of mental illness as a result of prolonged immigration detention that highlight Australia's obligations in relation to people's mental health while in the custody of the state. The HR Committee's view in response to one of these communications was that 'the continued detention of the author when the State party was aware of the author's mental condition and failed to take the steps necessary to ameliorate the author's mental deterioration constituted a violation of his rights under article 7 of the Covenant'.[24]

The views of TMBs in relation to inadequate medical care in prisons overseas is also illuminating. A complainant to the HR Committee from Kazakhstan was denied medical care and medication for more than a year, and not allowed access to his wheelchair while imprisoned.[25] He was unable to move without assistance and the prison authorities did not provide him with assistance for him to perform even 'basic needs'.[26]

---

23   Ibid [2.11]. As with many such communications there were a lot of other relevant circumstances that led to the finding that art 7 had been violated. In this communication, they included that the complainant had been gang raped while in state custody (see [2.3]) and had had her uterus removed without her consent (see [2.12]). For a discussion of the European Court of Human Rights consideration of solitary confinement see Bernadette Rainey, Elizabeth Wicks and Clare Ovey, *Jacobs, White and Ovey. The European Convention on Human Rights* (Oxford University Press, 7th ed, 2017) 207–8.

24   Human Rights Committee, *Views: Communication No 900/1999*, UN Doc CCPR/C/76/D/900/1999 (13 November 2002) ('*C v Australia*') [8.4]. See also Human Rights Committee, *Views: Communication No 1324/2004*, UN Doc CCCPR/C/88/D/1324/2004 (31 October 2006) ('*Danyal Shafiq v Australia*').

25   Human Rights Committee, *Views: Communication No 2146/2012*, UN Doc CCPR/C/119/D/2146/2012 (21 March 2017) ('*Suleimenov v Kazakhstan*') [2.5], [5.5].

26   Ibid [8.7].

The HR Committee found that he had not been treated with humanity and respect, in violation of art 10(1) of the ICCPR, and that art 7 of the ICCPR had also been violated.[27]

Another example comes from a communication to the HR Committee from a complainant from Sri Lanka. There were two aspects to the inadequate provision of medical treatment. The first was that he was experiencing chest pains. A doctor said he needed to be admitted to hospital, but the prison staff refused this. The doctor prescribed medication for the chest pains, but this was not provided to him by the prison staff. The second was that the complainant was a diabetic and was refused access to his diabetes medication while imprisoned.[28] Along with other ill-treatment experienced by the complainant, this contributed to the finding by the HR Committee that art 7 of the ICCPR had been violated.[29]

Prison an Inappropriate Environment

The indefinite detention of an Australian who was unfit to stand trial because of their disability has been the subject of three communications to the Committee on the Rights of the Persons with Disabilities (Disabilities Committee) (the TMB responsible for interpreting the *Convention on the Rights of Persons with Disabilities* (CRPD)). In response to all three communications, the Disabilities Committee found that Australia violated a number of articles in the CRPD, but most relevantly for the purposes of this discussion, art 15 that prohibits TCID.[30] Particular attention will be given to the communication by Mr Noble because the Australian

27   Ibid [8.7]–[9].
28   Human Rights Committee, *Views: Communication No 2412/2014*, UN Doc CCPR/C/118/D/2412/2014 (28 October 2016) ('*Samathanam v Sri Lanka*') [2.13].
29   Ibid [6.2]. Other ill-treatment included being beaten and being forced to watch others being beaten: at [2.8]–[2.9]. For further discussion of the HR Committee's views in relation to medical treatment see Alex Conte, 'Security of the Person' in Alex Conte and Richard Burchill (eds), *Defining Civil and Political Rights. The Jurisprudence of the United Nations Human Rights Committee* (Routledge, 2nd ed, 2016) 128–9. For a discussion of the European Court of Human Rights consideration of medical care in prisons see Rainey, Wicks and Ovey, above n 23, 208–10.
30   Committee on the Rights of Persons with Disabilities, *Views: Communication No 7/2012*, UN Doc CRPD/C/16/D/7/2012 (15 August - 2 September 2016) ('*Noble v Australia*') [9]. Australia was also held to have violated arts 5(1), 12, 13, 14(1)(b) and 14(2) of the CRPD: Committee on the Rights of Persons with Disabilities, *Views: Communication No 17/2013*, UN Doc CRPD/C/22/D/17/2013 (30 August 2019) ('*Leo v Australia*') [8.10]. Australia was also held to have violated arts 5, 12, 13 and 14 of the CRPD: Committee on the Rights of Persons with Disabilities, *Views: Communication No 18/2013*, UN Doc CRPD/C/22/D/18/2013 (30 August 2019) ('*Doolan v Australia*') [8.10].

Government has responded to the views of the Disabilities Committee, whereas there has been no response to the Committee's views in relation to the communications by Mr Leo and Mr Doolan.

Mr Noble was charged with 'sexual penetration of a child under the age of 13' and related charges when he was aged 19 in 2001.[31] A court found that Mr Noble was 'unfit to stand trial' due to his 'intellectual disability' and inability to understand the charges.[32] Mr Noble nevertheless spent more than 13 years in prison, even though he would likely have served less than three years in prison if he had been tried and convicted.[33]

The conditions that Mr Noble were subjected to in prison and that contributed to the Disabilities Committee's findings of a violation of art 15 were directly related to his disability. The other component of the Committee's finding of a violation was the indefinite nature of Mr Noble's detention. The Committee's comments are relevant to how the Subcommittee for the Prevention of Torture and Other Cruel, Inhuman or Degrading Treatment or Punishment (SPT) may view the circumstances of other people in similar situations to Mr Noble when they visit Australian prisons as part of their role under the OPCAT. This is why the Disabilities Committee's findings on this point will be extracted in full:

> [T]he Committee notes the author's [Mr Noble's] allegations that he was subjected to frequent acts of violence and abuse, that his disability prevented him from protecting himself against such acts, and that the State party authorities did not take any measures to sanction or prevent them or to protect the author therefrom. Additionally, the Committee notes that the author was detained for more than 13 years, without having any indication as to the duration of his detention. His detention was deemed indefinite in so far as, in compliance with section 10 of the Mentally Impaired Defendants Act, 'an accused found under this part to be not mentally fit to stand trial is presumed to remain not mentally fit until the contrary is found'. Taking into account the irreparable psychological effects that indefinite detention may have on the

---

31   Ibid [2.1].
32   Fiona McGaughey et al, 'UN Decision on Marlon Noble Case: Imprisonment of an Aboriginal Man with Intellectual Disability Found Unfit to Stand Trial in Western Australia' (2017) 42(1) *Alternative Law Journal* 67, 67.
33   Initially 10 years and three months, then another three years in civil detention in the same prison: see *Noble v Australia*, UN Doc CRPD/C/16/D/7/2012, [2.4], [2.8].

detained person, the Committee considers that the indefinite detention to which he was subjected amounts to inhuman and degrading treatment. The Committee therefore considers that the indefinite character of the author's detention and the repeated acts of violence to which he was subjected during his detention amount to a violation of article 15 of the Convention by the State party.[34]

The government's response to the Disabilities Committee's findings about the treatment of Mr Noble was dismissive. Freckelton and Keyzer describe the response as 'obdurate'.[35] This is unsurprising in light of the discussion in Chapter 2 about Australia's typical response to the views of TMBs. The response emphasises that Mr Noble did not provide evidence of the violence and abuse that he was subjected to and, therefore, the allegations should not have been admissible.[36] The response goes on to note that the government considers that the treatment 'does not meet the high threshold of harm required' and the Disabilities Committee should have applied a higher threshold.[37] This is disrespectful of the Disabilities Committee as the TMB responsible for interpreting the CRPD.

The timing of the government's response is significant. It was released in October 2017,[38] less than a year after the November 2016 release of a Senate Committee report on the subject of 'indefinite detention of people with cognitive and psychiatric impairment' that had been prompted by a 2015 Senate Committee inquiry into 'violence, abuse and neglect against people with disability in institutional and residential settings'. The Senate Committee recommended a Royal Commission on this topic.[39] A Federal Royal Commission into 'Violence, Abuse, Neglect

---

34   Ibid [8.9].
35   Ian Freckelton and Patrick Keyzer, 'Fitness to Stand Trial and Disability Discrimination: An International Critique of Australia' (2017) 24(5) *Psychiatry, Psychology and Law* 770, 781.
36   *Response of the Australian Government to the Views of the Committee on the Rights of Persons with Disabilities in Communication No 7/2012 (Noble v Australia)* [17]–[19].
37   Ibid [58].
38   The Attorney-General's Department does not date the responses, but Freckelton and Keyzer note they accessed the article on 20 October 2017: Freckelton and Keyzer, above n 35, 782 n 23.
39   Senate Community Affairs References Committee, *Indefinite Detention of People with Cognitive and Psychiatric Impairment in Australia* (2016); Senate Standing Committee on Community Affairs, *Violence, Abuse and Neglect Against People with Disability in Institutional and Residential Settings, Including the Gender and Age Related Dimensions, and the Particular Situation of Aboriginal and Torres Strait Islander People with Disability, and Culturally and Linguistically Diverse People with Disability* (November 2015). See also Parliament of Victoria Family and Community Development Committee, *Inquiry into Abuse in Disability Services Final Report* (May 2016).

and Exploitation of People with Disability' commenced in early 2019, which underscores the seriousness of the concern about the treatment of people with disabilities.[40]

The government's response, that there was insufficient evidence of violence and abuse that Mr Noble was subjected to, flies in the face of the evidence heard and accepted by both of these Senate Committee inquiries and the establishment of a Royal Commission. It also belies the evidence of violence in prisons more generally and the under-reporting of such violence that was presented in Chapter 1, as well as, most relevantly, the violence against vulnerable people in prisons. Mr Noble fell into two such categories of vulnerability: he had a disability and he was accused (although never convicted) of child sex offences.[41]

Problematic Practices in Australian Prisons

Throughout this book there has been frequent reference to the reports of Australian monitoring bodies, such as prison inspectorates, Ombudsmen and human rights commissions, that have highlighted seriously concerning practices in Australian prisons across all jurisdictions. There are four themes that emerge that are of particular relevance to this prerequisite: (1) use of solitary confinement, (2) access to medical care, (3) strip searching of women and (4) disrespectful treatment, particularly of Indigenous people.

Much of the discussion that follows reveals what appears to be problematic conduct by staff. In fact, such conduct is often appropriate in a formal sense. In many instances, problems occur when staff are complying with departmental policies. They lack the necessary autonomy to act differently

---

40 The terms of reference refer to 'the extent of violence, abuse, neglect and exploitation experienced by people with disability in all settings and contexts', suggesting that prisons would be relevant to the inquiry: Royal Commission into Violence, Abuse, Neglect and Exploitation of People with Disability, *Commonwealth Letters Patent (4 April, 2019)* <https://disability.royalcommission.gov.au/publications/commonwealth-letters-patent>.
41 In relation to the heightened risk of violence against people with disabilities see Human Rights Watch, *'I Needed Help, Instead I Was Punished': Abuse and Neglect of Prisoners with Disabilities in Australia* (2018). In relation to the heightened risk of violence directed to people convicted of child sexual abuse offences see Dot Goulding, 'Violence and Brutality in Prisons: A West Australian Context' (2007) 18(3) *Current Issues in Criminal Justice* 399, 407.

in the circumstances. This is a major problem. Policies too often do not promote any duty upon staff to act consistently with international human rights law. If change is to occur, it is crucial that laws, policies and individual behaviour all undergo a fundamental shift.

Solitary Confinement

As outlined above, the HR Committee has noted that 'prolonged solitary confinement of the detained or imprisoned person may amount to acts prohibited by article 7' (that is, TCID).[42] Mandela Rule 44 provides definitions of 'solitary confinement' and 'prolonged solitary confinement' as follows: 'solitary confinement shall refer to the confinement of prisoners for 22 hours or more a day without meaningful human contact. Prolonged solitary confinement shall refer to solitary confinement for a time period in excess of 15 consecutive days'.

Examples of solitary confinement from Tasmania and Queensland are discussed elsewhere in the book, but different instances are useful to the present analysis.[43] The Victorian Supreme Court has made several comments about the adverse effects of holding people in prolonged solitary confinement in the Acacia Unit at the Barwon maximum security prison, with one judge visiting the unit to see for themselves the conditions in which people were being kept.[44] In this particular unit, imprisoned people are kept in solitary confinement in their cells for 23 hours per day, meeting the definition of 'solitary confinement' in the Mandela Rules.[45]

In 2008, Bongiorno J ruled that a number of remandees who were being tried for complex terrorism offences could not receive a fair trial due to the combination of solitary confinement and inability to consult their legal representatives in the lead-up to the trial, the distance they were being transported from Barwon to the Supreme Court on a daily basis (approximately 60 km each way) and the strip searching and shackling

---

42   United Nations Human Rights Committee, above n 12, [6].
43   *Pickett v The State of Tasmania* [2011] TASSC 907 (20 April 2011) (discussed in Chapter 3). The conditions in the Woodford supermax prison regime in Queensland are discussed in Chapters 3 and 8. For a South Australian example see Ombudsman South Australia, *Department for Correctional Services – Unjust and Oppressive Separation of a Prisoner* (2017).
44   *R v Benbrika and Others (No 20)* (2008) 18 VR 410, 418.
45   Ibid.

they were subjected to.[46] The Court heard evidence from a forensic psychiatrist about the conditions at Acacia that included that they would cause 'a very significant degree of psychological and emotional distress'.[47]

In 2009, the Victorian Supreme Court accepted that the Acacia Unit was likely to cause psychological illness and this was found to be a breach of the *Charter of Human Rights and Responsibilities Act 2006* (Vic) ('*Charter*') s 22(1) requirement that people be treated with humanity and respect. The Court found that:

> [t]o place people in a custodial environment which is able to be foreseen as likely to result in their suffering a major psychiatric illness can hardly be said to be treating them with humanity. This is particularly so if, as here, no cogent grounds have ever been put forward as justifying such conditions for these prisoners.[48]

Psychological harm was also caused by the conditions in the Acacia Unit to Mr Dale. Mr Dale was remanded in custody in the unit from 27 February until 2 September 2009 and was being kept there for his own protection because he was a former police officer.[49] This is a period of six months, which definitely meets the Mandela Rules definition of 'prolonged' solitary confinement. Following this period (at the time of his bail application), he was 'suffering from a "moderate to severe" mental illness' and the Court opined that the conditions under which he had been held 'can cause significant psychological harm, and can do so quite quickly. Once the risk of such harm is identified, great care should be taken to prevent it eventuating, unless there is a compelling need for such repressive conditions to be maintained'.[50]

The final example from the Acacia Unit relates to Mr Tiba who was also on remand in the unit for two and a half years prior to being sentenced (from July 2011 to December 2013). The County Court accepted that Mr Tiba was subject to solitary confinement, which had caused 'a high degree of psychological disturbance, resulting in the clinical depression'. The Court noted that the *Charter* requirement that people be treated with

---

46 Ibid 428–9. The Court went on to stipulate the alterations that would need to be made before the trial could continue: at 430–1. For further analysis of this decision see Matthew Groves, 'Editorial: Prison Conditions and the Right to a Fair Trial' (2008) 32 *Criminal Law Journal* 133.
47 Ibid 422.
48 *R v Kent* [2009] VSC 375, [32].
49 *Dale v DPP* [2009] VSCA 212 (21 September 2009), [34].
50 Ibid [35].

humanity and respect was a relevant consideration, but did not make a finding as to whether it had been breached (although the Court did reduce the penalty imposed).[51]

The Victorian Courts have not considered whether solitary confinement in the Acacia Unit constitutes TCID under s 10 of the *Charter*. The Victorian Ombudsman has considered this in the context of an OPCAT-compliant inspection of the Dame Phyllis Frost Centre in Victoria. The report examined the conditions in an isolation unit where women were being kept locked in their cells for 22–23 hours per day, without access to fresh air daily, and where several women had been kept for more than a year.[52] The Ombudsman reported that this long-term separation may 'amount to treatment that is cruel, inhuman or degrading under the Charter and is incompatible with the Nelson Mandela Rules'.[53] This is something that will need to be considered in more detail as part of OPCAT compliance.

Human Rights Watch recently conducted an examination of the treatment of people with disabilities in prisons in Western Australia (WA), Queensland and New South Wales (NSW) between September 2016 and January 2018. They found many instances of people being kept in solitary confinement, sometimes without access to toilets, with one woman confined for 28 days having to 'use cardboard urine test containers' because of the lack of a toilet.[54] They reported multiple instances of people with disabilities who had been in solitary confinement for years at a time—in one instance, 19 years.[55] A Queensland psychologist told Human Rights Watch that '[i]n some cases, they are punished for behavior related to their disability. It's a systemic issue, there should be an alternative'.[56] Unsurprisingly, given the medical evidence before the Victorian courts about the effects of solitary confinement, the report noted that '[i]n most solitary confinement cases that Human Rights Watch documented, people with disabilities … said their psychological condition deteriorated after spending time in the sterile and isolating environment of solitary confinement units'.[57]

---

51   *DPP v Tiba & Ors* [2013] VCC 1075, [30]–[31].
52   Victorian Ombudsman, *Implementing OPCAT in Victoria: Report and Inspection of the Dame Phyllis Frost Centre* (2017) 52, 56.
53   Ibid 57.
54   Human Rights Watch, above n 41, 5.
55   Ibid 43.
56   Ibid.
57   Ibid 51.

This treatment is clearly in violation of international human rights law both because of its prolonged nature and because of Mandela Rule 45(2) which states, '[t]he imposition of solitary confinement should be prohibited in the case of prisoners with mental or physical disabilities when their conditions would be exacerbated by such measures'.

Access to Medical Care

People in prison tend to have poorer health than the general population, and people with mental illness or disability are over-represented (as documented in Chapter 1). These statistics indicate that most people in prison are likely to have health needs (physical and/or mental) that must be addressed while they are incarcerated.

The absence of adequate medical care violates a number of Australia's human rights obligations, most obviously the right to health found in art 12 of the *International Covenant on Economic, Social and Cultural Rights*.[58] It provides that '[t]he States Parties to the present Covenant recognize the right of everyone to the enjoyment of the highest attainable standard of physical and mental health'.[59] People in prison also have a right to medical care of an equivalent standard to that provided to people in the general community pursuant to Principle 9 of the Basic Principles for the Treatment of Prisoners, which provides that '[p]risoners shall have access to the health services available in the country without discrimination on the grounds of their legal situation'.[60] Inadequate medical care may constitute TCID, or failure to treat the person with humanity and respect, as seen from the discussion of individual communications earlier in this chapter.

In Australian prisons, the problem tends to be either inadequate health care provision, or keeping people in prison inappropriately because they should be in a specialised facility, such as a mental health hospital, to receive the treatment they require. Examples of both problems have arisen.

---

58   *International Covenant on Economic, Social and Cultural Rights*, opened for signature 16 December 1966, 999 UNTS 3 (entered into force 3 January 1976).
59   The Treaty was signed by Australia on 10 March 1976, but this Article has not been incorporated into domestic law.
60   Mandela Rule 24(1) provides a similar requirement: 'Prisoners should enjoy the same standards of health care that are available in the community, and should have access to necessary health-care services free of charge without discrimination on the grounds of their legal status'. The Australian Capital Territory has passed legislation to incorporate this principle: *CMA* s 53(1)(a).

The issue of lack of treatment for a mental health condition calls into question whether the detention is lawful, as required under art 9 of the ICCPR. This article provides that '[e]veryone has the right to liberty and security of person. No one shall be subjected to arbitrary arrest or detention. No one shall be deprived of his liberty except on such grounds and in accordance with such procedure as are established by law'. In essence, the legal position is that imprisonment becomes arbitrary if a person is being detained because of their mental illness. This is because prisons are not a therapeutic environment.

Inadequate Medical Care

There are some particularly shocking examples of imprisoned people— particularly women—being provided with inadequate medical care in prisons. These examples are additional to the other systemic problems referred to in earlier chapters, such as overcrowding causing people to be transferred frequently, which impacts on their medical care, and the problems connected with physical conditions that will be discussed in Chapter 8.[61]

On 11 March 2018, a woman gave birth in her prison cell in the Bandyup Women's Prison in WA. The Office of the Inspector of Custodial Services (OICS) report into this incident referred to it as 'a distressing, degrading and high risk set of events'.[62] The OICS made a number of findings, but the overarching finding was that there was 'no justification' for what occurred and that it resulted from 'cascading and intersecting failures'.[63] These failings may be divided into infrastructure and human failings.

The infrastructure failings include inadequate accommodation for pregnant women in WA. Corrections in WA has reportedly ignored earlier recommendations by the OICS about these inadequacies.[64] There are also inadequate medical facilities in the particular prison, which resulted in the woman being returned to her cell after she had indicated she was going into labour.[65]

---

61   See, eg, Australian Institute of Health and Welfare, *The Health of Australian Prisoners 2018* (2019) 7. See also the discussion in Chapters 1 and 4.

62   Office of the Inspector of Custodial Services (OICS), *The Birth at Bandyup Women's Prison in March 2018. Inspector's Summary* (2018) 1. The Inspector only released a summary of findings because releasing the full report would have compromised the privacy of the woman concerned. The full report was provided to the Minister for Corrective Services and other Western Australian government agencies: at 2.

63   Ibid 4, 2.

64   Ibid.

65   Ibid 1, 3.

The human failings are as follows. What the OICS described as 'poor communication' could also be described as failure to listen to, and believe, the woman when she said she was in labour.[66] She indicated this at 5.30 pm, was returned to her cell at 6 pm for the night time 'lock down', and the baby was born at 7.40 pm.[67] She should have been transferred to a hospital at 5.30 pm (if not in the preceding days, well in advance of her labour).

Once in the cell and the staff accepted that she was in labour, the OICS noted that staff were slow to respond. It took one hour for the nursing staff to arrive. When they arrived, they could not enter the locked cell because a person at the gatehouse ('a 2-3 minutes walk away') had the keys. After the baby was delivered (with staff outside the door), it took 7–12 minutes before the cell door was opened. The OICS noted it was 'inexplicable that nobody called a Code Red emergency until' this point.[68] Disturbingly, the OICS found that staff were 'desensitised' to the needs of this woman and of other women in the prison, something that they had drawn attention to in previous reviews.[69]

The OICS also considered the impact that this incident had on other women in the prison. They found that it had 'generated understandable fear on the part of prisoners that medical emergencies at Bandyup will not result in a proper response'.[70]

This situation was a clear violation of Mandela Rule 27, which provides that '[a]ll prisons shall ensure prompt access to medical attention in urgent cases. Prisoners who require specialized treatment or surgery shall be transferred to specialized institutions or to civil hospitals'. The Institute for Criminal Policy Research's *Handbook for Prison Staff* notes that pregnant women should preferably not even be in prison, but if they are, '[t]he presumption should always be that no expectant mother will give birth inside a prison'.[71]

---

66   Ibid 3.
67   Ibid 1.
68   Ibid 1, 3.
69   Ibid 3. In 2003, the Inspector described Bandyup as 'in a sense a male prison occupied by females. Security ratings accord with male criteria; staffing is predominantly by male officers; the role of women as mothers is inadequately recognised': OICS, *Report of an Announced Inspection of Bandyup Women's Prison June 2002* (2003) 6.
70   Ibid 4.
71   Andrew Coyle and Helen Fair, *A Human Rights Approach to Prison Management. Handbook for Prison Staff* (Institute for Criminal Policy Research Birkbeck, University of London, 3rd ed, 2018) 150.

Policy, as foreshadowed above, is sometimes the cause of breaches. The South Australian Department of Correctional Services introduced a policy in early 2011 that all imprisoned people receiving medical treatment in hospital have their legs shackled together, in addition to having one arm and one leg shackled to the hospital bed.[72] This policy was still in force in 2017.[73] The policy applies to women giving birth and to people receiving end-of-life care.[74]

This policy is a flagrant breach of international law, with Mandela Rule 48(2) providing, '[i]nstruments of restraint shall never be used on women during labour, during childbirth and immediately after childbirth'; a rule that is repeated in identical terms in Rule 24 of the Bangkok Rules. As a point of comparison, the European Court of Human Rights (ECtHR) found a violation of human rights in an instance where a women was shackled while in the maternity hospital *except* for when she was in labour (that is, before and after delivery of the baby).[75] The Court noted, '[a]ny risk of her behaving violently or attempting to escape would have been hardly imaginable given her condition';[76] that the 'unjustified shackling continued after the delivery, when she was particularly sensitive'; and that this constituted 'inhuman and degrading treatment'.[77]

This policy has been investigated by the South Australian Ombudsman on a number of occasions. In relation to women giving birth, the Ombudsman's investigation found that '[t]he restraints are only removed during the active stage of labour and are secured again immediately after the birth of the baby'.[78] The Ombudsman was also highly critical of male prison staff guarding women while they are in hospital and being in the room while they are in labour.[79] The Ombudsman drew a parallel to when a female imprisoned person is being searched. They are entitled under the *Correctional Services Act 1982* (SA) to be searched by a staff member of

72 The introduction of this policy followed the escape of three imprisoned people in 2010: Ombudsman South Australia, *Ombudsman Investigation into the Department for Correctional Services in Relation to the Restraining and Shackling of Prisoners in Hospitals* (2012) 1.
73 The policy was applied in the case investigated by the Ombudsman in 2017: Ombudsman South Australia, *Department for Correctional Services – Unlawful Shackling of a Mental Health Patient in Hospital* (2017).
74 Ombudsman South Australia, above n 72, 1.
75 *Korneykova and Korneykov v Ukraine* [2016] ECHR 56660/12, [14].
76 Ibid [112].
77 Ibid [113], [115].
78 Ombudsman South Australia, *Ombudsman Investigation into the Department of Correctional Services in Relation to the Restraining and Shackling of Prisoners in Hospitals* (2012) 28.
79 Ibid 28–9.

the same sex. The Ombudsman therefore concluded that the same criteria should apply when women are being guarded while 'undergoing medical procedures relating to childbirth'.[80]

The Ombudsman's overall finding was that the blanket application of the shackling policy—that is, application without regard to the dangerousness of the individual, or the risk of their escape—was contrary to the requirement to maintain the dignity of imprisoned people.[81] The Ombudsman recommended that '[p]regnant women should never be restrained during labour'.[82]

The Ombudsman has also commented on the effect the shackling policy is having on imprisoned people's willingness to access medical treatment more generally:

> [I]t is common for prisoners to refuse medical treatment. This is because the prisoners (particularly low risk prisoners) do not wish to face the humiliation and shame of attending medical facilities amongst the general public in prison clothing and shackles.[83]

A barrier to the provision of adequate health care that applies across every state and territory is that the Commonwealth Government does not provide any funding for prison health services through the Medicare Benefits Schedule (MBS), or medication through the Pharmaceutical Benefits Scheme (PBS). Funding is left to state and territory governments, which means that 'provision of services that would attract MBS and PBS rebates in the community [become] too expensive to offer at scale in prisons'.[84] Several peak medical bodies have called for this exclusion to end.[85]

---

80   Ibid 28.
81   Ibid 36.
82   Ibid 3, Recommendation 5. The Victorian Ombudsman has also reported that women in the Dame Phyllis Frost Centre are being shackled when attending medical appointments: Victorian Ombudsman, above n 52, 51.
83   Ombudsman South Australia, above n 78, 37. See also the Ombudsman's report about inadequate medical care for a diabetic: Ombudsman South Australia, *Department for Correctional Services – Handling of a Prisoner's Diabetes* (2018).
84   Craig Cumming et al, 'In Sickness and in Prison: The Case for Removing the Medicare Exclusion for Australian Prisoners' (2018) 26 *Journal of Law and Medicine* 140, 148–9.
85   Such as the Australian Medical Association and the Public Health Association of Australia: ibid 149.

Prison an Inappropriate Environment

There are two main categories of imprisoned people for whom prison is an inappropriate environment. The first is those who have not been convicted of a criminal offence because they are either unfit to stand trial or found not guilty by reason of mental impairment. The second is those who have been sentenced to imprisonment, but are mentally ill and have needs that cannot be catered for in the prison setting. Both are problems in Australian prisons.

As noted earlier in this chapter, the Disabilities Committee has expressed views about the indefinite detention of Mr Noble in WA and Mr Leo and Mr Doolan in the Northern Territory (NT), all of whom were unfit to stand trial due to their disabilities. WA and the NT are not the only Australian jurisdictions that indefinitely imprison people unfit to stand trial. This was the topic of a Senate Committee report in November 2016. The report noted that indefinite detention is possible in Victoria, in addition to the NT and WA.[86] The evidence before the Senate Committee was that there are approximately 100 people indefinitely detained nationally, and that 50 of them are Indigenous.[87]

The Senate Committee was of the view that it is inappropriate for forensic patients to be placed in prisons. They noted their concern about 'the lack of therapeutic support in this environment' and that it 'unnecessarily exposes them to physical risk and to isolation, both within the prison and from the community'.[88] The Senate Committee's preference was for people to be housed in 'secure care facilities and supported accommodation in the community' and they made two recommendations to support this.[89]

An example of a person found not guilty on grounds of mental impairment that should not have been in prison, but was imprisoned anyway, comes from Victoria. Mr White was found not guilty of murder on the grounds of mental impairment and the Court heard that it would be appropriate for him to be treated at the Thomas Embling Hospital. However, there was no bed available, so he was being held in prison. Bongiorno J

---

86   Senate Community Affairs References Committee, above n 39, 14.
87   Ibid. The report gives a breakdown by jurisdiction: at 14–20.
88   Ibid 179.
89   Ibid 179–80, Recommendations 19 and 20.

opined that 'his continued incarceration in a prison would appear to be contrary to the spirit, if not the letter of the *Charter of Human Rights and Responsibilities*'.[90]

The other category of people for whom prison is an inappropriate environment is those who have been sentenced to imprisonment, but have complex needs. The South Australia Ombudsman investigated one such instance. A woman who had repeatedly self-harmed had been restrained for 22 hours per day for a period of eight months as a way of managing her behaviour.[91] The Ombudsman found that 'the complainant presented with complex needs that are best dealt with outside of a custodial setting, and that a prison is not a therapeutic environment'.[92]

The NSW Coroner investigated another instance. Mr Simpson had paranoid psychosis and was placed in isolation in Goulburn Correctional Centre and provided with minimal psychiatric care.[93] The health professionals who did see Mr Simpson strongly advocated for him to be moved to a hospital.[94] Mr Simpson was later moved to the Long Bay correctional centre, where he was again kept in isolation. He was diagnosed with paranoid schizophrenia and medical professionals again recommended that he be hospitalised.

One doctor who gave evidence before the Coronial Inquest said, 'I have never had a higher index of concern about a patient. I felt powerless because it was absolutely apparent that he needed to be cared for in hospital and this was not happening'.[95] There was also evidence that the solitary confinement was making Mr Simpson's mental illness worse.[96] Mr Simpson ultimately hanged himself in his cell.[97]

Strip Searching of Women

This section on problematic practices in Australian prisons focuses specifically on women. While strip searching exacerbates many of the vulnerabilities of the female prison population referred to in Chapter 1,

---

90   *R v White* [2007] VSC 142, [4].
91   Ombudsman South Australia, *Final Report Department of Correctional Services* (2013) 16–17.
92   Ibid 16.
93   Magistrate Pinch, *Inquest into the Death of Scott Ashley Simpson*, 2006 [8].
94   Ibid [8]–[9].
95   Ibid [11].
96   Ibid [16].
97   Ibid [12], [19].

this is not to downplay the humiliation that may be experienced by imprisoned men subjected to strip searching.[98] Mandela Rule 52 requires that strip searching only be used 'if absolutely necessary' in recognition of this universal detrimental impact. International law has nevertheless recognised that strip searching is more traumatising for imprisoned women than imprisoned men. This has resulted in the introduction of Rule 20 of the Bangkok Rules, which requires alternative search methods to be developed so as 'to avoid the harmful psychological and possible physical impact of invasive body searches'.

In light of this international position, it is particularly concerning that in 2014 the Queensland Ombudsman documented a policy being applied at the Townsville Women's Correctional Centre whereby 'women taking a certain type of medication were strip searched both before and after the medication was provided for a period of 7 months. Some women were taking the medication twice per day and were therefore strip searched four times per day'.[99] The Queensland Ombudsman reported that this policy had a negative impact on the women subject to it, and some chose to come off the medication to avoid being strip searched.[100] The Ombudsman found it was 'intrusive', adversely impacted on the dignity of the women and was not justified, particularly because alternative less invasive measures (such as urine testing) could have achieved the intended aims.[101]

A 2017 Tasmanian Ombudsman investigation into strip searching raised concerns relating to a lack of clarity surrounding Tasmanian Prison Service's policy (as set out in a Director's Standing Order). The Ombudsman received a report that two women who did not comply with the request to be strip searched (in separate incidents) were searched by four staff in the Hobart Reception Prison. In one instance, two of the staff were male, and in the other, three were male.[102] The Ombudsman did not have any concerns with how strip searches were conducted when

---

98 For a recent detailed examination of strip searching of males and females in WA prisons see OICS, *Strip Searching Practices in Western Australian Prisons* (2019).

99 Anita Mackay, 'The Relevance of the United Nations Mandela Rules for Australian Prisons' (2017) 42(4) *Alternative Law Journal* 279, 283.

100 Queensland Ombudsman, *The Strip Searching of Female Prisoners Report. An Investigation into the Strip Search Practices at Townsville Women's Correctional Centre* (2014) 15.

101 Ibid 16–17. See also the discussion of the Victorian Ombudsman's recommendation about strip searching in the Dame Phyllis Frost Centre in Chapter 3, and in Victorian Ombudsman, above n 52, 57–60, 103, Recommendation 5.

102 Ombudsman Tasmania, *Investigation into the Strip Searching Procedures for Women at the Hobart Reception Prison* (2017) 6.

the imprisoned person complied, but found the policy relating to non-compliant searches and use of force was insufficiently clear, particularly as to how many staff were involved and whether only female staff were allowed to remove the clothing of female imprisoned people.[103]

The Tasmanian Prison Service had drafted a new Director's Standing Order that the Ombudsman considered had addressed some of these concerns. The Ombudsman also recommended that the prison service consider purchasing a body scanner, an approach taken by the Perth Watch House in response to an incident where a woman's finger was fractured during a strip search that involved force.[104] The OICS has recommended that 'new technology' be used to reduce strip searching in WA prisons, but the WA Government did not accept this recommendation.[105]

The Alexander Maconochie Centre (AMC) in Canberra has a scanner and accompanying policy that provides guidelines for its use, including matters such as the maximum radiation limits for women and men.[106] The ACT Human Rights Commission has reported that strip searching of women is being used minimally in the AMC, and when it does occur (usually on admission), it is never in the presence of a person of the opposite sex.[107]

A case decided by the ECtHR demonstrates that there may be two different human rights infringed by strip searching. The case involved the strip searching of a mother and her disabled son when they went to a prison in the UK to visit a family member. The ECtHR considered whether the strip searching violated the prohibition of TCID and the right to privacy.[108]

The ECtHR determined that a single strip search of these visitors did not constitute TCID.[109] However, the Court did clarify that the circumstances in prisons that would meet the threshold for TCID included:

---

103 Ibid 12–15.
104 Ibid 23–4.
105 OICS, above n 98, 29, 33.
106 *Corrections Management (SOTER XRay Body Scanner) Policy 2010* (No 2).
107 ACT Human Rights Commission, *Human Rights Audit on the Conditions of Detention of Women at the Alexander Maconochie Centre: A Report by the ACT Human Rights and Discrimination Commissioner* (2014) 70.
108 The relevant provisions of the *European Convention for the Protection of Human Rights and Fundamental Freedoms* are arts 3 and 8 respectively. These rights are protected in Australia by ss 10 and 12 of the *HRA*, ss 10 and 13 of the *Charter* and ss 17 and 25 of the *Human Rights Act 2019* (Qld).
109 *Wainwright v United Kingdom* [2006] ECHR 12350/04, [46].

- a search conducted by an officer of the opposite sex involving genitals being touched
- a search involving multiple officers who also verbally abused the person being searched
- when strip searching was being carried out in a 'systemic and long term' manner and could not be justified for maintenance of security and good order of the prison.[110]

The ECtHR made a finding that the strip searching of the visitors did violate their right to privacy because staff did not follow proper procedures. For example, the visitors were provided with a consent form to sign *after* the searches were carried out and when the son asked for his mother's help to read the form, this was refused.[111] The ECtHR commented that 'it behoves the prison authorities to comply strictly with those safeguards and by rigorous precautions protect the dignity of those being searched from being assailed any further than is necessary'.[112]

This decision is helpful for establishing the legal principles that apply to strip searching, and particularly the parameters of TCID in this context, for the purposes of OPCAT compliance.

Disrespectful Treatment

Disrespectful treatment is the opposite of treatment with humanity and respect. Based on qualitative research conducted in Victorian and WA prisons, Naylor has analysed the views of imprisoned people about their experience of the absence of respect in prisons. A number of imprisoned people interviewed perceived that they are treated like animals by staff. Naylor describes the interview data as follows:

> Many participants compared their treatment to that of animals, consciously or unconsciously illustrating the contempt they perceived.
> [T]hat's basically why they treat everyone like an animal. (prisoner 1)
> Some of the crap you wouldn't feed your dog. (prisoner 2)

---

110 Ibid [42] referring to previous decisions of the European Court of Human Rights including *Valašinas v Lithuania* [2001] ECHR 44558/98, *Iwańczuk v Poland* [2001] ECHR 25196/94 and *Van der Ven v the Netherlands* [2003] ECHR 50901/99.
111 *Wainwright v United Kingdom* [2006] ECHR 12350/04, [13], [15], [35], [45], [49].
112 Ibid [48].

> [Talking about meal times] … pushing through like cattle through the dining hall. (prisoner 3)
>
> You couldn't put animals in a place like that. (prisoner 4).[113]

Interviewees also referred to a lack of understanding of Indigenous culture by staff. An example of this is 'prisoners who are elders being shouted at and put on show, particularly by female officers, in front of younger Indigenous persons'. This was raised as an instance of a lack of acknowledgement of the respect normally accorded to elders in Indigenous culture.[114]

In addition, interviewees raised concern about the way staff treated them in front of family when they came to visit.[115] For instance, they reported 'instances where they were shouted at for touching, or getting out of their seat, sometimes when they were unaware of the applicable rules'.[116]

A study carried out by the OICS made similar findings, as follows:

> Surveys … across 13 prisons in WA between early 2010 and late 2012 … found that 46.8% of respondents 'felt that prison officers did not treat prisoners with dignity'. This view was more widely held amongst Indigenous people, with only 28.5% of Indigenous respondents indicating that they were treated with dignity by staff, compared to 41.1% of non-Indigenous respondents; (with 41.1% still being a low proportion). A further 53.7% of Indigenous respondents indicated that 'staff neither respected not understood their culture'.[117]

Human Rights Watch documented a lot of disrespectful treatment directed towards imprisoned people with disabilities, particularly Indigenous people. One man told Human Rights Watch the following: "'[An officer told me]: 'Why are you still living? It's time you die.' Officers are supposed to help us, not treat us like rubbish and run us down'".[118] In relation to Indigenous people, the report documented the following:

> In 11 out of 14 prisons, Human Rights Watch found evidence of staff and prisoners expressing racism in language and behavior towards Aboriginal and Torres Strait Islander prisoners. Racism in

---

113 Naylor, above n 4, 110.
114 Ibid.
115 Ibid 101.
116 Ibid.
117 Mackay, above n 16, 379, referring to OICS, *Prisoner and Staff Perceptions of WA Custodial Facilities from 2010-2012* (2014).
118 Human Rights Watch, above n 41, 34.

prison can manifest itself in many forms, such as name-calling, racial slurs, verbal abuse, harassment, biased treatment, and at times violence. ... Some officers are racist: '[they call us] "black cunt," "sheep," "mother fucker" or "pricks."'[119]

Lack of sufficient staff training may be a contributing factor. The same study by the OICS referred to above found that staff felt they had received inadequate training in matters including 'managing people with mental health issues' or 'drug issues'.[120] Approximately 70 per cent of staff working in the AMC also report feeling inadequately trained in these matters.[121] As noted in Chapter 1, this is a large proportion of the Australian prison population. Human Rights Watch also noted a lack of training for identifying and dealing with people with disabilities.[122] The next section undertakes further discussion about the need to improve training of prison staff.

There may also be perceptions held by staff that are not consistent with respectful or rights-respecting treatment. The same research project conducted by Naylor also interviewed prison staff. These interviews found that staff in both jurisdictions were wary about imprisoned people as 'rights-holders' and the impact that rights may have on security, with Naylor noting, '[t]here seemed to be concerns that prisoners would label all claims, no matter how minor, as "rights issues" and that this would undermine management and security regimes'.[123]

In WA, some staff perceived that imprisoned people had in fact lost their human rights, which, as outlined in Chapters 2 and 5, is inconsistent with the international and Australian legal position. Naylor noted, '[s]ome WA staff instead saw the loss of rights as part of prisoners' punishment, and suggested that they should be given only the basic minimum of entitlements and/or should have to relinquish certain rights as a part of their punishment for committing a crime'.[124]

119 Ibid 35.
120 OICS, above n 117, 20.
121 ACT Inspector of Correctional Services, *Report of a Review of a Correctional Centre by the ACT Inspector of Correctional Services: Healthy Prison Review of the Alexander Maconochie Centre* (2019) 66.
122 Human Rights Watch, above n 41, 66.
123 Bronwyn Naylor, 'Researching Human Rights in Prisons' (2015) 4(1) *International Journal for Crime, Justice and Social Democracy* 79, 87.
124 Ibid.

Strategies for Improving Interactions Between Staff and Imprisoned People in Australian Prisons

The problematic practices outlined earlier in this chapter need to be eradicated to achieve compliance with the prerequisite of staff treating imprisoned people in a human rights–consistent manner. It was noted prior to the discussion of these problematic practices that many of them stem from policies. Individual staff do not necessarily have the autonomy to act any differently. This is a matter that needs to be addressed by some of the macro-level prerequisites put forward in other chapters; those that address changes to law and the goals of imprisonment.

The specific strategies suggested for compliance with this prerequisite are instead focused on the actions of individual staff. They can be pursued alongside the macro-level prerequisites referred to in the previous paragraph. The three specific strategies are: (1) having the right leaders to drive the necessary reform, (2) comprehensive human rights–based training of prison staff and (3) ensuring the community value the work done by prison staff.

Leadership

Leadership in any organisation plays a pivotal role in setting the agenda and values that will apply within that organisation. This is even more so in hierarchical organisations, such as prisons, because everyone looks to the 'person at the top' for direction and to set the culture.[125] Prison managers set out their expectations of staff and it is possible for such expectations to include human rights–consistent treatment of imprisoned people. It is not suggested here that this is easy to achieve, but an illustration will be given from a prison in India to show that leadership can be extremely powerful, even in prisons that operate on a far larger scale than Australian prisons.

Kiran Bedi is described by Taylor and Rynne as one of five 'idealistic prison managers' that 'braved the punitive tide to apply reformative principles'.[126] Ms Bedi was put in charge of Tihar Central Prison in New Delhi for

---

125 Andrew Coyle, 'Governing, Leadership and Change' in Yvonne Jewkes (ed), *Handbook on Prisons* (Willan Publishing, 2007) 511.
126 A J W Taylor and John Rynne, 'Exemplary Prisoner Management' (2016) 49(4) *Australian & New Zealand Journal of Criminology* 512, 512.

two years from 1990. The facility was designed for 2,000 people but was imprisoning 9,000 people at the time Ms Bedi took over the management of the prison.[127] Her aim was 'to create mutual respect between staff and inmates'.[128] Strategies to implement this included carrying out 'daily inspections' and posting the expectations she had of staff on notice boards in full view of staff and imprisoned people.[129] This aligns with Coyle's recommended approach for ensuring humane treatment in prisons which, he says, requires 'visible and consistent leadership'.[130]

Taylor and Rynne summarise the effects of Ms Bedi's leadership as follows:

> Within 18 months Kiran Bedi converted the place into a relatively peaceful ashram in which open dialogue and problem solving were encouraged. She improved the morale and working conditions for the staff and introduced programmes to engage prisoners in education, crafts, horticulture, prayer, and meditation, and generally to help them take responsibility for improving their own lives.[131]

Comprehensive Staff Training

Earlier in this chapter there was some discussion about perceptions held by some prison staff that may be counterproductive to compliance with this prerequisite. This section considers how training might be used to achieve compliance, but it is first necessary to give a brief overview of the current training provided to prison staff. At present, it is not human rights focused.

Most corrective services departments operate their own training for new prison staff. Table 7.5 provides an overview of the duration of correctional staff training around Australia from the shortest to the longest.

---

127 Ibid 519.
128 Ibid.
129 Ibid 520.
130 Coyle, above n 125, 512.
131 Taylor and Rynne, above n 126, 519. An Australian example of human rights–committed leadership is the leadership when the Alexander Maconochie Centre (AMC) was opened in the Australian Capital Territory in 2009, which has been detailed elsewhere: see Anita Mackay, 'Operationalising Human Rights Law in Australia – Establishing a Human Rights Culture in the New Canberra Prison and Transforming the Culture of Victoria Police' in Bronwyn Naylor, Julie Debeljak and Anita Mackay (eds), *Human Rights in Closed Environments* (Federation Press, 2014) 282; Mackay, above n 16, 373–4.

Table 7.5: Prison Staff Training Duration

State/Territory	Duration of training for new staff
Victoria	42 days: equivalent to six weeks, with two of these weeks described as 'on the job'[132]
New South Wales	10 weeks[133]
Queensland	10 weeks[134]
Australian Capital Territory	Eight weeks: six weeks 'classroom based' and two weeks 'on the job'[135]
Northern Territory	11 weeks: eight weeks of training described as 'off the job' followed by three weeks of 'on the job' training[136]
Western Australia	12 weeks[137]
South Australia	12 weeks[138]
Tasmania	13 weeks[139]

It is difficult to access information about the content of these training courses in most jurisdictions. For example, the NT Information Pack simply notes that '[d]uring training recruits are required to establish and maintain an appropriate level of fitness and demonstrate an understanding of Correctional Centre practice and procedures'.[140] The ACT flyer notes that the training covers topics including 'legislation and policies, report writing and managing detainees with challenging behaviours'.[141]

---

132 Corrections Jobs, *The Application Process* <https://www.correctionsjobs.vic.gov.au/roles/prisons/prison-officers/the-application-process>.

133 NSW Government, Careers in Justice NSW, *Correctional Officer* <http://www.careers.justice.nsw.gov.au/Pages/our-roles/corrections-careers/correctional-officer.aspx>.

134 Queensland Corrective Services, *Work for Us* <https://corrections.qld.gov.au/about-queensland-corrective-services/work-for-us/>.

135 ACT Inspector of Correctional Services, above n 121, 67. The ACT Inspector of Correctional Services noted that this was reduced from 10 or 11 weeks recently.

136 Northern Territory Government, Department of Attorney-General and Justice, *Correctional Officers* <https://justice.nt.gov.au/correctional-services/corrections-careers/correctional-officers>.

137 Government of Western Australia, Department of Corrective Services, *Prison Officer* <https://www.wa.gov.au/organisation/department-of-justice/prison-officer>.

138 Government of South Australia, Department for Correctional Services, *Correctional Officer Recruitment Process* <https://www.corrections.sa.gov.au/careers/Working-with-prisoners-and-offenders/roles/applying-to-be-a-correctional-officer>.

139 Tasmanian Government, Prison Service, *Frequently Asked Questions* <http://www.justice.tas.gov.au/prisonservice/careers/frequently_asked_questions>.

140 Northern Territory Government, *Trainee Correctional Officer Information Pack* (2019) 4 <https://justice.nt.gov.au/__data/assets/pdf_file/0006/812949/NTCS-recrutiment-web.pdf>.

141 ACT Inspector of Correctional Services, above n 121.

The South Australian Information Pack provides some useful detail about the 'on the job' training, as follows:

> You will receive training, assistance, direction and guidance from qualified Correctional Officers, Accommodation Managers and functional specialists to gain experience in the safe, secure and humane containment of prisoners. You will learn to use a Case Management model which assists prisoners' care, rehabilitation, work skills, social and education development all of which contribute to 10 by 20 policy, reducing recidivism by 10% by 2020.
>
> Your work will include providing assistance to legal, medical, educational, social work, community and volunteer support agencies, which assist prisoners' welfare. You will be given practical experience and training in the preparation of incident reports, how to maintain records and operational procedures. You may also assist in interviewing, assessing and supervising prisoners concerning their development and behaviour.[142]

This appears to have some emphasis on the welfare and wellbeing of imprisoned people in the care of the prison staff, as well as training in maintaining safety and security.

There is also a national qualification to become a prison staff member: *Certificate III in Correctional Practice (Custodial)*. Prison staff often complete this course by part-time training undertaken after commencing their employment.[143] The Certificate involves five core units and 11 elective units. The core units are designed for staff becoming adult, juvenile or community correctional officers and are quite generic. They include 'contribute to achieving the goals of the organisation', 'communicate effectively' and 'maintain security'.[144]

---

142 This information is from the 'Trainee Correctional Officer Information and Application Pack' that can be downloaded from this website: Government of South Australia, Department for Correctional Services, *Become a Correctional Officer*, 4 <https://www.corrections.sa.gov.au/careers/Working-with-prisoners-and-offenders/roles/applying-to-be-a-correctional-officer>.
143 The website for the qualification does not indicate the amount of time required to undertake the qualification. However, the ACT Corrective Services advice to potential recruits notes that they are expected to complete the Certificate during their 12 month probationary period: ACT Inspector of Correctional Services, above n 121.
144 Australian Government, *Qualification Details CSC30115 - Certificate III in Correctional Practice (Release 1)* <https://training.gov.au/Training/Details/CSC30115#>.

All of the five elective units listed for the 'custodial' specialisation are security focused. They include 'maintain security system', 'control incidents using defensive tactics' and 'conduct searches'. There are general electives available that may be more likely to assist staff to comply with the duty to treat imprisoned people in a human rights–consistent manner. These include 'Protect the safety and welfare of vulnerable offenders', 'Maintain the health, safety and welfare of offenders' and 'Manage conflict through negotiation'. However, there are also more security-focused electives that staff could choose from the general list of electives, such as 'Maintain security during escort', 'Operate specialised security equipment', 'Monitor security from control room' and 'Maintain and use security database'. Thus, it may be possible for people to complete the qualification with little, if any, study of subjects that would promote compliance with this prerequisite.

The predominant focus of both corrective services training and the formal qualification for prison staff is maintaining security. It is not the rehabilitation or welfare of imprisoned people. It is also not how staff are to go about managing the vulnerabilities of the prison population outlined in Chapter 1. Nor does it address how to cater for the specific needs of groups that are over-represented, including Indigenous people (although staff may *elect* to do individual subjects on this as part of their Certificate).

There are also obvious limits to the content that can be covered in the number of weeks that these training courses last. This is especially so in the jurisdictions that have very short courses, such as Victoria, which only provides four weeks of training before new staff commence 'on the job' training in prisons. As a point of comparison, in Norway and Sweden, which are internationally recognised for having more humane prison systems than Anglophone countries, such training is much longer and more comprehensive.[145] In Norway, prison staff undertake a two-year university degree, and in Sweden they complete a 20-week training course (this was changed from a university-based course in 2012).[146]

---

145 For a comparison of Nordic and Anglophone prisons see John Pratt and Anna Eriksson, *Contrasts in Punishment – An Explanation of Anglophone Excess and Nordic Exceptionalism* (Routledge, 2013).
146 Anders Bruhn, Per Åke Nylander and Berit Johnsen, 'From Prison Guards to… What? Occupational Development of Prison Officers in Sweden and Norway' (2017) 18(1) *Journal of Scandinavian Studies in Criminology and Crime Prevention* 68, 73–4.

International human rights law has some particular requirements about the training that prison staff should be provided with, particularly in relation to the prohibition of TCID. Mandela Rule 75(2) requires that staff should be provided with 'training tailored to their general and specific duties, which shall be reflective of contemporary evidence-based best practice in penal sciences', and Rule 76 stipulates that this should include 'at a minimum' the following topics:

(1) (a) Relevant national legislation, regulations and policies, as well as applicable international and regional instruments, the provisions of which must guide the work and interactions of prison staff with inmates;

(b) Rights and duties of prison staff in the exercise of their functions, including respecting the human dignity of all prisoners and the prohibition of certain conduct, in particular torture and other cruel, inhuman or degrading treatment or punishment.

(2) Prison staff who are in charge of working with certain categories of prisoners, or who are assigned other specialized functions, shall receive training that has a corresponding focus.

The Bangkok Rules further provide, '[a]ll staff assigned to work with women prisoners shall receive training relating to the gender-specific needs and human rights of women prisoners'. One specific matter was picked up by the Tasmanian Ombudsman in response to their investigation of strip searching in the Hobart Reception Prison. The Ombudsman recommended that 'training material on strip searching specifically address the impact it can have on the victims of sexual assault'.[147]

GC 20 further requires that 'persons involved in the custody or treatment of any individual subjected to any form of arrest, detention or imprisonment must receive appropriate instruction and training' on the prohibition against TCID.[148]

---

147 Ombudsman Tasmania, above n 102, 25, Recommendation 4. This is supported by the international handbook for prison staff on a human rights approach to prison management: Coyle and Fair, above n 71, 48.
148 United Nations Human Rights Committee, above n 12, [10].

The Council of Europe's *European Code of Ethics for Prison Staff* is another useful resource.[149] It provides nine guidelines for staff conduct that relate specifically to the treatment of imprisoned people with humanity and respect. For example, guideline 13 provides that '[p]rison staff shall respect and protect the physical, sexual and psychological integrity of all prisoners, including against assault by fellow prisoners or any other person', and guideline 15 provides that '[p]rison staff shall only interfere with individual's right to privacy when strictly necessary and only to achieve a legitimate objective'. The Code also provides guidelines about acting with integrity (5–9); providing care and assistance (19–22); and behaving with fairness, impartiality and non-discrimination (23–27). It recommends specific groups have their needs catered for, as follows: '[p]rison staff shall be sensitive to the special needs of individuals, such as juveniles, women, minorities, foreign nationals, elderly and disabled prisoners, and any prisoner who might be vulnerable for other reasons, and make every effort to provide for their needs' (guideline 19).

A training provider would need a lot more guidance than the above to teach staff how these substantive obligations apply on a daily basis at an operational level. There is an Australian example of prison staff training that does encompass human rights. This is the training provided to staff at the AMC. The training covers the legal provisions in the *Human Rights Act 2004* (ACT) and *Corrections Management Act 2007* (ACT), which, as noted in Chapter 5, represent the most comprehensive human rights protections afforded to imprisoned people in Australia (at least on paper). Between the two Acts, they cover the prohibition of TCID, the requirement that people be treated with humanity and respect, and references to rehabilitation.[150]

Bartels and Boland have noted that:

> [n]ew officers also receive training on the detainee life cycle, giving them a deeper understanding of the detainee journey in, through and out of the criminal justice system, and their role in rehabilitation. In addition, new officers receive training on working with women detainees, which supports understanding of their particular vulnerabilities.[151]

---

149 *Recommendation CM/Rec (2012) 5 of the Committee of Ministers to Member States on the European Code of Ethics for Prison Staff* (Adopted by the Committee of Ministers on 12 April 2012 at the 1140th meeting of the Ministers' Deputies).
150 *HRA* ss 10 (prohibition of TCID), 19 (requirement for treatment with humanity and respect); *CMA* ss 7 (objects), 9 ('treatment of detainees generally').
151 Lorana Bartels and Jeremy Boland, 'Human Rights and Prison. A Case Study from the Australian Capital Territory' in Leanne Weber et al (eds), *The Routledge International Handbook of Criminology and Human Rights* (Routledge, 2017) 564.

Therefore, the ACT provides a model for prison staff training in other jurisdictions, regardless of whether those jurisdictions have statutory protections of the relevant human rights.

Valuing the Work Carried Out by Prison Staff

If staff feel that their role is valued by the community, they are more likely to treat imprisoned people with respect because they will feel respected themselves. Unfortunately, the literature suggests that prison staff do not currently feel that their work is valued. They feel that the good work they do remains 'invisible' and that their work only receives public attention when there are problems, such as escapes, riots, or suicides.[152]

This was the subject of a report by the NSW Inspector of Custodial Services entitled *The Invisibility of Correctional Officer Work*.[153] The report summarised international and Australian research about the lack of recognition of prison staff as an occupation, with the work generally accorded a low status.[154] This, combined with the lack of public attention about positive achievements of staff, led the Inspector to conclude that 'there remains a high degree of invisibility associated with the work … and as a consequence there is an absence of understanding of it or appreciation for the outcomes that work produces, even as it saves lives'.[155]

The report indicates that the work environment of the prison is extremely challenging and stressful, due to factors such as the complex needs of the prison population, propensity for violence and architecture and conditions in the buildings.[156] It examines the effects of this work environment on staff.[157] The report recommended that the NSW Parliament 'pass a motion recognising Correctional Officers'.[158]

Subsequently, in January 2017, NSW Corrective Services held the first 'National Corrections Day', which was followed by 'National Corrections Day' in January 2019 and 2020. The aim of this was to pay

---

152 Alison Liebling, David Price and Guy Shefer, *The Prison Officer* (Taylor and Francis, 2nd ed, 2010) 155.
153 NSW Inspector of Custodial Services, *Report No. 1 - The Invisibility of Correctional Officer Work* (2014).
154 Ibid 6–7.
155 Ibid 7.
156 Ibid 8–11, 14, 18–20.
157 This discussion is divided into 'cognitive', 'emotional' and 'behavioural' effects: ibid 26.
158 Ibid 3. It is unclear whether such a motion was in fact passed.

'tribute to corrections staff throughout Australia' and draw attention to 'the challenging and often dangerous work they do each day to keep the community safe'.[159]

The report and the national day of recognition represent positive steps towards valuing the work done by prison staff. Another important means by which the value placed on prison work could be increased is to establish it as a desirable, professional career for people—a career that requires professional training and accreditation.[160] Coyle writes that 'new prison staff need to be properly selected, assessed and trained and throughout their career they need to be given the opportunity to expand and develop their skills. If this does not happen then they are likely to remain one of the most undervalued sectors of public employees'.[161] Achieving this goal would involve increasing the level of qualifications required to become a prison employee beyond the current training requirements outlined in the previous section.

The value placed on prison work could also be increased by emphasising that the role is a social service, aimed at achieving rehabilitation and restoration in accordance with the third prerequisite (discussed in Chapter 6). Staff may be seen as role models for imprisoned people, helping them on their path to becoming law-abiding citizens upon their release.[162] This is likely to appeal to the community because the community would prefer that imprisoned people are no longer a threat to them upon their release.

It would also be helpful to increase the general public's understanding of the role. If it is emphasised that prison staff prepare people for re-entry into society as law-abiding citizens less likely to commit further crime, the public may be more likely to view the role of prison staff favourably. This could be pursued alongside the education of the public aimed at generating public support to reduce reliance on imprisonment, as recommended in Chapter 4.

---

159 NSW Government, Communities and Justice, *National Corrections Day* <https://www.correctiveservices.justice.nsw.gov.au/Pages/CorrectiveServices/national-corrections-day.aspx>.

160 Andrew Coyle, *Managing Prisons in a Time of Change* (International Centre for Prison Studies, 2001) 83.

161 Ibid 86.

162 Helen Arnold, 'The Prison Officer' in Yvonne Jewkes et al (eds), *Handbook on Prisons* (Routledge, 2016) 267–8. This sentiment is reflected in Principle 2.4.2 of the Guiding Principles, which requires that 'Staff model prosocial behaviour by treating all persons with decency, respect and fairness': Corrective Services Administrators' Conference (Cth), *Guiding Principles for Corrections in Australia* (2018) 14.

When OPCAT-compliant monitoring commences in Australia, because it will have a preventive focus, it should be highlighting examples of best practice. These examples should include best practice in the treatment of imprisoned people by staff. When the reports of the National Preventive Mechanism (established under the OPCAT) are made publicly available, this will serve multiple purposes. It will simultaneously reduce the invisibility of prison staff work, highlight to the community that this work is extremely valuable when it is done well, and hopefully counter prison staff perception that their work is misunderstood and undervalued, consequently increasing the respect they have for themselves and the imprisoned people in their care.

Conclusion

The problematic practices in Australian prisons detailed in this chapter clearly constitute human rights violations by prison staff, particularly the prohibition of TCID and duty to treat people with humanity and respect. This was shown by the outline of the international human rights law framework, followed by the discussion of problematic practices across a range of jurisdictions in the four areas of (1) use of solitary confinement, (2) access to medical care, (3) strip searching of women and (4) disrespectful treatment, particularly of Indigenous people.

While much of this chapter focused on the role of staff, it does not follow that any individual staff member in any individual prison can bear the entire burden of rights compliance. Many of the problematic practices stem from departmental policies that prison staff have no choice but to comply with. Other problems stem from inadequate training (due often to its short duration) and inadequate attention given during training to imprisoned people's welfare, managing people with complex needs or the duty to treat imprisoned people consistently with international human rights law obligations. Changes to these systemic problems will better enable individual staff to adopt more human rights–compliant conduct.

Other prerequisites proposed in this book are necessary for addressing this. Reduced reliance on imprisonment in accordance with the first prerequisite will assist because when there are fewer people in prisons there are better conditions for those that remain, and prisons become easier for staff to manage. When prisons are crowded it is easier for people to be reduced to numbers, rather than called by their names, and they can become 'bodies' or numbers to be delivered from one place to another.[163]

There also needs to be legislation that prohibits TCID, particularly prolonged solitary confinement, as detailed in Chapter 5. That legislation should also override policies such as the South Australian one requiring imprisoned people seeking medical care be shackled, regardless of whether they pose a danger or escape risk. The legislation should reduce the emphasis on security and good order. While recognising that security always remains a necessary priority for the welfare of imprisoned people and staff, a balance must be struck to accommodate other priorities, including treatment of people with humanity and respect.

These changes need to be overseen by regular OPCAT-compliant inspection that has a preventive focus. As was noted in Chapter 3, the reasons for continual oversight is that:

> regular monitoring helps keep the quality of correctional services high, because the staff's knowledge that an inspector could arrive at any time acts as a means of informal control over staff behavior. In other words, it 'keeps staff on their toes' and helps them avoid complacency, even when everything is going well.[164]

These systemic changes should be accompanied by specific strategies to improve staff compliance with their duty suggested in this chapter. These reforms include (1) having the right leaders to drive the necessary reform, (2) comprehensive human rights–based training of prison staff and (3) ensuring the community values the work done by prison staff. Some of these can be pursued on a state/territory-wide basis, particularly improvements to training and improving community perceptions of the work done by prison staff (as exemplified by NSW). Others, such as improved leadership, can be pursued in individual prisons.

---

163 Coyle, above n 160, 93.
164 Michele Deitch, 'Distinguishing the Various Functions of Effective Prison Oversight' (2010) 30 *Pace Law Review* 1438, 1443.

8

The Fifth Prerequisite: Ensure Decent Physical Conditions in All Prisons

Introduction

For those unfamiliar with prisons, it may seem that emphasis on physical conditions is misplaced, given the more serious problems, such as violence, that occur in prisons. However, physical conditions have great importance for imprisoned people. People in prison live in what Goffman termed a 'total institution', in that every aspect of their existence occurs within the prison surrounds.[1]

Perhaps it is for this reason that complaints about deficiencies in the physical conditions within prisons form a large proportion of the international communications to treaty monitoring bodies about the application of human rights law in prisons. Decent prison conditions are important for ensuring an absence of 'cruel, inhuman or degrading treatment or punishment' (TCID) (particularly important for compliance with the *Optional Protocol to the Convention against Torture and Other*

---

1   Erving Goffman, *Asylums. Essays on the Social Situation of Mental Patients and Other Inmates* (Aldine Publishing Company, 1962). See the discussion in Chapter 1.

Cruel, Inhuman or Degrading Treatment or Punishment (OPCAT)) and treatment with humanity and respect as required by art 10(1) of the *International Covenant on Civil and Political Rights* (ICCPR).[2]

Physical conditions are also a chief concern of organisations monitoring prisons. Thus it is also likely to be the case for both the Subcommittee for the Prevention of Torture and Other Cruel, Inhuman or Degrading Treatment or Punishment (SPT) and National Preventive Mechanisms (NPMs) (responsible for monitoring under the OPCAT at the international and domestic levels respectively). As Dame Anne Owers, former Chief Inspector of prisons in the United Kingdom (UK), argues, 'protecting human rights in closed environments has to start at the level of the everyday, not the extreme'. She refers to Colin Allen, former Deputy Chief Inspector, who, when he left Her Majesty's Inspectorate of Prisons (HMIP):

> posted only one message for his successor, which sat on his notice board until the day he too left. It simply said 'underpants': don't forget the importance of apparently mundane things in an environment where everything – what and if you eat, whether and if you get out of your cell, what you wear and do – is controlled by someone else.[3]

It can nevertheless be acknowledged that physical conditions may not be the highest priority when seeking to achieve human rights compliance in prisons. This is because deficiencies in physical conditions can be ameliorated by the way people are treated. For example, if a prison is old and the cells do not have enough natural light or ventilation, the harmful effects of this can be reduced if the cells are only occupied for sleeping.[4] Plenty of access to fresh air and natural light during the day can compensate. On the other hand, it does not matter how modern

---

2   The prohibition against torture, cruel, inhuman or degrading treatment or punishment stems from art 7 of the *International Covenant on Civil and Political Rights*, opened for signature 19 December 1966, 999 UNTS 171 (entered into force 23 March 1976) ('ICCPR'); art 15 of the *Convention on the Rights of Persons with Disabilities*, opened for signature 30 March 2007, 2515 UNTS 3 (entered into force 3 May 2008) ('CRPD'); and is required by the *Convention against Torture and Other Cruel, Inhuman or Degrading Treatment or Punishment*, opened for signature 10 December 1984, 1465 UNTS 85 (entered into force 26 June 1987) ('CAT') and *Optional Protocol to the Convention against Torture*, adopted 18 December 1992, UN Doc A/RES/57/199 (entered into force 22 June 2006) ('OPCAT').

3   Anne Owers, 'Comparative Experiences of Implementing Human Rights in Closed Environments: Monitoring for Rights Protection' in Bronwyn Naylor, Julie Debeljak and Anita Mackay (eds), *Human Rights in Closed Environments* (Federation Press, 2014) 217.

4   Andrew Coyle and Helen Fair, *A Human Rights Approach to Prison Management. Handbook for Prison Staff* (Institute for Criminal Policy Research Birkbeck, University of London, 3rd ed, 2018) 45.

a cell is if a person is kept in that cell in excess of 20 hours per day. This is cruel treatment for which even the best possible physical conditions are no compensation. Decent physical conditions should not be viewed as sufficient in themselves for achieving human rights compliance.

This is another example of the interdependence of the prerequisites proposed in this book. Good physical conditions become easier to achieve when there is reduced reliance on prison in accordance with the first prerequisite. People then have more space and better access to goods and services. This is in contrast to the current situation where overcrowding is the norm in most Australian prisons, such that people are sharing cells and competing for insufficient goods and services (as discussed in Chapter 4).

In defining the scope of physical conditions in prisons—which includes matters such as the built environment and access to basic necessities— reference to cases in which judges have found that physical conditions violate human rights is helpful. Because there is a limited amount of Australian case law, this discussion draws on international cases where relevant, including decisions of the European Court of Human Rights (ECtHR) (of which there is a much greater volume).[5] Moreover, the ECtHR's decisions in the past have also been considered by the Australian High Court to be 'instructive'.[6]

Concerns about physical conditions have also been raised by the SPT, which Australian prison administrators should be aware of, given that this Subcommittee will soon be visiting Australia. The recently published report of the visit to New Zealand is particularly instructive on these issues, given the similarities between Australian and New Zealand prisons.[7]

---

5   Manfred Nowak, 'The Need for a World Court of Human Rights' (2007) 7 *Human Rights Law Review* 251, 253. It has been noted that the 'conditions of imprisonment are frequent sources of individual applications' before the European Court of Human Rights (ECtHR): Bernadette Rainey, Elizabeth Wicks and Clare Ovey, *Jacobs, White and Ovey. The European Convention on Human Rights* (Oxford University Press, 7th ed, 2017) 204.
6   Gleeson CJ referring to the ECtHR decision in *Hirst v United Kingdom [No 2]* (2005) 42 ECHR 41: *Roach v Electoral Commissioner* (2007) 233 CLR 162, 178–9. Gleeson CJ cautioned that 'uncritical translation' is unwise, given the important differences in the Australian constitutional framework, but opined that 'aspects of the reasoning [of such cases] are instructive': at 178–9.
7   The Committee visited New Zealand in 2013, and the report was made publicly available in 2017: Subcommittee on Prevention of Torture and Other Cruel, Inhuman or Degrading Treatment or Punishment (SPT), *Visit to New Zealand Undertaken from 29 April to 8 May 2013: Observations and Recommendations Addressed to the State Party. Report of the Subcommittee*, UN Doc CAT/OP/ NZL/1 (10 February 2017).

The case law and reports by the SPT draw attention to the matters that are pertinent to the fulfilment of Australia's human rights obligations by identifying concrete circumstances that have been found to breach imprisoned people's human rights. It will be shown that Australian prisons generally do not meet the standards required for human rights–compliant physical conditions. Positive examples of ways to improve physical conditions in Australian prisons are then considered.

There is one preliminary point to be made prior to this discussion: lack of resources is not an acceptable reason for failing to comply with this prerequisite. Around the world, governments often claim they lack the resources to improve physical conditions in instances where they are imprisoning people in old buildings with design features that run counter to the human rights of imprisoned people. The Human Rights Committee (HR Committee) has made it clear, in an individual communication concerning Cameroon, that 'certain minimum standards regarding the conditions of detention must be observed regardless of a State party's level of development'.[8] The ECtHR has echoed the view that lack of resources does not absolve governments of their human right obligations. For example, in *Gusev v Russia*,[9] the ECtHR held that 'it is incumbent on the respondent Government to organise its penitentiary system in such a way as to ensure respect for the dignity of detainees, regardless of financial or logistical difficulties'.[10]

Physical Conditions and Human Rights Concerns

There are two relevant aspects of physical conditions in prisons: characteristics of the built environment (or architecture); and people's access to basic necessities of life, such as food, clothing and personal hygiene.

---

8   Human Rights Committee, *Views: Communication No 458/91*, UN Doc CCPR/C/51/D/458/1991 (21 July 1994) ('*Mukong v Cameroon*').
9   *Gusev v Russia* [2008] ECHR 67542/01.
10   Ibid [58]. See also *Dybeku v Albania* [2007] ECHR 41153/06, [50]; *Aliev v Ukraine* [2003] ECHR 41220/98, [151].

Built Environment

Building design is fundamental to how people in prison are able to meet basic living requirements. These requirements include adequate ventilation and natural light, sufficient personal space, and privacy when using the toilet and shower facilities. There also needs to be outdoor space for people in prison to get fresh air and exercise.

Although many international human rights obligations are relevant to such matters, international human rights law does not provide specific guidance about how to comply with these obligations in practice.[11] They do not, for example, specify how much cell space each imprisoned person should have. Rather, the Mandela Rules, in relation to accommodation, specify only that '[a]ll accommodation provided for the use of prisoners and in particular all sleeping accommodation shall meet all requirements of health, due regard being paid to climatic conditions and particularly to cubic content of air, minimum floor space, lighting, heating and ventilation'.[12]

As noted in Chapter 4, the 2012 *Standard Guidelines for Corrections in Australia* referred to the cell size being consistent with the 'Standard Guidelines for Prison Facilities in Australia and New Zealand (1990)'.[13] The Office of the Inspector of Custodial Services (OICS) in Western Australia has helpfully summarised these requirements (as noted in Chapter 4) as follows:

> The Standard Guidelines for Prison Facilities in Australia and New Zealand 1990 (Australasian Standard Guidelines 1990) provide that a single person cell without ablution facilities (toilet, shower, and basin) should be a minimum of 7.5 m² ('dry cells'). An additional 1.25 m² is required for cells that include ablution facilities ('wet cells'). If a cell is to be shared, a further 4.0 m² is required for each additional person.[14]

---

11 See, eg, the ICCPR arts 7 (the prohibition against cruel, inhuman or degrading treatment or punishment), 9 (security of the person), 10 (the requirement that people deprived of their liberty be treated with humanity and respect for inherent dignity), 12 (right to liberty and freedom of movement), 17 (right to privacy), 18 (right to freedom of freedom of thought, conscience and religion), 27 (rights of ethnic minorities to enjoy their own culture).

12 United Nations *Standard Minimum Rules for the Treatment of Prisoners* (the Nelson Mandela Rules), UN Doc A/RES/70/175 (17 December 2015) Rule 10 ('the Mandela Rules').

13 The Corrective Services Ministers' Conference (Cth), *Standard Guidelines for Corrections in Australia* (2012) 2, Guideline 2.3.

14 Office of the Inspector of Custodial Services (OICS), *Western Australia's Prison Capacity* (2016) 10. The ECtHR has held that shared cells must be at least three square metres, because cells smaller than this are likely to lead to degrading conditions: Rainey, Wicks and Ovey, above n 5, 206.

There remains a need to explore physical conditions in more depth. Space is only a superficial measure of the environment in which a person spends their entire existence for the duration of their incarceration.

There is no need to repeat here the detailed discussion about overcrowding and cell sharing (and their implications for human rights) included in Chapter 4. Instead, three other issues are considered: (1) the way architecture and prison regimes can be designed to be in violation of human rights from the outset, (2) prison buildings that are not built for the climate and (3) the specific needs of some groups within the prison population in relation to the built environment.[15]

Architecture and Prison Regimes

Four illustrations of problematic architecture and prison regimes will be provided here. The first two can be described as issues both of architecture and of regime. They are, first, the dormitory-style accommodation in the recently built New South Wales (NSW) 'rapid build' prisons, and, second, 'supermax' prisons. The second two illustrations are confined to architectural problems. These are, first, an underground facility in Victoria, and, second, the ongoing failure of prisons around Australia to remove hanging points.

Dormitory-Style Prisons in New South Wales

It was noted in Chapter 4 that NSW has recently built two 'rapid build' prisons, and there is another 1,700-bed facility planned. Jewkes has observed that '[t]he very fact that "rapid-build prison" has become part of the lexicon of prison planning is arguably shocking … conjuring up as it does an industrial scale, factory-line production of units in which to foment human misery'.[16] Then there is that fact that these prisons house imprisoned people in dormitories, with 25 cubicles in each dormitory and that '[e]levated catwalks overlook the dormitories so that staff can observe what is occurring within a dormitory without having to enter it'.[17]

---

15   For a more general discussion of the problems with prison architecture, which argues it shares features of 'sick building syndrome', see NSW Inspector of Custodial Services, *Report No. 1 - The Invisibility of Correctional Officer Work* (2014) 18–20.

16   Yvonne Jewkes, 'Just Design: Health Prisons and the Architecture of Hope' (2018) 51(3) *Australian & New Zealand Journal of Criminology* 319, 325.

17   New South Wales, Parliament Legislative Council Portfolio Committee No. 4 – Legal Affairs, *Parklea Correctional Centre and Other Operational Issues* (2018) 76. See also NSW Government, *Department of Justice Annual Report 2017-18* (2018) 52–3.

There are serious incursions on the human rights of imprisoned people inherent in this regime. They are the risks of violence (including sexual violence) and intimidation and the complete lack of privacy, due to the number of other people in the shared sleeping space and being monitored by staff from above.

It was also noted in Chapter 4 that cell sharing, even when it is only by two imprisoned people, causes increased risks of violence, with shared cells being one of the places in prisons where the risk of sexual assault is highest.[18] These risks are intensified in dormitories, and Australia's past experience with dormitory-style accommodation in prisons is informative in this regard.

A 1983 Victorian Parliamentary inquiry found that dormitory-style accommodation at the Pentridge prison (which closed in 1997) was 'unfit for human habitation' and went on to recommend that 'the first priority should be to move substantially from dormitory accommodation to single cells in Victorian gaols'.[19] There had been a series of sexual assaults in the Pentridge dormitories, a riot and a fire in the 1970s. When the Victorian Attorney-General announced the closure of these dormitories, he made it clear that '[t]he conditions in the dormitories are unacceptable in this day and age. They are intolerable for both inmates and staff … and can only be described as Dickensian'.[20]

Dormitory-style accommodation has also been dispensed with in juvenile detention centres, with a NSW Ombudsman's report finding that 'reliance upon dormitory accommodation is generally not conducive to detainees' safety or their privacy'.[21]

Other countries currently use dormitory-style accommodation in prisons and the parliamentary committee reviewing 'rapid build' prisons in NSW heard evidence of the problems in these countries, as follows:

---

18   Brian Steels and Dot Goulding, *Predator or Prey? An Exploration of the Impact and Incidence of Sexual Assault in West Australian Prisons* (November 2009) 50–1.
19   Victorian Parliament Legislative Council, Select Committee of the Legislative Council upon the Victorian Prisons Service, *Interim Report* (1984).
20   Referred to in Carolyn McKay, *Responses to Questions on Notice to the Inquiry into Parklea Correctional Centre and Other Operational Issues on Friday 28 September 2018* (October 2018) 2 <www.parliament.nsw.gov.au/lcdocs/other/11917/AQON%20-%20Dr%20Carolyn%20McKay.pdf>.
21   NSW Ombudsman, *Inquiry into Juvenile Detention Centres* (NSW Ombudsman, 1996) vol 1, cited in Australian Law Reform Commission, *Seen and Heard: Priority for Children in the Legal Process*, Report No 84 (1997) [20.40].

International experiences regarding the use of dormitory-style complexes have revealed significant problems for the security and safety of individuals inside them. In the United States and Romania, it has been reported that issues such as group and personal tension, increased assault against prisoners and staff, sexual assault and theft have increased within these prisons. The lack of privacy and personal space for prisoners in these facilities has exacerbated mental illnesses, which ultimately diminish a prisoners' capacity for reintegration upon release.[22]

In short, the combination of this architecture and regime in NSW prima facie violates the rights of imprisoned people to security of the person (ICCPR art 9), privacy (ICCPR art 17) and to be treated with humanity and respect (ICCPR art 10(1)), as well as potentially violating the prohibition against TCID.

'Supermax' Prisons

'Supermax' facilities were originally designed in the United States of America from the 1970s to impose a severe regime of isolation on the segments of the prison population seen to be the most difficult to manage (eg, due to being violent).[23] In a 'supermax' prison, imprisoned people spend 23 hours per day in their cell and, when out of their cell, have no contact with other imprisoned people or staff. If they are allowed contact with people outside, this may be via videoconference, rather than in person.[24] This is why this is described as a regime, in addition to an approach to architectural design.

There have been a number of examples of so-called 'supermax' facilities around Australia at various times, such as the high-risk management unit in Goulburn prison in NSW, the Melaleuca unit in Barwon prison in Victoria and the Woodford prison in Queensland.

The former Katingal unit within Sydney's Long Bay prison was specifically designed to have 'no natural light in the building and only from enclosed exercise yards surrounded by high walls could prisoners see the sky, and then only through roof bars'.[25] The unit operated for three years, closing in

---

22   New South Wales, above n 17, 85.
23   Derek Jeffreys, 'Segregation and Supermax Confinement. An Ethical Evaluation' in Yvonne Jewkes et al (eds), *Handbook on Prisons* (Routledge, 2016) 174–5.
24   Ibid 175.
25   Chris Cunneen et al, *Penal Culture and Hyperincarceration. The Revival of the Prison* (Ashgate, 2013) 126.

1978 after a Royal Commission finding that 'the cost of Katingal is too high in human terms',[26] with Grant and Jewkes noting the 'sensory deprivation conditions were considered to be an abuse of inmate human rights'.[27]

A current example of 'supermax' conditions is the Woodford prison in Queensland, which is specifically designed to house people convicted under anti-association legislation targeted at 'Criminal Motorcycle Gangs' (mentioned in Chapter 4). People in this prison are held in solitary confinement for 22 hours per day without access to sunlight during that period. The policy states, '[o]ut of cell time restricted to at least two daylight hours a day'.[28]

These type of 'supermax' conditions are quite likely to attract the criticism of the SPT, as they have done in New Zealand. The SPT has expressed the following concerns:

> the delegation noted with grave concern that the newly built management cells at the Auckland maximum security prison (where persons were held in solitary confinement) were extremely small, were under constant video surveillance, afforded little room for internal movement or activity and could best be likened to a tin can. The so-called exercise yard was a small cage situated immediately across the corridor from the cells and afforded no opportunity for exercise at all ... It considers the use of them for any prolonged period to amount to ill-treatment.[29]

Therefore, 'supermax' prisons in Australia are also likely to violate the prohibition against TCID.

Underground Prison in Victoria

The Melbourne Custody Centre is located underground—underneath the Melbourne Magistrates' Court—such that there is no natural light or fresh air. It is intended to be used to accommodate people on a short-term basis prior to their appearance in court. However, more recently, due to

---

26   Justice Nagle, *Report of the Royal Commission into NSW Prisons* (1978) 165; ibid 127. Another past example of such a unit is the Jika Jika unit in Pentridge Prison in Victoria: Bree Carlton, *Imprisoning Resistance: Life and Death in an Australian Supermax* (Institute of Criminology Press, 2007).

27   Elizabeth Grant and Yvonne Jewkes, 'Finally Fit for Purpose: The Evolution of Australian Prison Architecture' (2015) 95(2) *The Prison Journal* 223, 237.

28   Cited by Applegarth J in *Callanan v Attendee Z* [2013] QSC 342, [27]. For eight other examples of 'supermax' prisons see Mirko Bagaric, Richard Edney and Theo Alexander, '(Particularly) Burdensome Prison Time Should Reduce Imprisonment Length – and Not Merely in Theory' (2014) 38 *Melbourne University Law Review* 409, 414.

29   SPT, above n 7, 17–18.

overcrowding in Victorian prisons, it has been used to accommodate people for 14 days or longer.[30] Imprisoned people have described the conditions in the Centre in interviews as follows: '[t]hirty days. I did not see daylight for 30 days' and '[I] wouldn't keep my dog like this'.[31]

The General Manager has admitted to the Victorian Ombudsman that the facility fails to comply with the *Charter of Human Rights and Responsibilities Act 2006* (Vic) ('*Charter*'): 'It doesn't, we breach it [the *Charter*]. We all know that the Centre was designed to cater, to manage prisoners for a daily court occurrence, and then go to prison, or get bail or whatever. Not to be kept overnight and certainly not to be kept for 14 or 17 days'.[32] Further, the Victorian Coroner has described it as 'totally inappropriate, inhumane', and 'completely unacceptable in a modern society'.[33] The Victorian Ombudsman has concluded, '[i]n my view, detainees should not be held at the Melbourne Custody Centre for greater than five consecutive days'.[34]

The physical design of this facility arguably cannot be modified sufficiently to comply with the human rights of imprisoned people. Yet policies to ameliorate the effects of the physical environment, such as mandating a maximum length of stay, have not been employed.

Hanging Points

In the discussion about the failure to implement recommendations by monitoring bodies in Chapter 3, it was noted that in 1991 the Royal Commission into Aboriginal Deaths in Custody highlighted the serious risks posed by the prison environment for Indigenous people in general. A specific concern raised was hanging points in cells.[35] Despite more than 25 years having passed since this inquiry, many prisons in Australia have not made the necessary adjustments to implement the recommendations, and the built environment continues to pose risks to this vulnerable segment of the prison population.[36]

---

30 Ombudsman Victoria, *Investigation into Deaths and Harms in Custody* (2014) 10.

31 Bronwyn Naylor, 'Human Rights and Respect in Prisons: The Prisoners' Perspective' in Bronwyn Naylor, Julie Debeljak and Anita Mackay (eds), *Human Rights in Closed Environments* (Federation Press, 2014) 97.

32 Ombudsman Victoria, above n 30, 46.

33 Ombudsman Victoria and Office of Police Integrity, *Conditions for Persons in Custody. Report of Ombudsman Victoria and Office of Police Integrity July 2006* (2006) 49.

34 Ombudsman Victoria, above n 30, 51.

35 Royal Commission into Aboriginal Deaths in Custody, *National Report* (1991) [165].

36 Lorana Bartels, 'Twenty Years On: Indigenous Deaths in Police Custody and Lessons from the Frontline' in Isabelle Bartkowiak-Théron and Nicole Asquith (eds), *Policing Vulnerabilities* (Federation Press, 2012).

Even worse, there have been new prisons built in the Northern Territory (NT) with hanging points in the cells. The NT has the highest rate of Indigenous imprisonment in Australia, with 83.4 per cent of the prison population being Indigenous.[37] The NT Coroner stated in a coronial inquest report that 'it beggars belief that a prison designed and constructed in the 21st century has such classic hanging points with no mitigation of that risk'.[38] This comment relates to the Darwin Correctional Precinct which was opened in 2014.[39] Concerns about hanging points in other jurisdictions were noted in Chapter 3.

Climatic Conditions

The Australian climate is harsh and there are prisons built in some very hot and cold parts of the country. To begin with an example of a prison in an extremely hot part of the country, the OICS in WA has specifically reviewed the 'thermal conditions' in WA prisons and highlighted concerns about the Roebourne prison, described as being 'in one of the harshest climatic parts of Western Australia'.[40] The Inspector noted the prison had been built from unsuitable building material and the result was temperatures that were 'a significant threat to prisoner health', noting that '[t]he non-air-conditioned cells rarely recorded temperatures below 30°C and attained temperatures close to 40°C'.[41] The Inspector noted some of the points made in Chapter 1 about the prison as a 'total institution' and the poor general health of the prison population, specifically, that imprisoned people have no choice about when they are in these hot cells and also have higher rates of health conditions that make them more susceptible to the heat.[42]

In contrast, Hobart in Tasmania is a particularly cold part of Australia during winter. Yet the design of some of the prisons there was modelled on Californian prisons, making them inappropriate for Tasmanian winter temperatures.[43] The Tasmanian Office of the Custodial Inspector

---

37   Australian Bureau of Statistics, *Prisoners in Australia 2019* (5 December 2019) Table 14.
38   *Inquest into the Death of Roy Melbourne* [2017] NTLC 017 [47].
39   'New $500 Million Darwin Prison at Holtze Opens with Smoking Ceremony', *ABC News* (Australia), 9 September 2014.
40   OICS, *Thermal Conditions of Prison Cells* (2015) iii.
41   Ibid. See the summary of temperature data collected by the Inspector on page 10.
42   Ibid ii.
43   In relation to the Ron Barwick prison: Tasmanian Custodial Inspector, *Inspection of Adult Custodial Services in Tasmania, 2017 Care and Wellbeing Inspection Report* (October 2018) 44. In relation to the Risdon prison: Grant and Jewkes, above n 27, 227.

(TOCI) has raised concerns about the thermal conditions in the Ron Barwick Minimum Security Prison, noting that the 'cells are cold even in summer'.[44] In winter, there are problems with excessive condensation on cell walls to the extent that the paint peels of the walls and certain cells are unusable due to the build-up of mould.[45] Imprisoned people are also strip searched in a cold room.[46] The TOCI does not deal specifically with the health implications of this, but the OICS has insightfully noted that imprisoned people's poor health is likely to be exacerbated by thermal discomfort, whether due to cold or heat.[47]

Specific Needs of Some Groups Within the Prison Population

It has been emphasised throughout this book that the prison population display multiple vulnerabilities. The challenges faced by Indigenous people and older people in prisons demonstrate the importance of modifications being made to the built environment to cater for the needs of specific groups.

Indigenous People

Grant conducted qualitative research about the needs and preferences of Indigenous people in relation to prison accommodation in South Australia to document the ways in which they are not met by typical prison infrastructure.[48] Five matters of significance to have emerged from this research.

First, connection to country is vital for Indigenous people because this 'increased their feelings of wellbeing and decreased their feelings of disorientation'.[49] This is the case regardless of whether they are from an 'urban, rural or remote' area.[50] Most imprisoned Indigenous people in Australia are located a long distance from their country and denied the ability to practise their customary lore.[51]

---

44 Tasmanian Custodial Inspector, above n 43, 44.
45 Ibid 44–5.
46 Ibid 44.
47 OICS, above n 40, 4. That report also dealt with some West Australian prisons facing challenges with cold conditions: see the discussion of Bandyup and Albany prisons in ibid 12–15.
48 Elizabeth Grant, 'Prison Environments and the Needs of Australian Aboriginal Prisoners: A South Australian Case Study' (2008) 12(2) *Australian Indigenous Law Review* 66.
49 Ibid 69.
50 Elizabeth Grant, 'Designing Carceral Environments for Indigenous Prisoners: A Comparison of Approaches in Australia, Canada, Aotearoa New Zealand, the US and Greenland (Kalaallit Nunaat)' (2016) (1) *Advancing Corrections Journal* 26, 37.
51 Ibid 69.

Second, maintaining links to community, family and kin is essential to improve wellbeing and reduce incidence of suicide.[52] Yet, due to '[a] lack of affordable or reliable transport, the poor health of family members, and long distances to the prison', Indigenous people often do not get many, or indeed any, visits during their incarceration.[53]

Third, social groupings are an important form of support during imprisonment and Grant found these to be 'based on family/kin relationships, language groupings, shared histories of institutional life and mutual activities'.[54] However, these are complex, and Indigenous people preferred not to be forced to share with other Indigenous people solely because of their shared identity as such. In fact, problems can be created by putting certain groups in close proximity.[55]

Fourth, single cells are preferred for privacy and security. This is contrary to current policy where Indigenous people are housed in dormitories or shared cells, with overcrowding causing significant distress in many cases.[56]

Fifth, due to the poor health of many Indigenous people in prison (as referred to in Chapter 1), it is important that they are provided with a healthy prison environment with adequate health care. Grant notes that the design needs to take into account people's health needs.[57]

Elderly People

In Chapter 1, it was noted that the Australian Institute of Criminology defines elderly people in prison to be those over 50 years of age, which takes into account that the health of people in prison is generally worse than that of people in the general community.[58] The increase in elderly people in prisons and some of the reasons for this increase were also outlined.

---

52   Also recognised during the Royal Commission into Aboriginal Deaths in Custody, above n 35, [24.3.111]–[24.3.122], [25.3.1]–[25.3.2].
53   Grant, above n 48, 70.
54   Ibid 71.
55   Ibid 71–2.
56   Ibid 72; Grant, above n 50, 36.
57   Grant, above n 50, 41–2. This has led some prisons in Canada to introduce 'healing lodges': see further at 31–2.
58   Susan Baidawi et al, *Older Prisoners—A Challenge for Australian Corrections* (Trends and Issues in Crime and Criminal Justice No 426, 2011) 1.

The main challenge faced by elderly people in prison relate to their physical and mental health needs, which differ to those of younger people in the prison population. They are similar to those faced by older people in the general community. Physical health problems include 'frailty, reduced mobility, incontinence and sensory impairment' and mental health problems include dementia, Alzheimer's disease and depression.[59] Some of these problems may be exacerbated by the prison environment,[60] particularly when (if any) thought was given to the inhabitants of the building, the imagined inhabitants were fit, able-bodied young men. For example, shared cells have bunk beds, often without ladders, and older people find it difficult to access the top bunk. More generally, there are stairs and uneven surfaces in many prisons and the showers are not designed for people who cannot stand under them, nor the toilets for people who cannot easily sit and stand without a railing to hang on to.

Elderly people in prison do not all have special needs. However, of those who do have particular age-related requirements, their needs are diverse, depending on such matters as their mobility levels, general health and length of time spent in prison.[61] The focus of this discussion is how the needs of this group relating to the built environment may be accommodated.

It is not impossible to accommodate the needs of this group through changes to the built environment. The following suggestions are based on the NSW Inspector of Custodial Services review of managing elderly people in NSW prisons. However, some additional strategies and recommendations from HMIP in the UK have been included because the UK has been grappling with the challenges posed by the ageing prison population for longer than Australia.[62] The problems and the way they might be addressed are outlined in Table 8.1.

---

59   NSW Inspector of Custodial Services, *Old and Inside: Managing Aged Offenders in Custody* (2015) 26.
60   For an analysis of how the prison environment contributes to psychological distress see Susan Baidawi, Christopher Trotter and Catherine Flynn, 'Prison Experiences and Psychological Distress Among Older Inmates' (2016) 59(3) *Journal of Gerontological Social Work* 252.
61   Ibid 29. Her Majesty's Inspectorate of Prisons raised a similar concern: see Her Majesty's Inspectorate of Prisons (HMIP), *'No Problems – Old and Quiet': Older Prisoners in England and Wales. A Thematic Review by HM Chief Inspector of Prisons* (2004) v.
62   This is partly because, in 2001, the United Kingdom's Department of Health issued a 'National Service Framework for the Care of Older People' referring to the needs of older people in prisons, and this led to the HMIP examination of these needs: ibid. This topic has also been examined in Canada: The Correctional Investigator Canada, *Aging and Dying in Prison. An Investigation into the Experiences of Older Individuals in Federal Custody* (2019).

Table 8.1: Catering for the Needs of Elderly People in Prison

Problem identified by New South Wales Inspector of Custodial Services	Modification recommended by New South Wales Inspector of Custodial Services	Modification recommended by Her Majesty's Inspectorate of Prisons (HMIP)
Older people being allocated a top bunk. Older people find top bunks difficult to get into—particularly because no ladders are provided—and instances of people falling off them, leading to them requiring medical attention.[63]	Bunk beds should be fitted with ladders and protective rails.[64]	Elderly imprisoned people should be given single cells, or at least allocated the bottom bunk in shared cells.[65]
People requiring mobility aids, including walkers and wheelchairs, cannot get these into their cells due to narrow doorways and lack of space in the cells. This increases the risk of falls.[66]	Placement decisions include a consideration of the mobility needs of the person.[67]	
Lack of seating and shelter in the outdoor areas, where people are locked out during 'out-of-cell hours'.[68]	Ensure there is 'shelter and appropriate seating' to cater for elderly people in the outdoor areas.[69]	
Lack of rails to help people sitting and standing when using the toilet.[70]	Fixtures need to be improved so that they are suitable for elderly people.[71]	
Those with mobility problems having difficulty navigating stairs (eg, to get to the yard), 'steep gradient ramps, and high-gloss slippery, uneven surfaces' to access facilities such as the medical clinic and library.[72]	Placement decisions include a consideration of the mobility needs of the person.[73]	Special provisions, such as the installation of lifts, need to be made for people with limited mobility or in wheelchairs.[74]

63   NSW Inspector of Custodial Services, above n 59, 9. This is a concern that has also been raised in relation to the Alexander Maconochie Centre in the ACT: ACT Inspector of Correctional Services, *Report of a Review of a Correctional Centre by the ACT Inspector of Correctional Services Healthy Prison Review of the Alexander Maconochie Centre* (2019) 98.
64   Ibid 29, Recommendation 1.
65   HMIP, above n 61, 3.
66   NSW Inspector of Custodial Services, above n 59, 10, 30, 43.
67   Ibid 34, Recommendation 34.
68   Ibid 31.
69   Ibid 32, Recommendation 3.
70   Ibid 29, 43.
71   Ibid 43, Recommendation 11.
72   Ibid 27, 43. HMIP raised a similar concern: see HMIP, above n 61, 8.
73   NSW Inspector of Custodial Services, above n 59, 34, Recommendation 34.
74   HMIP, above n 61, 8.

As the number of elderly people in prisons continues to grow, it will become increasingly necessary for modifications to be made to the built environment to cater to their needs. The ACT Inspector has recently recommended that a specific policy be developed that 'articulates and responds to the needs of older detainees'.[75] This recommendation is broader than just considering the physical conditions in prison. It is advisable that all jurisdictions give this matter appropriate attention.

Access to Basic Necessities

There are other aspects of prison conditions, in addition to the physical design of buildings, relevant to the human rights of imprisoned people. These conditions are not just a matter of what is desirable; rather, they have a crucial impact on the mental and physical health of imprisoned people. The four factors discussed below—food and drink, personal hygiene, clothing and access to outside areas—are all examples of what Sykes termed 'deprivation of goods and services' (as summarised in Chapter 1). Medical care is also a basic necessity (and falls under what Sykes terms 'deprivation of autonomy'), but this was dealt with in Chapter 7.

While these basic necessities are discussed separately, for the purposes of clarifying the types of basic necessities prison authorities should give attention to, there are two important points to note about their interrelationships.

First, many of the cases discussed below involve complaints about a multitude of basic necessities. It is unlikely that a situation will ever be identified where an imprisoned person lacks only one basic necessity. The courts take into account the totality of the prison conditions when determining whether relevant human rights have been violated. This is encapsulated by the ECtHR statement, '[w]hen assessing conditions of detention, account has to be taken of the cumulative effects of these conditions, as well as of specific allegations made by the applicant'.[76]

Second, the courts are unlikely to find the mere absence of basic necessities to constitute TCID in breach of art 7 of the ICCPR. There is a threshold that must be reached, and the court's assessment will include consideration of the likely effect of the conditions on the particular person making the

---

75   ACT Inspector of Correctional Services, above n 63, 98.
76   *Bădilă v Romania* [2012] ECHR 31725/04, [70].

complaint. The statement of the HR Committee in its views in *Brough v Australia* is illustrative in this regard: 'The assessment of this minimum depends on all the circumstances of the case, such as the nature and context of the treatment, its duration, its physical or mental effects and, in some instances, the sex, age, state of health or other status of the victim'.[77]

These interrelationships provide important context for the case illustrations given in the following discussion. In particular, a human rights violation may have been found to have occurred, but this finding is likely to have been connected to the denial of multiple basic necessities as well as the effect of the deprivation on the particular complainant.

Food and Drink

The type, availability and variety of food and drink provided to people in prison are of major significance for their nutrition and wellbeing. They may also be of significance for their religious beliefs. This is recognised in the *Guiding Principles for Corrections in Australia*, which stipulate that food be 'nutritious', 'adequate for good health' and 'meets prisoners' cultural, religious and dietary needs'.[78] Three relevant cases illustrate how these concerns have arisen in Australian prisons.

First, Mr Islam sued the Australian Capital Territory (ACT) for failing to provide him with food consistent with his religious beliefs as a Muslim. The claim relied on the protection of freedom of religion by s 14 of the *Human Rights Act 2004* (ACT) ('*HRA*') and s 40 of the *Corrections Management Act 2007* (ACT) (*CMA*) which requires the Director-General to 'ensure, as far as practicable, that allowance is made for the religious, spiritual and cultural needs of detainees in relation to the provision of food and drink'.

The Court heard evidence that there are occasions where imprisoned people are not provided with food consistent with their dietary requirements (including their religious beliefs), but that on most occasions this is rectified at the time.[79] On one occasion, Mr Islam was provided with a roll for lunch containing processed chicken, which he does not eat, and

---

77 Human Rights Committee, *Views: Communication No 1184/2003*, UN Doc CCPR/C/86/D/1184/2003 (17 March 2006) ('*Brough v Australia*') [9.2]. The position of the ECtHR is similar. See, eg, *Husayn (Abu Zubaydah) v Poland* [2014] ECHR 7511/13, [500].

78 Principles 4.2.2 and 4.2.3: Corrective Services Administrators' Conference (Cth), *Guiding Principles for Corrections in Australia* (2018) 22.

79 *Islam v Director-General of the Department of Justice and Community Safety Directorate* [2018] ACTSC 322, [102], [109], [116]–[118].

the prison did not rectify the situation such that he did not have any lunch that day.[80] Prison staff gave evidence that imprisoned people with dietary requirements were required to fill in a 'special diet request' form, but Mr Islam and an imprisoned person involved in delivering food gave evidence that they had never heard of this form and Mr Islam had not had the opportunity to fill in such a form.[81]

The Court found that the kitchen at the prison generally accommodates dietary requirements 'as far as practicable' within the meaning of the *CMA*,[82] and that the *HRA* requires there to be a system in place for providing for dietary requirements. There was such a system, in the form of the 'special diet request' form. The Court found that non-compliance with that system was 'not of such a degree as to amount to a contravention of Mr Islam's human rights to practice his religion through adherence to a particular diet'.[83]

Second, Mr Minogue sued the Victorian Department of Corrections on the basis that he was not provided with nutritious vegetarian meals and was provided with meals consisting of 'identical ingredients presented in an identical manner' twice per day for three years.[84] His claim was based on two arguments: art 10(1) of the ICCPR, which the Court held was not enforceable in an Australian court (the case was decided before the *Charter* was enacted);[85] and the 'right to be provided with special dietary food' contained in s 47(1)(c) of the *Corrections Act 1986* (Vic), which the Court held did not provide an enforcement mechanism.[86] Therefore, Mr Minogue's claim was unsuccessful.[87]

Third, Mr Mahommed, a Muslim, made a complaint to the Queensland Anti-Discrimination Tribunal about the lack of availability of fresh halal meat. For some of the time Mr Mahommed was imprisoned, he was provided with the general menu containing non-halal meat.[88]

---

80   Ibid [103].

81   Ibid [86]–[90], [104], [108], [120].

82   Ibid [116]–[118].

83   Ibid [119]–[123]. The Court noted that there did need to be better communication about the process to follow: at [121].

84   See *Minogue v Williams* [1999] FCA 1585, [4].

85   Ibid [35].

86   Ibid [34].

87   The decision was upheld on appeal in *Minogue v Williams* [2000] 60 ALD 366. For another example of a claim concerning the provision of vegetarian food—one that was successful—see *Monteiro v State of New South Wales (No 2)* [2015] NSWSC 1901 (15 December 2015).

88   *Mahommed v State of Queensland* [2006] QADT 21 (4 May 2006), [3].

For a different period of time, he was provided with only vegetarian food.[89] Then, for yet a further period, he was provided with four cans of halal meat per week in addition to fresh vegetarian meals.[90] Due to limitation periods under the *Anti-Discrimination Act 1991* (Qld), the Tribunal was only able to consider the last two types of diet.[91] The Tribunal held that Mr Mahommed had been treated less favourably because he had been provided with vegetarian meals when he was not a vegetarian, and because he did not receive any fresh meat.[92] He was awarded $2,000 compensation.[93]

For the purposes of international law, the HR Committee has provided an opinion that failure to supply food or drink to a person in police custody for five days (followed by a period of very little thereafter) violated art 10 of the ICCPR.[94] The ECtHR has also found the provision of inadequate food—specifically, a daily ration of '100 grams of porridge with water twice a day and a soup consisting of mainly water for lunch, with an additional 400 grams of bread for the whole day'—to violate art 3 of the *European Convention for the Protection of Human Rights and Fundamental Freedoms* (ECHR)[95] (art 3 specifies that '[n]o one shall be subjected to torture or to inhuman or degrading treatment or punishment'). This was in the context of the deprivation of other basic necessities and also took into account the period for which the applicant was kept in such conditions.[96]

Of particular relevance, the SPT has raised concerns about the lack of nutritious food provided to imprisoned people in New Zealand, and the fact that no food was provided for a long period between 3.30 pm and 8.30 am the next morning. The SPT recommended that 'the quality, variety, nutritional value and times of meals be reviewed'.[97] These are the type of matters the SPT is likely to review when they visit Australia.

---

89   Ibid [4].
90   Ibid [6].
91   Ibid [8].
92   Ibid [29]–[31].
93   Ibid [65]. The Queensland Government's appeal of the decision was dismissed by the Supreme Court: *State of Queensland v Mahommed* [2007] QSC 18 (19 February 2007). Another example of a person of Muslim faith not being provided with halal meat lead to the claim in *Ali v State of Queensland* [2013] QCAT 319 (6 August 2013).
94   Human Rights Committee, *Views: Communication No 526/93*, UN Doc CCPR/C/59/D/526/1993 (2 April 1997) ('*Hill and Hill v Spain*').
95   *Ciorap v Moldova* [2007] ECHR 12066/02, [9].
96   Ibid [69]–[71].
97   SPT, above n 7, 17.

Personal Hygiene

There are two components to the basic necessity of personal hygiene. The first is ensuring people are not exposed to unhygienic conditions. The second is the positive obligation to provide facilities for people to maintain their personal hygiene. The latter includes having access to showers and other washing and personal grooming facilities. Access to such facilities is important for preventing skin problems and other diseases, and, more generally, for being able to take pride in one's appearance, which relates to a person's dignity. The international cases relating to personal hygiene most often arise in situations of severe overcrowding.

In relation to unhygienic conditions, the HR Committee has considered exposure to unhygienic conditions in circumstances where imprisoned people were forced to sleep on the floor, share a toilet with 150 other people, and use a bathroom that had defective drainage, 'forcing the authors to bath in six inches of dirty water'.[98] The ECtHR has also considered situations where cells 'were dirty and infested with cockroaches, bed-bugs and lice' to be problematic.[99]

The OICS has frequently criticised cell sharing in WA prisons leading to people having to use a toilet in front of others. In 2016, the Inspector noted that people locked in prisons for more than 12.5 hours per day were required to use an 'unscreened' toilet in front of others.[100] In 2013, they noted that '[t]his lack of privacy, now common throughout the Western Australian prison system, is fundamentally degrading'.[101]

In addition to being degrading, as the above quotation highlights, this is a situation contrary to the requirements of art 7 of the ICCPR, and in violation of imprisoned people's right to privacy under art 17 of the ICCPR. Having to use a toilet in front of another person, or people, is another reason that the physical environment in Australian prisons is not human rights compliant.

A South Australian Coroner's report referred to a lack of privacy for use of the toilet due to people sharing the cell, the lack of hygiene given that the deceased was sharing a cell with a person with a communicable disease,

---

98   Human Rights Committee, *Views: Communication No 676/1996*, UN Doc CCPR/C/62/D/676/1996 (30 March 1998) ('*Yasseen and Thomas v Guyana*') [2.3].
99   *Mayzit v Russia* [2005] ECHR 63378/00, [40]–[41].
100   OICS, *Western Australia's Prison Capacity* (2016) 15.
101   OICS, *Report of an Announced Inspection of Greenough Regional Prison* (2013) 26.

and the fact that the deceased was sleeping on a mattress on the floor next to the toilet.[102] Women were also found to be sleeping on trundle beds on the floor with their heads next to the toilet in a WA women's prison.[103]

The NSW Inspector of Custodial Services has also raised concerns about various unhygienic conditions in NSW prisons in reports, including:

- '[t]here is one bubbler in the yard. There is no separate tap for hand washing. So when inmates use the toilet they must wash their hands in the same bubbler as the inmates use for drinking'[104]
- following a review of bedding in correctional centres in NSW, the Inspector found that at one centre, the mattresses were 'dirty, stained, torn and unhygienic, with raw foam exposed'.[105]

In relation to the positive obligation to provide facilities to maintain personal hygiene, in the ECtHR case of *Bădilă v Romania*, being denied the ability to maintain personal hygiene in circumstances where no running water was provided was found by the Court to constitute TCID.[106] One of the 'cumulative' factors leading to an art 3 violation in *Bazjaks v Latvia* was that 'the applicant did not receive any personal hygiene products such as soap, toothbrush or toilet paper'.[107] Another instance was where people were only allowed to shower every 10 days.[108] The combination of this factor, and other conditions of detention, led to a finding that art 3 of the ECHR had been breached.[109]

A relevant problem identified in Queensland is that during a drought in 2009, a number of prisons imposed restrictions on the number of times toilets may be flushed per day (four to six times), as well as restrictions on the number and length of showers people could take (one shower per day lasting no more than three or four minutes).[110] This policy was applied

---

102 W C Chivell, *Inquest into Death of Marshall Freeland Carter*, South Australia Coroners Court, 2000, 14–15.
103 OICS, *Report of an Announced Inspection of Bandyup Women's Prison* (2014) vi, viii, 19.
104 NSW Inspector of Custodial Services, *Full House: The Growth of the Inmate Population in NSW* (2015) 61.
105 NSW Inspector of Custodial Services, *Prison Greens: The Clothing and Bedding of Inmates in NSW* (2017) 31. This concern was also raised in NSW Inspector of Custodial Services, above n 59, 30.
106 *Bădilă v Romania* [2012] ECHR 31725/04, [77]–[79].
107 *Bazjaks v Latvia* [2010] ECHR 71572/01, [116].
108 *Aliev v Ukraine* [2003] ECHR 41220/98, [139].
109 Ibid [151].
110 The different numbers relate to the different application of the policy in various prisons: Prisoners' Legal Service, *Inside Out* (Issue No 58, June 2013) 16, 23.

to women who were menstruating, arguably in breach of Rule 5 of the Bangkok Rules which requires that a 'regular supply of water' 'be made available for the personal care of children and women, in particular women [... who are] menstruating'.[111] This policy made it difficult for people to maintain personal hygiene, particularly in the hot, humid climate typical in Queensland.

Another concern relating to women being able to maintain their personal hygiene while menstruating was raised by the NT Ombudsman. Women in the Alice Springs prison were required to request sanitary products from male staff members.[112] The Ombudsman suggested this policy be reviewed and the processes be modified such that women could request these items from female staff, or access them from a vending machine.[113] There have also been problems with elderly males in NSW prisons with incontinence getting access to continence aids and sufficient access to clothing and bedding to maintain good hygiene.[114]

Clothing

The type of clothing people in prison wear, their access to appropriate clothing for the climatic conditions, and the frequency and process for these to be washed, are also important to their wellbeing. It may also contribute to an absence of personal hygiene if clothing is not washed frequently enough. Mandela Rule 19 stipulates:

1. Every prisoner who is not allowed to wear his or her own clothing shall be provided with an outfit of clothing suitable for the climate and adequate to keep him or her in good health. Such clothing shall in no manner be degrading or humiliating.

2. All clothing shall be clean and kept in proper condition. Underclothing shall be changed and washed as often as necessary for the maintenance of hygiene.

Clothing as a basic necessity is unlikely to, of itself, lead to the finding of a human rights violation. However, when considered in the context of other conditions and treatment, it will be a relevant factor. In the previously mentioned HR Committee case of *Brough v Australia*, all of

---

111 Ibid 23.
112 Ombudsman NT, *Ombudsman NT Investigation Report. Women in Prison II - Alice Springs Women's Correctional Facility* (2017) vol 2, 103.
113 Ibid vol 1, 62.
114 NSW Inspector of Custodial Services, above n 59, 32.

the applicant's clothes except his underwear were removed when he was put into an isolation cell because they may have been used to obstruct the cameras.[115] When he was later found trying to construct a noose using his underwear, this item was also removed.[116] The combined effects of the lack of heating, absence of clothing and blankets, and other conditions and treatment led the HR Committee to the view that art 7 of the ICCPR had been violated.[117]

The ECtHR has heard cases where complaints about clothing were made together with complaints about other aspects of conditions. Two examples will suffice. In *Dankevich v Ukraine*, an imprisoned person complained that he only had 'light' clothes to wear in temperatures of −20°C.[118] The ECtHR found that the totality of the prison conditions had violated art 3 of the ECHR. These conditions included being locked up for 24 hours per day with no access to natural light or contact with people outside the prison.[119] In *Bazjaks v Latvia*, the complainant's 'clothes were never taken to the prison laundry, so that he was obliged to wear the same underwear for two months'.[120] The ECtHR was not satisfied based on the evidence available that art 3 had been violated in this instance.[121]

There are two relevant Australian examples, the first relating to outerwear in Queensland and the second relating to underwear in Tasmania. In Queensland, a requirement was introduced that people convicted under Queensland 'Criminal Motorcycle Gang' legislation wear bright pink overalls in prison.[122] This was intended to be a form of humiliation, with Premier Newman reportedly stating that '[w]e know that asking them - well, not asking them telling them - to wear pink is going to be embarrassing for them'.[123] This is contrary to Mandela Rule 19(1) quoted above that specifically prohibits 'humiliating' clothing.[124] In addition to

115 Human Rights Committee, *Views: Communication No 1184/2003*, UN Doc CCPR/C/86/D/1184/2003 (17 March 2006) ('*Brough v Australia*') [2.8].
116 Ibid [2.10].
117 Ibid [3.3].
118 *Dankevich v Ukraine* [2003] 40679/98, [113].
119 Ibid [141].
120 *Bazjaks v Latvia* [2010] ECHR 71572/01, [27].
121 Ibid [95].
122 Andrew Trotter and Harry Hobbs, 'The Great Leap Backward: Criminal Law Reform with the Hon Jarrod Bleijie' (2014) 36(1) *Sydney Law Review* 1, 21. Legislation to control motorcycle clubs was discussed in Chapter 4.
123 David Lewis, 'Officers Who Question Qld Police Bikies Crackdown Told to "Reconsider Their Future"', *ABC News* (Australia), 22 October 2013.
124 Coyle and Fair, above n 4, 45.

the problematic nature of requiring people to wear particular clothing for the purposes of humiliation, it is also a discriminatory implementation of a clothing policy given that it only applies to one subset of the prison population in one particular prison (Woodford).[125]

In Tasmanian prisons, upon arrival, people were being issued with inadequate amounts of underwear and socks (two pairs of each) that had also previously been used by other people. This was not enough underwear for the maintenance of personal hygiene. The Tasmanian Custodial Inspector wrote of this situation, '[i]t is not considered acceptable for prisoners to wear previously used underwear, even if it has been freshly washed' and recommended that the prison service cease this practice.[126]

Access to Outside Areas

Access to outside areas to get fresh air, sunshine and exercise play a part in the health (both physical and mental) of imprisoned people. It affects, for example, people's ability to produce vitamin D and build or maintain physical health and fitness. Deprivation of natural light for 23 hours per day (other than one hour of daily recreation), in the view of the HR Committee, may amount to violation of art 10(1) of the ICCPR.[127] It was also a violation in a situation where a person was only allowed out of their windowless cell for one to two hours on weekdays, and not at all on weekends and holidays (due to a lack of staff availability).[128]

This is also something that has been raised by the SPT. For example, when inspecting prisons in New Zealand, the SPT noted that many imprisoned people only had a short time outdoors, for example, 30 minutes, and that the outdoor areas were covered, thus restricting access to sunlight. As a consequence, many had developed vitamin D deficiencies.[129]

---

125 This policy only lasted nine months. Following a change of government in Queensland, it was described by the incoming Police Minister as 'a brain snap; it was a stupid and ridiculous idea': Josh Bavas, 'Newman Government's Pink Bikie Prison Uniforms to be Sold Off as Breast Cancer Charity Fundraiser', *ABC News* (Australia), 2 June 2015.
126 Tasmanian Custodial Inspector, above n 43, 29.
127 Human Rights Committee, *Views: Communication No 676/1996*, UN Doc CCPR/C/62/D/676/1996 (30 March 1998) ('*Yasseen and Thomas v Guyana*') [7.6].
128 Human Rights Committee, *Views: Communication No 683/1996*, UN Doc CCPR/C/74/D/683/1995 (26 March 2002) ('*Wanza v Trinidad and Tobago*') [9.2].
129 SPT, above n 7, 17.

All people kept in solitary confinement in Australian prisons have insufficient access to outside, as detailed in Chapter 7, as do those kept in the 'supermax' prisons discussed earlier in this chapter.

Improving Physical Conditions in Australian Prisons

There is certainly huge scope for improvement in the prison conditions in Australian prisons, both in terms of the built environment and access to basic necessities. Nevertheless, there are some positive examples. The first is the way that human rights were taken into account in the design of the Alexander Maconochie Centre (AMC) in Canberra—a fairly new prison opened in 2009—which had the intended aim of being a human rights–compliant prison.[130] There has also been at least one attempt to meet the specific needs of Indigenous people.

These matters all relate to the built environment. In relation to access to basic necessities, it is hoped that the discussion of what not to do in the preceding sections will provide clear enough guidance about how to avoid human rights violations in future. It has certainly identified issues that the SPT and NPM will be looking for when they inspect Australian prisons.

The Alexander Maconochie Centre

The project manager for the ACT prison project that culminated in the building of the AMC was Dr John Paget, and the subject of his doctoral thesis was the role of architecture in the creation of human rights–compliant prisons.[131] Paget's thesis starts from the premise that the prison population is made up of people who are vulnerable, with the specific vulnerabilities including higher than average rates of mental illness, disability and victimisation. There are large numbers of Indigenous people in prison, people with mental illness and people from a low socio-economic background.

---

130 Anita Mackay, 'The Road to the ACT's First Prison (the Alexander Maconochie Centre) was Paved with Rehabilitative Intentions' (2012) 11(1) *Canberra Law Review* 33.
131 John Paget, *Human Rights and Prison Architecture: The Alexander Maconochie Centre from Conception to Construction* (PhD Thesis, Charles Sturt University, 2008).

Therefore, Paget explored aspects of architecture that may be calming, or healing, to the extent that this is possible within the institutional setting of a prison. He raised numerous architectural considerations, all of which are features in the design of buildings, such as hospitals. They include the importance of:

- having access to the natural environment, which can be therapeutic[132]
- minimising the amount of noise people in prison are exposed to, which may reduce their stress levels[133]
- having windows in cells, noting that '[i]n the prison cell or room the window provides sunlight penetration and a view which facilitates connection to the world outside the prison and to memories of normality'[134]
- research by the UK Home Office about the use of colour in correctional facilities to impact the mood of people in prison.[135]

These design features are reflected in modern prison design in Europe:

> An absence of hard fixtures and furnishings, the use of psychologically effective colour schemes, an attention to the maximum exploitation of natural light, and the incorporation of unevenness and differing horizons in the belief that distances, shadows and minimization of spatial repetition ward off monotony, are all to be found in prison buildings throughout Europe.[136]

The ways in which these features apply in practice is exemplified by the AMC, which makes use of secure glazing on cell windows instead of bars, and has been designed to ensure that the view from cell blocks is of open space, rather than of other cell blocks.[137] The AMC has cottages that allow people to live in a more normal environment. For example, they can cook

---

132 Ibid 126.
133 Ibid 138. The NSW Inspector of Custodial Services has reported that prisons are typically very noisy, writing: '[e]xcessive noise in the custodial setting arises from the clashing of steel doors against steel door frames and the continuous low frequency rumble of air-conditioning or other climate control systems together with the noise arising from the concentration of many people in limited spaces': NSW Inspector of Custodial Services, above n 15, 19.
134 Ibid 142.
135 The Home Office has produced a *Colour Design Guide* (2007) for correctional facilities which is discussed by ibid 156–8.
136 Philip Hancock and Yvonne Jewkes, 'Architectures of Incarceration: The Spatial Pains of Imprisonment' (2011) 13(5) *Punishment and Society* 611, 621.
137 John Hargreaves, '"Beyond Rehab": Where Does the Prison Fit?' (2009) 21(1) *Current Issues in Criminal Justice* 148, 151.

their own meals in the kitchen and are expected to do their own cleaning (until recently, all women were accommodated in the cottages).[138] The AMC is also 'a 'campus-style' facility with a central "town square", and program, education and industries blocks'.[139]

Consideration was given to the design of the visitors' area to ensure that it is 'welcoming and normalised'. There is a children's play area with toys, a café staffed by imprisoned people and 'café style' seats.[140] Paget noted that the design of the visiting area was intended to 'allow children to be seated with a prisoner to give effect to the principle that children should not suffer for the transgressions of their parents or relatives'.[141]

Designing for the Needs of Indigenous People

The specific needs of Indigenous people outlined earlier in this chapter were taken into account during the design of the new West Kimberley Regional Prison (Kimberley prison), which opened in late 2012. Before the design of this prison is outlined, a note of caution is in order. This prison is an example of positive steps being taken to overcome specific concerns; however, culturally sensitive prison design initiatives should *not* be used as a justification for imprisoning more Indigenous people. Instead, active steps should be taken to reduce Indigenous over-representation (justice reinvestment, as referred to in Chapter 4, may be a useful strategy in this regard). Further, regardless of the built environment, imprisonment will always be a damaging place for all people, and especially for Indigenous people.[142]

---

138 ACT Human Rights and Discrimination Commissioner, *Human Rights Audit on the Conditions of Detention of Women at the Alexander Maconochie Centre* (2014) 7, 38. Women were relocated out of the cottages in 2017 due to the number of women in custody exceeding capacity: ACT Inspector of Correctional Services, *Report of a Review of the Care and Management of Remandees at the Alexander Maconochie Centre* (2019) 10, 73. The accommodation that the women are currently in has been criticised by the Inspector of Correctional Services as unsuitable for a range of reasons: at 73–8.
139 ACT Auditor-General, *The Rehabilitation of Male Detainees at the Alexander Maconochie Centre (Report No 2 of 2015)* (2015) 27.
140 ACT Human Rights and Discrimination Commissioner, above n 138, 58–9.
141 Paget, above n 131, 277. It is noted that due to expansion of the Alexander Maconochie Centre, combined with the number of people detained exceeding the capacity of the prison, visits are restricted: ACT Inspector of Correctional Services, above n 138, 65.
142 See the discussion about daily life in Australian prisons in Chapter 1. In relation to Indigenous people, the damaging nature of prisons was well documented by the Royal Commission into Aboriginal Deaths in Custody, above n 35.

The Kimberley prison was designed in consultation with the local community.[143] The prison is located on the country of many of those sentenced to it, and people live in housing units arranged into clusters. Grant explains the rationale for this as follows:

> When people come into regional centers, they tend to locate their homes or camps in a radial manner aligning with the direction of their particular 'country' ... These arrangements are mirrored in the housing clusters at the prison, allowing inmates to live with countrymen in housing that is more closely aligned with their home 'country'.[144]

People are housed with others from their own family or language group, and attention is paid to separating groups who may be in conflict.[145] Each unit houses six to eight people, and each person has their own room. There are communal kitchens, living rooms and bathrooms.[146] Some units afford the opportunity for people to sleep outdoors on a secure veranda.[147] There is also an Australian Rules football field which provides an opportunity for people to play football together and gather with their family when they visit.[148]

Concluding Remarks on Improving Physical Conditions

The ACT's consideration of human rights when designing the AMC and Western Australia's consideration of the needs of Indigenous people when designing the Kimberley prison are in many ways atypical. Most jurisdictions around Australia are in a position of having to manage with very old buildings where there are structural features contrary to the human rights of imprisoned people. These include, for example, lack of in-cell sanitation, lack of windows and/or adequate heating and cooling.

There are also examples across Australia of brand new prisons built without taking into account human rights compliance, such as the new dormitory-style accommodation in NSW 'rapid build' prisons. There are hanging points in a recently built prison in the NT.

---

143 Elizabeth Grant, 'Innovation in Meeting the Needs of Indigenous Inmates in Australia' (2013) 75(4) *Corrections Today* 52, 57.
144 Ibid 54.
145 Ibid.
146 Ibid.
147 Ibid 56.
148 Ibid 54.

Whether a prison is old or new, neither the infrastructure nor a lack of resources can be used as a defence for failing to provide a built environment that is human rights compliant, or for sustaining a prison environment that exposes people to TCID. A similar point may be made here to that made in Chapter 3 about the cost of preventive monitoring versus the costs of imprisonment overall;[149] prison expansion; compensation payments;[150] and Royal Commissions, coronial inquests and other mechanisms to investigate deaths, harm and human rights violations after they have occurred. Ensuring decent physical conditions in prisons will cost a fraction of the cost of dealing with the human and economic costs of the problems caused by not having such conditions.

Conclusion

Physical conditions and the provision of basic necessities in prisons have been the subject of much litigation internationally and in Australia. This may be because it is easier to prove cases involving poor physical conditions than it is to prove other breaches of international human rights law, such as not being treated with 'dignity and respect' and denial of opportunities for rehabilitation. Nevertheless, it is true that physical conditions play a central role in people's experience of incarceration, largely because prisons are 'total institutions'. This, in turn, impacts on imprisoned people's overall wellbeing.

Once again, Australian prisons cannot be shown to meet the prerequisite of providing physical conditions that are human rights compliant. Problems have been identified in both the built environment and access to basic necessities. Appropriate provision of food and drink, the ability to maintain personal hygiene and access to outside areas have all been the subject of litigation. These problems are part of the deprivation of goods and services component of the 'pains of imprisonment'.[151]

---

149 Imprisoning people costs $3.8 billion each year nationally: Lorana Bartels, 'Criminal Justice Reform Challenges for the Future: It's Time to Curb Australia's Prison Addiction' in Ron Levy et al (eds), *New Directions for Law in Australia: Essays in Contemporary Law Reform* (ANU Press, 2017) 123.
150 For example, the Western Australian Government's $3.2 million compensation payment to the family of Mr Ward who died in a prison transport van: Chalpat Sonti, 'Multimillion-Dollar Payout to Mr Ward's Family After Prison Van Death', *WA News* (Western Australia), 29 July 2010.
151 Gresham Sykes, *Society of Captives; A Study of a Maximum Security Prison* (Princeton University Press, 1958). See the discussion of the relevance of this to Australian prisons in Chapter 1.

Some major adjustments are required to the physical conditions in Australian prisons to satisfy international human rights law requirements. The first priority must be to reduce reliance on imprisonment in accordance with the first prerequisite. Overcrowding is undoubtedly the number one barrier to decent physical conditions in Australian prisons.

When considering the built environment, there is an urgent need to reconsider harmful regimes such as 'supermax' facilities and 'rapid build' dormitory-style prisons. There is also a need to ensure adequate attention is given to the thermal conditions in prison cells. Specific attention needs to be given to groups with particular needs, particularly Indigenous and elderly people. There are some examples of best practice from around Australia that can be drawn on in this endeavour.

In relation to provision of basic necessities (food and drink, personal hygiene, clothing and access to the outside), it should be just that—basic. People should not have to use a toilet in front of another person, they should not be provided with second-hand underwear, if they need special dietary requirements they should be catered for, people need clothing that is suitable for the climatic conditions and they need regular access to sunlight and the outdoors. The cases discussed in this chapter should provide insight into the parameters of the human rights requirements for the provision of basic necessities.

Perhaps the simplest approach would be for policymakers and architects approaching prison design to consider this question: Would I want my brother or sister to be accommodated here in these conditions if they were convicted of a crime? If the answer is 'no', then it should be back to the drawing board.

Conclusions

There is a large gap between the international human rights law applicable to prisons, which Australia has chosen to be bound by, and daily prison operations in individual prisons across Australia. This gap exists for a number of reasons, including the lack of international enforcement mechanisms, lack of effective human rights protections nationally and difficulty in translating some of the requirements into practice. Australian imprisonment policy is formulated in the absence of human rights legislation in five jurisdictions out of eight, and in the absence of a well-established human rights culture in the broader community.

Most importantly, there are certain characteristics of Australian society as a whole, and also within its prisons, that are antithetical to both the spirit and the letter of international human rights law. Australian imprisonment policy prioritises punitiveness and related goals such as deterrence and retribution, at the expense of rehabilitation and restoration. This has arguably led to increasing prison populations, the over-representation of certain vulnerable groups in the community within the prison population and a consistent picture of overcrowded prisons across the country.[1]

The culture within Australian prisons is consistent with the observations of sociological literature on prisons as 'total institutions' and on the 'pains of imprisonment' detailed in Chapter 1.[2] There is also a heavy emphasis on 'security and good order' in both corrections legislation and training programs undertaken by staff. The latter two themes were addressed in Chapters 5 and 7.

---

1   Termed 'hyperincarceration' by Chris Cunneen et al, *Penal Culture and Hyperincarceration. The Revival of the Prison* (Ashgate, 2013).
2   In reliance on the sociological analyses of Goffman ('total institutions') and Sykes ('pains of imprisonment'): Erving Goffman, *Asylums. Essays on the Social Situation of Mental Patients and Other Inmates* (Aldine Publishing Company, 1962); Gresham Sykes, *Society of Captives; A Study of a Maximum Security Prison* (Princeton University Press, 1958).

It is undoubtedly the case that Australian prisons do not currently comply with Australia's international human rights law obligations. Indeed, the situation is such that it is easy to despair. Yet there is at least some reason for hope.

First, Australia's ratification of the *Optional Protocol to the Convention against Torture and Other Cruel, Inhuman or Degrading Treatment or Punishment* (OPCAT) in December 2017 represents a significant opportunity for a change to this situation.[3] The OPCAT shifts the focus to *prevention*, whereas the current monitoring regime in Australia is predominantly reactive (that is, dealing with deaths and harms after they have occurred). Australia's ratification was voluntary and opens it to a level of ongoing monitoring that will make the ingrained non-compliance with international human rights law in Australian prisons (both in policy and practice) more difficult to ignore.

Second, it is clear what needs to be done to improve Australia's compliance with its international human rights obligations in line with the commitment displayed by the ratification of the OPCAT. To this end, this book has proposed five prerequisites that will help to achieve the preventive aims of the OPCAT, particularly the prevention of 'torture and other cruel, inhuman or degrading treatment or punishment' (TCID). They are:

1. reduce reliance on imprisonment (Chapter 4)
2. align domestic legislation with Australia's international human rights law obligations (Chapter 5)
3. shift the focus of imprisonment to the goal of rehabilitation and restoration (Chapter 6)
4. support prison staff to treat imprisoned people in a human rights–consistent manner (Chapter 7)
5. ensure decent physical conditions in all prisons (Chapter 8).

The prerequisites provide clarity about how international human rights law should be operationalised in Australian prisons, including by clarifying abstract terms such as 'rehabilitation' and treatment 'with humanity and with respect for the inherent dignity',[4] identifying the parameters of the

---

3   *Optional Protocol to the Convention against Torture*, adopted 18 December 1992, UN Doc A/RES/57/199 (entered into force 22 June 2006) ('OPCAT').

4   As required, respectively, by arts 10(3) and 10(1) of the *International Covenant on Civil and Political Rights*, opened for signature 19 December 1966, 999 UNTS 171 (entered into force 23 March 1976) ('ICCPR').

obligations and providing practical strategies that should be put in place to achieve compliance with the international human rights law obligations. Moreover, the prerequisites reinforce each other. There are connections between these prerequisites that suggest that striving to achieve one may have positive implications for achieving all five.

Achieving prerequisite one (reduced reliance on imprisonment) can contribute to the achievement of all other prerequisites except for two (legislative change). Prison occupancy rates have a significant impact on the physical conditions in prisons (prerequisite five). It is crucial for avoiding cell sharing and the concomitant risk of violence and lack of privacy. Reducing the prison population is also of assistance in ensuring there are enough resources to provide programs and facilities for the purposes of rehabilitation and restoration (prerequisite three), and to ensure the prison population is small enough to foster positive relationships, based on care and respect, between staff and imprisoned people (prerequisite four).

Prerequisite two (domestic legislation), if achieved, also has considerable potential to assist with the implementation of several others. The Treaties Australia has signed require domestic incorporation of the human rights contained in therein.[5] It is important that the National Preventive Mechanism (NPM) has domestic legislation to refer to when carrying out inspections of prisons, in the way that the Australian Capital Territory (ACT) Inspector of Correctional Services is required by legislation to provide reports to the ACT Legislative Assembly containing 'an assessment about whether the rights under international and territory law of detainees at a correctional centre subject to review are protected'.[6]

Australian legislation across all jurisdictions (that is, beyond the ACT, Victoria and Queensland) needs to incorporate the prohibition against TCID and *International Covenant on Civil and Political Rights* (ICCPR) art 10(1) requirement that '[a]ll persons deprived of their liberty shall be treated with humanity and with respect for the inherent dignity of the human person'. Then there can be an Australia-wide commitment to the preconditions both for the staff duty to treat imprisoned people in a human rights–consistent manner (prerequisite four), and decent physical

5   ICCPR art 2; *Convention on the Rights of Persons with Disabilities*, opened for signature 30 March 2007, 2515 UNTS 3 (entered into force 3 May 2008) art 4 ('CRPD').
6   *Inspector of Correctional Services Act 2017* (ACT) s 27(2)(c).

conditions (prerequisite five). Moreover, this legislation can establish the goal of the prison system as rehabilitation in accordance with art 10(3) of the ICCPR (prerequisite three), contrary to current corrections and sentencing legislation that prioritise other goals.

If a focus on rehabilitation and restoration can be established (prerequisite three), it will soon become clear that this is more difficult to achieve in overcrowded conditions and that prerequisite one must be addressed. Nor can rehabilitation and people's early release from prison be achieved without the support of staff—staff who need to be trained and assisted to develop appropriate attitudes and skills to provide respectful and caring treatment, as required by prerequisite four.

Respectful treatment in and of itself has been found in empirical research to be extremely important to imprisoned people's experience of incarceration. Respectful treatment can improve wellbeing, whereas the absence of respect can cause distress, anxiety and depression.[7] When respectful treatment is prioritised, TCID is less likely to occur.

Respectful treatment and avoidance of TCID (prerequisite four) are both easier to foster in smaller prisons, where it is more likely that staff can build interpersonal relationships with imprisoned people. Reduced reliance on imprisonment is thus important for achieving human rights–consistent treatment. Respectful treatment also supports the prerequisite of rehabilitation. An important way to prepare people for their release from prison is to improve their ability to relate to others. It is useful when respectful treatment is mandated by law (prerequisite two), although a legal requirement is merely a starting point. Factors such as staff training and human rights–focused leadership are necessary for this to work in practice.

Finally, decent physical conditions (prerequisite five) are difficult, if not impossible, to achieve when prisons are overcrowded. It was argued that the prerequisite for decent physical conditions is lower in the hierarchy of prerequisites than others because it can be ameliorated by compliance with other prerequisites in a way that they cannot. However, it still forms a crucial concern from the perspective of imprisoned people who spend 24 hours per day seven days per week in the physical environment of

---

7   Karin Beijersbergen et al, 'Procedural Justice and Prisoners' Mental Health Problems: A Longitudinal Study' (2014) 24 *Criminal Behaviour and Mental Health* 100, 101.

the prison. It is also likely to be a subject that takes up a lot of time of the NPM if the experience of existing prison inspectorates and other monitoring organisations is anything to go by.

International case law demonstrates that unsatisfactory physical conditions may breach the prohibition of TCID. This is something both the Subcommittee for the Prevention of Torture and Other Cruel, Inhuman or Degrading Treatment or Punishment (SPT) and NPM will be examining. It is also important that the physical conditions are modified to cater for the needs of particular groups in the prison population, including Indigenous and elderly people. The physical conditions of prisons may also play a part in fostering rehabilitation because there needs to be enough space available for educational programs and work opportunities (prerequisite three).

Towards Human Rights Compliance: One Prerequisite at a Time

The picture of Australian prisons painted throughout this book is not positive. There is no state or territory operating prisons without human rights violations occurring, or that are entirely human rights compliant. These violations occur because of macro-level goals across prisons that have a surprising degree of consistency, despite the fact that prisons are the responsibility of the states and territories. Those goals place too much emphasis on punishment and punitiveness, security and good order— at the expense of goals such as rehabilitation and humane treatment.

There are numerous state and territory legislative provisions and policies that preclude humane treatment of imprisoned people by prison staff. These include policies relating to shackling of imprisoned people seeking medical assistance, policies mandating strip searching and legislation that overrides imprisoned people's right to consent to medical treatment (this is not to suggest that daily interactions between staff and imprisoned people are never positive).

The Australian Government's ratification of the OPCAT indicates a commitment to improving prison conditions around Australia. This preventive focus should lead to a significant shift in emphasis for prison monitoring domestically, as well opening up places of deprivation of liberty to scrutiny by the expert members of the SPT. In particular, the

OPCAT's preventive focus identifies ways that TCID can be prevented and prison policy and operations improved. Therefore, the government's ratification of the OPCAT is a reason for hope.

The prerequisites identified in this book echo this preventive focus. Each prerequisite has provided an illustration of national best practice and/ or a combination of strategies that may be employed to work towards improvements. Moreover, while many of the practices identified in earlier chapters are disheartening, there are signs of movement towards positive changes. Some can be identified in relation to most prerequisites.

With respect to the first prerequisite, justice reinvestment has led to some reductions in prison populations overseas, with the State of Texas in the United States of America often referred to as a success because of the reduction in prison growth and redirection of funds to community-based programs such as substance abuse treatment programs.[8] Some Australian trials also indicate some early successes with this approach (eg, Bourke in New South Wales (NSW)), although the trials are in preliminary stages. The ACT has also extended its justice reinvestment strategy due to the initial success of some trials.[9] If the recommendations about justice reinvestment made by the Australian Law Reform Commission in 2017 (including the establishment of a national coordinating body)[10] are implemented, justice reinvestment may help curb Australia's 'addiction to prisons'.[11] This will need to be pursued alongside other reductionist strategies, including amendments to sentencing legislation, outlined in Chapter 4.

There is a very good model of a legislative scheme aligned with Australia's international human rights law obligations in the ACT. This is a comprehensive model for the second prerequisite. The ACT has statutory protection of human rights by the *Human Rights Act 2004* (ACT) ('*HRA*'), as well as corrections legislation that is the most recent in

---

8   Australian Institute of Criminology (AIC), *Justice Reinvestment in Australia: A Review of the Literature* (Research Report No 9, 2018) 51.

9   Jordan Hayne and Niki Burnside, 'Canberra's Only Jail is Running Out of Cells, But the Government Wants to "Build Communities Not Prisons"', *ABC News* (Australia), 15 February 2019.

10   Australian Law Reform Commission (ALRC), *Pathways to Justice—An Inquiry into the Incarceration Rate of Aboriginal and Torres Strait Islander Peoples*, Report No 133 (2017) 137–8, Recommendations 4-1, 4-2.

11   Lorana Bartels, 'Criminal Justice Reform Challenges for the Future: It's Time to Curb Australia's Prison Addiction' in Ron Levy et al (eds), *New Directions for Law in Australia: Essays in Contemporary Law Reform* (ANU Press, 2017) 119.

Australia (passed in 2007) and aligned with the *HRA*.[12] It has appointed a new Inspector of Correctional Services required by legislation to monitor how well the Alexander Maconochie Centre complies with the *HRA* and international human rights law.[13] The Inspector has published detailed inspection standards based on the World Health Organization's 'healthy prison' test, which has been used as a basis for prison inspections by Her Majesty's Inspectorate of Prisons in the United Kingdom for over a decade.[14] A set of human rights principles provide further detail to that contained in the *HRA*, Corrections Act and standards and may also be of assistance to the Inspector when carrying out inspections.[15] Other Australian jurisdictions need look no further than the ACT to find a model of best practice for domestic legislative protection of imprisoned people's rights (prerequisite two).

Making the goal of imprisonment consistent with art 10(3) of the ICCPR to achieve the third prerequisite is complex. There is a lack of guidance from the United Nations Human Rights Committee about how this article is to be implemented by states parties to the ICCPR. For this reason, is has been recommended that Australia focus on rehabilitation *and restoration*. Restorative justice is well established in Australia, which may make transferring restorative principles into prisons easier. The 'Sycamore Tree' program operated in West Australian prisons may provide a starting point for development of restorative prisons.[16]

The fourth prerequisite—staff duty to treat imprisoned people in a human rights–consistent manner—has two sides to it: a positive duty to treat people with humanity and respect for their human dignity (as required by art 10(1) of the ICCPR) and the prohibition of TCID. Many policies need to be revised to achieve compliance with this prerequisite because it is recognised that staff are bound to follow policies.

---

12 *Corrections Management Act 2007* (ACT).

13 *Inspector of Correctional Services Act 2017* (ACT) s 27(2)(c).

14 ACT Inspector of Correctional Services, *ACT Standards for Adult Correctional Services* (2019).

15 ACT Government, Justice and Community Safety, *Human Rights Principles for ACT Correctional Centres* (January 2019).

16 Dot Goulding, Guy Hall and Brian Steels, 'Restorative Prisons: Towards Radical Prison Reform' (2008) 20(2) *Current Issues in Criminal Justice* 231, 236, 239–40. For a more recent discussion of the 'Sycamore Tree' program see Jane Anderson, 'Introducing and Theorising an In-Prison Restorative Justice Programme: The Second-Generation Sycamore Tree Project' (2018) 1(2) *International Journal of Restorative Justice* 210.

There are also specific practical strategies that can be pursued in addition to policy and legislative changes. The first is training. The human rights–focused training provided by the ACT to give staff a solid grounding in their human rights obligations is a useful starting point for other states and territories to learn from.[17] The second is increasing the value placed on prison work by the wider community. The 'National Corrections Day' held in NSW is a positive step in this direction.[18] Improving the length of training provided to Australian prison staff would help both to improve their preparedness for the work and increase recognition by the community, because they would be gaining accreditation in provision of a social service (helping prepare staff to be law-abiding citizens upon their release). Expanded training is also required to ensure that training covers all the international human rights law requirements comprehensively, and to support staff to manage the complex vulnerabilities found within the Australian prison population. The third is leadership, and the changes made in the Tihar Central Prison in New Delhi demonstrate that one progressive leader can achieve a lot in a short amount of time.[19]

Finally, the improvement of physical conditions in prisons, to achieve the fifth prerequisite, will require that all new prisons are built with human rights at the forefront of design, in the way that the Alexander Maconochie Centre was designed.[20] It is unlikely that all older prison buildings will be decommissioned or rebuilt, but modifications can be made to existing buildings. These should include removing hanging points; installing air-conditioning and heating to protect against climatic conditions; and providing appropriate sleeping, toilet and shower arrangements for elderly people. Serious consideration needs to be given to the use of 'supermax' and dormitory-style 'rapid build' prisons because these are unlikely to be able to be modified to be human rights compliant. Architecture is no barrier to provision of basic necessities, including food and drink, personal hygiene,

17   Lorana Bartels and Jeremy Boland, 'Human Rights and Prison. A Case Study from the Australian Capital Territory' in Leanne Weber et al (eds), *The Routledge International Handbook of Criminology and Human Rights* (Routledge, 2017) 564.
18   NSW Government, Communities and Justice, *National Corrections Day* <https://www.corrective services.justice.nsw.gov.au/Pages/CorrectiveServices/national-corrections-day.aspx>.
19   A J W Taylor and John Rynne, 'Exemplary Prisoner Management' (2016) 49(4) *Australian & New Zealand Journal of Criminology* 512, 519–20. Taylor and Rynne's discussion of other innovative prison managers is also useful.
20   John Paget, *Human Rights and Prison Architecture: The Alexander Maconochie Centre from Conception to Construction* (PhD Thesis, Charles Sturt University, 2008).

clothing and access to outside areas, and there should be no excuse for Australian prisons not providing these. The minimum living conditions guaranteed by legislation in the ACT are a useful starting point.[21]

Concluding Remarks

It may be trite to say that 'prevention is always better than cure', but when one considers the litany of human rights abuses occurring in Australian prisons across all jurisdictions on a daily basis, it is important to remember it. For there is no 'cure' in the sense that deaths are irreversible, and an already vulnerable population is being harmed by practices including solitary confinement, strip searching, being shackled while receiving medical care, being left to give birth unaided in a prison cell, being forced to share overcrowded prison cells and other practices.

The OPCAT requires that human rights abuses be prevented before they occur. This book has demonstrated that there are a range of practical ways this may be achieved, with five overarching prerequisites, and detailed consideration of practical strategies that will help to implement each of them. Australia will benefit from the assistance of the SPT in establishing an NPM. The branch of the NPM responsible for prison monitoring will build on the monitoring expertise of existing prison inspectorates, Ombudsmen and human rights commissions. It will hopefully plug the gaps in the existing monitoring regime and offer the benefit of a national coordinated approach to improving prison operation across the states and territories. A national approach will provide opportunities for good practices to be transferred between prisons and between jurisdictions, consistent with the preventive aim of the OPCAT.

The OPCAT is nevertheless not a panacea, as shown by the erratic progress made in some of the countries that ratified the OPCAT many years ago.[22] But the OPCAT does represent an opportunity to reimagine

---

21   *Human Rights Act 2004* (ACT) s 12; *Corrections Management Act 2007* (ACT) ch 6. However, case law demonstrates that there are problems in practice with the provision of food and drink. See, eg, *Islam v Director-General of the Department of Justice and Community Safety Directorate* [2018] ACTSC 322 (discussed in Chapter 8).

22   For example, the United Kingdom has had a National Preventive Mechanism (NPM) in place since 2009. A recent annual report of the NPM raised concerns about a range of matters relating to prisons, including the number of self-inflicted deaths and insufficient time out of cells: NPM, *Monitoring Places of Detention. Ninth Annual Report of the United Kingdom's National Preventive Mechanism 1 April 2017 – 31 March 2018* (2019) 13.

the purpose of imprisonment in Australia, focus attention on the inherent risks associated with the deprivation of people's liberty and proactively counter those risks. Australia has elected to ratify the OPCAT, as well as the Treaties that protect the human rights of imprisoned people. People in prison deserve the benefit of any protection international human rights law may provide and any improvement it may offer to their treatment and the prison conditions in which they live their lives.

Select Bibliography

Journal Articles

Aertsen, Ivo and Tony Peters, 'Mediation and Restorative Justice in Belgium' (1998) 6 *European Journal on Criminal Policy and Research* 507

Anderson, Jane, 'Introducing and Theorising an In-Prison Restorative Justice Programme: The Second-Generation Sycamore Tree Project' (2018) 1(2) *International Journal of Restorative Justice* 210, doi.org/10.5553/ijrj/258908912018001002003

Bagaric, Mirko, 'An Argument for Uniform Australian Sentencing Law' (2013) 37(1) *Australian Bar Review* 40

Bagaric, Mirko, Richard Edney and Theo Alexander, '(Particularly) Burdensome Prison Time Should Reduce Imprisonment Length – and Not Merely in Theory' (2014) 38 *Melbourne University Law Review* 409

Baidawi, Susan, Christopher Trotter and Catherine Flynn, 'Prison Experiences and Psychological Distress Among Older Inmates' (2016) 59(3) *Journal of Gerontological Social Work* 252, doi.org/10.1080/01634372.2016.1197353

Bartels, Lorana, 'The ACT Prison: Human Rights Rhetoric Versus Crowded and Bored Reality' (2015) 9 *Court of Conscience* 13

Bartels, Lorana et al, 'Bail, Risk and Law Reform: A Review of Bail Legislation Across Australia' (2018) 42 *Criminal Law Journal* 91

Bartels, Lorana, Robin Fitzgerald and Arie Freiberg, 'Public Opinion on Sentencing and Parole in Australia' (2018) 65(3) *Probation Journal* 269, doi.org/10.1177/0264550518776763

Bateman, Will and James Stellios, 'Chapter III of the Constitution, Federal Jurisdiction and Dialogue Charters of Rights' (2012) 36 *Melbourne University Law Review* 1

Beijersbergen, Karin et al, 'Procedural Justice and Prisoners' Mental Health Problems: A Longitudinal Study' (2014) 24 *Criminal Behaviour and Mental Health* 100, doi.org/10.1002/cbm.1881

Bower, Alicia, 'Unconstitutionally Crowded: Brown v Plata and How the Supreme Court Pushed Back to Keep Prison Reform Litigation Alive' (2012) 45 *Loyola of Los Angeles Law Review* 555

Brown, David, 'The Nagle Royal Commission 25 Years On. Gaining Perspective on Two and a Half Decades of NSW Prison Reform' (2004) 29(3) *Alternative Law Journal* 135, doi.org/10.1177/1037969x0402900306

Brown, David, 'The Limited Benefit of Prison in Controlling Crime' (2010) 22(1) *Current Issues in Criminal Justice* 137, doi.org/10.1080/10345329.20 10.12035873

Brown, David, Melanie Schwartz and Laura Boseley, 'The Promise of Justice Reinvestment' (2012) 37(2) *Alternative Law Journal* 96, doi. org/10.1177/1037969x1203700206

Bruhn, Anders, Per Åke Nylander and Berit Johnsen, 'From Prison Guards to... What? Occupational Development of Prison Officers in Sweden and Norway' (2017) 18(1) *Journal of Scandinavian Studies in Criminology and Crime Prevention* 68, doi.org/10.1080/14043858.2016.1260331

Buckland, Ben and Audrey Olivier-Muralt, 'OPCAT in Federal States: Towards a Better Understanding of NPM Models and Challenges' (2019) 25(1) *Australian Journal of Human Rights* 23, doi.org/10.1080/132323 8x.2019.1588061

Burgess, Alannah and Catherine Flynn, 'Supporting Imprisoned Mothers and Their Children. A Call for Evidence' (2013) 60(1) *Probation Journal* 73, doi. org/10.1177/0264550513478318

Butler, Tony et al, 'Injury Surveillance in the New South Wales Prison System' (2004) 15(2) *Health Promotion Journal of Australia* 151, doi.org/10.1071/ he04151

Butler, Tony et al, 'Mental Disorders in Australian Prisoners: A Comparison with a Community Sample' (2006) 40 *Australian and New Zealand Journal of Psychiatry* 272

Butler, Tony et al, 'Sexual Behaviour and Sexual Health of Australian Prisoners' (2013) 10 *Sexual Health* 64, doi.org/10.1071/sh12104

Charlesworth, Hilary, 'Australia's Accession to the First Optional Protocol to the International Covenant on Civil and Political Rights' (1991) 18 *Melbourne University Law Review* 428

Charlesworth, Hilary, 'The Australian Reluctance About Rights' (1993) 31(1) *Osgoode Hall Law Journal* 195

Charlesworth, Hilary et al, 'Deep Anxieties: Australia and the International Legal Order' (2003) 25 *Sydney Law Review* 423

Chen, Bruce, 'The *Human Rights Act 2019* (Qld): Some Perspectives from Victoria' (2020) 45(1) *Alternative Law Journal* 1, doi.org/10.1177/1037969x19899661

Clear, Todd and James Austin, 'Reducing Mass Incarceration: Implications of the Iron Law of Prison Populations' (2009) 3 *Harvard Law & Policy Review* 307

Cramp, Taylah and Anita Mackay, 'Protecting Victims and Vulnerable Witnesses Participating in Royal Commissions: Lessons from the 2016–2017 Royal Commission into the Protection and Detention of Children in the Northern Territory' (2019) 29(1) *Journal of Judicial Administration* 3

Crewe, Ben, 'Soft Power in Prison: Implications for Staff–Prisoner Relationships, Liberty and Legitimacy' (2011) 8(6) *European Journal of Criminology* 455, doi.org/10.1177/1477370811413805

Cumming, Craig et al, 'In Sickness and in Prison: The Case for Removing the Medicare Exclusion for Australian Prisoners' (2018) 26 *Journal of Law and Medicine* 140

Debeljak, Julie, 'Parliamentary Sovereignty and Dialogue Under the Victorian *Charter of Human Rights and Responsibilities*: Drawing the Line Between Judicial Interpretation and Judicial Law-Making' (2007) 33(1) *Monash University Law Review* 9

Debeljak, Julie, 'The Rights of Prisoners Under the Victorian Charter: A Critical Analysis of the Jurisprudence on the Treatment of Prisoners and Conditions of Detention' (2015) 38(4) *University of New South Wales Law Journal* 1332

Deitch, Michele, 'Distinguishing the Various Functions of Effective Prison Oversight' (2010) 30 *Pace Law Review* 1438

Dhami, Mandeep, Greg Mantle and Darrell Fox, 'Restorative Justice in Prisons' (2009) 12(4) *Contemporary Justice Review* 433, doi.org/10.1080/10282580903343027

Dixon, Rosalind, 'An Australian (Partial) Bill of Rights' (2016) 14(1) *International Journal of Constitutional Law* 80

Dolan, Kate et al, 'Incidence and Risk for Acute Hepatitis C Infection During Imprisonment in Australia' (2010) 25 *European Journal of Epidemiology* 2

Edney, Richard, 'To Keep Me Safe From Harm? Transgender Prisoners and the Experience of Imprisonment' (2004) 9(2) *Deakin Law Review* 327, doi. org/10.21153/dlr2004vol9no2art247

Evans, Richard, 'Prison Rape: Is it Okay to Make Jokes About Rape in Prison?' (2014) *Arena* 26

Evans, Simon and Carolyn Evans, 'Legal Redress Under the Victorian Charter of Human Rights and Responsibilities' (2006) 17 *Public Law Review* 264

Fortune, Clare-Ann, Tony Ward and Gwenda Willis, 'The Rehabilitation of Offenders: Reducing Risk and Promoting Better Lives' (2012) 19(5) *Psychiatry, Psychology and Law* 646, doi.org/10.1080/13218719.2011.6158 09

Freckelton, Ian, 'Cruel and Unusual Punishment of Prisoners with Mental Illnesses: From Oates to Plata' (2011) 18(3) *Psychiatry, Psychology and Law* 329, doi.org/ 10.1080/13218719.2011.599927

Freckelton, Ian and Patrick Keyzer, 'Fitness to Stand Trial and Disability Discrimination: An International Critique of Australia' (2017) 24(5) *Psychiatry, Psychology and Law* 770, doi.org/10.1080/13218719.2017.1379 105

Freiberg, Arie, 'Suspended Sentences in Australia: Uncertain, Unstable, Unpopular, and Unnecessary Alternatives to Imprisonment' (2019) 82(1) *Law and Contemporary Problems* 81

Freiberg, Arie et al, 'Parole, Politics and Penal Policy' (2018) 18(1) *QUT Law Review* 191

Fuller, Jacqueline, 'The David Eastman Case: The Use of Inquiries to Investigate Miscarriages of Justice in Australia' (2020) 45(1) *Alternative Law Journal* 60, doi.org/10.1177/1037969x19886348

Gerber, Paula and Joel Gory, 'The UN Human Rights Committee and LGBT Rights: What Is It Doing? What Could It Be Doing?' (2014) 14 *Human Rights Law Review* 403, doi.org/10.1093/hrlr/ngu019

Goulding, Dot, 'Violence and Brutality in Prisons: A West Australian Context' (2007) 18(3) *Current Issues in Criminal Justice* 399, doi.org/10.1080/10345 329.2007.12036401

Goulding, Dot, Guy Hall and Brian Steels, 'Restorative Prisons: Towards Radical Prison Reform' (2008) 20(2) *Current Issues in Criminal Justice* 231, doi. org/10.1080/10345329.2008.12035806

Grant, Elizabeth, 'Prison Environments and the Needs of Australian Aboriginal Prisoners: A South Australian Case Study' (2008) 12(2) *Australian Indigenous Law Review* 66

Grant, Elizabeth, 'Innovation in Meeting the Needs of Indigenous Inmates in Australia' (2013) 75(4) *Corrections Today* 52

Grant, Elizabeth, '"Pack 'em, Rack 'em and Stack 'em": The Appropriateness of the Use and Reuse of Shipping Containers for Prison Accommodation' (2013) 13(2) *Australasian Journal of Construction Economics and Building* 35, doi.org/10.5130/ajceb.v13i2.3269

Grant, Elizabeth, 'Approaches to the Design and Provision of Prison Accommodation and Facilities for Australian Indigenous Prisoners after the Royal Commission into Aboriginal Deaths in Custody' (2014) 17(1) *Australian Indigenous Law Review* 47

Grant, Elizabeth, 'Designing Carceral Environments for Indigenous Prisoners: A Comparison of Approaches in Australia, Canada, Aotearoa New Zealand, the US and Greenland (Kalaallit Nunaat)' (2016) (1) *Advancing Corrections Journal* 26

Grant, Elizabeth and Yvonne Jewkes, 'Finally Fit for Purpose: The Evolution of Australian Prison Architecture' (2015) 95(2) *The Prison Journal* 223, doi. org/10.1177/0032885515575274

Groves, Matthew, 'Administrative Segregation of Prisoners: Powers, Principles of Review and Remedies' (1996) 20 *Melbourne University Law Review* 639

Groves, Matthew, 'International Law and Australian Prisoners' (2001) 24(1) *University of New South Wales Law Journal* 17

Groves, Matthew, 'Ombudsmen's Jurisdiction in Prisons' (2002) 28 *Monash University Law Review* 181

Groves, Matthew, 'Editorial: Prison Conditions and the Right to a Fair Trial' (2008) 32 *Criminal Law Journal* 133

Groves, Matthew, 'Prisoners and the Victorian Charter' (2010) 34 *Criminal Law Journal* 217

Guthrie, Jill, Michael Levy and Cressida Forde, 'Investment in Prisons: An Investment in Social Exclusion. Linking the Theories of Justice Reinvestment and Social Inclusion to Examine Australia's Propensity to Incarcerate' (2013) 1(2) *Griffith Journal of Law & Human Dignity* 254

Hancock, Philip and Yvonne Jewkes, 'Architectures of Incarceration: The Spatial Pains of Imprisonment' (2011) 13(5) *Punishment and Society* 611, doi. org/10.1177/1462474511422171

Hardcastle, Lesley, Terry Bartholomew and Joe Graffam, 'Legislative and Community Support for Offender Reintegration in Victoria' (2011) 16(1) *Deakin Law Review* 111, doi.org/10.21153/dlr2011vol16no1art96

Harding, Richard, 'Australia's Circuitous Path Towards the Ratification of the OPCAT, 2002–2017: The Challenges of Implementation' (2019) 25(1) *Australian Journal of Human Rights* 4, doi.org/10.1080/132323 8x.2019.1588062

Harding, Richard and Neil Morgan, 'OPCAT in the Asia-Pacific and Australasia' (2010) 6(2) *Essex Human Rights Review* 99

Hardwick, Nick and Rachel Murray, 'Regularity of OPCAT Visits by NPMs in Europe' (2019) 25(1) *Australian Journal of Human Rights* 66, doi.org/10.1 080/1323238x.2019.1588054

Hargreaves, John, '"Beyond Rehab": Where Does the Prison Fit?' (2009) 21(1) *Current Issues in Criminal Justice* 148, doi.org/10.1080/10345329.2009.120 35837

Heffernan, Edward, Kimina Andersen and Stuart Kinner, 'The Insidious Problem Inside: Mental Health Problems of Aboriginal and Torres Strait Islander People in Custody' (2009) 17(17) *Australasian Psychiatry* S41, doi. org/10.1080/10398560902948696

Hefler, Marita, Robyn Hopkins and David Thomas, 'Successes and Unintended Consequences of the Northern Territory's Smoke-Free Prisons Policy: Results From a Process Evaluation' (2016) 26(2) *Public Health Research and Practice* 1, doi.org/10.17061/phrp2621619

Henderson, Emma and Nicole Shackleton, 'Minority Rights Advocacy for Incarcerated Indigenous Australians: The Impact of Article 27 of the ICCPR' (2016) 41(4) *Alternative Law Journal* 244, doi. org/10.1177/1037969x1604100406

Heydon, Georgina and Bronwyn Naylor, 'Criminal Record Checking and Employment: The Importance of Policy and Proximity' (2018) 51(3) *Australian & New Zealand Journal of Criminology* 372, doi. org/10.1177/0004865817723410

Hillgenberg, Harmut, 'A Fresh Look at Soft Law' (1999) 10(3) *European Journal of International Law* 499, doi.org/10.1093/ejil/10.3.499

Houseman, Lilith, 'Reducing Reliance on Incarceration in Texas: Does Finland Hold Answers?' (2010) 46 *Texas International Law Journal* 209

Jewkes, Yvonne, 'Just Design: Health Prisons and the Architecture of Hope' (2018) 51(3) *Australian & New Zealand Journal of Criminology* 319, doi. org/10.1177/0004865818766768

Jones, Robin and Andrew Day, 'Mental Health, Criminal Justice and Culture: Some Ways Forward?' (2011) 19 *Australasian Psychiatry* 325, doi.org/10.310 9/10398562.2011.579613

Kerr, Anne and Rita Shackel, 'Equality with a Vengeance: The Over-Incarceration of Women' (2018) 147 *Precedent* 20

Lansdell, Gaye et al, '"I am Not Drunk, I Have an ABI": Findings From a Qualitative Study into Systematic Challenges in Responding to People with Acquired Brain Injuries in the Justice System' (2018) 25(5) *Psychiatry, Psychology and Law* 737, doi.org/10.1080/13218719.2018.1474818

Law Institute, 'Calls for Independent Prisons Inspection Body' (2008) 82(6) *Law Institute Journal* 22

Lawson, Anna, 'Disability, Equality, Reasonable Accommodation and the Avoidance of Ill-Treatment in Places of Detention: The Role of Supranational Monitoring and Inspection Bodies' (2012) 16(6) *The International Journal of Human Rights* 845, doi.org/10.1080/13642987.2012.706003

Lerman, Amy and Joshua Page, 'The State of the Job: An Embedded Work Role Perspective on Prison Officer Attitudes' (2012) 14(5) *Punishment & Society* 503, doi.org/10.1177/1462474512464135

Lewis, Sam, 'Rehabilitation: Headline or Footnote in the New Penal Policy?' (2005) 52(2) *Probation Journal* 119, doi.org/10.1177/0264550505052645

Liebling, Alison, 'Moral Performance, Inhuman and Degrading Treatment and Prison Pain' (2011) 13(5) *Punishment & Society* 530, doi. org/10.1177/1462474511422159

Loughnan, Arlie, 'Drink Spiking and Rock Throwing. The Creation and Construction of Criminal Offences in the Current Era' (2010) 35(1) *Alternative Law Journal* 18, doi.org/10.1177/1037969x1003500104

Loughnan, Arlie, '"The Very Foundations of Any System of Criminal Justice": Criminal Responsibility in the Australian Model Criminal Code' (2017) 6(3) *International Journal for Crime, Justice and Social Democracy* 8, doi.org/10.5204/ijcjsd.v6i3.420

Lynch, Sam and Lorana Bartels, 'Transgender Prisoners in Australia: An Examination of the Issues, Law and Policy' (2017) 19 *Flinders Law Journal* 185

Mac Suibhne, Seamus, 'Erving Goffman's *Asylums* 50 Years On' (2011) 198 *The British Journal of Psychiatry* 1, doi.org/10.1192/bjp.bp.109.077172

Mackay, Anita, 'The Road to the ACT's First Prison (the Alexander Maconochie Centre) was Paved with Rehabilitative Intentions' (2012) 11(1) *Canberra Law Review* 33

Mackay, Anita, 'Human Rights Law Compliance in Prisons: What Can Australia Learn From the Nordic Approach?' (2014) 20(1) *Australian Journal of Human Rights* 31, doi.org/10.1080/1323-238x.2014.11882140

Mackay, Anita, 'Stubbing Out Smoking in Prisons. Bans are an Ineffective Mechanism' (2014) 39(2) *Alternative Law Journal* 99, doi.org/10.1177/1037969x1403900207

Mackay, Anita, 'Human Rights Protections for People with Mental Health and Cognitive Disability in Prisons' (2015) 22(6) *Psychiatry, Psychology and Law* 842, doi.org/10.1080/13218719.2015.1015207

Mackay, Anita, 'The Human Rights Implications of Smoking Bans in Closed Environments: What Australia May Learn From the International Experience' (2016) 46 *International Journal of Law, Crime and Justice* 13, doi.org/10.1016/j.ijlcj.2015.12.005

Mackay, Anita, 'Article 10(1) of the International Covenant on Civil and Political Rights (ICCPR) and Australian Prisons' (2017) 23(3) *Australian Journal of Human Rights* 368, doi.org/10.1080/1323238x.2017.1397095

Mackay, Anita, 'The Relevance of the United Nations Mandela Rules for Australian Prisons' (2017) 42(4) *Alternative Law Journal* 279, doi.org/10.1177/1037969x17732706

Mackay, Anita, 'Human rights guidance for Australian prisons: Complementing implementation of the OPCAT' (2020) (Online Advance) *Alternative Law Journal*, doi.org/10.1177/1037969X20962863

Maconochie, Kenneth, 'Captain Alexander Maconochie: Sociologist and Penal Reformer' (2009) 9(3) *The Howard Journal of Criminal Justice* 235, doi. org/10.1111/j.1468-2311.1956.tb00990.x

Malacova, Eva, 'Attitudes Towards Sex: A Comparison of Prisoners and the General Community' (2011) 8 *Sexual Health* 355, doi.org/10.1071/sh10113

Marchetti, Elena, 'Critical Reflections upon Australia's Royal Commission into Aboriginal Deaths in Custody' (2005) 5 *Macquarie Law Journal* 103

Mathieson, Thomas, 'The Politics of Abolition' (1986) 10 *Contemporary Crises* 81

McDonnell, Michelle and James Farrell, 'Tough, Tougher, Toughest? A New Government's Approach to Sentencing Laws in Victoria' (2012) 37(3) *Alternative Law Journal* 238, doi.org/10.1177/1037969x1203700405

McGarrity, Nicola, 'From Terrorism to Bikies. Control Orders in Australia' (2012) 37(3) *Alternative Law Journal* 166, doi.org/10.1177/1037969x1203700305

McGaughey, Fiona, Tamara Tulich and Harry Blagg, 'UN Decision on Marlon Noble Case: Imprisonment of an Aboriginal Man with Intellectual Disability Found Unfit to Stand Trial in Western Australia' (2017) 42(1) *Alternative Law Journal* 67, doi.org/10.1177/1037969x17694790

McGregor, Judy, 'The Challenges and Limitations of OPCAT National Preventive Mechanisms: Lessons From New Zealand' (2017) 23(3) *Australian Journal of Human Rights* 351, doi.org/10.1080/1323238x.2017.1392477

McKay, Carolyn, 'Digital Access to Justice from Prison: Is There a Right to Technology?' (2018) 42 *Criminal Law Journal* 303

McNamara, Luke and Julia Quilter, 'High Court Constitutional Challenges to Criminal Law and Procedure Legislation in Australia' (2018) *University of New South Wales Law Journal* 1047

Meijer, Sonja, 'Rehabilitation as a Positive Obligation' (2017) 25 *European Journal of Crime, Criminal Law and Criminal Justice* 145, doi.org/10.1163/15718174-25022110

Minogue, Craig, 'Why Don't I get the Joke? Prison Rape in the Public Discourse' (2011) 36(2) *Alternative Law Journal* 116, doi. org/10.1177/1037969x1103600209

Moffa, Monique, Greg Stratton and Michele Ruyters, 'Parole Populism: The Politicisation of Parole in Victoria' (2019) 31(1) *Current Issues in Criminal Justice* 75, doi.org/10.1080/10345329.2018.1556285

Moore, John, 'Alexander Maconochie's "Mark System"' (2011) 198 *Prison Service Journal* 38

Naylor, Bronwyn, 'Criminal Records and Rehabilitation in Australia' (2011) 3(1) *European Journal of Probation* 79

Naylor, Bronwyn, 'Researching Human Rights in Prisons' (2015) 4(1) *International Journal for Crime, Justice and Social Democracy* 79

Naylor, Bronwyn, 'Protecting Human Rights in Detention. Rights, Monitoring and OPCAT' (2016) 41(3) *Alternative Law Journal* 151, doi. org/10.1177/1037969x1604100302

Naylor, Bronwyn, Julie Debeljak and Anita Mackay, 'A Strategic Framework for Implementing Human Rights in Closed Environments' (2015) 41 *Monash University Law Review* 218, doi.org/10.1080/1323238x.2015.11910938

Naylor, Bronwyn and Stan Winford, 'Implementing the OPCAT Through Prison Monitoring: The Relevance of Rehabilitation' (2019) 25(1) *Australian Journal of Human Rights* 113, doi.org/10.1080/1323238x.2019.1588060

Nowak, Manfred, 'The Need for a World Court of Human Rights' (2007) 7 *Human Rights Law Review* 251, doi.org/10.1093/hrlr/ngl026

O'Connor, Claire, 'Victims or Offenders? Mental Health Issues in Women's Prisons' (2007) 81 *Precedent* 26

Odgers, Stephen, 'Uniform Evidence Law at 21' (2017) 28(3) *Current Issues in Criminal Justice* 311, doi.org/10.1080/10345329.2017.12036077

Orr, Graeme and George Williams, 'The People's Choice: The Prisoner Franchise and the Constitutional Protection of Voting Rights in Australia' (2009) 8(2) *Election Law Journal* 123, doi.org/10.1089/elj.2008.0016

Owers, Anne, 'Prison Inspection and the Protection of Human Rights' (2004) 2 *European Human Rights Law Review* 107

Owers, Anne, 'The Protection of Prisoners' Rights in England and Wales' (2006) 12 *European Journal on Criminal Policy and Research* 85

Owers, Anne, 'Prison Inspection and the Protection of Prisoners' Rights' (2010) 30(5) *Pace Law Review* 1535

Prisoners' Legal Service, *Inside Out* (Issue No 58, June 2013)

Raynor, Peter and Gwen Robinson, 'Why Help Offenders? Arguments for Rehabilitation as a Penal Strategy' (2009) 1(1) *European Journal of Probation* 3, doi.org/10.1177/206622030900100102

Reisig, Michael, 'The Champion, Contender, and Challenger: Top-Ranked Books in Prison Studies' (2001) 81(3) *The Prison Journal* 389, doi. org/10.1177/0032885501081003006

Ritchers, Juliet et al, 'Consensual Sex Between Men and Sexual Violence in Australian Prisons' (2012) 41 *Archives of Sexual Behavior* 517

Roos, Oscar and Anita Mackay, 'A Shift in the United Nations Human Rights Committee's Jurisprudence on Marriage Equality? An Analysis of Two Recent Communications from Australia' (2019) 42(2) *University of New South Wales Law Journal* 747

Rosenberg, Sebastian et al, 'National Mental Health Reform: Less Talk, More Action' (2009) 190(4) *Medical Journal of Australia* 193, doi. org/10.5694/j.1326-5377.2009.tb02346.x

Sarre, Rick, 'Beyond "What Works?" A 25-Year Jubilee Retrospective of Robert Martinson's Famous Article' (2001) 34(1) *Australian and New Zealand Journal of Criminology* 38, doi.org/10.1177/000486580103400103

Sarre, Rick, 'The Importance of Political Will in the Imprisonment Debate' (2009) 21(1) *Current Issues in Criminal Justice* 154, doi.org/10.1080/10345 329.2009.12035838

Scheerer, Sebastian, 'Towards Abolitionism' (1986) 10 *Contemporary Crises* 5

Schetzer, Louis, 'Queensland's Human Rights Act: Perhaps Not Such a Great Step Forward' (2020) (Advance) *Alternative Law Journal* 1, doi. org/10.1177/1037969x19898538

Schwartz, Melanie, 'Building Communities, Not Prisons: Justice Reinvestment and Indigenous Overimprisonment' (2010) 14(1) *Australian Indigenous Law Review* 2

Shammas, Victor, 'The Pains of Freedom: Assessing the Ambiguity of Scandinavian Penal Exceptionalism on Norway's Prison Island' (2014) 16(1) *Punishment & Society* 104, doi.org/10.1177/1462474513504799

Shinkfield, Alison and Joseph Graffam, 'Community Reintegration of Ex-Prisoners' (2009) 53(1) *International Journal of Offender Therapy and Comparative Criminology* 29, doi.org/10.1177/0306624x07309757

Stathopoulos, Mary, 'Addressing Women's Victimisation in Custodial Settings' (2012) 13 *ACSSA Issues* 1

Steinerte, Elina, 'The Jewel in the Crown and Its Three Guardians: Independence of National Preventive Mechanisms Under the Optional Protocol to the UN Torture Convention' (2014) 14 *Human Rights Law Review* 1, doi. org/10.1093/hrlr/ngt042

Subedi, Surya, 'Protection of Human Rights Through the Mechanism of UN Special Rapporteurs' (2011) 33(1) *Human Rights Quarterly* 201, doi. org/10.1353/hrq.2011.0011

Suzuki, Masahiro and William Wood, 'Co-Option, Coercion and Compromise: Challenges of Restorative Justice in Victoria, Australia' (2017) 20(2) *Contemporary Justice Review* 274, doi.org/10.1080/10282580.2017.1311194

Taylor, A J W and John Rynne, 'Exemplary Prisoner Management' (2016) 49(4) *Australian & New Zealand Journal of Criminology* 512, doi. org/10.1177/0004865815604194

Thornton, Margaret, 'Sex Discrimination, Courts and Corporate Power' (2008) 36 *Federal Law Review* 31, doi.org/10.1177/0067205x0803600102

Tran, Christopher, 'Facts and Evidence in Litigation Under the *Charter of Human Rights and Responsibilities Act 2006* (Vic) and the *Human Rights Act 2004* (ACT)' (2012) 36 *Melbourne University Law Review* 287

Trotter, Andrew and Harry Hobbs, 'The Great Leap Backward: Criminal Law Reform with the Hon Jarrod Bleijie' (2014) 36(1) *Sydney Law Review* 1

Tubex, Hilde and Roger Houchin, 'Opportunities for Restorative Justice in the Contemporary Penal Climate' (2009) 11(2) *Journal of Police Studies* 173

Tubex, Hilde et al, 'Penal Diversity Within Australia' (2015) 17(3) *Punishment & Society* 345, doi.org/10.1177/1462474515590891

Tubex, Hilde et al, 'Western Australian Penal Culture and Indigenous Over-Representation: Evaluating 25 Years of Law, Policy and Practice' (2018) 43(1) *The University of Western Australia Law Review* 264

Vernon, Alikki, 'The Ethics of Appropriate Justice Approaches: Lessons From a Restorative Response to Institutional Abuse' (2017) 35(1) *Law in Context* 139, doi.org/10.26826/law-in-context.v35i1.36

Wallace, Rebecca and Karen Wylie, 'Changing on the Inside: Restorative Justice in Prisons: A Literature Review' (2013) 19 *Journal of Bahamian Studies* 57, doi.org/10.15362/ijbs.v19i1.180

Walsh, Tamara, 'Is Corrections Correcting? An Examination of Prisoner Rehabilitation Policy and Practice in Queensland' (2006) 39(1) *Australian and New Zealand Journal of Criminology* 109, doi.org/10.1375/acri.39.1.109

Ward, Tony and Astrid Birgden, 'Human Rights and Clinical Correctional Practice' (2007) 12(6) *Aggression and Violent Behaviour* 628, doi.org/10.1016/j.avb.2007.05.001

Ward, Tony and Robyn Langlands, 'Repairing the Rupture: Restorative Justice and the Rehabilitation of Offenders' (2009) 14 *Aggression and Violent Behavior* 205, doi.org/10.1016/j.avb.2009.03.001

Ward, Tony, Kathryn Fox and Melissa Garber, 'Restorative Justice, Offender Rehabilitation and Desistance' (2014) 2(1) *Restorative Justice: An International Journal* 24, doi.org/10.5235/20504721.2.1.24

Watchirs, Helen and Gabrielle McKinnon, 'Five Years' Experience with the *Human Rights Act 2004* (ACT): Insights for Human Rights Protection in Australia' (2010) 33(1) *UNSW Law Journal* 136

Weatherburn, Don, 'Australian Imprisonment 2002-2016: Crime, Policing and Penal Policy' (2018) 51(4) *Australian & New Zealand Journal of Criminology* 537, doi.org/10.1177/0004865818757585

Weller, Penelope, 'OPCAT Monitoring and the Convention on the Rights of Persons with Disabilities' (2019) 25(1) *Australian Journal of Human Rights* 130, doi.org/10.1080/1323238x.2019.1588056

Wemmers, Jo-Anne, 'Where Do They Belong? Giving Victims a Place in the Criminal Justice Process' (2009) 20 *Criminal Law Forum* 395, doi.org/10.1007/s10609-009-9107-z

White, Paul and Harvey Whiteford, 'Prisons: Mental Health Institutions of the 21st Century?' (2006) 185(6) *Medical Journal of Australia* 302, doi.org/10.5694/j.1326-5377.2006.tb00581.x

Williams, George and Daniel Reynolds, 'A Human Rights Act for Queensland? Lessons From Recent Australian Experience' (2016) 41(2) *Alternative Law Journal* 81, doi.org/10.1177/1037969x1604100202

Zedner, Lucia, 'Dangers and Dystopias in Penal Theory' (2002) 22(2) *Oxford Journal of Legal Studies* 341, doi.org/10.1093/ojls/22.2.341

Zehr, Howard and Harry Mika, 'Fundamental Concepts of Restorative Justice' (1997) 1(1) *Contemporary Justice Review* 47, doi.org/10.4324/9781351150125-4

Books

Aertsen, Ivo, Tom Daems and Luc Robert (eds), *Institutionalizing Restorative Justice* (Willan Publishing, 2006)

Anthony, Thalia and Chris Cunneen (eds), *The Critical Criminology Companion* (Hawkins Press, 2008)

Baldry, Eileen et al, *A Predictable and Preventable Path: Aboriginal People with Mental and Cognitive Disabilities in the Criminal Justice System* (UNSW, 2015)

Barry, John, *Alexander Maconochie of Norfolk Island. A Study of a Pioneer in Penal Reform* (Oxford University Press, 1958)

Bartkowiak-Théron, Isabelle and Nicole Asquith (eds), *Policing Vulnerabilities* (Federation Press, 2012)

Bentham, Jeremy, *Introduction to the Principles of Morals and Legislation* (Clarendon Press, 1789)

Bentham, Jeremy, *A Fragment on Government* (Clarendon Press, 1891)

Blouin-Genest, Gabriel, Marie-Christine Doran and Sylvie Paquerot (eds), *Human Rights as Battlefields: Changing Practices and Contestations* (Springer Nature Switzerland, 2019), doi.org/10.1007/978-3-319-91770-2

Braithwaite, John, *Restorative Justice and Responsive Regulation* (Oxford University Press, 2002)

Bronitt, Simon and Bernadette McSherry, *Principles of Criminal Law* (Lawbook Co, 3rd ed, 2010)

Brown, David and Meredith Wilkie (eds), *Prisoners as Citizens* (The Federation Press, 2002)

Brown, David et al, *Justice Reinvestment. Winding Back Imprisonment* (Palgrave Studies in Prisons and Penology, 2016)

Campbell, Tom and Seumas Miller (eds), *Human Rights and the Moral Responsibilities of Corporate and Public Sector Organisations* (Kluwer Academic Publications, 2004)

Carlton, Bree, *Imprisoning Resistance: Life and Death in an Australian Supermax* (Institute of Criminology Press, 2007)

Carrington, Kerry et al (eds), *Crime, Justice and Social Democracy: International Perspectives* (Palgrave Macmillan, 2012)

Cavadino, Michael and James Dignan, *Penal Systems: A Comparative Approach* (SAGE, 2006)

Cavadino, Michael and James Dignan, *The Penal System. An Introduction* (SAGE, 2007)

Cohen, Stanley, *Visions of Social Control: Crime, Punishment and Classification* (Polity Press, 1985)

Conte, Alex and Richard Burchill (eds), *Defining Civil and Political Rights. The Jurisprudence of the United Nations Human Rights Committee* (Routledge, 2nd ed, 2016), doi.org/10.4324/9781315576244

Coyle, Andrew, *The Prisons We Deserve* (Harper Collins Publishers, 1994)

Coyle, Andrew, *Managing Prisons in a Time of Change* (International Centre for Prison Studies, 2001)

Coyle, Andrew, *Humanity in Prison. Questions of Definition and Audit* (International Centre for Prison Studies, 2003)

Coyle, Andrew and Helen Fair, *A Human Rights Approach to Prison Management. Handbook for Prison Staff* (Institute for Criminal Policy Research Birkbeck, University of London, 3rd ed, 2018)

Cunneen, Chris et al, *Penal Culture and Hyperincarceration. The Revival of the Prison* (Ashgate, 2013), doi.org/10.4324/9781315599892

Davis, Angela, *Are Prisons Obsolete?* (Seven Stories Press, 2003)

Debeljak, Julie and Laura Grenfell (eds), *Law Making and Human Rights: Executive and Parliamentary Scrutiny Across Australian Jurisdictions* (Lawbook Co, 2020)

Deckert, Antje and Rick Sarre (eds), *The Palgrave Handbook of Australian and New Zealand Criminology, Crime and Justice* (Palgrave, 2017), doi.org/10.1007/978-3-319-55747-2

Durnescu, Ioan and Fergus McNeill, *Understanding Penal Practice* (Taylor and Francis, 2013)

Fletcher, Adam, *Australia's Human Rights Scrutiny Regime. Democratic Masterstroke or Mere Window Dressing?* (Melbourne University Press, 2018)

Freckelton, Ian and Kerry Peterson (eds), *Tensions and Traumas in Health Law* (Federation Press, 2017)

Freiberg, Arie, *Fox & Freiberg's Sentencing: State and Federal Law in Victoria* (Lawbook Co, 3rd ed, 2014)

Garland, David, *The Culture of Control: Crime and Social Order in Contemporary Society* (Oxford University Press, 2001)

Garland, David (ed), *Mass Imprisonment. Social Causes and Consequences* (SAGE, 2001)

Gerber, Paula and Melissa Castan (eds), *Contemporary Perspectives on Human Rights Law in Australia* (Lawbook Co, 2013)

Goffman, Erving, *Asylums. Essays on the Social Situation of Mental Patients and Other Inmates* (Aldine Publishing Company, 1962)

Groves, Matthew and Colin Campbell (eds), *Australian Charters of Rights a Decade On* (Federation Press, 2017)

Groves, Matthew, Janina Boughey and Dan Meagher (eds), *The Legal Protection of Rights in Australia* (Bloomsbury Publishing, 2019)

Hayward, Keith, Shadd Maruna and Jayne Mooney (eds), *Fifty Key Thinkers in Criminology* (Routledge, 2010)

Hertogh, Marc and Richard Kirkham (eds), *Research Handbook on the Ombudsman* (Edward Elgar Publishing, 2018)

Ireland, Jane et al (eds), *The Routledge International Handbook of Forensic Psychology in Secure Settings* (Routledge, 2017)

Jesuit Social Services, *All Alone. Young Adults in the Victorian Justice System* (2018)

Jewkes, Yvonne (ed), *Handbook on Prisons* (Willan Publishing, 2007)

Jewkes, Yvonne et al (eds), *Handbook on Prisons* (Routledge, 2016)

Johnstone, Gerry and Daniel Van Ness (eds), *Handbook of Restorative Justice* (Willan Publishing, 2003)

Joseph, Sarah and Melissa Castan, *The International Covenant on Civil and Political Rights. Cases, Materials and Commentary* (Oxford University Press, 3rd ed, 2013)

Keyzer, Patrick et al (eds), *Access to International Justice* (Routledge, 2014)

Levy, Ron et al (eds), *New Directions for Law in Australia: Essays in Contemporary Law Reform* (ANU Press, 2017)

Liebling, Alison, David Price and Guy Shefer, *The Prison Officer* (Taylor and Francis, 2nd ed, 2010)

Mackenzie, Geraldine, Nigel Stobbs and Jodie O'Leary, *Principles of Sentencing* (The Federation Press, 2010)

Maconochie, Alexander, *Report on the State of Prison Discipline in Van Diemen's Land* (London, 1838)

Mannheim, Hermann (ed), *Pioneers in Criminology* (Patterson Smith Publishing Corporation, 1972)

Maruna, Shadd and Russ Immarigeon (eds), *After Crime and Punishment. Pathways to Offender Reintegration* (Willan Publishing, 2004)

Mathieson, Thomas, *Prison on Trial* (Waterside Press, 3rd ed, 2006)

Max Planck Yearbook of United Nations Law, Volume 19, 2015 (Brill, 2016)

Moeckli, Daniel et al (eds), *International Human Rights Law* (Oxford University Press, 2014)

Moore, Linda et al (eds), *Women's Imprisonment and the Case for Abolition: Critical Reflections on Corston Ten Years On* (Routledge, 2017), doi. org/10.4324/9781315204819

Morris, Norval, *Maconochie's Gentlemen. The Story of Norfolk Island and the Roots of Modern Prison Reform* (Oxford University Press, 2002)

Murray, Rachel et al, *The Optional Protocol to the UN Convention Against Torture* (Oxford University Press, 2011)

Naylor, Bronwyn, Julie Debeljak and Anita Mackay (eds), *Human Rights in Closed Environments* (Federation Press, 2014)

Neal, David, *The Rule of Law in a Penal Colony: Law and Power in Early New South Wales* (Cambridge University Press, 1992)

Owen, Tim and Alison Macdonald (eds), *Livingstone, Owen, and Macdonald on Prison Law* (Oxford University Press, 5th ed, 2015)

Pratt, John et al (eds), *The New Punitiveness: Trends, Theories, Perspectives* (Willan Publishing, 2005)

Pratt, John and Anna Eriksson, *Contrasts in Punishment. An Explanation of Anglophone Excess and Nordic Exceptionalism* (Routledge, 2013), doi. org/10.4324/9780203096116

Rainey, Bernadette, Elizabeth Wicks and Clare Ovey, *Jacobs, White and Ovey. The European Convention on Human Rights* (Oxford University Press, 7th ed, 2017)

Raynor, Peter and Gwen Robinson, *Rehabilitation, Crime and Justice* (Palgrave Macmillan, 2005)

Reeves, Carla (ed), *Experiencing Imprisonment. Research on the Experience of Living and Working in Carceral Institutions* (Routledge, 2017), doi. org/10.4324/9781315764177

Roberts, Andrew and Jeremy Gans (eds), *Critical Perspectives on the Uniform Evidence Law* (The Federation Press, 2017)

Rodley, Nigel, and Matt Pollard, *The Treatment of Prisoners Under International Law* (Oxford University Press, 3rd ed, 2009)

Rotman, Edgardo, *Beyond Punishment. A New View on the Rehabilitation of Criminal Offenders* (Greenwood Press, 1990)

Rutherford, Andrew, *Prisons and the Process of Justice: The Reductionist Challenge* (Heinemann, 1984)

Scott, David (ed), *Why Prison?* (Cambridge University Press, 2013)

Steels, Brian and Dot Goulding, *Predator or Prey? An Exploration of the Impact and Incidence of Sexual Assault in West Australian Prisons* (Centre for Social and Community Research, Murdoch University, Perth, Western Australia, 2009)

Sykes, Gresham, *Society of Captives; A Study of a Maximum Security Prison* (Princeton University Press, 1958)

Van Zyl Smit, Dirk and Sonja Snacken, *Principles of European Prison Law and Policy: Penology and Human Rights* (Oxford University Press, 2009)

Wallace, Jack et al, *Regulating Hepatitis C: Rights and Duties. Preventing Hepatitis C Transmission in Australian Adult Correctional Settings* (La Trobe University, 2009)

Weber, Leanne et al (eds), *The Routledge International Handbook of Criminology and Human Rights* (Routledge, 2016)

Weber, Leanne et al (eds), *The Routledge International Handbook of Criminology and Human Rights* (Routledge, 2017)

White, Rob and Fiona Haines, *Crime and Criminology* (Oxford University Press, 4th ed, 2008)

Williams, George, Sean Brennan and Andrew Lynch, *Blackshield & Williams Australian Constitutional Law & Theory. Commentary & Materials* (The Federation Press, 6th ed, 2014)

Williams, George and Daniel Reynolds, *A Charter of Rights for Australia* (UNSW Press, 4th ed, 2017)

Australian Government, Statutory Agency and Other Official Publications

A WA Human Rights Act: Report of the Consultation Committee for a Proposed WA Human Rights Act (2007)

ACT Auditor-General, *The Rehabilitation of Male Detainees at the Alexander Maconochie Centre (Report No. 2 of 2015)* (2015)

ACT Government, *ACT Drug Strategy Action Plan 2018-2021: A Plan to Minimise Harms from Alcohol, Tobacco and Other Drug Use* (2018)

ACT Government, Justice and Community Safety, *Human Rights Principles for ACT Correctional Centres* (January 2019)

ACT Health Services Commissioner, *Review of the Opioid Replacement Program at the Alexander Maconochie Centre* (2018)

ACT Human Rights and Discrimination Commissioner, *Human Rights Audit on the Conditions of Detention of Women at the Alexander Maconochie Centre* (2014)

ACT Human Rights Commission, *Human Rights Audit on the Operation of ACT Correctional Facilities Under Corrections Legislation* (2007)

ACT Human Rights Commission, *Annual Report 2011/12* (2012)

ACT Human Rights Commission, *Annual Report 2012–2013* (2013)

ACT Human Rights Commission, *Response to the Australian Human Rights Commission's May 2017 'OPCAT in Australia Consultation Paper'* (21 July 2017)

ACT Inspector of Correctional Services, *Review into the Treatment and Care of Remandees at the Alexander Maconochie Centre* (2018)

ACT Inspector of Correctional Services, *ACT Standards for Adult Correctional Services* (2019)

ACT Inspector of Correctional Services, *Report of a Review of a Correctional Centre by the ACT Inspector of Correctional Services: Healthy Prison Review of the Alexander Maconochie Centre* (2019)

ACT Inspector of Correctional Services, *Report of a Review of the Care and Management of Remandees at the Alexander Maconochie Centre* (2019)

Adult Parole Board Victoria, *Parole Manual Adult Parole Board of Victoria* (Adult Parole Board of Victoria, 2018)

Angus, Chris, *Older Prisoners: Trends and Challenges* (NSW Parliamentary Research Service, 2015)

Anti-Discrimination Board of New South Wales, *C Change. Report of the Enquiry into Hepatitis C Related Discrimination* (2001)

Anti-Discrimination Commission Queensland, *Women in Prison. A Report by the Anti-Discrimination Commission Queensland* (2006)

Anti-Discrimination Commission Queensland, *Women in Prison* (2017)

Anti-Discrimination Commission Queensland, *Women in Prison 2019: A Human Rights Consultation Report* (2019)

Australian Bureau of Statistics, *Prisoners in Australia 2013* (2014)

Australian Bureau of Statistics, *Prisoners in Australia 2018* (2018)

Australian Bureau of Statistics, *Prisoners in Australia 2019* (5 December 2019)

Australian Human Rights Commission, *Implementing the Optional Protocol to the Convention Against Torture: Options for Australia. A Report to the Australian Human Rights Commission by Professors Richard Harding and Neil Morgan (Centre for Law and Public Policy, The University of Western Australia)* (2008)

Australian Human Rights Commission, *OPCAT in Australia Consultation Paper* (May 2017)

Australian Human Rights Commission, *OPCAT in Australia Consultation Paper: Stage 2* (June 2018)

Australian Institute of Criminology, *Guilty Outcomes in Reported Sexual Assault and Related Offence Incidents* (Crime Facts Info No 162, 2007)

Australian Institute of Criminology, *Australian Crime: Facts and Figures: 2013* (2014)

Australian Institute of Criminology, *How Much Does Prison Really Cost? Comparing the Costs of Imprisonment with Community Corrections* (Research Report No 5, 2018)

Australian Institute of Criminology, *Justice Reinvestment in Australia: A Review of the Literature* (Research Report No 9, 2018)

Australian Institute of Health and Welfare, *The Health of Australian Prisoners 2015* (2015)

Australian Institute of Health and Welfare, *The Health of Australian Prisoners 2018* (2019)

Australian Institute of Health and Welfare, *National Drug Strategy Household Survey 2016 Detailed Findings* (2017)

Australian Law Reform Commission, *Seen and Heard: Priority for Children in the Legal Process*, Report No 84 (1997)

Australian Law Reform Commission, *Connection to Country: Review of the Native Title Act 1993 (Cth)*, Report No 126 (2015)

Australian Law Reform Commission, *Traditional Rights and Freedoms— Encroachments by Commonwealth Laws*, Report No 129 (2016)

Australian Law Reform Commission, *Pathways to Justice—An Inquiry into the Incarceration Rate of Aboriginal and Torres Strait Islander Peoples*, Report No 133 (2017)

Australian Law Reform Commission and New South Wales Law Reform Commission, *Uniform Evidence Law* (2006)

Baidawi, Susan et al, *Older Prisoners—A Challenge for Australian Corrections* (Trends and Issues in Crime and Criminal Justice No 426, 2011)

Callinan, Ian, *Review of the Parole System in Victoria* (2013)

Commonwealth and Northern Territory, *Royal Commission into the Protection and Detention of Children in the Northern Territory, Final Report* (2017)

Commonwealth Ombudsman, *Commonwealth Ombudsman Implementation of the Optional Protocol to the Convention Against Torture and Other Cruel, Inhuman or Degrading Treatment or Punishment (OPCAT) Baseline Assessment of Australia's OPCAT Readiness Report No. 3/2019* (September 2019)

Community Development and Justice Standing Committee (WA), *'Making Our Prisons Work': An Inquiry into the Efficiency and Effectiveness of Prisoner Education, Training and Employment Strategies* (2010)

Corrective Services Administrators' Conference (Cth), *Guiding Principles for Corrections in Australia* (2018)

Department of Justice and Regulation, *Annual Report 2017–18* (2018)

Freiberg, Arie et al, *Drug and Specialist Courts Review* (Department of Justice and Attorney-General, Queensland, 2016)

Government of Western Australia Department of Corrective Services, *Annual Report 2010/11. Contract for the Provision of Court Security and Custodial Services* (2011)

Heseltine, Karen, Andrew Day and Rick Sarre, *Prison-Based Correctional Offender Rehabilitation Programs: The 2009 National Picture in Australia* (Australian Institute of Criminology Reports Research and Public Policy Series 112, 2011)

House of Representatives Standing Committee on Aboriginal and Torres Strait Islander Affairs, *Doing Time – Time for Doing. Indigenous Youth in the Criminal Justice System* (2011)

Independent Inquiry into the Treatment in Custody of Mr Steven Freeman, *'So Much Sadness in Our Lives'* (2016)

Independent Investigation into the Metropolitan Remand Centre Riot, *Final Report* (December 2015)

Justice Nagle, *Report of the Royal Commission into NSW Prisons* (Government Printer, 1978)

National Human Rights Consultation, *National Human Rights Consultation Report* (September 2009)

New South Wales, Parliament Legislative Council Portfolio Committee No. 4 – Legal Affairs, *Parklea Correctional Centre and Other Operational Issues* (2018)

NSW Government, *Department of Justice Annual Report 2017–18* (2018)

NSW Inspector of Custodial Services, *Inspection Standards for Adult Custodial Services in New South Wales* (2014)

NSW Inspector of Custodial Services, *Report No. 1 – The Invisibility of Correctional Officer Work* (2014)

NSW Inspector of Custodial Services, *Full House: The Growth of the Inmate Population in NSW* (2015)

NSW Inspector of Custodial Services, *Old and Inside: Managing Aged Offenders in Custody* (2015)

NSW Inspector of Custodial Services, *Prison Greens: The Clothing and Bedding of Inmates in NSW* (2017)

NSW Inspector of Custodial Services, *The Management of Radicalised Inmates in NSW* (2018)

Office of the Custodial Inspector Tasmania, *Inspection Standards for Adult Custodial Services in Tasmania* (2018)

Office of the Inspector of Custodial Services, *Report of an Announced Inspection of Bandyup Women's Prison June 2002* (2003)

Office of the Inspector of Custodial Services, *Vulnerable and Predatory Prisoners in Western Australia: A Review of Policy and Practice* (2003)

Office of the Inspector of Custodial Services, *Report of an Announced Inspection of Adult Prisoner Transport Services* (2004)

Office of the Inspector of Custodial Services, *Code of Inspection Standards for Adult Custodial Services, Version 1* (19 April 2007)

Office of the Inspector of Custodial Services, *Thematic Review of Custodial Transport Services in Western Australia* (2007)

Office of the Inspector of Custodial Services, *Issues Paper. Smoking in Prison* (2008)

Office of the Inspector of Custodial Services, *Prisoner/Detainee Transportation 1 July 2011 – 31 December 2011* (2012)

Office of the Inspector of Custodial Services, *Directed Review into an Incident at Banksia Hill Detention Centre of 20 January 2013* (2013)

Office of the Inspector of Custodial Services, *Funeral Attendances by Incarcerated People in Western Australia* (2013)

Office of the Inspector of Custodial Services, *Report of an Announced Inspection of Greenough Regional Prison* (2013)

Office of the Inspector of Custodial Services, *Prisoner and Staff Perceptions of WA Custodial Facilities from 2010–2012* (2014).

Office of the Inspector of Custodial Services, *Report of an Announced Inspection of Bandyup Women's Prison* (2014)

Office of the Inspector of Custodial Services, *Thermal Conditions of Prison Cells* (2015)

Office of the Inspector of Custodial Services, *Fine Defaulters in the Western Australian Prison System* (2016)

Office of the Inspector of Custodial Services, *Western Australia's Prison Capacity* (2016)

Office of the Inspector of Custodial Services, *Access to Funerals and Other Compassionate Leave for People in Custody in Western Australia* (2017)

Office of the Inspector of Custodial Services, *Annual Report 2017–18* (2018)

Office of the Inspector of Custodial Services, *The Birth at Bandyup Women's Prison in March 2018* (2018)

Office of the Inspector of Custodial Services, *The Digital Divide: Access to Digital Technology for People in Custody* (2018)

Office of the Inspector of Custodial Services, *Contact with Family and Friends While in Custody* (2018)

Office of the Inspector of Custodial Services, *Strip Searching Practices in Western Australian Prisons* (2019)

Ombudsman New South Wales, *Managing Use of Force in Prisons: The Need for Better Policy and Practice* (2012)

Ombudsman New South Wales, *Annual Report 2017–2018* (2018)

Ombudsman for the Northern Territory, *Women in Prison Northern Territory. Report of the Investigation into Complaints from Women Prisoners at Darwin Correctional Centre* (2008)

Ombudsman Northern Territory, *Ombudsman NT Investigation Report. Women in Prison II – Alice Springs Women's Correctional Facility* (2017)

Ombudsman South Australia, *Department for Correctional Services – Port Augusta Prison Disturbance* (2010)

Ombudsman South Australia, *Department for Correctional Services – Prisoner Amenities Levy* (2011)

Ombudsman South Australia, *Department for Correctional Services – Continuing Separation of a Prisoner* (2012)

Ombudsman South Australia, *Ombudsman Investigation into the Department of Correctional Services in Relation to the Restraining and Shackling of Prisoners in Hospitals* (2012)

Ombudsman South Australia, *Final Report Department of Correctional Services* (2013)

Ombudsman South Australia, *Department for Correctional Services – Treatment of a Prisoner* (2013)

Ombudsman South Australia, *Department for Correctional Services – Restraint of a Prisoner* (2014)

Ombudsman South Australia, *Department for Correctional Services – Prohibition of Correspondence* (2016)

Ombudsman South Australia, *Department for Correctional Services – Shackling of a Prisoner in Hospital* (2016)

Ombudsman South Australia, *Department for Correctional Services – Unreasonable Shackling of a Prisoner in Hospital* (2016)

Ombudsman South Australia, *Department for Correctional Services – Failure to Ensure that a Prisoner Understood the Induction Process* (2017)

Ombudsman South Australia, *Department for Correctional Services – Failure to Induct Prisoner* (2017)

Ombudsman South Australia, *Department for Correctional Services – Unjust and Oppressive Separation of a Prisoner* (2017)

Ombudsman South Australia, *Department for Correctional Services – Unlawful Shackling of a Mental Health Patient in Hospital* (2017)

Ombudsman South Australia, *Department for Correctional Services – Failure to Amend Record of Gender Media Release* (2018)

Ombudsman South Australia, *Department for Correctional Services – Handling of a Prisoner's Diabetes* (2018)

Ombudsman South Australia, *Department for Correctional Services' – Handling of a Physical Altercation* (2019)

Ombudsman South Australia, *Restraint of Prisoner During Hospitalisation – Compliance with Standard Operating Procedures in Relation to Checking of Restraints* (2019)

Ombudsman Tasmania, *Report on an Inquiry into Risdon Prison. The Risdon Prison Complex* (2001)

Ombudsman Tasmania, *Report on an Inquiry into Risdon Prison. Risdon Prison Hospital & Forensic Mental Health Service* (2001)

Ombudsman Tasmania, *Risdon Prison Complex Tamar Unit and Behaviour Management Program. Investigation Report* (2010)

Ombudsman Tasmania, *Investigation into the Strip Searching Procedures for Women at the Hobart Reception Prison* (2017)

Ombudsman Victoria, *Investigation into Deaths and Harms in Custody* (2014)

Ombudsman Victoria and Office of Police Integrity, *Conditions for Persons in Custody. Report of Ombudsman Victoria and Office of Police Integrity July 2006* (2006)

Ombudsman Western Australia, *Annual Report 2017–18* (2018)

Palmer, Mick, *Risdon Prison Complex Inquiry* (March 2011)

Parliament of Tasmania Legislative Council Select Committee, *Correctional Services and Sentencing in Tasmania* (1999)

Parliament of Victoria Family and Community Development Committee, *Inquiry into Abuse in Disability Services Final Report* (May 2016)

Productivity Commission, *Disability Care and Support, Productivity Commission Inquiry Report* (2011)

Queensland Ombudsman, *The Classification and Movement of Prisoners Report. An Investigation of Queensland Corrective Services' Process for the Classification, Placement and Transfer of Prisoners* (2009)

Queensland Ombudsman, *The Strip Searching of Female Prisoners Report. An Investigation into the Strip Search Practices at Townsville Women's Correctional Centre* (2014)

Queensland Ombudsman, *Overcrowding at Brisbane Women's Correctional Centre Report* (2016)

Queensland Productivity Commission, *Inquiry into Imprisonment and Recidivism. Final Report* (2019)

Response of the Australian Government to the Views of the Committee in Communication No 1184/2003 (Brough v Australia)

Response of the Australian Government to the Views of the Committee on the Rights of Persons with Disabilities in Communication No 7/2012 (Noble v Australia)

Royal Commission into Aboriginal Deaths in Custody, *National Report* (1991)

Select Committee on the Increase in Prisoner Population (NSW), *Final Report* (2001)

Senate Community Affairs References Committee, *Indefinite Detention of People with Cognitive and Psychiatric Impairment in Australia* (2016)

Senate Legal and Constitutional Affairs References Committee, *Value of a Justice Reinvestment Approach to Criminal Justice in Australia* (2013)

Senate Select Committee on Mental Health, *A National Approach to Mental Health – From Crisis to Community, First Report* (2006)

Senate Select Committee on Regional and Remote Indigenous Communities, *Indigenous Australians, Incarceration and the Criminal Justice System* (2010)

Senate Standing Committee on Community Affairs, *Violence, Abuse and Neglect Against People with Disability in Institutional and Residential Settings, Including the Gender and Age Related Dimensions, and the Particular Situation of Aboriginal and Torres Strait Islander People with Disability, and Culturally and Linguistically Diverse People with Disability* (November 2015)

Sentencing Advisory Council, *Gender Differences in Sentencing Outcomes* (2010)

Sentencing Advisory Council, *Does Imprisonment Deter? A Review of the Evidence* (2011)

Sentencing Advisory Council, *Minimum Standard Non-Parole Periods. Final Report* (2011)

Sentencing Advisory Council, *Victoria's Prison Population 2002–2012* (2013)

Shuard, Jan, *Critical Incident Review into the Events at Greenough Regional Prison on 24–25 July 2018* (2018)

Sofronoff, Walter, *Queensland Parole System Review, Final Report* (Department of Justice and Attorney-General, 2016)

Standing Committee on Justice and Community Safety, ACT Legislative Assembly, *Inquiry into the Establishment of an ACT Prison: Justification and Siting* (1999)

Standing Committee on Justice and Community Safety, ACT Legislative Assembly, *The Proposed ACT Prison Facility: Philosophy and Principles* (1999)

Steering Committee for the Review of Government Service Provision, *Report on Government Services 2018, Volume C: Justice* (Commonwealth of Australia, 2018)

Steering Committee for the Review of Government Service Provision, *Report on Government Services 2019, Part C: Justice* (Commonwealth of Australia, 2019)

Steering Committee for the Review of Government Service Provision, *Report on Government Services 2020, Volume C: Justice* (Commonwealth of Australia, 2020)

Tasmania Law Reform Institute, *A Charter of Rights for Tasmania*, Report No 10 (2007)

Tasmanian Custodial Inspector, *Annual Report 2017–18* (2018)

Tasmanian Custodial Inspector, *Inspection of Adult Custodial Services in Tasmania, 2017 Care and Wellbeing Inspection Report* (October 2018)

The Corrective Services Ministers' Conference (Cth), *Standard Guidelines for Corrections in Australia* (3rd ed, 2004)

The Corrective Services Ministers' Conference (Cth), *Standard Guidelines for Corrections in Australia* (2012)

Trimboli, Lily, *NSW Trends in the Age-Specific Rates of Offending, 1995 – 2018* (Issues Paper No 143, NSW Bureau of Crime Statistics and Research, 2019)

Victorian Auditor-General, *Prison Capacity Planning* (2012)

Victorian Equal Opportunity and Human Rights Commission, *Unfinished Business. Koori Women and the Justice System* (2013)

Victorian Equal Opportunity and Human Rights Commission, *2013 Report on the Operation of the Charter of Human Rights and Responsibilities* (2014)

Victorian Equal Opportunity and Human Rights Commission, *Annual Report 2017/18* (2018)

Victorian Government, Submission 324 to Scrutiny of Acts and Regulations Committee, *Review of the Charter of Human Rights and Responsibilities Act 2006*, 2011

Victorian Ombudsman, *Investigation into the Handling, Storage and Transfer of Prisoner Property in Victorian Prisons* (2005)

Victorian Ombudsman, *Investigation into Contraband Entering a Prison and Related Issues* (2008)

Victorian Ombudsman, *Investigation into Prisoner Access to Health Care* (2011)

Victorian Ombudsman, *The Death of Mr Carl Williams at HM Barwon Prison – Investigation into Corrections Victoria* (2012)

Victorian Ombudsman, *Investigation into Children Transferred from the Youth Justice System to the Adult Prison System* (2013)

Victorian Ombudsman, *Investigation into Deaths and Harms in Custody* (2014)

Victorian Ombudsman, *Ombudsman's Recommendations. Third Report on Their Implementation* (Report for Parliament, 19 February 2014)

Victorian Ombudsman, *Investigation into the Rehabilitation and Reintegration of Prisoners in Victoria* (2015)

Victorian Ombudsman, *Implementing OPCAT in Victoria: Report and Inspection of the Dame Phyllis Frost Centre* (2017)

Victorian Ombudsman, *Investigation into the Imprisonment of a Woman Found Unfit to Stand Trial* (2018)

Victorian Ombudsman, *Annual Report 2018* (2018)

Victorian Parliament Legislative Council, Select Committee of the Legislative Council upon the Victorian Prisons Service, *Interim Report* (1984)

Weatherburn, Don, Jiuzhao Hua and Steve Moffatt, 'How Much Crime Does Prison Stop? The Incapacitation Effect of Prison on Burglary', *Crime and Justice Bulletin* (NSW Bureau of Crime Statistics and Research, 2006)

International Reports and Committee General Comments

Committee on the Elimination of Racial Discrimination, *Decision 2(54) on Australia: Concluding Observations/Comments*, UN Doc CERD/C/54/Misc.40/Rev.2 (1999)

Correctional Investigator Canada, *Aging and Dying in Prison. An Investigation into the Experiences of Older Individuals in Federal Custody* (2019)

Guidelines of the Subcommittee on Prevention of Torture and Other Cruel, Inhuman or Degrading Treatment or Punishment in Relation to Visits to States Parties Under Article 11 (a) of the Optional Protocol, CAT/OP/5 (14 February 2015)

Her Majesty's Inspectorate of Prisons, *'No Problems – Old and Quiet': Older Prisoners in England and Wales. A Thematic Review by HM Chief Inspector of Prisons* (2004)

Her Majesty's Inspectorate of Prisons, *Report on HMP Aberdeen Full Inspection 6 – 10 October 2008* (2009)

Human Rights Committee, *Concluding Observations of the Human Rights Committee: Australia*, UN Doc CCPR/C/AUS/CO/5 (7 May 2009)

Human Rights Committee, *Concluding Observations on the Sixth Periodic Report of Australia*, UN Doc CCPR/C/AUS/CO/6 (1 December 2017)

Human Rights Council, *Report of the Special Rapporteur on the Right of Everyone to the Enjoyment of the Highest Attainable Standard of Physical and Mental Health, Anand Grover*, UN DOC A/HRC/14/20/Add.4 (3 June 2010)

Human Rights Council, *Report of the Special Rapporteur on the Rights of Indigenous Peoples on Her Visit to Australia*, UN Doc A/HRC/36/46/Add.2 (8 August 2017)

Human Rights Council, *Report of the Special Rapporteur on Violence Against Women, Its Causes and Consequences on Her Mission to Australia*, UN Doc A/HRC/38/47/Add.1 (17 April 2018)

Human Rights Watch, *'I Needed Help, Instead I Was Punished': Abuse and Neglect of Prisoners with Disabilities in Australia* (2018)

Independent Monitoring Boards, *'Slopping Out?' A Report on the Lack of In-Cell Sanitation in Her Majesty's Prisons in England and Wales* (National Council for Independent Monitoring Boards, 2010)

Joseph, Sarah, Katie Mitchell and Linda Gyorki, *Seeking Remedies for Torture Victims. A Handbook on the Individual Complaint Procedures of the UN Treaty Bodies* (World Organisation Against Torture, 2006)

National Preventive Mechanism (UK), *Monitoring Places of Detention. Ninth Annual Report of the United Kingdom's National Preventive Mechanism 1 April 2017 – 31 March 2018* (2019)

Quaker Council for European Affairs, *The Social Reintegration of Ex-Prisoners in Council of Europe Member States* (Quaker Council for European Affairs, 2011)

Recommendation CM/Rec (2012) 5 of the Committee of Ministers to Member States on the European Code of Ethics for Prison Staff (Adopted by the Committee of Ministers on 12 April 2012 at the 1140th meeting of the Ministers' Deputies)

Secretary-General of the United Nations, *Compilation of Guidelines on the Form and Content of Reports to be Submitted by States Parties to the International Human Rights Treaties*, UN Doc HRI/GEN/2/Rev.5 (29 May 2008)

Subcommittee for the Prevention of Torture and Other Cruel, Inhuman or Degrading Treatment or Punishment, *The Approach of the Subcommittee on Prevention of Torture to the Concept of Prevention of Torture and Other Cruel, Inhuman or Degrading Treatment or Punishment Under the Optional Protocol to the Convention Against Torture and Other Cruel, Inhuman or Degrading Treatment or Punishment*, CAT/OP/12/6 (30 December 2010)

Subcommittee for the Prevention of Torture and Other Cruel, Inhuman or Degrading Treatment or Punishment, *Fifth Annual Report of the Subcommittee on Prevention of Torture and Other Cruel, Inhuman or Degrading Treatment or Punishment (January – December 2011)* (2012)

Subcommittee on Prevention of Torture and Other Cruel, Inhuman or Degrading Treatment or Punishment, *Visit to New Zealand Undertaken from 29 April to 8 May 2013: Observations and Recommendations Addressed to the State Party. Report of the Subcommittee*, UN Doc CAT/OP/NZL/1 (10 February 2017)

United Nations Committee against Torture, *CAT General Comment No. 2 Implementation of Article 2 by States Parties* (24 January 2008)

United Nations Committee against Torture, *Concluding Observations of the Committee against Torture: Australia*, UN Doc CAT/C/AUS/CO/3 (22 May 2008)

United Nations Committee on the Rights of Persons with Disabilities, *CRPD General Comment No. 6: Equality and Non-Discrimination* (26 April 2018)

United Nations Committee on the Rights of Persons with Disabilities, *Concluding Observations on the Initial Report of Australia*, UN Doc CRPD/C/AUS/CO/1 (21 October 2013)

United Nations Human Rights Committee, *CCPR General Comment No. 20: Article 7 (Prohibition of Torture, or Other Cruel, Inhuman or Degrading Treatment or Punishment)* (10 March 1992)

United Nations Human Rights Committee, *CCPR General Comment No. 21: Article 10 (Humane Treatment of Persons Deprived of Their Liberty)* (10 April 1992)

United Nations Human Rights Committee, *General Comment 29, States of Emergency (Article 4)*, UN Doc CCPR/C/21/Rev.1/Add.11 (2001)

United Nations Human Rights Committee, *Consideration of Reports Submitted by States Parties Under Article 40 of the Covenant Sixth Periodic Reports of States Parties Due in 2013 Australia*, UN Doc CCPR/C/ AUS/6 (2 June 2016)

United Nations Human Rights Council, *Report by the Special Rapporteur on the Situation of Human Rights and Fundamental Freedoms of Indigenous People, James Anaya, Addendum, Situation of Indigenous Peoples in Australia* (1 June 2010)

United Nations Office on Drugs and Crime, *Handbook on Strategies to Reduce Overcrowding in Prisons* (United Nations, 2013)

World Health Organization, *Health in Prisons. A WHO Guide to the Essentials in Prison Health* (2007)

www.ingramcontent.com/pod-product-compliance
Lightning Source LLC
Chambersburg PA
CBHW040149270326
41929CB00032B/3393